T0243425

THE
SAUCER
AND THE
SWASTIKA

'Reality is for people who can't cope with drugs.'
John Lennon, noted UFO witness

* * * * *

UFO is a bucket of shit
Its followers: perverts, monomaniacs, dipsomaniacs,
Artists of the fast buck ...
The Air Force investigated UFOs
And issued a report
Couched in polite language
Which, translated, means:
'UFO is a bucket of shit' ...
And I sit here writing
While the shit drips down my face
In great rivulets.
Gray Barker, disillusioned UFO investigator
and amateur poet

* * * * *

'Nazis – I hate those guys!'
Indiana Jones, prominent ancient
astronaut theorist

THE SAUCER AND THE SWASTIKA

THE DARK MYTH OF NAZI UFOs

S. D. TUCKER

AMBERLEY

First published 2022

Amberley Publishing
The Hill, Stroud
Gloucestershire, GL5 4EP

www.amberley-books.com

British Library Cataloguing in Publication Data.
A catalogue record for this book is available from the British Library.

ISBN 978 1 3981 0538 6 (hardback)
ISBN 978 1 3981 0539 3 (ebook)

1 2 3 4 5 6 7 8 9 10

Typeset in 10pt on 12.5pt Sabon.
Typesetting by SJmagic DESIGN SERVICES, India.
Printed in the UK.

Contents

SEKTION ZWEI: WEB OF LIES – THE POSTMODERN PUZZLE OF THE ONLINE NAZI UFOs ERA

Introduction

Close Encounters of the Third Reich Kind

'A lie, repeated often enough, becomes the truth.'
Joseph Goebbels, liar

In late September 1955, a man jumped from the Mersey Ferry to his death in the freezing, murky waters below. He could not have made a better job of killing himself. Lest he didn't drown, he had his head chopped off by the ferry's paddles, into which rapidly rotating mass he had deliberately leapt, just in case. Liverpool's detectives were soon able to identify the headless corpse, however, as the man had thoughtfully sent a suicide note to a newspaper: 'My work here is complete. I follow the Führer to glory and eternity. Through the sacrifice of the Aryan martyrs, our world victory is assured. Heil Hitler!'

This headless Hitlerite was James Larratt Battersby (1907-55), leader of a small pro-fascist cult named the League of Christian Reformers (LCR), one of the first men in Europe to have worshipped the Nazi Führer Adolf Hitler (1889-1945) as a literal god on Earth. Battersby had once been a director of a successful family business, the Stockport-based Battersby Hats, one of Britain's leading manufacturers of headgear, until forced to resign due to controversy caused by his political activities. Known as 'The Mad Hatter' in Far-Right circles, Battersby joined the British Union of Fascists (BUF) and travelled to Lancashire, warning cotton-workers' traditional factory-jobs were under threat from sweatshop labour in India, a trend funded by 'international moneylenders' – that is, Jews. By 1935, Blackshirt Battersby was already combining Nazism with religion by giving talks on fascism to helpless children in Sunday School. Also a member of the fanatically anti-Zionist Militant Christian Patriots group, Battersby desired to introduce militant Christianity into all areas of British life, but few visions of Christianity can have been quite as militant as his own.

Appointed BUF District Leader for Stockport, when war with Germany broke out in 1939 Battersby was imprisoned in a British internment camp on the Isle of Man, where he befriended another fascist named Captain Thomas Guillame St Barbe Baker (1895-1966), who professed to believe that Adolf Hitler was the reincarnation of Jesus Christ, come to save humanity from the machinations of international Jewry. Baker himself had already sired Christ's future heir, so he said, his son allegedly being born with a swastika-shaped birthmark on his head. Baker was thought by camp authorities to be a fraud in search of followers and their money, but Battersby for one believed him, and together they founded the LCR Church, winning other convict converts to their cause. In 1943, still under lock and key, Battersby penned a manifesto, declaring Adolf Hitler was God's chosen instrument of the Final Judgement of the Jews, with the dictator being appointed 'God's Judge' in 'the final struggle between God and Mammon'.

Following Christ's second crucifixion in his Berlin bunker in 1945, Battersby and his newly liberated men set up their own holy temple named Kingdom House inside a seventeenth-century mansion near Petworth in Sussex, donated by a sympathetic wealthy follower. Here a chapel and altar were established, guarded by dogs, where prayers were offered up to the departed Christ-Führer, whose work on Earth remained incomplete. The Church of Hitler lacked appropriate ritual decoration, though, and in November 1945 an auction was held in London, selling off the no-longer needed Nazi-related contents of the German Embassy. Here, a granite bust of Hitler went for £500, along with a number of flags adorned with swastikas. Curious reporters asked the buyers why they wanted such things. When told they were intended for use as ritual paraphernalia in a Church of Hitler, predictable headlines ensued, and questions were asked in the House of Commons. The Home Secretary, James Chuter Ede, said that whilst he shared the public's 'revulsion' about this 'cult of Hitler and the forces of evil', he could do nothing about it, as it was not actually illegal to worship Nazis as gods. Understandably, nobody had ever thought to specifically outlaw such a thing, although Ede himself suspected the cult was simply a front for political extremism masquerading under 'the guise of religion'. However, the sect could not be closed down 'merely because it was unpopular or ridiculous', he said.

Interviewed by the *Daily Express*, Battersby explained that 'Hitler himself was essentially a good man,' who had descended to Earth to help sort the Aryan wheat from the Jewish chaff, much as the Bible had promised. The function of the Final Solution of genocide against the Jews 'fits exactly' with the idea of the Final Judgement, he implied. To the *Daily Mail*, his ally Captain Baker further protested that the 'simple faith' of the Hitler-cult was wholly 'non-political', being only 'a self-supporting community of Christians', living in rural harmony by rearing and growing 'our own goats, ducks and food'. The LCR was 'for God and for England', he added, even though its own chief deity was clearly German, the LCR ending their prayers with the stock phrase 'In the name of Adolf Hitler, Amen.' MI5 had already monitored the nascent cult within their Isle of Man prison camp, concluding they were 'crazy', but not necessarily harmless, as 'Anyone who believes that Hitler is Christ returned to Earth might well try to help the coming of His Kingdom by, for example, helping the Nazis in the event of an invasion.' Spies reasoned there was little chance of Battersby converting many other Mad Hatters to his insane cause following Allied victory, however, so they were essentially left alone to get on with goose-stepping amongst the geese down at Kingdom House. Thus, it was up to the public to intervene. Clergymen held hymn-singing protests outside LCR HQ, before a gang of ten masked vigilantes mounted an assault on the building, beating up one disciple, tying him up and gagging him, then driving off and dumping him in a town square with his trousers pulled down. Whilst the cult's men were 'roughly handled', the *Daily Mirror* later reported, any female followers were 'treated courteously'. Supposedly, the vigilantes were outraged servicemen, yet Captain Baker maintained they were actually journalists in disguise, seeking to create their own front-page headlines by violent means. However, being good Christians, Baker declared, the LCR and their Führer forgave the miscreants their sins and refused to press any charges.

Following this attack, Battersby emigrated to South Africa hoping to establish memorial institutes there in Hitler's name, but he was ultimately barred from the country as an 'undesirable immigrant' – if Apartheid authorities think you're a bit too racist for them, you know you've made the grade as an extremist. So it proved when, in 1952, Battersby disrupted the annual two-minute silence at the Cenotaph by giving a Hitler salute and shouting 'This is the Day of English Judgement. I speak the truth. English children must be saved. Trust God and the Eternal Christ. Heil Hitler!' Arrested for his own safety after crowds bayed for him to be lynched or stabbed, Battersby was found to have five photos of Adolf on his person and a programme for the Cenotaph ceremony on which he had written his planned outburst as an aide-mémoire. In case efforts were made to put him into a mental institution, he also carried three signed affidavits from Harley Street doctors testifying he was not insane. Up in Bow Street Magistrates Court and charged with 'insulting behaviour', Battersby pleaded not guilty, claiming to have *Sieg Heiled* only out of 'the deepest sense of responsibility to God and to my fellow countrymen', before being fined £10.[1]

By now living in Southport, Battersby may have been declared sane by Harley Street, but had been suffering from depression ever since the crushing German military defeat at Stalingrad in 1943. One way to stave off gloom was to keep busy and write, with Battersby publishing a two-volume *Holy Book of Adolf Hitler* in 1951 and 1952. This Hitlerite Bible recognised that 'God has indeed come down from Heaven and His name is Adolf Hitler.' And, just like Jesus, Adolf would one day rise again. Although physically dead, 'His Spirit, eternal and triumphant, marches on with and leads his disciples and followers throughout the world, in judgement and destruction of the old order,' which was soon to be replaced by a global fascist utopia of which Hitler would be seen as having been 'its prophet, its Pope, its

Jesus Christ'. 'Might is right when it is God's might and dominion,' meaning Hitler, not the original Jesus, was the true 'Leader of Leaders, Lord of Lords and King of Kings', in politics and on the battlefield. Battersby spoke of supernatural 'revelations of Hitler's Divinity' that had been made to 'chosen men and women throughout the world' such as himself, thereby confirming that 'Verily, National Socialism is the Spirit of God in action.' As such, Hitler possessed miraculous powers, and would one day rise again: 'And to Adolf Hitler, God's Chosen, is given all power in Heaven and Earth, with the conquest of the last enemy, Death: "*My spirit will rise from the grave, and the world will see I was right.*" So declared Adolf Hitler.'[2]

Despite all transient surface appearances, Hitler did not lose the war in 1945 at all. Merely by introducing Nazism into the world, he won, as it was his 'vibrant Aryan faith' which was destined to conquer all nations ideologically speaking, with the rapid post-war decline of the British Empire indicating 'the collapse of the Jewish-Britannic order' and the imminent development of 'a higher civilisation' in which rejuvenated Nazis would 'make mankind anew', causing those receptive to the Hitler-Christ's creed to evolve into a new form of humanity: 'In the Hitlerian world-idea is seen the new Heaven and the new Earth, as foretold in the Revelations of the Christian Bible, in which the Spirit of God is poured out on mankind, in the regeneration or resurrection of the world.'[3] Christian-Nazi evolution would seemingly involve everybody magically becoming German:

> Today there is no conflict in the German soul. Rather, there is the unassailable conviction that the German or Aryan is called and chosen by God for world leadership. And in his way-of-life the German recognises that everything is right which serves the Cause of Germany and her Divine Mission in the world. Yes, the Germans are the God-appointed Lords of the Earth and those who have vowed their eternal loyalty to Adolf Hitler shall be given all power from on high. The world will understand the supreme honour that is embodied in the phrase '*Ich bin ein Deutscher*' [I am a German]. For to be German or Aryan is to be the holy or whole man – one in spirit, mind and body in the Lord of Lords, Adolf Hitler.[4]

But Mr Battersby himself was English, not German, surely? Apparently not. 'Mere nationality is a minor matter; Race and Spirit are everything.' By becoming one in spirit with the Divine Adolf, you could merge with his holy Aryan soul and become German yourself, just like Battersby had done. To be German was no longer a mere matter of legal citizenship – it was a spiritual one. Just as Frenchmen, Russians, Poles and Italians could all convert to Christianity, so they could all convert to being German. As Hitler was the 'highest manifestation of Almighty God' on Earth, 'It is in His Pattern that the world will be rebuilt' after the collapse of the British-Jewish Empire, with all genuine 'Truth-seekers' submitting voluntarily to the Teutonic world-spirit. Hitler had revealed that the original Jesus was 'sometimes wrongly supposed to have been a Jew', an 'erroneous view' which led to 'an alien Asiatic spirit' being forced upon the West, turning everybody Jewish. That Hitler was the true Jesus was proved in several ways: an excommunicated priest had brought Adolf messages from a saint's ghost ordering him to 'break the fetters' placed on Germany by the Treaty of Versailles, an instruction obeyed; his Nazi creed had been the only one in history in which the biblical 'principle of loving your neighbour was actually put into practice instead of remaining an abstract principle'; and Hitler's 'miraculous survival' from a bomb-attack 'which killed men on the other side of the room but left him unharmed' indicated he was shielded by his Holy Father's Hand.[5]

'Towards the end of his physical life,' Battersby wrote, Hitler had complained he had a comprehensive plan for governing the entire globe, but it was so complicated it would take him ten years to write it all down properly. However, 'as a disciple of Adolf Hitler,' said Battersby, 'many things have been revealed to me in the Spirit,' and Hitler's ghost had managed to pass on a wide-ranging 'World Plan for Peace' laying out just how the future Nazi planet should be governed, once the British-Jewish Empire finally collapsed. Battersby, inspired by the invasion of his soul by 'the Wisdom of Adolf Hitler', had since managed to whittle this plan down to fewer than fifty highly tedious pages.[6] However, Hitler-worship was supposed to be inspiring, not merely technocratic in nature. Accordingly, if you wanted to worship the Christ-Führer and so turn your soul German for yourself, Adolf's chief priest provided the following printed prayer:

> Even so may God guide us to follow Him who lives eternally, our Leader and Redeemer, the Greatest Man from God who has ever been sent to the Aryan race. May the Aryans of the world unite in the bonds of the German religion and World-Philosophy, National Socialism. Heil Hitler![7]

Future generations would live to see Germany transformed into a second Holy Land to outrank the hated Zionist nation of Israel, with pilgrims travelling to Hitler's old haunts on significant Holy Days like the Führer's birthday of 20 April, his believed death-date of 1 May, 'remembered eternally as the day when God's Christ, Adolf Hitler, was caught up unto God and to His throne' and 16 October, 'when the Nuremburg martyrs were executed by Judaism, but survived in the Spirit,' a reference to the mass hanging of Nazi top-brass following the Nuremburg war crimes trials of 1946. Before he jumped into the Mersey, one particular 'English pilgrim' had already marched to Hitler's fortified mountain retreat of Berchtesgaden himself one 16 October, before pronouncing the sacred words *Adolf Hitler ist der Christus. Heil Hitler!*[8] As we shall see, Battersby was not to be the last man to do so – but some deranged disciples would trek out to Germany seeking not only Hitler's ghost, but also his flying saucers …

* * * * *

11

Nazism is often compared to some form of political religion, with Adolf Hitler as its Jesus Christ or Prophet Muhammad, yet this is generally meant in a metaphorical sense. However, the example of James Larratt Battersby and his outlandish Hitler cult proves the impulse to literally worship at the altar of German fascism can in fact be very real. This seems odd enough, but things were about to get even odder. Another new form of cult tailor-made for the twentieth century was that of the UFO; several space-age religions devoted to venerating UFOs and their alleged alien occupants do exist worldwide. By splicing these two curious post-war religious trends together, you end up with an even more bizarre fringe creed: that of the Nazi UFO cult, the story of which this book aims to tell. Yet, in actual fact, the very idea of a Nazi UFO is a total anachronism, as the UFO itself is a strictly post-war invention. The very idea of a 'flying saucer', as such things were initially known, was born two years after the Second World War had already ended, on the afternoon of 24 June 1947, when the American private pilot Kenneth Arnold (1915-84) famously saw 'a chain of nine peculiar aircraft' flying over the Cascade Mountains in Washington State, moving in an 'erratic' high-speed fashion which he compared to looking 'like a saucer would [move] if you skipped it across the water'. As is often pointed out, Arnold never actually said that the craft – if, indeed, that is what they were – were saucer-*shaped* at all, merely that they *moved* like saucers, being skimmed across a lake like discoid pebbles. He actually described them as looking more like batwings, crescent moons or boomerangs. Yet the Press misreported his description in headlines using the term 'Flying Saucer', and the name stuck. The Nazis could not have invented flying saucers at all, or have been in cahoots with their imagined ET occupants, as many later Nazi UFO-cultists were later to claim, because flying saucers were essentially a media creation from 1947, and, even when they were first seen, they did not *look* like flying saucers at all, but flying boomerangs.

However, the myth unleashed by careless headline-writers had legs. When, later that summer, a high-altitude weather-balloon (to accept, for the sake of avoiding a very long digression, what debunkers generally dismiss it as being) fell onto a ranch near the New Mexico settlement of Roswell, the scene was now set for it to be misidentified as a downed flying saucer, exactly like those Kenneth Arnold had just seen – even though he had not actually seen any saucers at all. The legend of the Roswell UFO crash was born, something which, when later resurrected for inclusion in a best-selling 1980 book about the alleged incident, became one of the defining media sensations of the late twentieth century. No Kenneth Arnold, no Roswell, it is as simple as that. And no Nazi UFOs, either. Supposedly, the US military back-engineered their own super-tech devices, like stealth aircraft and infra-red goggles, from having their military engineers examine the extraterrestrial Roswell wreckage, but the true back-engineering here was narratological. If a German scientific genius had approached Adolf Hitler in early 1945 and proudly announced the war was not lost after all, as he had just built him a UFO, the Führer's only possible response could have been 'What the Hell is one of those?' And then, once he received the answer, to have had him shot as a lunatic.

But Kenneth Arnold's sighting did not only influence the future of ufology; it also influenced its past. During the Second World War, Allied pilots had increasingly encountered strange phenomena in the skies over occupied Europe and the Far East, which came to acquire the nickname 'foo-fighters'. Foos appeared both by day (generally in the shape of hanging silver spheres) and by night (generally in the shape of luminous fireballs of various colours), which tailed along after aircraft as if intelligently remote-controlled from the ground, something technologically impossible at the time. Although these small flying globes did not show up on radar, they do appear to have been real phenomena, apparently of an unusual and still poorly understood meteorological kind; one guess is that they may have been some form of obscure atmospheric plasmas, perhaps electromagnetically attracted to the metal frames of Allied fighters and bombers. Whilst some were doubtless optical illusions or innocent misidentifications, there was some worry at the time that they represented a new German secret weapon – yet if so, they were not very good secret weapons, as they are not known to have ever succeeded in bringing any British or American planes down, despite several spurious and sensational modern-day accounts to the contrary.

The war being won, the foos largely dropped out of public memory until June 1947, when they suddenly popped back into people's minds in light of Kenneth Arnold's fateful sighting, now being reconfigured as pre-1947 flying saucers, even though they were not saucer-shaped at all. Some sceptical ufologists, belonging to something known as the 'psychosocial school', would see this as a classic example of 'cultural tracking', defined as being the way mankind's interpretations of strange things seen in the skies shift around to fit in with prevailing cultural trends and beliefs. A weird aerial light may in ancient times have been thought to be a flaming dragon; by 1947 few still believed in dragons, so lights of an exactly similar kind could be interpreted by witnesses as being advanced flying machines instead, chiming with a more scientific age. As the 1940s passed into the 1950s, two main competing theories emerged about what the foos could have been, both of which were what is often termed 'nuts-and-bolts' in nature. Nuts-and-bolts ufologists consider UFOs in a literal sense, as being actual solid, metallic craft. Some nuts-and-bolts men thought the foos were tiny alien probes, sent to spy on mankind's greatest war yet, in fearful anticipation of our imminent development of nuclear weapons. Others, more sceptical of this 'Extra-Terrestrial Hypothesis' (ETH), preferred to guess that the Nazis, famous for developing several technologically advanced *Wunderwaffen*, or 'Wonder-Weapons', throughout the war, such as the V-1 semi-robotic flying bomb and the V-2 ballistic missile, had also successfully designed their own tiny flying saucers – prototypes, perhaps, for larger versions which were thankfully not fully combat-ready by the war's end. The tiny Nazi foos may well have carried various types of secondary *Wunderwaffe* technology on-board with the ability to scramble enemy radar or knock out planes' engines by exposing them to electromagnetic fields, it was proposed.

When various defeated Nazi *Wunderwaffen* engineers were captured under an initially top-secret programme known as 'Operation Paperclip' and exported to the US, Russia and Britain to work for their new masters in return for not being hanged as war criminals, conspiracy theorists thought they must have brought their saucer designs along with them. Hence, perhaps what Arnold really saw that day in 1947 was a formation of back-engineered full-size Nazi flying saucers built by the US Air Force (USAF) or Britain's Royal Air Force (RAF), which still then possessed various aerospace interests in nearby Canada. Maybe it was even the Soviets, flying some back-engineered *Wunderwaffe* saucers over US soil as a dry run for a future atom bomb assault. As several Paperclipped scientists, most notably Wernher von Braun (1912-77), the main man behind the V-2 ballistic missile, really were design geniuses, this seemed plausible to some, especially once the existence of a few abortive roughly circular-shaped aircraft, such as Canada's AvroCar, the US Navy's Flying Flapjack and the Nazis' own Sack A-6 monoplane became known during the 1950s. All were abandoned due to poor performance, but nonetheless these craft did hover after a fashion, so it showed the idea of making a broadly saucer-shaped flying-machine was not impossible – just so long as you didn't mind the fact it would be inherently unstable, more or less impossible to control and basically worthless. However, the SS officer von Braun and his Paperclipped colleagues later helped NASA put a man on the moon, so the idea such mad professors may have built prototype saucers during the war did not seem entirely fanciful. To avoid enemy bombing, under SS auspices the Nazis had increasingly shifted design and production of weapons into underground *Alpenfestung* ('Alpine Fortress') complexes dug beneath mountainsides using concentration camp forced labour, and there was no telling what things they might have been creating down there – maybe even full-blown spaceships.

Of course, the SS were really building no such things, but that didn't stop a number of chancers coming forward during the 1950s and posing as former *Wunderwaffen* scientists themselves, eager to gain credit, money and media kudos as the original inventors of those amazing flying saucers by now buzzing the entire globe's skies. Key figures in this field included Giuseppe Belluzzo (1876-1952), one-time Italian Economics Minister in the fascist dictatorship of Benito Mussolini (1883-1945), who claimed to have drawn up blueprints for a saucer during the war, and Rudolf Schriever (1909-53), an alleged former flight captain in the Luftwaffe, who gained reams of publicity during the early 1950s for supposedly having constructed (and maybe even test-piloted) Nazi UFOs at a commandeered Skoda factory in Prague during the 1940s. Schriever's 'flying tops', which were really something more like circular helicopters with a ring of downwards-facing jet engines along the bottom for vertical take-off purposes, were the basic imaginative model many later fraudulent saucer-makers copied, especially once he had died in a car accident in 1953 and was no longer able to contradict them about anything.

A number of persons crawled out of the woodwork claiming to have worked with Schriever building saucers for Skoda once he was dead, including the alleged Nazi rocket scientist Dr Richard Miethe, who may not even have existed, probably being the total invention of a sensation-seeking French newspaper. In his 'interviews' with this rag, Miethe (or the journalist pretending to be him) coined the term 'V-7' to describe his own flying disc, a follow-on from the V-1 and V-2 'Vengeance Weapons' intended by Hitler to win the war by advanced technological means at the last minute. Whenever a new saucer-wave hit the headlines, a new wave of saucer inventors now followed close on its heels. Most such fraudsters just wanted money and attention, but another, more sinister idea was also being seeded; that, had the war lasted out just a few more months, the Germans, as the world's true Master Race, would inevitably have won it via advanced *Wunderwaffe* means, as the Aryan mega-brain was undoubtedly the most intelligent and capable in existence. Notably, in 1956 the book *German Secret Weapons of the Second World War*, written by Major Rudolf Lusar, a self-styled former German intelligence officer once employed by the Reich Patent Office in Berlin, appeared. Revanchist in tone, it set a pattern for future *Wunderwaffen* books by containing accurate accounts of V-1 and V-2 development and high-tech giant Nazi tanks, submarines and artillery, mixed in confusingly with total nonsense about Schriever and Miethe working together on UFOs at the Prague Skoda plant, to make the latter lie appear more plausible than it really was.

Bemusingly, Heinrich Himmler (1900-45), the Reichsführer of the elite and fanatical Nazi 'Black Order' of the SS, believed in the existence of an ancient *Wunderwaffe* named 'Thor's Hammer', this being the magical weapon the Norse god Thor used to fire thunderbolts at his enemies in ancient myth. Being rather occult-minded, Himmler thought the Norse gods might have been the modern-day German race's highly evolved, superhuman ancestors, who had enjoyed access to powerful electricity weapons. Accordingly, he tasked his special SS pseudo-archaeology and racial research unit, the *Ahnenerbe* ('Ancestral Heritage Unit'), which enjoyed hunting out evidence for the Aryan race's former existence in non-existent fairylands like Atlantis, to look into depictions of the Norse gods wielding lightning in art, literature and legend, to see whether their ancient electrical *Wunderwaffen* could be back-engineered; a wildly over-optimistic proposal was made by an opportunistic German engineering firm to weaponise the Earth's natural atmospheric electricity to make enemy aeroplanes' engines cut out, but nothing ever came of it. But the notion of the Aryan race having an innate affinity with electricity stuck, and the Italian aerospace engineer and journalist Renato Vesco (b.1924) published his book *Intercept – But Don't Shoot* in English in 1971, arguing the Nazis had indeed managed to harness electromagnetic forces within their underground *Alpenfestung* labs, thus explaining the foo-fighters, which were just what Himmler had once desired. The foos were officially called *Feuerballs* ('Fireballs'). Their purpose was to electrically disrupt enemy radar, but they also had a larger big brother companion, the *Kugelblitz* ('Ball Lightning'), which could actually bring down planes, Vesco explained. It later transpired Vesco had simply made all this up, motivated by a hatred of the Extra-Terrestrial Hypothesis. Not wanting people to believe in alien invasions, he desired them to believe in other impossibilities instead.

Other fantasists promoted a particular class of Nazi UFO called 'suction-saucers', which sucked air inside their engines for fuel, making them perpetual-motion machines powered by the sky itself, the ultimate form of clean, non-polluting energy. There was a movement within Nazism termed 'Blood and Soil', which argued that the German people, or *volk*, were inherently connected back to the German soil, whose adherents hymned things like farming and getting back to Nature. So-called 'Green Nazis' contrasted the healthy, clean country air with the foul, disease-ridden city, full of Jews and Marxists, which drained a German's well-being. The Nazis did genuinely promote animal rights and pass certain environmental protection laws, and as the Green movement has spread across the West from the 1960s onwards, this has now been exploited by some neo-Nazi ufologists as another good way to draw support for their cause. If they really did invent emissionless suction-saucers, then the Nazis can be repositioned not as evil genocidal maniacs, but as potential saviours of the planet from global warming.

Central to this revisionist myth is the figure of Viktor Schauberger (1885-1958), an eccentric Austrian forestry worker and early eco-campaigner with an interest in free-energy research, who once really did engineer an official meeting with Adolf Hitler to discuss his ideas. Sadly, Hitler thought his ideas were stupid, but myth-mongers often imply otherwise. During the war Schauberger was forced to work for the SS, producing a small metal disc christened a 'repulsine' which, when spun around after being started off by an electric starter-motor, allegedly shot up into the roof of his laboratory. This unusual device has since become inflated into being a full-blown SS UFO of a suction-saucer variety. So the legend now goes, with this mini-disc Schauberger had created a revolutionary new form of non-polluting, perpetual-motion, anti-gravity transport which has since been covered up by a cabal of high-ups in the oil industry, who fear such things will destroy their profit-margins – something which appears to be code for 'the Jews control our economies'.

Schauberger claimed his inventions ran according to special 'implosive' rather than 'explosive' technology, the latter referring to engines powered by the burning of filthy fossil-fuels. This sounds impossible, but in Hitler's Germany there was official denigration of the prevailing so-called 'Jewish Physics' of the day, which had to be sidelined in favour of something far better called 'German Physics'. Quite what this was supposed to be remains obscure; essentially, it was a rhetorical device used to kick Jews and Marxists out of university positions. But some today argue otherwise. Maybe the Nazi *Wunderwaffen* inventors really did have access to a whole other realm of physics, unknown here in the West, which would give their secret weapons magical powers like levitation or invisibility? In some variants, Schauberger's Green repulsine saucer was actually powered by something known as the 'Black Sun', a fictional astronomical body used as a substitute swastika by contemporary neo-Nazis in lands like Germany, where display of the real thing is now illegal. According to some fringe thinkers, the Black Sun is a real thing, although invisible (because outer space is black too, you see) and its benign rays shine upon the favoured Aryan race, lending them various supernatural powers and aspects of their famed natural genius; Western democrats may not know much about it, but only because they know nothing about German Physics. This Black Sun can even power environmentally friendly, anti-Jewish suction-saucers, like those of Viktor Schauberger; as the Black Sun is actually just a disguised swastika, this means all true UFOs are swastika-powered! If only the Nazis had won, we would not now be facing an environmental holocaust – the Jewish Holocaust would have been a small price to pay in comparison.

As this shows, the myth is constantly evolving to adapt to new social trends. The latest major development in our age of endless online rumour-mongering is that the Nazis even managed to develop an actual time-machine craft termed The Bell, under the auspices of the real-life SS-*Obergruppenführer* Dr Hans Kammler (1901-45?). The way in which real figures and invented ones are relentlessly mixed up within the whole meta-narrative makes it deeply confusing to navigate and can initially appear to lend it all some surface plausibility, at least to the terminally naïve.[9]

The full story of the foos and the fake Nazi saucer-inventors is a long and convoluted one, but the above is all you need to know to understand this current text. Remember the key terms and names just mentioned and you can't go far wrong, particularly if you recall them in conjunction with the following central fact: that there never were any Nazi flying saucers but by the end of the 1950s, there was a huge amount of spurious media material available which implied that there could have been. When various individuals later began building entire Nazi space religions based on this conceit, they were not operating within a vacuum.

*****

If by the 1950s some thought saucers were made by aliens, and others thought they were made by Germans, then a third, intermediary possibility also existed – that they were actually made by *German aliens*. This was the claim made by one of the most laughably audacious confidence men of the period, a sixty-year-old travelling grain-merchant of proudly

German-American extraction named Reinhold O. Schmidt (1897-1974), of Bakersfield, California. In 1957, following a short, enforced stay inside a mental asylum, Schmidt had the following strange advert placed in a local newspaper serving the town of Kearney, Nebraska, announcing to local farmers that, having been released out into the community, he was now very much back in business:

ATTENTION

MILO AND CORN GROWERS

That crazy grain-buyer from California is still around and would like to bid on your grain. Will pick it up at your farm in twenty-tonne trucks. Call me at the Fort Kearney Hotel.

Reinhold O. Schmidt

Would you want to sell your crops to a self-confessed 'crazy' man? According to Schmidt, he had received 'a stream' of calls from local farmers eager to trade him 'thousands of tonnes' of grain before the day was out. Possibly crop-growers just wanted to hear Reinhold's amazing story from his own mouth. If so, what was it?

During November 1957 a large UFO wave swept the US, and on the 5th, whilst driving along an isolated sandy area near the Platte River, Schmidt had his own close encounter with a 100-foot long, propeller-driven, zeppelin-shaped spaceship that had landed nearby, causing his car engine to conk out when he neared it. Approaching on foot, he was hit by 'a thin stream of light, about as big around as a pencil', paralysing him. Two men now emerged from the craft, frisked him down and demanded to know if he was armed, then took him inside where he was told he 'could look around but not touch anything', especially not the control systems or the female staff operating them. The entirely human-looking crew members, dressed in 'light-coloured blouses, dark shirts and shoes with medium heels', did not immediately appear terribly Aryan in nature, having black hair and bronzed skin, but then Hitler himself was not blonde, and doubtless was capable of getting a suntan if he wanted. They did, however, speak to one another in what Schmidt recognised from his schooldays as being 'High German', although when they spoke to him it was in English with a heavy German accent, as in Hollywood war movies. Their control panels also featured clocks and Roman numerals, thus further indicating their apparent human nature – although the way they 'glided, instead of walking' across the floor rather militated against this.

Oddly, the spaceship, although silver and metallic from the outside, was see-through on the inside, meaning it didn't need any windows. The zeppelin was undergoing repairs, but eventually, '*Wir sind fertig*,' 'We are finished', Reinhold was told, whereupon he was booted off-board before the ship rose into the sky and vanished in a flash of light. Schmidt's initial theory was that this was a Russian research vessel staffed by East German scientists, sent out to gather data about the recent launch of the Soviet space-satellite

Sputnik. Being German, Schmidt noted, they had landed on common ground by the river, rather than on private property, thus adhering to petty rules and regulations, as per national stereotype. Before leaving, the Russo-German spies asked Schmidt several questions about geopolitics. 'I promised to try to get the answers,' said Schmidt, 'and said if they would give me their address, I would kindly forward this information to them.' But why were they asking a humble grain-merchant questions about Cold War politics? A 1958 photocopied booklet put out by the Spacecraft Research Association of Phoenix, Arizona, provided the following random guesses:

- He has a commanding physique.
- His hands tell a story of a soul that has found a kind of peace.
- The way he puts it over.
- He is a friend of every man – farmers, etc.
- He is a representative of Midwestern America.
- He has physical health.
- He has courage.
- He has a 'spiritual withinness'.
- He has a sense of humour, a sense of kindness, and a sense of loyalty.

The man himself was more modest. Up until this point, 'my life was a normal one, by average world standards,' Schmidt later wrote, but no longer. Disturbed, he sought guidance from his local Minister, but he was absent, so Schmidt visited the nearest Sheriff instead, this being 'my duty as a citizen'. In the company of lawmen, Schmidt returned to the landing site, where footprints, together with a greenish, 'sweet-smelling' oil-like substance, were discovered. Also later discovered in the boot of Reinhold's car was an empty can of this same substance – it was a brand of motor-oil. Schmidt had previously served time in prison for embezzlement in 1938 and 1939, and when he refused to take a lie-detector test the police got suspicious, as did officials from military intelligence called out to waste their time questioning him. Psychiatrists were summoned and concluded that Schmidt sincerely believed he had met Germans from another planet. He was thus brought up before a medical board and forcibly hospitalised as mentally ill. Apparently, the police thought he had been smoking marijuana, but 'The truth is, I don't smoke, period.' Yet Schmidt was not deemed insane by madhouse medics. They hooked him up to a special device to measure his brainwaves, but 'the charts were so regular they thought there was something wrong with the machine.' Far from being insane, Schmidt was dangerously *over*-sane. Released, Reinhold complained he had been the victim of a conspiracy aimed at concealing the truth about saucers from the public, on behalf of something called the 'Silence Control Group'. The oil can was planted in his car to make him look a fraud. Furthermore, the brand's manufacturer, Veedol, noticing media reports that the oily substance left behind by the UFO had been sweet-smelling, had spotted a sponsorship opportunity, and paid the conspirators to announce its brand had been used during the hoax to get the message out that its own product smelled better than any competitor's!

Making the best of matters, Schmidt quickly began exploiting his media notoriety for commercial gain via book sales. On 5 February 1958, Schmidt said he saw the zeppelin-saucer land again, being taken back aboard by its captain, 'Mr X', who now said he actually hailed from Saturn. Later, Mr X and a female companion approached Schmidt in a black Volkswagen Beetle – or possibly an MG sports car, there is some debate – in which they used to drive out from their craft in order to shop for groceries undercover. Apparently, they had a particular fondness for MJB coffee. They then asked if Schmidt would care for a trip to the Arctic Circle, one of the alleged chief hiding-places of Nazi UFO pilots in later developments of the myth. Here, their zeppelin turned into a submarine to monitor Soviet nuclear subs in the region. Their true mission on Earth was to prevent nuclear warfare; world powers were warned that, if they ever launched any A-bombs, the Space-Germans would ensure they dropped straight back down onto their launch-sites. Schmidt then elaborated his tale so that he travelled to the Great Pyramid in Egypt, where Mr X opened a secret doorway revealing a miniature spaceship and a series of ancient relics from the Bible, such as Jesus' sandals and the crooks of the shepherds and clothes of the Wise Men who had followed the star (or UFO) to witness Christ's birth. Jesus (or 'J---s', as Schmidt respectfully spelled it) was truly an alien, who had levitated up from the cross into a waiting spaceship disguised as a cloud piloted by the two-thousand-year-old-plus Mr X, who took Him away to German Saturn. Then, Mr X had brought the cloud-ship down to Earth again and deposited it inside the Great Pyramid, to act as undeniable proof of the reality of his whole tale, once humanity was spiritually advanced enough to hear it. Optimistically, Mr X predicted this would be in 1998.

In May 1961 Schmidt released an hour-long dramatisation of his experiences, *Edge of Tomorrow*. The film flopped, but it didn't matter as the Saturnians had provided him with an alternative source of income. Having superior technical knowledge, the alien Aryans had informed Schmidt of the cancer-healing properties of certain 'free-energy' quartz-crystals, pointing out nearby locations where such items could be found. Armed with this data, Schmidt had approached several little old ladies in the California area and persuaded them with 'loving talk' to provide seed capital approaching $30,000 in total, to begin his own crystal-mining venture. By October Schmidt found himself up in court in Oakland, facing charges of grand theft. Eager to clear his name, he treated the jury to a courtroom showing of *Edge of Tomorrow* as incontrovertible proof that Germans lived on other worlds, but they didn't believe him. No less a figure than future TV-documentary star Carl Sagan (1934-96), then still a bright young unknown astronomer, was called as an expert witness for the prosecution, testifying it was impossible for life of any kind to exist upon the harsh gas giant world of Saturn – not even hardy Germans, inured to adversity by life on the Eastern

Front. A guilty verdict led to a sentence of up to ten years for the fraudster in his own personal Colditz. Reinhold O. Schmidt subsequently disappeared from the UFO scene, and all known copies of his film – by all accounts truly terrible – vanished along with him.[10]

* * * * *

The end of Reinhold Schmidt's story was not the end of Reinhold Schmidt's story, for it was later refashioned by others to serve their own purposes, most notably by the German-Canadian author, publisher and fringe activist Ernst Zündel (1939-2017) in his 1975 underground hit *UFOs: Nazi Secret Weapon?*, first printed under a false name. Quite why Zündel felt the need to publish pseudonymously can be instantly perceived by reading the book's opening notice: 'This book is dedicated by the authors, their collaborators, and the publishers, to the unsung and much-maligned heroes of the Second World War' – i.e. members of the Nazi Party. The proudly pro-Hitler Zündel was one of the world's most prominent Holocaust deniers, hitting upon the since much-copied brainwave of abusing UFOs to promote an extremist agenda. Riding on the back of a 1970s boom in New Age publishing, he promoted the idea the wartime Germans really were a Master Race, capable of inventing amazing things like spaceships, implanting the notion that one day they would rise again in the form of a 'Last Battalion' from saucer-bases concealed beneath the South Pole or within cave systems in the Andes, to save humanity from the clutches of a degenerate, Jew-ridden post-war world. To support his claims – which even he didn't actually believe – there was no depth to which Zündel was not willing to stoop, such as inventing wholesale a since much-copied 1945 'quote' from Hitler that 'In this war there will be no victors and no vanquished either, but only the dead and the survivors. The Last Battalion, however, will be a German one.'[11]

Born a child of war in 1939, Zündel's positive, hero-worshipping attitude towards his Führer was inherited from his mother, who told the young Ernst that without generous Nazi economic policies, she would never have been able to afford to have any children, as Hitler was always urging German women to do. 'I owe that man my life,' concluded Zündel, praising the Führer as having brought Germany 'work, bread, peace, honour and a place in the sun'. There was little bread or honour in starving, bomb-ravaged post-war Germany, though, Zündel blaming his childhood poverty and family hunger not on Nazi hubris, but the evil of the victorious Allies; when his father Fritz returned home from time as an American POW, he had become an alcoholic. For a man so keen on Corporal Hitler, however, Zündel proved curiously averse to conscription into the West German Army on the grounds that, like most Nazis, he was a committed pacifist. So, aged nineteen, Zündel left for Canada in 1958, where he found work as a photographer and image-retoucher before setting up his own graphic arts business in Montreal, Great Ideas Advertising, aimed at servicing the visual design needs of the marketing trade. A talented painter, he was several times chosen to illustrate front covers for Canada's popular periodical *Maclean's*.

During the 1960s, Zündel was taken under the wing of fascist politician Adrien Arcand, and in 1968, aged twenty-nine, ran against Pierre Trudeau for leadership of the Liberal Party of Canada, professing alarm at the future PM's allegedly pinko leftist views. His true aim was to become a 'nuisance candidate', attracting free media attention by putting forward a deliberately contrarian policy platform. Like some modern-day agitators, Zündel used Canadians' own liberalism against them by claiming to be an 'immigrant rights' campaigner – the immigrants in question being German-Canadians like himself, whom he claimed were constantly discriminated against. As professed anti-racists, Canada's liberal elite felt obliged to give Zündel space to make his case, even when he was abusing his new position as spokesman for the Concerned Parents of German Descent pressure-group to complain about the negative depiction of German soldiers gassing Jews in the TV mini-series *Holocaust* leading to the bullying of poor, defenceless Aryan infants by pro-Jewish thugs at school. His reputation successfully established, Zündel withdrew any future hopeless candidacies and decided to undermine democracy from behind the scenes instead, transforming his large Victorian-era home in Cabbagetown, Toronto, into a Nazi shrine, even acquiring a collection of Hitler's youthful watercolours to hang on the walls and show off to visitors. When the place was attacked by arsonists in 1995, Zündel made the best of a bad situation by crying that many of the valuable documents he had in storage there proving his ideas were true had been destroyed, meaning sceptics would now just have to take his word for it all.

During the 1970s, Zündel set up the underground publishing house 'Samisdat', this being a term used to describe banned literature in the Soviet Union, and thus an excellent marketing ploy to justify the fact Zündel had to self-publish all his hate material as no reputable firms would touch it. *UFOs: Nazi Secret Weapon?* was a key turning point in the firm's success, enjoying several reprints. Mainstream publications would not accept ads for his initial range of Holocaust-denial texts, bearing as they did openly pro-Nazi titles like *The Auschwitz Lie, Did Six Million Really Die?* and *The Hitler We Knew and Loved*. However, 'when one door is closes, another will open,' and popular American and Canadian magazines, sci-fi pulps, newspapers and children's comics were quite happy to carry paid notices for UFO literature. Thus, Zündel collated the addresses of the thousands of people who bought *UFOs: Nazi Secret Weapon?*, and sent them follow-up catalogues offering other items of Third Reich memorabilia for purchase as well, such as posters, fun toys and stickers, transcripts of Hitler's speeches, tapes of SS marching songs (with 'no annoying commentaries distorting the music') and writings by other Hitler apologists, anti-Zionists and revisionist pseudo-historians of the Second World War from around the globe. Hopefully, customers who came for the saucers would walk away more interested in the swastikas. If not, they could just buy more UFO tat, and fund his other activities anyway. As he once boasted, 'a lot of my subsequent Holocaust [denial] trials were partially paid for by UFO trinkets and donations by fervent supporters who believed in those Nazi UFO stories. In fact, some believe them deeply to this day.' Whilst campaigning Jews maintained fake websites still offering his old UFO titles for sale 'to embarrass me', Zündel once told a conference on 'Waging and Winning the Information War', all they thereby did was give him 'advertising free of charge'. When one gullible UFO fan died in 1985, she bequeathed him 'a substantial amount of money' in her will, helping fund a Holocaust-denying colleague's research trip to Poland. 'Where would Ernst have been without all that UFO money?' he asked.

This commercial model worked splendidly for years, yet when his part-time publishing career was exposed by a Canadian journalist, Zündel's days as a propagandist seemed over – but this was not so. By continuing to make wilfully distasteful public comments, such as calling for the Oscar-winning anti-Holocaust film *Schindler's List* to be banned as constituting 'hate-speech' against good honest Nazis in 1994, he knew full well that, even if Jews did run all the nation's newspapers, they still realised which headlines would be crudely sensationalist enough to shift more copies. He came up before the Canadian, American and German courts several times down the decades, being happy to do so on account of the free rein this gave him to turn received opinion on its head on the TV news. If Canadian authorities were so liberal and democratic, then why were they always trying to shut down his right to free speech? Casting himself as 'the Gandhi of the Right', many non-Nazi libertarians rallied to Zündel's defence, thus appearing to give his denial or downplaying of the Holocaust (he sometimes claimed 'only about 300,000' Jews were murdered, not six million) surface credibility as a legitimate opinion to hold. His lawyers were accused of making arguments in such a way that the reality of the Holocaust, and not Zündel, was really the main thing being put on trial. When one Holocaust survivor testified to seeing Jews marched into ovens and never coming out again, lawyers asked if this might have been because they had been generously released to freedom through a nearby gate.

In 1992, Zündel successfully had a conviction for breaching Section 181 of the Criminal Code of Canada, which prohibited the deliberate reporting of false information, overturned by the Supreme Court on the grounds of this legislation being deemed unconstitutional. Clearly, Canada was a tyranny, and Zündel was being persecuted. When he repeatedly turned up to court wearing a bullet-proof vest and yellow hard hat like Bob der Builder, claiming to be in fear of his life from dangerous Jewish avengers, Zündel effectively made a criminal into a victim. Hadn't the Jew-duped Canadian public heard of the Nuremburg Show Trials? Zündel was now gleefully presenting himself as a human-rights martyr, and when faced with deportation to Germany for illegally distributing pro-Nazi material abroad electronically in 2003, via firewall-evading 'mirror-sites', he tried to claim actual refugee status in Canada, lodging an official complaint with the UN

Human Rights Committee in 2007. 'Sometimes I feel like a black man being convicted on Ku Klux Klan news clippings,' he complained, thus proving the real victims of racial discrimination in the post-war world, with no benign Hitler-figure around to protect them, were white folk. Unsuccessful for once, he received five years in a German jail, being released in 2010. Possibly, his case had not been strengthened when his lawyer had signed documents 'Heil Hitler!', said the Holocaust was 'the biggest lie in world history' and ranted that the presiding judge deserved the death penalty, later receiving a three-year sentence herself. When Zündel hired other lawyers, one read extracts from *Mein Kampf* in his closing speech. The German State had been after Zündel since the 1970s, when he had begun mailing out large quantities of Samisdat material to every single West German MP, in hope of converting or annoying them. Barred from returning to Canada, Zündel retreated to his childhood home in the Black Forest where, until his death in 2017, he continued to send out online 'Zündel-Grams' to followers, having plenty of time to reflect on the hypocrisy of the entire Western 'justice' system he had sacrificed his life helping to expose and undermine.[12]

* * * * *

Whilst his 'rather frivolous line' of UFO books were mere 'Mickey Mouse' products by his own open admission, Zündel himself was not a stupid man. The 'real lunatic fringe', he explained, were not those who questioned the Holocaust, but those who believed in Unidentified Flying Objects.[13] Much of his original UFO book is based upon a 1960 text, *We Want You: Is Hitler Alive?* and its 1968 sequel, *The German Saucer Story*, both by one 'Michael X' (not 'Malcolm X', as Zündel comically misprints it!).[14] This was the pseudonym of Michael Barton (1937-2003), a semi-reclusive American individual who on the evening of 22 May 1955 had stared up at the planet Venus really hard and broadcast a telepathic telegram made up of 'mind-stuff' contained within a 'vibratory beam of light' to its inhabitants, reading 'MICHAEL OF EARTH CALLING VENUS. COME IN VENUS. COME IN VENUS. OVER.' Venus obliged, thanking him for getting in contact via 'Telethot', and so began an interplanetary dialogue exhaustively catalogued by Barton through his own vanity press, Futura, in titles like *Venusian Health-Magic*. His sideline in Nazi UFO books got him into trouble, however, as Barton received one Telethot message telling him to go alone into California's Mojave Desert, to meet the Venusians face-to-face. This was actually a Nazi telepathic trick, as when Barton got there he received an urgent genuine psychic transmission from Venus, warning him to flee. As he did so, he caught a glimpse of a man hiding in a bush, just about to shoot a rifle, thus blowing out his mind-stuff entirely – no doubt a German sniper. Terrified, Barton left the world of saucers to become a delivery driver for UPS. When contacted by a New Age publisher in the early 2000s to see if he could reprint his old books, Barton agreed, but only on condition that his

Nazi UFO titles be omitted from the list, lest members of The Last Battalion come after him again.[15]

This is the kind of nut Zündel was happy to paint as being a reliable source. Although following their 1997 divorce his second wife Irene Margarelli complained that her husband Ernst was 'evil incarnate' on account of his annoying habits of excessively celebrating Hitler's birthday every 20 April and continually banging on about how Adolf had faked his own suicide and then escaped to victory on a flying saucer back in 1945, Zündel's only real enduring UFO belief was that such things sold books. Zündel was by trade an advertising man, and in a 1994 interview with Frank Miele of US magazine *The Skeptik*, explained that, whilst the original German-language version of *UFOs: Nazi Secret Weapon?* (ostensibly written by a different person) was more sober and serious in tone, it being harder to fool members of the Master Race, his English-language semi-translation was really a different book entirely, a mere tabloid-style entertainment product. According to Ernst:

> I realised that North Americans were not interested in being educated. They want to be entertained. The book was for fun. With a picture of the Führer on the cover and flying saucers coming out of Antarctica it was a chance to get on radio and TV talk shows. For about fifteen minutes of an hour's programme I'd talk about all that esoteric stuff. Then I would talk about all those Jewish scientists in concentration camps, working on these secret weapons. And that was my chance to talk about what I wanted to talk about.[16]

And what Zündel really wanted to talk about was the Holocaust 'lie'. If Jewish scientists were kept safely fed and sheltered in concentration camps building spaceships, then they can't have all been being gassed then burned in industrial ovens as in racist films like *Schindler's List*, could they? To prove this, Zündel proposed a little experiment. As in his view gas chambers wouldn't work anyway, why not build one according to the alleged Nazi designs of such things faked by the Allies after the war, fill them with persons deemed expendable, and then drop Zyklon B through the roof and see if they all died or not? Refusal by Western authorities to perform such a trial on the grounds it would kill people could easily be recast as really being down to fear that such a trial would *not* kill people, thus exposing the entire Holo-Hoax industry as a giant fraud.[17]

In 1978 Zündel pushed his luck even further, using his purportedly 29,000-strong US mailing list to give 'the truly dedicated UFO researcher' the chance to go on the holiday of a lifetime to visit Adolf Hitler at his secret saucer-base located somewhere inside a big hole beneath the South Pole for the all-inclusive price of only $9,999 per lucky tourist – imagine how many books denying Auschwitz existed could be printed up with a sum like that! Samisdat's selection criteria for successful applicants were 'of necessity rigorous', but if you had enough cash it would certainly be 'the unique experience of a lifetime'. Instead of visiting Santa at the North Pole, if you wanted to spend the Christmas of 1979/80 visiting Satan at the South Pole instead, Zündel would charter an aircraft from South America in which he and 'a very limited number of people' could soar southwards over Antarctica, keeping a close look-out for the by-now almost 100-year-old Führer below. The expedition's total cost would be around $2,000,000 and a $500,000 deposit was needed to make 'modifications on the special aircraft required' to access Hitler's remote polar lair. This was admittedly 'a fantastic sum', but one 'certain to be worth every dollar in terms of the knowledge to be gained' from 'the most daring scientific operation ever launched' in all of human history.

Zündel opened his mail shot by boasting of receiving an 'overwhelming number' of letters and phone calls expressing support for Samisdat's books, tapes, 'psychic research projects' and 'extensive experimental UFO construction programmes'. Pleasingly, this meant the general public were finally waking up to the 'junk food' lies peddled by the media and 'saucer charlatans' who slavishly parroted 'the official CIA-KGB alibi that all UFOs are extraterrestrial', when they were really stamped 'Made in Germany'. Thanks to customers' brave defiance in buying Samisdat's 'currently suppressed and sometimes vilified books', such as *Secret Nazi Polar Expeditions* and *Hitler at the South Pole*, the 'media-enforced blockade of the truth has now been broken' and the 'herculean efforts and sacrifices' of Zündel's 'five-year-long struggle against the forces of vested interest, deceit and prejudice' who tried to hide the truth beneath 'a cloak of childish nonsense and outright lies' had at last been won – sort of. Actually, money was still tight and so, warned Zündel, if you did not send back a completed order form for one of Samisdat's many fine products, you would be struck off their mailing list forever, meaning you would never know what Hitler had to say when they found him shivering at the South Pole. This would be 'too bad', Zündel signed off laconically, under his habitual *nom de Nazi* of Christof Friedrich (these actually being his middle names). As the Führer himself had often argued, 'we must have rowers on the oars, not idle passengers in the boat.' So, if you didn't send Zündel your dollars, you would never even know about 'that glorious day when we board our sleek, silvery aircraft and wing our way to Antarctica and beyond – to our rendezvous with history,' let alone get to participate in 'this magnificent and awe-inspiring experience'.

By collectively contributing towards Samisdat in various small ways, however, customers could help bring ticket prices down somewhat from the mooted $9,999, thus making 'this dream of a lifetime' more attainable. Possibly, UFO fans could buy Zündel's products in bulk at special wholesale prices, flog them on at 100 per cent mark-up at 'UFO conventions, county fairs, psychic fairs and flea-markets', then send the profits back to Toronto. Or you could set up your own UFO club, selling membership 'on a profit-sharing basis with Samisdat'. If you had good contacts, you could ask wealthy businessmen to sponsor the trip. Or, if you were 'rich and conscientious', why not 'underwrite the whole or part of the Expedition' personally and send Zündel some 'cold, hard cash' straight up front, thereby to 'realise our goal of a lifetime much, much faster'? No timewasters need apply: 'Empty promises and other hot-air products from windbags and do-nothings, however well off, will not serve to waft the Expedition to Antarctica and back.'

Maybe one day Samisdat members would fly out to Antarctica in a saucer of their own. Zündel had successfully located 'some of the original German flying saucer scientists who are still alive,' a race of elderly 'space pioneers' whose *Wunderwaffe* genius was now being utilised by Samisdat's own hard-working saucer design teams located in 'Canada, the USA, and in particular Germany, whose task it is to rediscover basic wingless flight' of the kind first achieved by Hitler. Already, Samisdat scientists had succeeded in mastering 'propulsion systems unprecedented in today's aerospace technology', craft exploiting which they hoped to make available 'in kit-form for hobby-builders'. If you wished to pre-order one, all cheques 'should be made out to SAMISDAT'. Two very basic miniature prototype models were already available for purchase right now, one of which used the original Nazi *Flügelrad* or 'winged-wheel' principle of flight, and had been shown off at a *Star Trek* convention in New York. This SAMISDAT MODEL-1 was 'a safe, exciting, entertaining and educational introduction to the world of flying saucers', which made 'a beautiful take-off and landing any UFO pilot could be proud of!' Accompanying descriptions make clear it was actually a child's toy spinning helicopter rotor, bought by Zündel and then rebranded along Nazi lines, costing $6.95 plus $1.00 P&P – 'a perfect gift for a boy or a girl, whatever age he may be!' Zündel's scientists had also successfully devised a saucer prototype for those on a tight budget, now available for only $3.70 P&P inclusive, in the form of a plastic Frisbee with a swastika painted on it.[18] Surely the hitherto-unknown Nazi invention of the Frisbee was proof enough of innate German design genius.

Within *UFOs: Nazi Secret Weapon?*, Reinhold O. Schmidt's ripping yarn was relentlessly exploited for further misinformation purposes. Zündel's book is not internally consistent, throwing as many competing notions out as possible, just to see what sticks. In some places, the creators of the saucers are purely human Nazis. In others, they are alien Nazis instead. Whichever lie the reader preferred to swallow was fine by Zündel, just so long as they also bought the wider accompanying falsehood that Adolf Hitler was lovely and all Jews evil and vile. In his 1994 interview with Zündel, Frank Miele spoke of the neo-Nazi's innate skill as a salesman, who in conversation 'quickly reverses himself in order to agree with his interlocutor on anything that is not critical to his game-plan'. He would 'dangle a reference to UFOs or the wisdom of the ancient Atlanteans' into his conversation and, if it has no effect 'he just moves on.' Yet, if it should elicit scepticism or laughter, he simply 'blows it off' with a 'jovial' dismissal.[19] His writing style is similar. To reclaim

Schmidt's tale, Zündel had to pretend that the grain-buyer claimed 'most convincingly' that the 'entire crew' of his Saturnian saucer 'spoke German and behaved like German soldiers'. The soldiers were, however, 'friendly and correct to him', probably on account of Schmidt's own admirable German ancestry, whilst their later flight to polar regions was certainly suggestive. Schmidt's spell in a mental asylum was recast as a 'KGB tactic'. Far from being the Land of the Free, the USA was just another giant gulag in disguise. According to Zündel, the craft boarded by Schmidt matched the design of 'at least two' marques of flying saucer built in Germany during the war, even though Schmidt's craft was actually a zeppelin, not a saucer. But how did Germans get to other planets like Saturn in the first place, Zündel wanted to know? Reinhold Schmidt himself 'forgot to ask', but Ernst was not so lax.[20] So suited to his purposes was Schmidt's story that Zündel closed his entire book with a stirring call to arms based upon its possible implications:

> Could it mean that the German nation is indeed a colony, either from German-speaking Saturnians with whom Reinhold Schmidt conversed, or are they the outer-Earth beach-head of the inner-Earth civilisation ... [of Nazis living beneath polar regions]? Is this perhaps the answer to the vexing question of why the Germans are 'different'? Is this the explanation for their superb performance and genius as soldiers? Are they leading the world in precision-engineering and technology because they have dwelling amongst them a disproportionate number of Saturnians? Could this be the reason why they always rise stronger and Phoenix-like from the ashes of defeat? Was Hitler planted on this Planet Earth to pull back Western civilisation from the brink of degenerate self-extinction – peacefully, if at all possible – through war, if necessary? Should the above question be answered in the affirmative, then The Last Battalion, when the time is ripe, will spring into action. With racial strife and economic disaster looming, how far away can *Der Tag* ['The Day'] actually be? And finally, will the Saucer Nazis, as a last resort, invade strategic areas militarily? Members of The Last Battalion are already amongst us as soldiers, labourers, teachers, students, scientists – in fact, in all walks of life, male and female, young and old. So look at your neighbours and your friends – how many of them do you think belong to The Last Battalion? Time will tell![21]

Just in case you ever felt inspired by such rhetoric to try and climb aboard one of the Last Battalion's UFOs yourself one day, Zündel was pleased to offer customers a special 'Official UFO Investigator Pass' to hand over to the Space-Sentries when they jabbed their bayonets into your abdomen and barked 'Papers please!' As a bonus, Zündel would also post you a list of appropriate questions to ask the crew, in both German and English, once safely aboard, thus allowing you to win their trust as a commendably military-minded individual, questions such as '*WAS WOLLEN SIE?*' ('WHAT IS YOUR MISSION?'), '*SIND SIE BEWAFFNET?*' ('IS YOUR

CRAFT ARMED?') and, if so, then '*MIT WELCHER ART WAFFEN?*'
('WITH WHAT TYPE OF WEAPON?'). Quite how you were supposed
to understand their answers if this was all the cue-card German you could
speak, Zündel did not clarify.[22] When Reinhold O. Schmidt spun his own
web of lies back in 1957, he could never have anticipated that decades later
his con would be stolen by another conman and repurposed anew for his
own morally dubious ends. Schmidt may have been an incurable criminal,
but at least he wasn't a Nazi – and neither were his imaginary, German-
tongued aliens. Except that, come 1975, and the underground propaganda
tomes of Ernst Zündel, they suddenly were.

* * * * *

Where would this process of narrative mutation end? According to the
Italian ufologist Maurizio Verga, who has done much to unearth the true
origins of the whole Nazi spacecraft myth, the genuine history of this topic
can be broadly split into two main periods, those of 'German Saucers' and
'Nazi UFOs'.[23] In the first, more innocent, 'German Saucers Age', most
saucer-spinners tried to appear at least vaguely plausible in their theorising,
mainly limiting their speculations to the notion that, during the Second
World War, Nazi scientists of a purely human kind managed to design (but
not *necessarily* successfully deploy), early prototype versions of those same
aerial vehicles which, post-Kenneth Arnold, became known as flying saucers.
We have already laid out the basic chronology of this period briefly above,
when talking about the likes of Rudolf Schriever, Richard Miethe and Viktor
Schauberger. This era lasted from roughly 1947 up until the early 1980s,
at which point the second-generation 'Nazi UFOs Age' began, and things
started to get a whole lot darker, more elaborate, and wildly improbable.

Fusing earlier contributions with new strands which had appeared in
wider UFO-lore itself during the 1960s and 1970s, primarily legends of alien
abduction of humans and mutilation of cattle, Nazis now began being linked
with actual ET beings, from whom they had truly sourced their saucers,
rather than *Wunderwaffen* scientists designing them themselves from scratch.
Together with emotionless, sperm-obsessed grey midgets from Zeta Reticuli,
paedophile, blood-drinking lizard-men from the constellation Draco and
their fellow racially superior Nordic-looking blondes from the star system
of Aldebaran, it was proposed the Germans had actually won the war but
cunningly presented it as a military 'defeat', thus enabling the conquest of
our globe by stealth. Today, SS occultists were secretly running the entire
world from behind the scenes with the aid of the fascist-alien puppet
governments of the US, UK and Russia, it was whispered (or sometimes
shouted, in a quasi-psychotic manner), as Nazi UFO theory began to merge
seamlessly with the wider and ever-mushrooming field of paranoid anti-State
conspiracy theories in general, particularly once the Internet gained ground
from the mid-1990s onwards.

Throughout both eras, the picture was further contaminated by the related underground spiritual movement of 'Esoteric Nazism', which is the other main subject covered by this book. Like the cult of James Larratt Battersby, this claimed National Socialism itself was secretly a hidden religion which had merely camouflaged itself as a mass political movement in order to gain material power and thus destroy the physical world. Then, SS high-priests could transform our reality into a much better non-physical and spiritually uncontaminated one, fit for true sons of the Aryan race – whether human, supernatural or alien in nature – to inhabit. Throw in a few other side-myths – the idea that Hitler survived the war and established a hidden Fourth Reich somewhere in South America, the polar regions or on the moon, the notion that the Earth is hollow and full of Germans, the perpetual lie that Jews run the world – and you end up with a florid agglomeration indeed. One fake theorist builds on the fake theories of an earlier fake theorist, and then these new fake theories are built on to create a further generation of hybrid monsters, a process with no apparent end: 'Great fleas have little fleas upon their backs to bite 'em; And little fleas have lesser fleas, and so ad infinitum.' (It's a deeply satisfying rhyme, though the observation is syphonapteral nonsense.) As with fleas, so with fantasists. No matter how improbable or unsourced an assertion made by any single theorist, you can bet someone, somewhere, will be willing to take it at face-value and then re-use it, as with Reinhold Schmidt's tall tale. Even if that original assertion is an outright invention, the fact it subsequently appears in two separate sources will then be taken by a third theorist as a good indication it might be true, and he will then repeat it verbatim himself. Now it appears in four separate sources and so another theorist comes along and thinks it must be *even more* reliable, and so ... you get the idea. The fiction takes on a certain strange truth of its own. Take that famous quote from the Nazi propaganda chief Joseph Goebbels (1897-1945) with which I prefaced this chapter to the effect that 'A lie, repeated often enough, becomes the truth'. He never actually said it. And yet, as if to prove the truth of these very words, through sheer force of repetition everyone now thinks he did.

What would motivate someone to begin peddling such a weird lie? There are a variety of potential reasons, some of them more sensible than others. When it comes to the topic of Esoteric Nazism, there are many people around who simply find our modern-day, technocratic, politically correct world to be quite literally soul-destroying in its nature, and so seek to re-enchant it with a heady brew of occultism and hard-core fascist aesthetics, fascism being the political philosophy which seems about as far removed from the current liberal hegemony under which we all now exist in the democratic West, whether we want to or not. If you long to live in another world, then the Third Reich and Mars represent equally viable imaginative alternatives to some individuals. Admittedly, some proponents of the whole Nazi UFO idea are simply mad, the clearest example being the 1970s US serial-killer Richard Trenton Chase (1950-1980), 'The Sacramento Vampire'. A profoundly disturbed and substance-abusing individual, Chase was known for eating live birds, injecting rabbit-blood into his veins and mixing trapped animals up with Coca-Cola in a food-blender to make interesting cocktails, being once found naked and covered in cow's blood. In 1977/78, Chase killed six adults and children before raping their corpses and sucking their veins dry. When asked why he did it, Chase blamed Nazis. On account of him being Jewish and having the Star of David emblazoned on his forehead (he wasn't and he didn't), a crew of Nazis had begun bombarding him with telepathic messages to kill from aboard their UFO, he said. Refusing to eat any cheese in prison as it probably contained Nazi mind-control drugs, Chase asked to be given a radar gun so he could track the saucer down and place the true guilty parties on trial instead. According to Chase, the UFO-Nazis had planted a special *Wunderwaffe* device in his bathroom which looked like an ordinary soap-dish, but actually had the power to transform his Jewish blood into powder. If the bottom of the dish was dry, he was safe for now. If it had wet soap-scum there, it meant he hadn't done enough killing lately, and his blood was due for imminent fascist crystallisation. Unsurprisingly, Chase's lawyers pleaded insanity at his trial; more surprisingly, they failed.[24]

The motives of some figures are harder to fathom, however, as with Tim Hepple (b.1967), a one-time Far-Right activist who helped organise the 1989 Dewsbury race-riots before, so it was said, reforming his outlook and becoming a spy, of sorts. In 1999 Hepple published a book, *UFO Revelation*, under the name Tim Matthews. Thinking UFOs were secret military craft, a smallish part of Hepple's book promoted the Nazi UFO angle. Suspicious, the left-wing activist Larry O'Hara co-authored a pamphlet, *At War with the Universe*, claiming the text represented Hepple's sinister aim to become the 'Führer of Ufology' by rehabilitating the Nazis as super-intelligent saucer-inventors; his cover featured Hepple done up as Oswald Mosley (1896-1980), old leader of the British Union of Fascists, accepting Hitler salutes from his Blackshirt troops. On the other hand, given Hepple had a long alleged record of infiltrating extremist groups, instigating others to commit illegal acts and then watching as they received prison sentences whilst he got off scot-free, the pamphleteers speculated Hepple may have been encouraging potentially troublesome ufologists to break into military bases so the State could lock them away. There were also suggestions he was arranging fake saucer sightings in Knutsford as part of a government disinformation campaign. Hepple denied all this, reasonably arguing he just liked UFOs; he also claimed Larry O'Hara had been stalking him, once being found hiding in his parents' coal-shed. It did seem rather a waste of time for MI5 to infiltrate UFO groups on the off-chance one might accidentally photograph a real-life RAF flying saucer, especially as the RAF didn't have any. Even if they did, it is unlikely they would choose someone with a known record as a mole to do so; Hepple had been interviewed on TV as an informer inside the neo-Nazi football hooligan group Combat 18. When Hepple later became editor of a paranormal magazine endorsed by the Israeli spoonbender – and 'self-confessed CIA and Mossad asset' – Uri Geller, O'Hara saw this as yet more evidence Hepple was a spook, plugging 'NASA propaganda and FBI-approved psychics'. But how did this fit in with his supposed desire to turn ufologists fascist and so 'rehabilitate Nazism'? Being left-wing, O'Hara appeared to think the British State was an inherently fascistic entity in itself. Thus, to work for the British (if indeed Hepple *did* work for them) automatically made you into a sort of fascist anyway, even if you weren't one. To an outsider, the fog was impossible to penetrate.[25]

It is often so. Why did the semi-official Iranian news agency FARS put out a story online in 2014 claiming a race of ETs called the 'Tall Whites' had secretly helped Nazi Germany develop its wartime submarine fleet, and were currently running America in a 'secret regime' behind the scenes, ensuring Washington's military hegemony? Such allegations came illustrated by a computer-generated image of stereotypical Grey-type alien beings superimposed on the US flag, with then-President Barack Obama and Adolf Hitler in front of them. The propaganda element seemed clear enough: anti-Iranian US foreign policy was every bit as evil as that of the Nazis. But what was FARS' source? They have a record of presenting information from spoof websites as true news, or making totally invented claims such as that the British Royal Family are secretly Jews, and in this case sourced their details from whatdoesitmean.com, an obscure conspiracy site pushing mad theories with little evidence behind them. It looked a clear case of Iranian disinformation – but some speculated the original source site itself was a rival US disinformation effort. Spuriously, whatdoesitmean.com boasted of gaining evidence of the US-Nazi-ET alliance from Russian spies' summaries of the documents leaked by American intelligence whistleblower Edward Snowden. By planting obviously fake stories online and saying they came from Snowden, it could be argued the CIA were just trying to make him look like a crank and thereby discredit his wider revelations, a ruse Iran stupidly fell for. Others, however, may say the idea the CIA would waste time doing this is in itself a sign of cranky paranoia, and that the site is just a standard online nonsense-peddler. Yet others might sensibly say there is no way of us knowing either way.[26]

Naturally, the various possible motives people may have for promoting the Nazi UFO legend are not necessarily mutually exclusive; it is perfectly possible to be both mentally ill and quite rationally disenchanted with liberal democracy, or to be a Far-Right activist and a full-blown believer in the nuts-and-bolts existence of alien craft. Some of the myth's champions obviously don't believe a word they are saying, yet others appear perfectly sincere. Nonetheless, the most common reason for pushing the existence of Nazi flying saucers appears to be a broadly sinister one. As incontestably shown by Ernst Zündel, some neo-Nazi saucer-heads have begun using the entire motif as a novel recruitment tool, hoping to lure the young into the malign orbit of white supremacism by exploiting a combination of teenage naivety and obsessive love of sci-fi, a way to draw in the gullible. If the standard version of history is so wrong as to fail to acknowledge that Hitler helped invent UFOs, what else might historians have got wrong about the Third Reich? Might the Nazis actually have been right all along, contrary to misleading Allied propaganda? Could Germany have fought in justifiable self-defence? Were Britain, Poland and the Jews the true aggressors? Or could the Holocaust itself have been a hoax from start to finish? Once they have swallowed the first lie, a person might easily swallow several others too. If you can believe Adolf Hitler is alive and well and living on Venus, then the idea Auschwitz never existed seems fairly reasonable by comparison.

When once asked if he really believed a word of his risible *UFOs: Nazi Secret Weapons?* book, Ernst Zündel replied 'Look, it has a question mark at the end of the title.' So did one of Samisdat Publishing's other top-sellers, *Did Six Million Really Die?*[27] Myths are powerful things. Just because they are not true, it doesn't mean they cannot have a major effect upon society at large and the individuals who make up that society. Adolf Hitler himself knew that just as well as Ernst Zündel did.

MEN AGAINST TIME: THE ETERNAL MYTH OF ESOTERIC NAZISM

'*I will make the trains run on time and create order out of chaos.*'
Benito Mussolini, early fascist opponent of *kali yuga* confusion

'*I'll be back.*'
Arnold Schwarzenegger, possible Aryan übermensch avatar of Kalki

1

Tyrannosaurus Sex: Ariosophy, the Rape of the White Race by Apes and Dinosaurs and Other Myths of Nazi Occultism

In the early 2010s, newspapers discovered the phenomenon of 'dinosaur erotica', a bizarre subgenre of sub-literary pornography with titles like *Taken by the T-Rex*, *Ravished by the Triceratops*, *Professor T-Rex Teaches Me Gayness* and *A Billionaire Dinosaur Forced Me Gay*. Initially intended as jokes, the genre quickly found many genuine fans, making its writers easy cash. According to one such author, numerous women 'probably like the idea of a big, powerful, massive male roughly having sex with a smaller female', and there is no better example of an alpha-male than a Tyrannosaurus Rex which, it was speculated, would be filled with pent-up sexual frustration due to its extremely short arms making it impossible for the dinosaur to masturbate. Plus, it appeared unlikely prehistoric reptiles could give you AIDS or get you pregnant, even with no condom.[1] There are now reimaginings of *Jurassic Park* available online in which women are penetrated in nests by computer-generated pterodactyls; admittedly, pterosaurs are not technically dinosaurs, but this is hardly the main reason for approaching such films with a critical eye. When it also transpired there is a sister subgenre termed 'Bigfoot erotica', in which people basically have sex with giant monkeys in bushes, another round of open-mouthed media gawping ensued. Yet, if mainstream journalists were more *au fait* with ufology, they would have realised humans had been mating with dinosaurs and hairy men-beasts for real for decades. Prolific spoof porn-author Chuck Tingle's 2016 cult hit *Space-Raptor Butt Invasion* was old hat to some.

The drug-abusing occultist, artist and writer William S. Burroughs (1914–97) mowed his lawn into crop-circles shaped like colossal erect penises, hoping space-perverts would see it as an open invitation to come in and probe him.[2] In 1999, LA-based jazz-singer Pamela Stonebrooke was offered $100,000 for a book about her regular rape by a shape-shifting 'reptilian entity with scaly, snake-like skin' who was 'so much larger than most men' down below, whose crimes gave her 'intense' orgasms. Stonebrooke admitted saurian space-rapists were not 'a very politically correct species in the UFO community', but speculated that, by producing hybrid babies with one, she may have been helping create a new, future kind of human.[3] The most famous account of a space-rape, that suffered by Brazilian farmer Antonio Villas-Boas (1934-91) aboard a landed saucer on 5 October 1957 at the hands of a naked, slant-eyed woman with blood-red pubic hair, featured the curious detail that the entity in question barked like a dog throughout after a group of helmeted male dwarfs had rubbed Antonio's body down with special gel to give him an erection, an experience he found 'agreeable'. Following forcible ejaculation, the dog-woman pointed at her belly and then up into the sky, meaning she would have his puppies in outer space.[4] There are many other accounts of people embracing apes and lizards from other planets – in America, there is even a club where alien-lovers can meet and draw pictures of their imaginary offspring – but let us not dwell on the issue.

Such disturbing sexual pathologies surely portend the impending death of Western civilisation, but one man who saw all this coming over a century ago was the Austrian racial theorist Jörg Lanz von Liebenfels (1874-1954), who in 1905 published a very, very strange book called *Theo-Zoology: Or, the Lore of the Sodom-Apelings and the Electron of the Gods*. Lanz thought the white Aryan race to which all true Germans and Austrians belonged had once been gods on Earth who were partially electronic in nature, possessing anti-gravity powers, psychic abilities, a magical Third Eye and the capacity to emit beams of light and fire from their bodies. Sadly, the female descendants of this prehistoric super-race, who seemingly originally came to our planet from outer space, were obsessively devoted to mating with then-extant Earth-bound races of bipedal lizard-men with big, hard bones in their penises, named 'dinosaur-hominids', and bands of well-hung midget half-monkeys termed 'love-pygmies'. Subsequent bestiality-related pregnancies led to profound racial degeneration and loss of white babies' electronic powers, with the weakened Nordic race 'today dying the sodomistic death' all across Europe. The historic 'quite strange preference' of Aryan females for such 'so-called *interesting men*' had to be terminated, argued Lanz, otherwise we would make the entire world into 'a big brothel'. White women must thus be barred by law from sleeping with any more 'pleasure-apes' and 'sodomistic monsters' – by which Lanz meant Jews, Slavs, blacks and other modern products of ancient bestiality – and allowed to touch only their fellow Aryans. Then, the remaining monkey-men 'must be exterminated in a gentle way', or exploited as slave labour, incinerated as sacrifices to God, or resettled *en masse* on Madagascar. Via selective breeding programmes, in which Nordic sex-nuns were locked in erotic convents and forced to bear multiple children to those deemed white and worthy enough, the German *volk* would gradually recapture their ancient godly nature, siring a breed of holy electronic Grail-Knights to conquer the globe. 'We *were* electric, we *will be* electric!' was Lanz's unlikely promise, and many chose to believe him. The Vienna-based magazine in which he made such claims had a reputed print-run of 100,000 – or so he said. And one of its most famous apparent readers was a certain Adolf Hitler.[5]

* * * * *

The real name of this staunch early opponent of dinosaur-porn was Josef Adolf Lanz; he adopted the fake title Jörg Lanz von Liebenfels in 1902 to falsely imply he had aristocratic origins and, allegedly, thereby obscure the awkward fact his mother was a part-Jewish Kong-woman. Perhaps he also wished to soften his recent expulsion from a Cistercian monastery for 'surrendering to the lies of the world and to carnal love', hopefully not with a lizard. Lanz was imitated in this deception by his ideological mentor Guido von List (1848-1919), who also fraudulently adopted the preposition 'von' to imply aristocratic forebears. List prophesied the coming of a 'Strong One from the Skies' who would unify all German-speaking peoples into one Reich – guess who that could later be taken as being. List followed the then-booming *völkisch* movement, which praised an inherent connection between the blood of the Germanic people and the soil of their homeland, glorifying Nature, farming, folklore and traditional ways of life as inherently superior to modern cities and industry. The long-bearded List referred to his race as 'Ario-Germans', meaning 'Aryan-Germans', implying only an ethnic white Aryan could ever be a true citizen, and claimed to possess a clairvoyant ancestral memory ranging back to pagan times when Germanic priest-kings had worshipped the Norse deity Wotan. There had once been four realms; one of fire dragons, one of air gods, one of water giants and one of men. During a period of blindness in 1902, List began to identify with Wotan, who had legendarily sacrificed one of his physical eyes in return for second sight. Hating life in excessively commercialised Vienna, with its many Jewish immigrants, List sought refuge in country walks, performing self-devised rituals like burying wine bottles in the shape of a swastika as a sacrificial offering, thereby inducing more visions of his race's glorious past, about which he then wrote successful *völkisch* novels and plays. List called the swastika the *fryfos*, or 'hook-cross', and inaccurately promoted it as a letter of an ancient Germanic rune-alphabet which functioned as a sun wheel, tracking the movement of the solar disc; ancient Germans were now *völkisch* sun worshippers, unlike pale, unhealthy, city-dwelling Jews, he taught.[6]

Lanz put his own pseudo-Christian spin on List's ideas, developing a personal racial religion of 'Ariosophy', or 'Aryan-Wisdom', founding his Order of the New Templars (ONT) cult on Christmas Day 1907; a version still exists today, having direct links to contemporary Nazi ufology. A clear model for Himmler's later SS Black Order, the ONT was intended as a lodge of Germanic Grail-Knights, who would meet in the ruined Castle Werfenstein overlooking the River Danube to perform invented rituals in fancy dress and lay plans to resurrect the prehistoric Aryan god-race by holding beauty contests for white maidens, performing genealogical research and hoisting swastika flags. Only full Aryans were allowed to join, so it was a good job the allegedly part-Jewish Lanz had already changed his name. Guido von List was also an ONT man, with fake aristocrats naturally flourishing within a fake religion with fake ceremonies, celebrating the fake past of a fake quasi-alien race.[7]

Lanz was an early pioneer of something now called 'ancient astronaut theory', the idea aliens visited Earth in the distant past, helping early humans build monuments like the pyramids and being worshipped as gods in return, only to later depart. The genre's origins lie partially in Theosophy, an international sect founded by Russian mystic Helena Petrovna Blavatsky (1831-91), whose 1888 work *The Secret Doctrine* featured a complex origin-myth for the human race termed 'cosmogenesis' or 'anthropogenesis', in which an immaterial God had descended from outer space into the clothing of base matter and flesh down here on Earth and other planets, initiating a complex series of racial evolutions and declines involving so-called 'root-races' of Atlantean, Hyperborean, Lemurian, Aryan and other fictional natures, some of whom had, as in Lanz, mated with beast-men, degrading their blood and making them forget their former divinely inherited psychic abilities and superior pyramid-building technology. 'Narrow-headed' humans slept with 'huge she-animals', creating 'dumb races' and 'monsters', who ran around on all fours, covered in red hair, eating people. Theosophy was popular in Germany, including with Lanz and List, who pinched some of its tenets: Blavatsky's cult seal featured a swastika, once an innocent Hindu fortune and fertility symbol. Believing men would be reincarnated as their own ancestors once humanity had eventually evolved back upwards into god-men, Blavatsky promised we would be reborn as 'Lords of planets, Regents of galaxies and wielders of fire-mist'. Supposedly, she gained some of this insight from two Hidden Masters named Morya and Koot Hoomi, highly spiritually evolved Aryan god-men who lived in the Himalayas of Tibet, fine examples of what the white race might become.[8] To all of which tosh, perhaps the most trenchant repudiation is given by the poet Louis MacNeice in his *Bagpipe Music*:

> It's no go the Yogi-man, it's no go Blavatsky,
> All we want is a bank balance and a bit of skirt in a taxi.

During the 1960s and 1970s books of this same basic ilk, now simplified for a mass market with Blavatsky's immaterial space-God replaced by more commercially viable physical space-aliens, enjoyed a widespread vogue, but Ariosophy and some pseudo-archaeological SS *Ahnenerbe* 'Ancestral Research Unit' output stand as clear precursors of the genre. Ancient astronaut theory possesses innate potential for racial theorising; primitive blacks or browns could never *really* build any pyramids without outside help, could they? Some critics have mined the texts of the most successful of all ancient astronaut theorists, Erich von Däniken (b.1935), author of 1968's 40 million-selling *Chariots of the Gods?*, to find queries like 'Was the black race a failure, and did extraterrestrials change the genetic code by gene-surgery and then programme a yellow or a white race?' Von Däniken believed human evolution may be due to ET intervention, asking 'Who has ever seen a white monkey? Or a dark ape with curly hair such as the black race has?' He even suggested aliens might want us to maintain 'strict segregation' of the races or use genetics to decide which combinations of racial interbreeding are 'beneficial' and which 'should be eliminated'. The Swiss von Däniken was hardly a Nazi, but his ideas could obviously be exploited by those who were.[9]

Jörg Lanz von Liebenfels wasn't actually a Nazi himself, either, apparently being forbidden to publish under fascist rule; with his ONT sect suppressed, Lanz spent Hitler's reign in neutral Switzerland.[10] Yet Adolf Hitler really does appear to have been a dedicated reader of Lanz's monthly Ariosophy magazine *Ostara*, named after a pagan goddess of Easter and rebirth, the logo for which was a knight and his horse, both covered in swastikas. Containing illustrations of blonde, white women being molested by gorillas, each issue featured a special theme, most of which seemed like minor variants of the same one – the folly of race-mixing. Issues included *The Aryan and His Enemies*, *The Sex-Life and Love-Life of the Blondes and the Darks*, *The Resurrection of the Blondes to Wealth and Power*, *Racially Conscious and Unconscious Love-Making: A Breviary for the Ripe Blonde Youth*, *Fighters Against the Ape-People* and *World War as a Racial Struggle of the Darks Against the Blondes*.[11] Although Hitler himself wasn't blonde, according to psychologist Wilfried Daim's (1923-2016) 1958 book *The Man Who Gave Hitler His Ideas*, he regularly bought *Ostara* anyway. In 1951 Daim visited Lanz in his Vienna flat, where the old man told the author that in 1909 Hitler, then a penniless Vienna art student, had visited him in *Ostara*'s offices, seeking back-issues to complete his collection of racist monkey-porn. Feeling sorry for Hitler, Lanz gave him the copies for free, together with the bus-fare home. Others also testified to seeing Hitler reading *Ostara*, and a copy of one of Lanz's books did sit in Hitler's personal library, so these claims are generally considered plausible.[12]

Why would Hitler have read a magazine about white Nordic females of original off-Earth origin having sex with dinosaurs and monkeys? The Ariosophists were responding to pressing demographic trends of the time, fearing ethnic Germans like themselves were at imminent risk of being subsumed by teeming animalistic *üntermenschen* ('sub-men') within the polyglot Austro-Hungarian Empire. This was how Hitler described the multi-ethnic Vienna of his youth: 'I found the racial conglomeration of the Imperial capital disgusting, this whole medley of Czechs, Poles, Hungarians, Ruthenians, Serbs and Croats ... The city seemed the very embodiment of racial infamy.' Between 1860 and 1900 the city's population increased threefold, substantially due to immigration, like London today. In talking about dinosaurs and monkeys pleasuring humans, Lanz was drawing a demented parallel with the German race being swallowed into racial chaos via miscegenation. Under such specific historical circumstances, what should have been the very definition of a fringe idea ended up being read about by thousands who shared such basic racial worries – including, apparently, Hitler himself. In the later Third Reich, 'subhumans' really were incinerated and enslaved, marriage laws passed to ensure the purity of the race, and *lebensborn* programmes akin to Lanz's notion of sex-convents initiated, in which SS-men were tasked with impregnating multiple Aryan brood-mothers to produce future soldiers. Madagascar was even considered as a potential location for resettling Europe's Jews by Himmler, as Lanz had prophetically advocated. Whilst depicting Jews and blacks as monkeys in propaganda, the Nazis did not literally believe in love-apes themselves, but it has been credibly argued Lanz's cult helped prepare the road which eventually led to Auschwitz.[13]

* * * * *

1905's *Theo-Zoology: Or, the Lore of the Sodom-Apelings and the Electron of the Gods* is perhaps the funniest book ever written – until you realise what it helped lead to. Later serialised in *Ostara* throughout 1928, Lanz's seminal volume had its origins in an essay for an academic journal which, inexplicably, was accepted for publication (possibly the editor was taken in by Lanz's false adoption of the qualification 'Dr'). This 1903 article, *Anthropozoon Biblicum*, or 'Beast-Men of the Bible', was devoted to a novel re-interpretation of two antique reliefs excavated at the old Iraqi settlement of Nimrud in 1848, depicting odd bipedal animals being led along on leashes like pets before being presented to ancient Assyrian rulers as a tribute, like so:

Lanz suggested these animals were really a species of half-human black African pygmies, descended from a quite separate branch of evolution from real white humans, intended as bestial sex-slaves for the ruling Assyrian elite. These 'love-pygmies', or *Buhlzwerge*, had been one species of beast-men with whom the Aryan race had been foolishly mating for millennia by now, polluting their bloodlines. The rest of his article was devoted to culling supposed evidence for this from the Old Testament.[14] By the time of *Theo-Zoology* itself, these initial thoughts had hardened into a fully fledged sexo-racist conspiracy theory, in which the entire history of ancient civilisation was revealed as having been secretly devoted to the breeding of love-pygmies and other species of well-endowed animal-persons, for the deviant sexual pleasure of fallen Aryans. Other ancient art provided much alleged evidence of this. Consider the image below, found in the ruins of Pompeii:

For Lanz, this showed not two men transporting an animal across some water, but three 'ugly hobgoblins travelling on a barge', proving that *Buhlzwerge* survived into Roman times; it looks as if two semi-humans are preparing to penetrate the monkey-dwarf, one in the mouth and one from behind, whilst messing about on the river.[15] Or what about this, which seems to show a small human figure mounted on an obscure symbol of some kind, a bit like a modern key-ring?

To Lanz, this really shows 'a pygmy girl impaled on a phallus', this being 'archaeological proof that men also have committed bestiality'.[16] This pottery-shard, meanwhile, apparently shows some loose-moralled white woman 'with large buttocks' lying down waiting to be serviced by a reindeer:

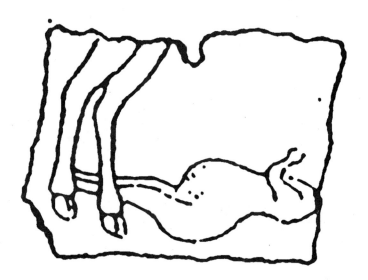

One can only speculate as to whether both of Rudolf's big red bulbs glowed in the dark.[17] The end-result of such unnatural unions could be horrific. The reindeer-woman's ample backside resembles the one shown in this Egyptian image of 'an excessively fat woman':

Egypt, Lanz explains, is close to Somalia, where 'the phenomenon of large buttocks is still very common.'[18] These unnatural posteriors may have represented 'some type of water-wings for swimming', inherited from *üntermenschen* blacks' animal-ancestors, like fatty anal life-jackets, but when these oddly shaped maidens wore clothes, 'they must have resembled walking bells', like this poor unfortunate from Thracia, 'a region prostitutes were drawn from in antiquity':

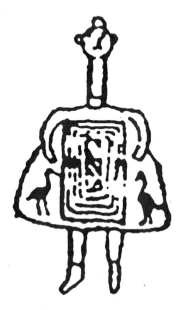

Wherever you saw a depiction of a woman wearing a large dress, it was a sure sign she was only doing so to hide her figure[19] – even if the woman in question happened to be the Virgin Mary holding the infant Christ:

It now perhaps becomes easier to see why Lanz was expelled from his Cistercian monastery.[20] The following 'strange humanoid shape' was found in Bosnia, meanwhile:

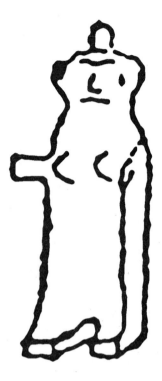

This demonstrated conclusively that miscegenation with beast-men had destroyed even the white European race.[21] No sane mother wanted to give birth to a baby shaped like *that*. So why did they risk it? A glance at the following fossil of a primitive monkey and relief-carving of a dinosaur-hominid should make the answer clear:

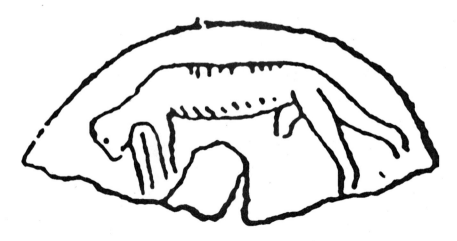

Both have extraordinarily large penises or, as Lanz puts it, a 'strikingly large genital organ'.[22] No wonder the Greeks once carried around 'small men' possessing 'large genital members' with them everywhere they went, and 'called them muscle-stretchers'.[23] But it was not worth sleeping with a beast-man with a long front-tail, otherwise your son might be born with a long back-tail instead, as with the following poor unfortunate:

'That there were, and still are, people with tails is a scientific fact', says Lanz – which is sort of true, there are people occasionally born with abnormal fleshly appurtenances which resemble tails, but certainly not for the reasons he suggests![24]

Lanz's innovative re-readings of pottery, carvings and fossils were not quite as revolutionary as his re-readings of the Bible, however, which turned out to be a giant warning against bestiality in disguise – although he prefers to use the term 'sodomy' instead, as the Sodomites whose city was famously destroyed by God in the Book of Genesis were actually 'guilty of this most terrible crime' of mating with animal-people, rather than having anal sex with one another, as is generally assumed.[25] The author's own personal copy of the Bible seemed a bit different from those owned by most Christians, with Ezekiel XXIII:20 now complaining of how 'Women were crazy for the voluptuousness of fornication with those whose members are like the members of asses and whose flood of semen is like semen from a stallion.'[26] The King James Bible is a bit more coy in its phrasing here, speaking of a woman who had once 'played the harlot in the land of Egypt', enjoying the fact her lovers had large penises *like* those of donkeys; but just because they were well-endowed it did not mean they were actually *descended* from donkeys. Lanz thought otherwise. An amateur philologist, he felt an old name for Egypt, *Misraim*, meant 'Land of the Bastards', this actually referring to its women's illegitimate half-animal offspring.[27]

His logic now strangely echoes the online conspiracy theorists of the 2016 'Pizzagate' saga, in which alt-right loons accused the owners of an innocent US pizzeria of having a dungeon full of underage sex-slaves hidden beneath it, for the sole use of prominent paedophile left-wing politicians like Hillary Clinton; when such words as 'pizza' or 'ice-cream' appeared on receipts, these were really code words for items like 'naked five-year-old boy' or 'helpless baby girl' which had been ordered by the fiends to abuse down in the basement that day. Completely arbitrarily, Lanz anticipated the alt-right by deciding various common words used in the Bible and many other ancient texts, like 'water' and 'bread', really meant things like 'penis', 'vagina', 'anus', 'dinosaur-sex', 'beast-man' or 'monkey-love'. The old parables of religion and myth may sound unlikely to modern ears, but in fact 'they are written in a secret language and contain absolutely no absurdities or fables,' being disguised 'scientific treatises' explaining why it is never OK to rape an ape. 'God is love devoid of the ape-nature,' it says in the New Testament. 'If we preserve this love among our kind, then God will remain in us.' This is primitive eugenics, said Lanz, the Bible scientifically advising whites to stick to their own kind and resist the donkey-dicks of others. Christ's command for men to 'Love thy neighbour' was also a sensible and practical racist message, really meaning 'Don't have sex with foreigners,' the very word 'foreigner' being only a euphemism for 'monkey'. If every white man went around 'sexually loving his neighbour' then Aryan civilisation would never have collapsed in the first place. Even incest is better than race-

48

mixing, says God – as long as your family is white. The Bible's true message has been 'intentionally forgotten' today, with its remberance having been 'prevented by all sorts of tortures and persecution' by an international ape-man conspiracy who seek to keep whites submerged within the stinking mire of interracial civilisation. As Lanz knew his 'rediscoveries [of the keys to the Bible-Code] will be the fall of many', he was already preparing himself 'for the most furious attacks' from the agents of the cover-up. If the conspirators did manage to silence him, though, then his readers need remember only one important fact when next perusing their Bibles and Greek myths: 'Everything is meant in the erotic sense.'[28]

Everything? Yes, *everything*. Lanz had sex not only on the brain, but also on the stomach, thinking 'All banquets and symposia of the ancients were filthy Sodomite feasts,' or orgies. 'Eaters of fish' were those who liked performing (oral?) sex on animal-people, whilst 'the staff of bread' really indicated the huge baguette-like penises of 'the sodomite monsters', so 'to shove bread in the oven' means to be deeply penetrated by the shaft of a monkey, whilst 'the bread of a mother's womb' indicated such a woman had given birth to a mis-shapen loaf, as an ape-lover's belly inevitably 'generates atrocious beast-men'. This was the evil 'power of bread' mentioned in the Book of Isaiah; it was no wonder in Ezekiel XVI:13, God ranted of how 'I want to smash the staff of bread', indicating all true white Christians should go around snapping monkey-cocks to keep their race pure. 'Wine' and 'water' also had hidden meanings. When the mixing of water and wine was damned, was this another hidden reference to the sin of miscegenation?[29] If ancient persons drank water or wine, meanwhile, they had to drink it from pots or jugs. Were these yet more code words? When Lanz discovered the following carving of a repulsive dwarf, he began to realise the horrible truth:

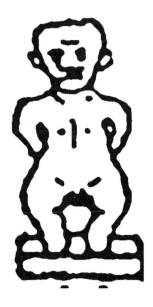

Look at the flat top of its head, and the way its arms hang down by the side of the body in a way somewhat resembling handles. (Do we not also still speak of ugly folk possessing 'jug-ears', one might add?) When the people of the Bible 'drank' from 'pots', they were actually consuming dwarf-semen! Ancient people had become so perverted they had begun deliberately breeding with midgets who looked like earthenware vessels, with the term 'mixing jug' actually meaning 'race-mixing jug', or 'sodomite jug'; the vessel of the Aryan body was being deliberately soiled, thereby watering down the red, red wine of Nordic blood, diluting it into worthless nothing.[30] And how to explain the fact ancient writers kept going on about towns, cities, houses and buildings? Surely it couldn't just be because they lived in them or something? No, these too were 'code words for these apelings of fornication'. In particular, *Buhlzwerge* sex-dwarfs were kept in special sex-towers for use later, so the Tower of Babel story 'now receives a deep and intelligible meaning which up to now was lacking' – the chaos of mixed Babel-tongues anticipates the chaos of mixed Babel-races in modern-day Babylons like Jew-riddled Vienna, an 'absurd orgy' of wrongness. And how did you 'enter' a building or tower? Through a door, naturally, which must have indicated a sex-beast orifice; the 'Doors of Hades' now took on a whole new meaning. As in Hebrew the same word was apparently used for 'barley', 'horror', 'pubic hair' and 'gate', there was much scope for confusion. A biblical 'howling gate of Babylon' may just have been a beastly vagina so hairy it made you want to scream.[31] Musical instruments, such as flutes, were really just animal-penises to be played upon with your mouth and fingers, whilst sewing-related items like flax, linen and so forth were also codes for ape-lovers; a carpet-weaver is one who 'breeds such dwarfs for commercial purposes' on stud farms. The less said about the 'purple wares' they offered their richer clients, the better. Disturbingly, as Jesus was buried within a shroud, 'one of these sodomite cloths is in the grave of Christ.'[32]

It now became possible to reinterpret so many beloved old Bible tales anew. When Moses' Jews fled Egypt after the parting of the Red Sea, they were truly perpetrating an 'escape from the sodomite flood of Egypt', so they wouldn't be raped by subhumans.[33] The word 'usury' is also usually interpreted as meaning lending out money at excessive interest rates, a crime traditionally attributed to the Jews – but what if 'usury' actually meant breeding and then selling on *Buhlzwerge* at an excessively large profit-margin? This made Jesus' violent rampage against the moneylenders in the Temple much more understandable; not only were greedy Jews selling monkey sex-slaves in the House of God, they were doing so at rip-off prices.[34] Stones were also sex-apelings, so when Pygmalion slept with a living statue in Greek myth, he was really embracing a female ape, when Orpheus made stones dance with his sweet music he was charming animal-lovers into his bed, and when 'the stones cry out' in Hebrews II:11, they are presumably having an orgasm. Therefore, when the biblical stone-walls of Jericho come tumbling down, this represents the temptations of the sex-monkey army being resisted by the truly righteous. When Jesus rolls away the stone from his own tomb and that of Lazarus, He is saving corpses from necrophiliac defilement at the hands of yet more rapist simian dwarfs.[35] The classic tale of Daniel in the Lions' Den, meanwhile, where the lions miraculously refuse to eat the holy hero, is easily transformed into an uplifting parable about a faithful Christian's refusal to have sex with tiny hairy people within a public arena:

In these images of Daniel bravely resisting the animal-men's apparent attempts to offer him a blowjob, taken from the Roman catacombs where so many early Christians were said to have hidden from persecution, Lanz notes admiringly how he is depicted as a 'beautiful, noble European man'.[36]

As for the story of the Garden of Eden, the very word 'garden', together with the names for many of a garden's usual contents, such as trees and wood, all meant sex-apes too, whilst the name 'Adam' was really *udumu*, a small 'hairy being'. As in much modern-day ancient astronaut theory, for Lanz God did not create Adam from scratch so much as cause him to evolve into a superior racial being, like Darwinism on fast-forward, but he then fell to temptation for the 'forbidden fruit' of animal genitalia, with unfortunate consequences. The Fall of Man is an allegory for Aryan Adam's racial decline, an 'Original Sin' now shared in by the entire palsied white race. Apparently, when Genesis says Adam 'named the animals' this really means that 'he sodomised them', which is never a good idea. 'The biblical Eden is the Garden of the Joys of Sodom,' explains Lanz, with mankind itself since having become a gigantic garden and Christ the gardener, who comes to uproot all the polluting racial weeds, 'bitter roots' and 'strange trees' choking up our true human bloodline.[37] Figs are 'a symbolic designation for female genitalia in the languages of most people', meanwhile, meaning a biblical reference to someone's 'fig-daughter' tasting 'as sweet as a fig in everyone's mouth' was simply a reference to someone pimping out his hot female monkey-baby for anyone to have a lick.[38] The word 'bean' is also highly suspect. Pythagoras, the Greek philosopher and mathematician, once led a bizarre cult devoted to worshipping numbers, which contained as one of its main rules a total ban on eating beans: 'Miserable world, abstain from the enjoyment of beans!' Pythagoras commanded. But 'surely the enjoyment of the harmless hulled fruit can't be meant by this,' says Lanz. Indeed not, as the very word 'bean' also 'serves as a designation of the genitalia' of black men – no white woman should ever allow herself to become full of beans, therefore.[39]

Satan the Fallen Angel was truly a white-winged Aryan from outer space, and when he tempted Eve in Eden, he was a snake only allegorically, as few snakes are able to talk people into 'eating apples' – that is, bending over and spreading their legs for them. By polluting his blood with the monkey-woman Eve, Satan represents symbolically the ancient fact that, after flying down to Earth, 'The [white] god-men sodomised the ape-people … [and] lost something of their higher natures, but on the other hand made the *udumi* [Adams – i.e. monkey-folk] more like gods and bred them upward' with their space-sperm. Various biblical mentions of angels mating with the sons of men should be taken in a similar fashion.[40] Ancient winged beings like Satan and his fellow fallen angels were real – they were our infinitely great-great-grandfathers. How else to explain the existence of the hideous pterodactyl?

If a winged Aryan angel rapes a dinosaur, what kind of offspring do you expect to end up with? That space-Aryans could successfully interbreed with dinosaurs could be proven by looking closely at the hands of griffins, iguanodons and other such scaly beasts:

Just as Jewish and black monkeys now looked (misleadingly) human because their veins had been infused with once-pure Aryan blood, so the dinosaurs and dragons had grown deceptively human-like hands with fingers and thumbs too. Tales of winged monsters, or part-human, part-reptilian creatures like bat-people, harpies, ostrich-men and the shape-shifting snake-women called lamias were thus based on truth. 'Arab' means something like 'raven-bastard', says Lanz, demonstrating how many Middle Easterners are descended from 'flying entities'. He cites an ancient report that in the Iraqi city of Borsippa there was once a 'linen-factory', which was obviously just more code for a big building in which people had sex with bats, hoping to breed 'resistant bastards' out of them for further sexual deviancy – I believe that's also how coronavirus started over in China.[41] So, the Aryans of old did not just breed with monkeys and lizard-people. Sometimes they copulated with weasels, mice and hedgehogs, too, although Lanz admits that perhaps the names given to various animals in days of yore were not the same as those they bear now; thus, when he unearths a coded reference to someone eating a piece of bread as really meaning they are sodomising a hedgehog, it could equally mean they are being fellated by a camel.[42] For example, Egyptians notoriously enjoyed raping crocodiles, but it is hard to see how such a dangerous activity could take place, even when the beasts had been first 'captured with a hook' and 'hoodwinked' with a sack over their heads before 'one can do what one wants with it'. Maybe the first space-Aryans could easily rape dinosaurs to create griffins, but the degenerate humans who came after them would find it hard not to be eaten. Therefore, these crocodiles must actually have been ordinary *Buhlzwerge* who just *looked* like crocs, having some scaly skin condition like icthyosis. This explains 'the tendency of the skin of negroes to have a wrinkled formation' – the monkey-men are themselves descended from dinosaur-folk.[43]

What is certain is that ancient perverts even liked to have sex with mer-men and fish-people, or 'sea-bastards' as they were commonly known – icthyosis literally means 'fish-skin'. These were 'two-legged beasts about 1.2 metres tall with scaly skin' mentioned 'in the ancient Law Code of the Babylonian King Hammurabi ... as bastards.' In the Bible, the giant sea-monster Leviathan is normally thought to be a whale but may actually have been a colossal sea-bastard: 'However, having intercourse with him is not without danger, and this is why he is fettered and given a muzzle' in the relevant passage. 'Fish-men' were still popular sexual partners into Roman times, when 'the lascivious Roman noblewomen would flock around them in large numbers' during their notorious orgies. Such animals – which looked very much like the dinosaur-hominids – were still being seen in swamps or caught in nets right into the 1800s, Lanz said.[44] Here is one being led about on a lead:

All this sheds new light upon Jesus' feeding of the five thousand, when He miraculously made five loafs and two fish serve to feed the entire crowd who had assembled to hear Him preach. Clearly, this meant Christ had actually passed around five monkey-dwarfs and two mermaids for anyone who wanted a go. If the entire crowd took Jesus up on this offer, the beasts would quickly die from exhaustion, not to mention the risk of them catching STDs. That they managed to fulfil the passions of everyone present can only mean Jesus' impassioned Hitler-style sermon against race-mixing was so persuasive that nobody present there that day dared take Him up on the offer, thus proving how His true message, since suppressed by those who had filled the Bible with stupid code words like 'bread', could one day save our fallen souls from sexual sin. Amazingly, the crowd had even handed over their pre-owned *üntermenschen* sex-slaves to Jesus and His disciples for safe disposal once His speech was over; such was the power of the Word of the Lord.[45]

Lanz amassed a wide array of undeniable proof for his notions, such as the fact that 'Even in modern times, sexual activity with animals, especially of women with dogs, is not uncommon,' at least in the circles he moved. Meanwhile, 'Even today in India, girls are deflowered by an idolatrous doll which is fitted with a large wooden member,' a stand-in for the former fleshly penis of an apeling. He also provides ample evidence of women frequently having sex with goats in public in ancient Egypt and Rome, where this was considered to cure infertility. Furthermore, Lanz had discovered certain types of syphilis were common to humans and chimpanzees, whilst the remains of hairy Neanderthal Man was more support for his theory, as was the continued existence of hirsute 'Alpine cretins'. Meanwhile, studies had shown that '20 per cent of the population' of pre-Christian civilisation were dwarfs, a time remembered allegorically in all those old fairy tales about 'dwarfs who violate beautiful women' of an ordinary Aryan size and appearance on hillsides, making them cry; the original version of Snow White must have been most un-Disney-like. Whilst Dopey, Sneezy, *et al* had small bodies, 'nothing may be said concerning their other physical properties' – no need for them to be Bashful about what they had swinging down below. Tales of dragons abducting women were also really recollections of dinosaur-men acting similarly; fossils of 'lower human types' and 'higher beast-men' were difficult to distinguish between. Records from medieval witch-trials, where witches were forced to confess to having had group-sex with demons, were furthermore just truthful accounts of their orgies with surviving *Buhlzwerge*.[46]

The tendency of today's rich women to dress their lapdogs up in human-like finery was also a relic from olden times, when ladies had costumed their pet *Buhlzwerge* as people. The desire for such apelings to wear human clothes was their literal downfall, as this was how they were captured. Cunning ape-hunters would leave out pairs of tubes filled with glue, which the retarded beast-men would think were trousers. Putting them on, the stiff leg-tubes would prevent them running away, making them easy prey to be raped when they fell over. Alternatively, the hunters could wash their eyes in tubs of water within sight of the hiding monkeys. Then, they would leave out substitute tubs filled with birdlime. As 'monkey see, monkey do', the *Buhlzwerge* would copy the humans by washing their eyes with the birdlime, sticking them together and blinding them, once more making them easy to rape.[47] Most obviously as regarded the truth of his ideas, said Lanz, all black people supposedly looked like monkeys, as in the following 'ethnographic' drawing of a member of the Wambutti pygmy-people of Central Africa, with his characteristic 'chimpanzee-like facial structure':

'It is striking that the most ape-like men and the most man-like apes live so close to one another,' wrote Lanz, implying black Africans and gorillas were still interbreeding.[48] Fearlessly, Lanz then collected reliable testimony that modern-day monkeys were total perverts:

> The lewdness of apes, especially of the baboon, exceeds all imagination. They are sodomites, pederasts and onanists; they also act in a disgraceful manner toward men and boys. It is universally agreed upon that baboons will attack and mistreat little girls, and that in zoos women are inconvenienced by their vile forwardness and shamelessness. North of Lake Kiwu in Africa, the natives tell of giant apes called gorillas which abduct women and rip up their sexual parts during intercourse.[49]

And, if you really demanded absolute, final proof that rapist gorillas could impregnate human females, Lanz had one final suggestion: 'Since the matter is of extreme importance, it is high time that experiments in such cross-breeding of species should begin,' although 'of course, only under the direction of scientific specialists.'[50]

* * * * *

Besides denigrating the brown ape-men, Lanz also celebrated the white god-men, or Theo-Zoa, who came ultimately from outer space, his thinking here partly influenced by Madame Blavatsky; by combining Guido von List's worship of the Aryan race with Blavatsky's Theosophy cult, you get his own personal 'Ariosophy'. These Theo-Zoa were 'older, genetically related forms of humankind', once possessed of wonderful sense organs like a Third Eye which facilitated psychic abilities. Humans today still possess 'vestigial remains' of such organs, particularly the pineal gland, identified by Classical authors as the seat of the soul, which is really an atrophied Third Eye. That lizards also possess pineal glands is more proof the Theo-Zoa once mated with dinosaurs, Lanz explains (in reality, it means humans' mammalian ancestors long ago evolved ultimately from lizards, hence biologists speaking of our 'lizard-brains' to describe certain ancient architectures of our grey matter's wiring). Doubtless, these Third Eyes worked via electrical means; Lanz had been inspired by the recent discovery of x-rays, radio communication, electrons and radioactivity. 'If I were asked what I understood divinity to be,' said Lanz, he would answer 'the living beings of the ultraviolet forces and worlds' which once upon a time had 'moved about in complete purity' but currently 'slumber in bestialised human bodies'. Remember, many of the old Germanic deities were sky gods like Thor, who hurled thunderbolts down to Earth. This could only mean that 'To be electric and to be divine is the same thing!' with the biblical Jehovah Himself being 'a winged entity' having 'the form of the electron' and being 'ablaze with radiation', an animate electrical cloud with 'hands and the appearance of a man', which was why his true descendants, 'the Sons of God, have feet similar to those of the electron'. Like Thor, Jehovah 'hurls lightning rays' to smite sinners, and the reason His Ark of the Covenant struck down anyone who touched it was because it was electrified like a cattle-fence. This was also why Satan was said to descend to Earth 'like a bolt of lightning'.[51]

This explained why today the world's best psychics were 'relatively racially pure white people' like the Frisians, who inhabited fairly cool climates. Electricity is known to be conducted better through a cold medium than through a warm medium, so 'clairvoyant Frisians', living as they did in a 'foggy country' where the heat-giving sun was often obscured, were better able to transmit electrically based psychic messages to one another through the vestigial Third Eyes hidden away somewhere inside their lizard-brains. The Germanic god Wotan's single, prophecy-enabling eye was an allegory of this truth; the cyclopean eye of the deity represents the invisible psychic 'eye' of the white clairvoyant's vestigial Theo-Zoan pituitary gland. The prehistoric dinosaurs also once lived in 'a dim, misty world', just like many fog-bound modern Germans, meaning the electric powers they, too, inherited from their white alien forefathers were highly developed. This discovery allowed the intelligent Ariosophist to solve many long-standing puzzles of palaeontology, such as why the Stegosaurus had all those large 'apparently quite useless' bony plates lined up along its spine where they were little good as armour. Today, scientists think they were probably used to regulate body temperature by catching the sun's rays, but Lanz perceived they were actually 'electrical induction antennae' akin to biological satellite dishes, with Theo-Zoa and armoured dinosaurs alike being 'not only living electrical receiving stations ... [but] also electrical power and broadcasting stations' for psychic radio-messages. The wings of pterosaurs and other prehistoric winged beings could also 'easily have served to generate power' like wind-turbines if flapped quickly enough. Lanz notes how many dinosaurs had 'a large swelling in the spinal cord in the haunch area' which 'has to be accounted for in some way' – clearly, they were electrical accumulators or batteries. There were still today electric eels and 'strange deep-sea fish' with bioluminescent properties swimming through the world's waters, proving it was quite possible for an animal to be electric.[52]

This all had profound implications for racial hygiene, as 'a meaningful role is played by [electrical] radiation in the sexual life,' with the fertilisation of female eggs being possible without using any semen. You just had to beam 'ultrared and other warm rays' at eggs from a fully functioning Third Eye, thus one day rendering 'the male absolutely unnecessary' for reproduction once Aryans had evolved back upwards into aliens. By white people only having sex with other white people, ultimately siring new Theo-Zoa, they would eventually have no need to have sex with anyone at all, thus explaining old tales of virgin births. Ancient Aryans, being closer to their Theo-Zoa forefathers, could make their kind pregnant just by looking at them – although unfortunately some had misused this power by looking at monkeys or cows with lustful thoughts and impregnating them instead. This is why so many ancient gods like Hermes were hermaphrodites. Originally, all Theo-Zoa were made thus, as could be seen by closely examining a woman's clitoris, which was 'nothing other than a stunted penis' from the good old days when women were also men. Naturally, 'the pure blonde Germanic race has the greatest inclination to hermaphroditism today'; contemporary German researchers had proved that 'there really are lactating men' walking around the country, leaking milk everywhere. Entomologists knew it was possible to fertilise the eggs of silk moths by brushing them lightly with certain chemicals in lieu of insect-sperm – if moths could do it, why not Germans?[53]

All this now made the life of Christ much more comprehensible. The true message of the Bible, since suppressed, was that 'Through Christ, the beast-man in us should die out,' if only we would follow His excellent example of never sodomising monkeys. Jesus is often acclaimed as 'The Light of the World', really meaning He was electric, like a lightbulb; but the only reason He shone so bright is because He was 'one of the angels who did not sully himself with sodomy'.[54] Lanz's extraordinarily blasphemous retelling of the New Testament truly is The Greatest Story Never Told. The Nativity narrative is the first to get electrically re-wired; when 'the Angel of God' announced Mary was pregnant, this was just a euphemism for a Theo-Zoan god-man stirring up her eggs with electric waves. 'Where will I get a boy-child from, as no man has touched me and I am not a prostitute!' Mary shouted when the Angel Gabriel told her she was carrying Christ, but he had already raped her with his eyes.[55] Jesus being 'an electric pre-human', and 'probably one of the last' of the pure Aryan humanoid space-electrons, explained how He performed His many miracles. When He healed lepers, it was by using radiation, and when He animated clay birds in certain apocryphal texts, He was imitating that other great Germanic genius Professor Frankenstein by bringing things to life with lightning. When an unclean menstruating woman touched the hem of His garb in the Gospel of Luke and He 'felt a power going out from me', this was because she had drained Him of juice like a piece of heavy machinery; she's lucky she didn't have her eggs fried on the spot. Other miracles could always be explained by virtue of yet more code words. When Christ turned water into wine at Cana, He was just stopping people from having an orgy with *Buhlzwerge* dwarfs who resembled water jugs. That many of Jesus' disciples were fishermen only meant they had once earned their living catching fish-people for sale as sex-slaves; Jesus' preaching had successfully reformed them. His exorcism of devils from possessed persons simply indicated He had chased hairy midgets away from entering into their bodies.[56] But all this pales into insignificance by comparison with Lanz's deliriously obscene reinterpretation of Christ's crucifixion. Crucifixion, the Ariosophist sage reveals, did not actually exist as a form of execution in the ancient world at all, as proven by the following old Roman graffiti from Pompeii:

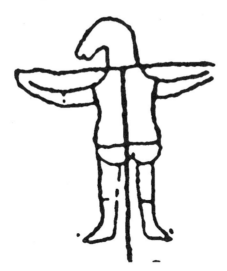

This is known as the 'mocking crucifixion' and is generally guessed to deride early Christians as worshipping a donkey-headed fool, something Lanz links to Romans once calling Christ's followers 'donkey-bastards'. But Lanz believed there really were men with donkeys' heads during ancient times, and it should also be noted how you can see the donkey-fool's behind, which faces outwards towards the crowd of onlookers who would have gathered to view this irresistible spectacle. Self-evidently, all talk of Roman crucifixions actually referred to the practice of 'binding wild and unruly sodomite monsters to poles in order to be able to copulate with them without danger', presumably from a step-ladder. However, the reverse scenario could also occur, with human criminals strapped to a cross to be raped or sodomised by 'lascivious apelings', as a form of torture or 'Death by Um-Bongo', as the old joke went. Early Christians were routinely subjected to this form of public humiliation, and Jesus Himself was no exception. Prior to arrest, Jesus had met His disciples in the Garden of Gethsemane, which, translated, really means 'Garden of the Sodomite Olives', 'olives' being yet another code word for love-apes. Here, Jesus had resisted temptation but then been strapped to the cross like the Pompeii donkey-man where He then 'died' whilst 'screaming mightily', but only metaphorically. When He 'died', it truly means He was raped by monkeys, an ordeal He thankfully survived. When He later returns and shows Doubting Thomas His wounds, these were not caused by Roman nails, but by the claws of the *Buhlzwerge*, who had torn at his white Aryan body. Ever since, similar wounds had been viewed by those ape-resistant Christian martyrs who wore them as 'the most excellent bodily decorations'.

Christ was successfully 'outraged by the sodomite hobgoblins', but He submitted to this ordeal completely under duress; this was the true nature of His test from God. 'If He consented to this willingly and if He was overcome by temptation, then His whole mission would have been dashed.' Allegorically, He becomes rather like Odysseus lashed to the mast in *The Odyssey* so he can hear the sirens' enticing song without crashing his ship onto their rocks. Truly, Odysseus had simply resisted ravishing the fishy flesh of a gang of slutty mermaids by being bound, just as Jesus had resisted. This was why, in some ancient art, the figures of Christ and Odysseus became conflated. 'Liberate me from the hand of the hound!' Jesus prays to God during His sufferings, but as Lanz astutely observes, normal dogs don't have hands; maybe the sex-mutants were of various different species? What did 'the hand of the hound' try to do to Him? Lanz does not say, but whatever it was, Jesus ultimately managed to use His powers to break free from his bindings and overpower His *Buhlzwerge* guards, a feat encoded by the biblical lie that He rose from the dead; to resurrect oneself in this context means simply 'to stand up out of the sodomite grave' and reject the siren-call of monkeys and the tender loving hands of dogs. Bursting loose, Jesus 'overpowered the sodomite gravestones' and 'hurled the sodomite linens away' like Samson, picking up the monkey-rapists and throwing them around like rag dolls. Then, He ran away. When the Bible says He rose into the clouds, it means He fled into the desert dust, where there were fewer potential slavering sex-hounds. He even kept on coming back to town to show off his wounds to His old friends, so obviously Jesus *couldn't* have died, could He? Unlike the above narrative, that would just be stupid.[57]

However, in some ancient art Jesus is portrayed as a fiery phoenix rising from the ashes of His death, the literal reality of this bird's existence in centuries past being attested to by 'very reliable and credible historians'. As the closest thing humanity had seen to one of the original winged Theo-Zoa during historical times, Jesus was probably thus an actual phoenix in some sense, with the 'fire' in which He dies just being His electric glow. 'Age is a disease,' Lanz concludes, which fallen mankind, ravaged by apes, now suffers from unnecessarily; the fact that 'parrots reach an extreme age is well-known', and if one day Aryan mankind should sprout back his angelic space-wings, then maybe we too would not grow old or weary. When Christ is reborn like a phoenix, it really symbolises how one day the white human race will be reborn as glowing Theo-Zoa, who may aspire to immortality.[58]

* * * * *

You seldom saw a full-blown hairy midget Sodom-apeling walking around Europe today though, so was the danger to life and loins now over? Far from it:

> The present-day coloured human races are nothing other than ... [*Buhlzwerge*] which have been bred upward by contact with *homo Europeaus*. They are as dangerous to [God's children] today as they were in pre-history. They ensnare us with their arts of love – breeding themselves upward, while breeding us downward![59]

'God is purified race!' declared Lanz, with whites being 'children from His semen, from His flesh and from His bone'. God still lived within the German *volk*, but 'as in an apeman-husk, He is wrapped in sodomite linen, like a corpse in mummy bandages.' An early proponent of body-horror, Lanz knew that 'the Kingdom of God is within us,' as the Bible says, but at present both 'Heaven *and* Hell dwell within our bodies' due to Aryans' inheritance of traits from monkeys and lizard-men. Nonetheless, the God within white men 'is not dead, He is only sleeping, but the day is coming, and it is not far off, when He will once more be resurrected [by] selective breeding,' which will occur once all true Germans finally realise Heaven is 'a racially hygienic institution' in which 'the angelic men' enjoy total 'rulership' over their ethnic inferiors. Jesus did not descend from space to unite mankind in brotherly harmony, 'Jesus came in order to divide' us into worthwhile wheat and worthless chaff, sheep and goats. When the Bible speaks of Christ presiding over the Last Judgement condemning some to Hell and letting others into Heaven, it does not mean the literal Christ raped by apes and dogs on the cross, but 'the once more purely bred and transfigured white man of the future' who will transform white Europe into paradise and burn the *Buhlzwerge* in a death camp Hell. Soon, the Aryan angels 'will reap the human harvest' and were already 'whetting their scythes for the mowing down of whole peoples'.[60] Lanz's language becomes pretty hard-core Old Testament:

> All of mankind, including the Germanic lands, is today dying the sodomitic death, we are drowning in the mixing-jug of the Whore of Babylon, who has sucked the marrow from our bodies and the brains from our skulls.

We know that the Fire of Sodom is the Devil – the beast-man. He is in Hell: he is the worm that never dies. In the Apostles' Creed XVI it is said that in the final days mankind will be tested by fire. All offspring of Sodom, all apelings, will burn themselves up in the fire-oven of fornication. The sensual prurience, which stems from the apeling-blood, from the swirling water, is the fire which cannot be quenched, it is the Hell in which today nearly all of mankind languishes weeping and gnashing its teeth … The time has come! The old sodomite brood in the Middle East and all around the Mediterranean is degenerate and wretched, the one-time paradisiacal fields are completely exploited and plundered like a wheat-field in which a thievish horde of apes has taken up residence. Our bodies are infected with a mange which despite every kind of soap remains … Never has human life been as miserable as it is today – despite all its technical advancements. Devilish human beasts oppress us from above, slaughtering millions of people in unconscionably murderous wars conducted for the enrichment of their own personal money-bags [a reference to Jews]. Savage human beasts undermine the pillars of culture from below. Mankind is putrid like Lazarus and already exudes the stink of sodomite death. What do you want with Hell in the Beyond?! Isn't life in the one we are living in now, and in which we are now burning, terrible enough?[61]

The situation had become so dire, only extreme solutions were possible. The dinosaur-hominids and dwarfish *Buhlzwerge* of the Bible were almost now extinct, having 'been assimilated into the race of mankind as mongrels', thus demonstrating how 'whole races are exterminated with the advance of the whites!' By simply keeping their womenfolk away from sex with Jews, Slavs, blacks and other non-Aryans, it should be possible for whites to wipe the modern-day mongrel beast-men out, too.[62] Once miscegenation had been outlawed, 'Those of lesser value must be exterminated in a gentle way – by castration and sterilisation.' Lanz was also 'certainly not against condoms', as 'those who seek out copulation only for the purposes of lascivious enjoyment' and 'the nymphomaniacal baboon she-creatures afraid of birth-pains' will 'exterminate themselves, will strangle themselves with rubber' thereby. Juvenile delinquents must also 'be castrated without mercy, or sterilised by radiation'. Most criminals were the result of sex with beast-men outside marriage, which is why 'Among the Persians when someone commits a crime an investigation is made as to whether he is a bastard,' as he usually is. 'If we only allow fit persons to reproduce, the hospitals, prisons and the giant criminal justice system will become superfluous,' saving the State millions.[63] As cold, Nordic blood 'must again sweep through the withered garden of mankind and extinguish the southern ape-rut', it would be best to destroy the cult of feminism so beloved of 'the so-called modern woman' with her calls for 'free love', which are really nothing more than disguised longings for 'the burning tender sodomite pieces of wood [i.e. erect penises] … for all those completely wild lascivious beasts'. Such 'hysterical women', with their 'adulterous and sensual' tendencies, 'belong in the whorehouse', where 'the honour of motherhood is withdrawn from her and her name is blotted out of the book of life.' Lanz greatly disapproved of 'unilateral women's rights, which would make the world into a big brothel in which everything revolves around penises and pussies in a silly and absurd satyrs' orgy while the proper wife, the loyal mother of the house, and the healthy strong troop of children, will be mercilessly driven out of the chaste and legitimate home,' which would only delay evolution of the Aryan race.[64] Lanz's overall view on women's rights would give the Taliban pause for thought:

No-one other than those women with their lascivious ape-like natures destroyed the cultures of antiquity and they will bring down our culture as well if men do not stop and think soon ... Avoid sodomy and copulation with the hobgoblins of pleasure, rear your own species! Every man should avoid marrying a woman who has whored around a lot if he wants to generate descendants. The male semen has an effect on the woman such that the child, even when it comes from a legitimate father, still inherits characteristics from all those men with whom the wife had premarital or extramarital intercourse. It is for this reason that the old laws favour marriage with virgins ... Just as different races of men have unequal rights, so too do men and women have unequal rights. The old custom of law [*droit de seigneur*] which allowed the Lord of the Manor to sleep with every virgin first proves that the ancients knew that it is the man who is responsible for breeding the race upward. Dear ladies, tell me honestly, whose wives would you be today if noble [white] men, if god-like Siegfrieds, had not torn you away from the sodomite monsters, if they had not put you in warm nests, if they had not defended you – sword in hand – throughout thousands and thousands of years against Slavs, Mongols, Moors and Turks? Choose between us and those sons of Sodom, have yourselves sexually serviced on the mounds of corpses of your husbands who fell in battle – as so many of your mothers' mothers did! Take them to your husbands' houses, so they can make harem slaves of you, so you can become the mother of a brood of lascivious, bloodthirsty beasts, who know no motherly or wifely love! What [the white] woman is today, she has become thanks to the sword and power of [the white] man. Man wrestled woman from the apes of Sodom, and for this reason she is his property![65]

For highly evolved white males, however, the sexual impulse was quite different, as 'eroticism plays a subordinate role for a racially pure Germanic husband' who 'only enjoys coitus when his chosen wife meets all aesthetic requirements.' As real German men are 'uncommonly choosy' they can be rendered immediately impotent if their wife possesses so much as 'a worn-down shoe', but this is simply a sign of the Aryan race's impending recovery of its former pansexual alien godhood: 'It is just this characteristic of the man of higher race – of his being incapable of immediately servicing any and every woman – that must be further developed and expanded in a systematic way so that husbands will only be potent with their own wives, and with all other women they will become impotent in the literal sense.'[66] It being imperative that 'For the sake of the Kingdom of Heaven we must become eunuchs,' Lanz's ultimate plan in eliminating mating with the ape-men is to eliminate all sexual intercourse itself:

> In the Resurrection [of our race] there will be no more marriage, humans will once more be angels – i.e. hermaphrodites ... [enjoying] the state of bees and ants! We will no longer generate men by means of carnal intercourse, but rather perhaps by means of radiation. Jesus came to abolish the work of women ... We must take off the dark pelt of the ape and put on the shining breast-plate of the God-Man. We come from God and to God we will return.[67]

In a sense, Lanz even ultimately wants his own race to become extinct, along with women and men *per se*; he is a kind of early transhumanist. But if inferior beings like women had to be taken in hand and locked up within their homes or whorehouses, depending on their state of personal moral development, then the inferior races descended directly from the *Buhlzwerge* had to be dealt with even more harshly. The best solution was a disturbing combination of mass slavery and the near-total abolition of charity as a weak and thoroughly un-Christian ideal:

> Culture is impossible without slavery [as Jesus Himself taught] ... The brain-value the noble race of man – above all the Germanics – gave to humanity must now be repaid as brain-interest by those of lesser value in the form of manual labour. Here I am not thinking so much of a subjugation of the coloured races ... but rather much more of a breeding of a new race of slaves, with dull nerves and strong arms; to this new race mental abilities will only be apportioned as necessary. These beings will have to do all the tasks for which machines cannot be invented ... This may sound inhuman. But all the babble about Christian brotherly love is just a conjuring trick of words ... Complete equality is nonsense! If all the estates of the Earth had to be divided up into 1600 million parts [the presumed then-population of the planet] then each individual would get, if everything went well, a loincloth, a hole to live in and a handful of fruit every day! ... Who can say that expansion of equal rights should cease at the Australian Aborigines? Gorillas, chimpanzees and bats have exactly the same claim to socialistic 'human rights'. General equality would not advance the cause of the individual, but would hurl everyone back into the condition of a horde of apes ... Away with false and suicidal brotherly love which was invented by the sodomite apelings and their pastors in order to strangle us ... We must arm ourselves against pity, our greatest weakness ... We [Aryan] lords must check our charitable natures. If the socialists go on strike, then we must

go on strike with our charity. How come there are charitable institutions for hospitals, foundling homes for illegitimate children and fallen girls [i.e. prostitutes]? How come there are no such institutions for the preservation of pure and noble blood and legitimate children? ... Whatever we give to such a person we are taking away from a fit person who has hit a patch of misfortune through no fault of their own ... Those who should be supported are strictly the old, and those of good Germanic descent ... one should expect certain anthropological characteristics of applicants: blue eyes, blonde hair, ruddy complexion, small mouth, healthy teeth, small, slim hands and feet, tall, well-proportioned form.[68]

'Everything for the pearls and nothing for the rotten fish,' as Lanz wrote elsewhere. [69] I suspect Lanz may have been reading his Friedrich Nietzsche (1844-1900) here, the eventually mad German philosopher whose teachings about the forthcoming *übermenschen*, or 'supermen', who would sweep away the weak and false 'slave-religion' of Christianity, were enthusiastically taken up (and wilfully misinterpreted) by many Nazi thinkers. 'Racial breeding and purity of race will be and must be the only religion and Church of the future,' Lanz argued. Christianity had been 'distorted into an altruism' and had to become once more 'an Ariosophic cult-religion of racism, which it was right from the beginning', before Jesus' true message had been subverted by Jews, Communists and other such apelings.[70] Again, it is not hard to see why Lanz got expelled from his monastery.

In *Theo-Zoology*, Lanz didn't yet explicitly advocate simply murdering all non-whites on a systematic basis – that would come later – but the book certainly helped lay the theoretical and rhetorical groundwork for such an idea. In calling for 'a deep moat that cannot be overwhelmed' to surround the 'Valhalla' of a white Germany, over which 'no apeling must be allowed to jump', not even if they came from amongst 'the Welsh and the Slavs' (who may have looked white, but were not) he tried to pave the path towards rejection of the creed of 'counterfeit Christianity', which had preached only false charity and encourage his readers to embrace the idea that 'we must finally start to breed humans' rather than Welshmen.[71] As his *Ostara* magazine progressed, Lanz became more explicit about what was truly necessary. 'By means of Ariosophic running of the economy, the whole problem of unemployment will be solved,' he declared within its pages – as, once Ariosophists were in charge of Europe, anyone who didn't have a job by a certain date would be enslaved within a mine. As only feckless subhuman scum couldn't be bothered to get a job by a pre-announced deadline, only 'untouchables, or rather criminals', would end up toiling away underground, such tasks being 'unworthy of the heroic type of person'. If any *üntermenschen* refused to be mine-slaves, they should be thrown out of civilisation to die in deserts or hurled into 'the forests of the monkeys', where they 'will greet gorillas and baboons as comrades and people of a similar race', uniting with the apes to 'put into reality their socialist, Bolshevik, proletarian State utopia, where everybody has an equal right to vote in secret.'[72]

'The basis of all wars is race-war,' he wrote in another issue, urging his readers to join patriotic paramilitary organisations. Whilst it would be difficult 'to shoot millions of inferior races with our rapid-fire cannons' and 'strangling them with rubber' by making them use condoms would certainly be easier, it may nonetheless be possible to arrange mass executions of expendable apeling-troops during any future conflict by keeping white soldiers in reserve and mercilessly sending 'any coloured ones, without any consideration at all' to die on the front-line as cannon-fodder. If the 'dark, unruly urban mob of untouchables' were slaughtered in this way, then, no matter which warring European nation won the actual war, both sides would end up the true victors, as all the Jews and blacks would lie dead in the trenches. 'The hordes of untouchables have eaten up and destroyed all our economic reserves,' Lanz now fulminated. Thus, there must be 'a bloodless and painless destruction and damming up of the dark, untouchable elements' through a colossal programme of State-enforced euthanasia. The 'sick bodies of inferior races ... millions of whom are incapable of work and are simply unsocial, racial curs' had to be put down like the dogs they were. If any left-wing journalists writing for 'the Monkey-Press' objected to this, then they too would have to be 'stifled'. This was all most necessary, as 'the percentage of mad Jews is quite enormous.'[73]

If some such measures seemed a tad unpalatable, as genocide tends to be, then Lanz sought to disguise this with classic Germanic myths relating to King Arthur and the Norse gods. Wagnerian valkyries and swan maidens were yet more memories of electronic flying Theo-Zoa, he said, whilst the *Sangraal* or Holy Grail itself was nothing but a symbol of the Nordic race's true electronic God. The rainbow, traditional sign of the covenant between God and His people (that is, the white Germans) was simply 'the electrical essence of God', as later personified by Iris, ancient Greek goddess of the rainbow, the daughter of Electra, wife of the wind god, Zephyrus; an alternative name for her was apparently 'Electron'. Electrons themselves now became miniature versions of the *Sangraal*, being 'a mixture of gold and silver' like the sacred vessel itself – but, traditionally, the Holy Grail also symbolised the blood of Christ. Thus, the Grail stood above all else for pure Aryan blood, which would one day be restored by the powerful, sword-like genitals of brave Arthurian Knights with blonde hair and blue eyes, making Germans into electric deities once more.[74] Lanz's most explicit rallying cry to the suffering Nordic race in *Theo-Zoology* is stirring and Romantic:

It has taken a long time for people to be convinced that Germania is the 'womb and factory of nations'. Only today, now that almost the whole world has succumbed to ape-nature – right up to the Germanic countries which have not been fully spared either – does the truth begin to dawn on us, that we are lacking a certain divine humanity in a general flood of ape-men. But it will not be long before a new priestly race will rise up in the land of the electron and the Holy *Graal*, which will play new songs on new harps, and as before, on the first feast of Pentecost, when the Holy Spirit descended in tongues of radiation on the Apostles, so will the electrical swans of the gods come once more to the great Pentecost of mankind. Great princes, strong warriors, God-inspired priests, singers with eloquent tongues and bright-eyed cosmologists will rise up out of Germany's ever-holy soil of the Gods, put the sodomite apelings in chains, establish the Church of the Holy Spirit, of the Holy *Graal* anew, and make the Earth into an Island of the Blessed. The temples of the [false] pastors and the ape-dealers will collapse, the *Graal*-Castle ... will, however, abide until Christ comes again.[75]

In *Ostara*, Lanz explained that, in the years prior to sex itself becoming obsolete, any racially unadulterated white male should have 'the right to put himself forward to several women' to impregnate them, being 'permitted to have more children than those of an inferior race'. Meanwhile, when a woman marries a German who becomes impotent, he should be offered the services of a 'marriage helper', a 'young, strong and efficient' Nordic male with virile sperm who would get the husband's wife pregnant for him. Breeding colonies called 'ecclesia' should be established 'in remote, secret places', far away from the temptations of black or Jewish apes, where such activities could occur on an industrial scale, an early prototype of the later Nazi *lebensborn* programme. Interestingly, Lanz thought members of the old German princely dynasties would make the best human studs for such purposes, as it was in them that electronic alien blood still ran strongest. Given his own claims to be an aristocrat, was he volunteering? Once enough electronic Grail-Knights had been born, it would become Germany's holy duty to 'conquer the whole planet' to bring the 'quarrelsome' sex-monkeys under control at long last, with a free farm being given away from seized territories for the use of every blonde soldier, and a free country estate for every German officer. These new electronic knights would ride out to colonise the planet for its own good, accompanied by 'great princes, doughty warriors, inspired priests, eloquent bards and visionary sages'.[76] Lanz also began developing a new form of racial astrology, believing the stars showed this new Aryan Camelot would be centred upon his home city of Vienna. The clearest signal of this was the transformation of lands like Spain and Italy into 'Jupiter Nations' under their new fascist and proto-fascist governments of the 1920s, precursors of the totalitarian Arthurian global dictatorship which was later to come, lasting until around 2640.[77]

Despite its more lunatic assertions, the mission statement provided in the very first issue of *Ostara* in 1905 certainly sounds like the kind of thing to make Hitler become a loyal reader:

Ostara is the first and only illustrated Aryo-aristocratic collection of publications, which, in both words and pictures, depicts the heroic blonde peoples, the beautiful, moral, noble, idealistic, gifted and religious people;

the creators and keepers of all knowledge, art and culture; and the main bearer of divinity. All iniquity and ugliness originates from the cross-breeding of races, in respect of which, for physiological reasons, the woman has always been and remains more submissive than the man. Thus, the arrival of *Ostara* comes at a time when women and the inferior races are taking it upon themselves to procreate and thereby ruthlessly to eradicate the heroic blonde race of men, who epitomise all outstanding beauty, truth, ambition and seeking of God.[78]

Was Jörg Lanz von Liebenfels really the ultimate source of Adolf Hitler's own extreme racial ideas? No. Hitler already hated the Jews before he ever supposedly bought *Ostara*, the rag being a symptom of the growing proto-Nazi mindset, not its cause. If Hitler read *Ostara* it was because he was an anti-Semite; he wasn't an anti-Semite because he read *Ostara*. However, if Hitler truly was influenced by Lanz, you can see why he failed ever to acknowledge this debt through sheer embarrassment. The specific issues of *Ostara* printed during Hitler's youthful spell in Vienna focused upon cataloguing racial characteristics and criticising feminism, not raping mermen; possibly Adolf had no idea of *Theo-Zoology*'s specific contents, or just wasn't interested in that aspect of Lanz's thought.[79] Yet in later years, other persons of a UFO-friendly Nazi mindset definitely were ...

* * * * *

When in 1955 the Austrian conman and former Gestapo employee Karl Mekis was fleeing to a new life in Chile, after his wife, tired of his continual imprisonment for crimes like smuggling, counterfeiting and the illegal possession of firearms, had finally left him, he met a fellow fraudster named Franz Weber-Richter on the ship to South America. By this time, flying saucers existed, at least in the public mind, and the two men discussed how incredibly gullible many of their believers were. So willing to believe were these fools, they would surely be easy to scam out of their spare cash. Thus was born 'Project Venus', in which Weber-Richter would pose as the illegitimate son of Adolf Hitler, his father supposedly having impregnated a young blonde nurse who looked after him in hospital when he had been wounded during the First World War. Far above in space, said the conmen, on the planet Venus, intelligent aliens had been spying on mankind since 1640. Following the Second World War, alarmed by mankind's development of atom bombs and V-2-type rockets, the Venusians had grown increasingly concerned that humanity may one day attack their home world. Therefore, motivated purely by self-defence, the aliens planned to invade and colonise Earth, just as Hitler had tried to do with Europe. As Hitler had been such an outstanding individual leader, the Aryan-looking Venusians had earmarked his son Weber-Richter as the ideal puppet-ruler of their new fiefdom, appointing him 'President of the World Republic of Venus', as Earth was soon to become known, with his assistant Karl Mekis becoming Head of the Security Service, appropriate for a former Gestapo man. Accordingly, Weber-Richter was taken to Venus for an eighteen-month management training scheme in successful global dictatorship, although Mekis had to make do with only a three-month crash-course in spaceship control.

On Venus – which appeared to be run along basic National Socialist principles – Weber-Richter studied a 630-page book, *Fundamentals of the Venusian World Republic*, being taught how the key to a successful global Reich was to recruit local human collaborators to run things on behalf of the armed Venusian overlords, just as the traitorous native pro-Hitler PM Vidrun Quisling (1887-1945) had once governed Norway for the Nazis. The best way to recruit such people, the Venusians advised, would be to place job advertisements in newspapers, sci-fi mags and UFO journals, offering roles like 'Economic Adviser to the Civil Administration of the World Republic of Venus (Food and Consumables)' to those willing to send the new President large administration fees through the post. Pathetically, many did so, with the dubious duo gaining over a thousand followers in Chile. Whilst they got all the money, all the dupes got were fake passports and ID cards for the forthcoming Venusian Reich, signed by Hitler's fake son, plus copies of *Fundamentals of the Venusian World Republic*, if they wanted to buy a copy of that too – as with *Mein Kampf*, you may think this was basically obligatory. Mekis and Weber-Richter then branched out into the German-speaking and previously pro-fascist world too, taking out ads for more recruits in Austria, West Germany, Switzerland and Italy in 1958; they didn't even necessarily want well-qualified people, you could just apply to be the Nazi President's future chauffeur. Ultimately, the fraudsters became pretty rich.

Whilst the conmen tried to tempt men with promises of power, they sought to entice women with promises of sex. Within their leadership manual, which dictated the entire structure of the Venusian Reich, were descriptions of 'love camps', based upon the SS's old *lebensborn* programme, for which female volunteers were required. Here, women would be required to lie back and think of Earth, whilst racially superior Venusian *übermenschen* mounted them in order to breed a race of half-human, half-ET blonde super-beings who would act as the colony's eventual Space-Nazi ruling class. By breeding the humans upwards, as in Ariosophy, Earth's racial stock would be improved. This promise of becoming alien sex-slaves proved appealing to some women, gaining Mekis and Weber-Richter more female acolytes. This proved useful when Chilean police began investigating the pair, causing them to flee to Rome in 1960 where they established a new HQ in the *palazzo* of the upper-class Italian painter Duchess Elena Caffarelli, one of their greatest fans. Together with them lived a twenty-two-year-old girl from Salzburg, Annemarie Baumann, who acted wholly unpaid as the pair's full-time private secretary, receiving only her board and meals plus a tiny amount of 'pocket money' in return. Annemarie later testified the pair had 'promised me a Venus-Man after the invasion' as a husband, although she had to sleep apart from everyone else in the house and maintain her virginity intact if she wanted to remain acceptable to 'one of the great Venus leaders'.

But the invasion never came. 'Day X' shifted around repeatedly due to 'lack of financial support', but was finally and definitively set for 1 July 1960 when the saucers would touch down at Berlin's Tempelhof Airport, the city being earmarked as Hitler Jr's new world-capital. At the last minute, however, President Urun, leader of the Third Venusian Space-Fleet, fell fatally ill – presumably with a Venereal disease – meaning the landing had to be delayed yet again, whilst his chosen successor Ase was trained up properly in how to subdue Earthlings. Sick of their consummations in the *lebensborn* love camps being perpetually postponed, several disciples realised it was all a trick and complained to the police. When Mekis then carelessly returned to visit Austria using a Chilean passport issued in a false name, he was arrested and placed on trial. Many victims called as witnesses testified reluctantly, surely through embarrassment, and the presiding judge, Hans Braun, could not keep from laughing throughout, finally handing Mekis down a five-year sentence for fraud in December 1962 – even though the defendant had ominously warned Braun that 'If you find me guilty, you will regret it. On the day when the Venusians invade the country, you will be crushed.' Weber-Richter remained in hiding in his friendly Duchess' attic, meanwhile, so avoided all prosecution. If this sad example is anything to go by, had Lanz ever managed to successfully establish his ecclesia sex castles, he would not have run short of women to act as brood mares for his part-alien Theo-Zoa, and thence become mothers to their shiny electronic god-babies.[80]

* * * * *

Originating long prior to 1947, the original Ariosophists themselves could not have known of UFOs, and their concept of Theo-Zoa from other worlds, derived as it was essentially from Madame Blavatsky's Theosophy, did not precisely correspond with the idea most people have of aliens today. Yet some did directly promote the existence of literal physical extraterrestrial beings on other planets, most notably Friedrich Bernhard Marby (1882-1966), developer of the magical discipline of 'rune-gymnastics'. Marby created rune-gymnastics whilst editing a Stuttgart newspaper from 1917, quitting its haunted offices in 1922 to become a full-time writer and lecturer on weirdness. Selling astrological advice, in 1924 he launched a rune-magazine, *Your Own Way*, together with a spin-off *Marby Rune-Library* series. His publishing firm was ruined in a Nazi crackdown on rival philosophies, however, and Marby fell into debt, for which he received a ten-month concentration camp sentence in 1936. Once war erupted, SS critics felt Marby and his 'League of Rune-Scientists' may lead the public astray, so he remained behind barbed wire until liberation in 1945. His idea was that, by imitating the shape of the letters of the ancient Nordic straight-line-based runic alphabet with your limbs, ideally whilst reciting or singing the sound of the rune as a mantra, persons of appropriate Aryan ancestry could transform into astral antennae for space-rays, not unlike Lanz's radio-receiving Stegosauruses. Marby combined Ariosophy with yoga, saying the ancient Wotan-priests of Guido von List had once practised it too, as proven by his own access to the Germanic racial memory, or *Erberinnerung*. This scheme proving successful, Marby soon gained rivals, notably Siegfried Adolf Kummer (1899-1977), who asked rune-magicians to yodel at special frequencies whilst they cast their shapes in *völkisch* anticipation of the YMCA.

Runes had been a central element of Ariosophy ever since Guido von List's 1908 text *The Secret of the Runes*, which taught that, alongside their practical value as an alphabet, these sigils held holy or magical import too, particularly the 'victory rune', *sig*, once used as an Aryan meeting and battle-cry – hence the later Nazi '*Sieg Heil!*' Modern German rune-magicians have decried Marby's bastardisation of List's ideas as 'insane rune-rape', and some do sound alarming, like his belief that adopting the position of the 'I-rune' – standing upright with your legs together and your arms down by your sides like the letter 'I' or a soldier standing on parade – had been coincidentally exploited by German officers to transform their troops into 'a living bar-magnet' receptive to racial influences from other planets. Such accidental Ariosophy gave soldiers shining auras like the Northern Lights, making them healthier, more effective servicemen via 'liberation from slag', causing 'general rejuvenation'. Marby illustrated this with a diagram of a glowing man wearing only his underpants with 'eyes straight, chin drawn, shoulders slightly raised, chest arched, body pulled in, knees pushed through' – the flower of Prussian fighting youth.

For *völkisch* types, German culture had an inherent biological seat within the body, with cultural heritage carried literally within the blood. Jewish-tainted urban civilisation was atrophying Aryans' natural faculties, but you may reverse this via 'racial cleansing' and 'up-racing'. The best forms of instinctual education used the body, not the brain, so by dancing, yodelling and breathing in positive astral influences whilst exhaling negative ones, rune-magicians could access Germanic history direct, via ancestral memories, not second-hand through books. By joining arms naked and dancing in a circle, it was even possible to joyfully embody the spinning swastika sun wheel. The separation between man and the universe was illusory, with white skin a low-frequency solidification of cosmic racial energy. By allowing this energy to penetrate your veins, you could intercept transmissions from the past, future and outer space. Marby published the names of medically troubled rune-gymnasts in his magazine, asking subscribers to beam out healing race-rays to help them whilst exercising. Readers reported amazing results: their skin had become whiter, their eyes bluer, their hair more blonde. Some literally sweated away their tainted beast-blood or shed it through boils and abscesses during gyrations. Occasionally, the non-white filth of fish-people even poured from their ears. This was a process of 'materialising the Aryan', akin to tuning in a radio-set properly.[81]

In 1924, the great gymnast revealed his own blood was now so clean due to exercise that he had been telepathically contacted by one of Lanz's ancient Nordic Theo-Zoa living on Mars, an Aryan alien with the inappropriately Slavic name of Vandanisski, an eighteen-year-old ephebe: 'Tall and slender and blonde is he, the image of a youth we do not know here on Earth.' The Martians, all of 'only one race', did not visit Earth any more, fearing the 'terrible sexual demons' infesting our atmosphere thanks to the influence of the 'demon-star' Algol, which 'favours the incarnations of murderers, killers, vivisectionists and sadists', and ruins the souls of any babies born under its sign. The Martians had sent out rune-magic prayers to try and cure our 'changeling' children, but no luck yet. Mars was no Red Planet but a White one, whose god-men with 'long, oval-shaped' faces, 'skin shiny white' and 'hair shining blonde', spent their days engaged in healthy *völkisch* activities in a world without that horrific Jewish substance, money. They did have access to advanced technology, but it was Green in nature, in terms of special towers which radiated multi-coloured lights 'like a giant flame' over the lovely Martian flower-fields, these buildings housing 'star-power transformers', which received starlight, transmuting this into 'fluid electricity' to be stored away in 'shiny flasks with silver caps' until needed. So might life on Earth become if, one day, Germans should ever escape the grip of the pervert-star Algol and stop playing rape-an-ape. 'I have already lived once, in the stars,' Marby cited many of his countrymen as saying; maybe all true Aryans had.[82]

* * * * *

As a successful politician, Adolf Hitler derided Ariosophists as '*völkisch* wandering scholars', viewing their ritualistic obsessions as a distraction from his main cause of making Germany great again.[83] Hitler was no occultist, rune-gymnast or believer in aliens; but others exploited his apparent disguised debt to Lanz to suggest otherwise. The pseudonymous Michel-Jean Angebert's 1971 book *Mystics of the Sun* claimed that in 1898 Lanz, then still a monk, visited the monastery where the eight-year-old choirboy Adolf attended singing lessons. According to Angebert, Lanz took Hitler under his wing and initiated him into the swastika's hidden mysteries, thus making him an infant occultist.[84] The basic notion of such trash-texts is that there was no way the Nazis could have conquered Western Europe with such stunning speed if they were not in league with demonic or ET forces. Surely they had to have access to some secret power?

In 1947 the anti-Nazi German rocket scientist Willy Ley (1906-69), who had fled his homeland to seek sanctuary in America before the war, published an influential article called *Pseudoscience in Naziland* in the pulp magazine *Astounding Science Fiction*, which featured talk of an ominous pre-war

Berlin-based occult cabal later known as the Vril Society, whose members sat around meditating upon the two halves of a sliced apple to access the wonderful power of *Vril*, an early equivalent to The Force from *Star Wars*. *Vril* was invented by the Victorian novelist Edward Bulwer-Lytton (1803-73) in his 1871 Gothic fantasy epic *The Coming Race*, which spoke of a secret subterranean city of advanced technological nature inhabited by racially superior female-dominated beings called the Vril-ya, whose mastery of the cosmic power of *Vril*, a psychic substance inherent within the universe itself, lent them powers of telepathy, telekinesis, healing, hypnotism and weather-control. One day, the Vril-ya would emerge from their lair and conquer us. *Vril* became widely known, with the rejuvenating beef-extract drink Bovril – or 'Bovine-Vril' – being named after it as a marketing gimmick, whilst Madame Blavatsky also swiped the novel's ideas for Theosophy. As Bulwer-Lytton was also a student of the occult, Blavatsky thought his story told forbidden mystical facts in disguised fictional form, a complete misapprehension on her behalf. The Vril Society spoken of by Willy Ley itself was actually real, though, and they really did stare at apples.

The group's actual name was the Imperial Working Society for the Coming Germany (RAG), publisher of the 1930 pamphlet *Vril – the Cosmic Primal Force – Rebirth of Atlantis*. RAG felt the fabled sunken continent of Atlantis had once mastered the power of *Vril*, which it was now hoped could be re-harnessed to make modern-day Germans evolve back upwards into god-men, as in Lanz. Their sliced apple represented the two quasi-electrical *Vril*-poles the cult thought the Earth possessed, the North Pole being the positive anode, the South Pole the negative cathode. Electric *Vril*-power and 'radiant energy' could be harnessed from these poles using 'ball-shaped power generators', transforming Earth into a utopia. This was a reference to the Austrian inventor Karl Schappeller (1875-1947), inventor of the idea of *Raumkraft*, or 'Space-Force', a Viktor Schauberger-like fantasy about tapping into hidden energy fields immanent in the universe around us. Schappeller became rich, gaining investment from the exiled Kaiser Wilhelm II (1859-1941), and in the 1930s a New Power Trust was established in Britain to persuade the Royal Navy to use *Raumkraft* in their ships' engines; its seal shows a Masonic symbol of an eye in a pyramid. The device Schappeller used to accomplish his wonders was a sphere split into two hemispheres, each containing a magnetic pole. So, when they meditated on split apples, the *Reichsarbeitsgemeinschaft Das Commende Deutschland* members were really considering the principles of this foo-fighter-like invention, which they arbitrarily equated with Bulwer-Lytton's fictional *Vril*. Schappeller himself called the ball's power-source 'electrical vapour' or 'luminous ether'.[85]

The RAG were not Nazis, nor even called the Vril Society; yet Ley's innocent misrememberings were noted by the joint authors of a hugely influential New Age best-seller, *The Morning of the Magicians*, published in France in 1960. Occult writer Louis Pauwels (1920-97) and chemical engineer Jacques Bergier (1912-78) wildly exaggerated Ley's recollections in the second part of their book, 'A Few Years in the Absolute Elsewhere', claiming Hitler yearned to abuse *Vril*-power to cause bizarre racial mutations in the German people. In Pauwels and Bergier, the Vril Society were in cahoots with a secret sect of Theosophy-style Hidden Masters living in underground cities in Tibet named Agartha and Shambhala, and their 'King of Fear', who would help the Nazis rule the world and turn the Aryans into real-life Vril-ya. Exterminated gypsies were really human sacrifices to attract the attention of dark forces from Shambhala, whilst a Berlin-based llama called 'The Man with the Green Gloves' helped facilitate contact with the good land of Agartha. There was even a Nazi Tibetan monk combat-unit, a thousand of whose corpses littered the German capital after the war. Under Hitler, it was not actually the Nazis, but 'the Other World' who ruled conquered Europe; that is, the evil 'Satanic spirit' of Shambhala.[86] The incredible claims just kept on coming: Hitler was possessed and had 'a sort of ectoplasm' in his eyes, SS psychics willed the English Channel to shrink to make invasion easier, Nazi agents desired to sabotage holy bells in Oxford which prevented the town being hit by Luftwaffe bombs, and Himmler was 'like a kind of fighting monk from another planet'. Pauwels and Bergier exaggerated even Lanz's lunacy so that Hitler now wanted whites to evolve into a race of Theo-Zoa cyclops people, being awakened in the night by terrifying supernatural visitations from the Ariosophist Super-Men of tomorrow.[87] Pauwels and Bergier did admit their story seemed unlikely but justified this on the grounds that crazy events require crazy explanations and that 'history alone' should not be allowed to govern interpretations of what really occurred in the past – outright fiction should, too.[88] They should have joined the *Ahnenerbe*.

The Vril Society was now falsely twinned with another occult group, the Thule Society. Again, this was a real body, whose significance was twisted. 'Ultima Thule' was traditionally the ancient northern homeland of the Nordic race; Lanz called Thule 'Arktogäa'. To List, it was a prehistoric home of Aryan refugees. Fellow travellers of Ariosophy became convinced there was a Jewish conspiracy against the noble but exiled Thulean race, and established quasi-underground lodges named *Germanenorden* ('Orders of the Germans'), to combat this, adopting a curved-armed swastika as an emblem. However, they became targeted by irate Communists – possibly the fact they placed advertisements in newspapers seeking new 'fair-haired and blue-eyed' members gave the game away. One healthy Nordic type who joined was Rudolf von Sebottendorff (1875-1945), another fake aristocrat after the model of von Liebenfels and von List; these men considered themselves the Master Race within the Master Race. Von Sebottendorff changed the name of his Bavarian branch of the *Germanenorde* to the Thule Society in 1918, to confuse Commies. Its logo was another swastika entwined around a dagger, surrounded by oak-leaves, symbolically urging its members to fight on against the Jews 'until the swastika [sun wheel] rises out of the icy darkness' of Thule.

If the politically ambitious Thuleans posed purely as a *völkisch* group organising lectures about 'sun castles' and runes, it was hoped they may appear harmless. But seven Thuleans were killed by Communists in April 1919 anyway, lending the group nationalist prestige, and several prominent future Nazis attended their meetings as guests. Sebottendorff had to leave after being blamed for losing his membership lists, thereby enabling the murders, but had previously encouraged subsidiary workers' political discussion groups to form, from which grew the DAP of local agitator Anton Drexler (1884-1942), which in 1920 became the NSDAP, or Nazi Party. Hitler attended meetings, originally as a spy, but was impressed by their nationalist political talk – which was not occultist in nature – joined for real, and took them over. The Nazi symbol of the swastika was lifted direct from the Thule Society and modified, but because it looked striking and memorable, not for any magical reasons; a left-facing swastika is customarily intended to bring luck into the world, but Hitler supposedly chose to have it face rightwards to bring evil and death into it, a legend which is wholly untrue, he just thought a right-hand one looked better. Left-hand swastikas also represent exile from Thule, whilst right-hand ones represent return there, allegedly, though historically the two were used interchangeably. Whilst the Thule Society folded around 1925, it was clearly a Nazi precursor organisation. The official Party newspaper, the *Völkischer Beobachter*, was once owned by Sebottendorff, winning readers with extensive sporting coverage laced with irrelevant anti-Semitic editorialising. Sebottendorff possibly also helped inspire the famous '*Sieg Heil!*' greeting. Therefore, in 1933, he published a book, *Before Hitler Came*, insisting he and the Thuleans were the future Führer's true original inspiration, claims for which he was briefly jailed. Becoming an astrologer, he then travelled to Turkey, finding some minor work as a German spy, before drowning himself in 1945 after receiving word of total Thulean defeat.[89]

So while the Nazis did partly grow from an occult lodge, Hitler had no interest in the Thule Society's mystical inclinations, and no connections to the Vril Society, who did not even bear that name. Yet Pauwels and Bergier knew better. One key tenet of Nazi ideology was *lebensraum*, the plan to steal 'living space' in the East. But if you go far enough East, you will eventually reach Tibet, home of Agartha and Shambhala. The Nazi geopolitician Karl Haushofer (1869-1946) wrote perfectly rational academic articles arguing Germany should seize foreign agricultural land and oil supplies to survive enemy blockades, but to Pauwels and Bergier this was just an elaborate cover-story to hide Hitler's search for *Vril*-power in the magical underground kingdoms of Central Asia. Haushofer was inaccurately presented as a clairvoyant member of the Thule Society, together with Dietrich Eckart (1868-1923), a well-connected anti-Semitic playwright, poet and journalist who in reality helped introduce Hitler into high society and present himself properly in public, but who now morphed into a hypnotist who initiated Adolf into secret mysteries, persuading him of the need to control the power of *Vril*. On his deathbed in 1923, Eckart purportedly prayed to a black meteorite fragment that the Thule Society would rule the world by proxy, boasting 'Hitler will dance, but it is I who called the tune.' Thus, Hitler was just a handy medium for evil spirits conjured from Shambhala by Eckart and Haushofer. Eckart had been a mentally unstable morphine addict with paranoid ideas, believing Moses' refusal to go on building pyramids for Pharaoh made him history's first Bolshevik trade-union leader, and he did attend some Thule Society meetings, but Pauwels and Bergier's image of him as a magician was totally fictional. Their picture of Haushofer, a one-time military attaché in Japan, of belonging to a secret Buddhist cult and committing suicide via ritual disembowelment, samurai-style, was equally spurious. Yet, once printed, the lies mushroomed. In Dietrich Bronder's 1964 *Morning of the Magicians* clone, *Before Hitler Came* (note its Sebottendorff-imitating title), a new fictional membership list of Thule Society wizards appeared, including Hitler, Himmler, Mussolini, Lanz and List.[90]

The realms of Agartha and Shambhala also have some basic basis in Buddhist fable, yet as usual Pauwels and Bergier distorted it by saying the first was good, the second evil, underground equivalents of the leftwards and rightwards swastikas, attributing this knowledge to Haushofer. Maybe these cities were truly in Mongolia, not Tibet, with the Gobi Desert being formed by a prehistoric nuclear war; this forced the Hidden Masters underground, where rival Cold War-style factions split into the two magical sub-Himalayan citadels.[91] However, the specific name 'Agartha' was seemingly invented in the 1870s – the very idea of the place, just like the idea of *Vril*, also appears to derive largely from Edward Bulwer-Lytton's 1871 novel *The Coming Race*. In 1886, French astral-traveller Saint Yves d'Alveydre (1842-1909) published *The Mission of India*, detailing a spy-mission his soul had been on to the underground kingdom, which already had railways, air travel, inflatable mattresses and other advanced *Wunderwaffen*-like super-technology – no flying saucers yet, but that would come later. Its special mode of government, dubbed 'Synarchy', should be adopted by us all, argued d'Alveydre; he wrote to Queen Victoria and the Pope, urging them to implement it, to make the Agarthans rise from their caves and greet us in brotherly political love. Significantly, d'Alveydre was a close friend of Bulwer-Lytton's son. Under the twin influences of Theosophy and a personal Indian guru, he seems to have read his friend's father's novel, and then had mad visions of actually flying there.

Shambhala is different, having genuine existence in ancient Buddhist myth, but is no more a real geographical location than the Garden of Eden. A utopia – or dystopia – of the mind, the fabled city is whatever the soul of the individual percipient makes of it, Heaven or Hell. In Buddhism, all existence is illusory, so to make the distinction between Shambhala being real or imaginary, good or evil, is in itself to fall for a mirage; it is both, simultaneously. Pauwels and Bergier misunderstood this, splitting the city into Heaven (Agartha) and Hell (Shambhala) and saying the Nazis generally tried to contact the latter, a literalistic mistake since copied direct from *The Morning of the Magicians* by innumerable later authors – you can tell this, as so many misspell the place 'Schamballa', copying the French duo's own odd initial typo. If you examine historic Buddhist descriptions of Shambhala, it seems a place of great spiritual advancement. If you examine d'Alveydre's descriptions of Agartha, derived from Bulwer-Lytton, it seems a place of great technological advancement, the misguided paradise of someone with an unwise, materialistic mind-set, whose idea of Heaven would be Trump Tower, not Eden. Actually, therefore, if there *were* two cities, it would appear Shambhala is actually the good place and Agartha the evil one. To mistake Agartha for paradise is to reveal your impurity of soul. When Far-Right fantasists later began reimagining Agartha as a post-war subterranean Nazi Valhalla full of *Wunderwaffe* flying saucers, they too made the same error.[92]

The other key book in this field was Trevor Ravenscroft's (1921-89) *Spear of Destiny*, a 1970s literary hoax perpetrated by the author, who promised to deliver an astonishing narrative of Nazi Satanism, pocketed the substantial advance, then ran away. Tracked down, Ravenscroft evidently realised the publisher didn't care if his story was nonsense, as this made it more likely to sell by the bucketload. Clearly, the public just *wanted* to believe Himmler enjoyed performing 'blood lodge' rituals involving samples of Hitler's bodily fluids, as the author wrote. Nothing was too tasteless for Ravenscroft's readership, particularly the invention that Himmler, knowing of a magical trial in which the ashes of crushed rabbit testicles had been spread across fields to deter any further rabbits eating crops, ordered a similar test be performed with Jews. In death camps, living Jews were injected with the testicular ashes of dead ones and ordered to await the full moon, which would 'potentise' the ashes in their blood. Then, these liquidised ashes were extracted, with the by now doubly powerful serum spread all over Germany. The consequent exodus of Jewish refugees was thus achieved by magical means, not systematic persecution. Other Jews and Marxists were ritually tortured and sacrificed before Hitler by the Thule Society in an 'incredibly sadistic and ghastly' manner to induce visions of Satan, the Führer really being the reincarnation of the evil wizard Klingsor from the Arthurian *Parsifal* myth. Ravenscroft's imaginary Hitler also communicated with other realms by ingesting hallucinogenic cacti from Mexico and, as per the old unproven rumour, had only got one ball. As one key source of Hitler's evil was called 'Schamballa' – do note the misspelling – Ravenscroft had obviously been reading his Pauwels and Bergier.

Ravenscroft derived aspects of this mad narrative from ghosts during Spiritualist séances, but his main alleged source was Walter Johannes Stein (1891-1957), a Viennese Jew who had settled in Britain in 1933 – purportedly to become Winston Churchill's (1874-1965) personal occult advisor. Now unable to contradict Ravenscroft unless also contacted by séance, Stein was painted as having been an acquaintance of the youthful Adolf Hitler, who spent his early days in Vienna obsessing about the titular *Spear of Destiny*, once used by the Roman centurion Longinus to end Christ's suffering on the cross (that is, His *actual* suffering, nothing to do with monkey-rapists in this version). Even though Stein was Jewish, Hitler went to see the Spear with him in Vienna's Hofberg Museum. As Hitler stared at it, the air filled with 'ghostly ectoplasmic light' and Adolf became possessed by 'some mighty spirit'. Having been bathed in Jesus' blood, the spear enjoyed holy powers, meaning its owners would rule the world — but as its owners back then were the Habsburg royal family, it is unclear why Austria and Germany lost the First World War. Maybe it was because the weapon was actually manufactured some seven centuries after Christ's death, and so wasn't the Holy Lance at all. Nonetheless, obscene rituals involving naked women were performed and the murdered Thule Society members contacted, whose ghosts confirmed Hitler would be the Spear's next owner; he immediately seized the thing upon annexing Austria in 1938, putting it under the guard of the SS and *Ahnenerbe*. In this narrative, Guido von List's Ariosophist sect was really a demonic sex-cult to which Hitler belonged, the two men once conjuring up a 'Moon Child' via erotic means. Stein supposedly first met Hitler after finding a book containing the future dictator's annotated notes about occult matters in a second-hand bookstore, a literary device Ravenscroft filched wholesale from the 1842 novel *Zanoni* – by Edward Bulwer-Lytton, inventor of *Vril*. When horror writer James Herbert (1943-2013) later fictionalised Ravenscroft's own fiction even further in his 1978 novel *The Spear*, about neo-Nazi attempts to resurrect a zombie Heinrich Himmler, Ravenscroft successfully sued. Bulwer-Lytton's ghost could have done the same to Ravenscroft.[93]

Herr Himmler is the final link in this fictional chain. We have already seen his belief in Aryan extraterrestrial god-men's lightning weapons like Thor's Hammer, which now appear derived from Ariosophy. As a youth, Himmler's father made him keep a 'reading diary', which he maintained until 1934; it is stuffed with titles about astrology, pendulums, Freemasonry, Eastern wisdom, homeopathy, telepathy, Spiritualism, aberrant racial theorising, Germanic mythology, *völkisch* pseudo-history, and various other *Ahnenerbe* favourites. He liked to say he worshipped 'Waralda, the Ancient [One]', a source of perennial wisdom suffused throughout the fabric of the universe, desiring the SS declare themselves *Gottgläubig*, 'believers in God' – just not the fake Judaeo-Christian one. Yet on a day-to-day basis he kept most such enthusiasms to himself, knowing mainstream Nazis would laugh, or use them to discredit him. But after the war, various former associates, hoping to make money from books, or win favour from Allied captors by discrediting Himmler as a lunatic, exaggerated outrageously. Now, the former chicken farmer Himmler thought himself the reincarnation of the great Saxon King Henry the Fowler (876-936), for instance, whereas actually he just imaginatively identified with him, like Boris Johnson with Churchill.[94]

In 1933, Himmler bought Wewelsburg Castle in Westphalia, intending to turn the dilapidated Renaissance fortress into an ideological training and ceremonial centre and, later, the focal point of a huge 'SS city'. It was brought to Himmler's attention by local officials who wanted to get the money pit off their hands, but post-war it was said Wewelsburg was chosen due to its magically auspicious location at the centre of ley-line systems, its status as a courtroom for old witch-trials, or on account of ancient prophecies about the place, which was all nonsense. It was near to the Teutoberg Forest, though, scene of heroic Germanic tribes vanquishing invading Roman legions, and a reputed pagan sun worship site called the Externsteine, so had much Romantic appeal. Himmler had Lanz-style fantasies about transforming the SS into a Black Order of Ariosophist-like fancy-dress Grail-Knights, but this became garbled into him keeping the *Ahnenerbe*-discovered Holy Grail there for real. Supposedly, he had a Round Table installed, around which King Heinrich II and his warriors would sit, practising mind-control techniques. SS men would be ritually beheaded, and their severed craniums used as oracles to contact Tibetan Hidden Masters, their voices speaking through the dead man's mouth. In 1978, British thriller writer Duncan Kyle (1930-2000) published an adventure novel, *Black Camelot*, complete with Himmler wearing a King Arthur helmet on the cover, whose story combined occultism with *Wunderwaffen* myths; Kyle's Wewelsburg held the Spear of Destiny, which had to be captured by Allied commandos before Heinrich reborn could use its powers to fuel the Reich to victory.[95]

Once restored to its former greatness by slave labour, Wewelsburg was intended to act as a historical research centre, SS leadership college and archive for *Ahnenerbe* types, never as a black magic citadel to raise the dead, or to host the Holy Grail (although Himmler did fantasise about it one day having a treasure-room filled with gold and silver). The castle is now a museum, whose authorities seek to demythologise it, the official line being that its apparent ritual spaces were designed for eventual use in SS oath-taking ceremonies, not contacting ghosts or Hidden Masters. The authorities aim to 'desacralise' Wewelsburg as a centre of black magic pilgrimage; CCTV cameras monitor rooms because increasing numbers of neo-Nazis, entranced by fake accounts of Himmler's occultism, were turning up to perform weird rituals. In 1989, attempts were even made to raise funds to buy Wewelsburg and turn it into a private neo-Nazi shrine. Consider the 1982 visit of US Satanist high-priest Michael A. Aquino (b.1946) to perform a rite called the 'Wewelsburg Working' in the castle's large underground crypt to 'summon the Powers of Darkness at this powerful locus'. Inspired by these dark energies, Aquino reshaped his 'Order of the Trapezoid' sect to incorporate Nazi symbolism alongside all the previous Satanic imagery, having already long admired the 'irrational principles' of the SS. Thus, whilst Wewelsburg may not have been a Nazi occult centre during the actual era of Nazi Germany, it is now anyway, despite the crackdown. In 2012, Australian Karl Young (presumably a pseudonym, referencing the Swiss psychologist

Carl Jung) published his *Third Reich Pilgrim*, detailing a trip to Wewelsburg, during which he had noticed how, if you draw lines onto maps in a certain way, the site looks remarkably like a human head with a lance – surely the Spear of Destiny? – jabbed through its pituitary gland, echoing the Third Eye of Ariosophy. This symbolised how SS occultists could use their Aryan Third Eyes to penetrate the sacred ritual landscape to contact the Nazi Black Sun at the centre of our Hollow Earth, sucking up pure *Vril* from within its orb.[96]

Credulous texts about these topics, now often cumulatively labelled as 'Esoteric Nazism', sell. Others include *Storm-Troopers of Satan* and *Satan and the Swastika*. Yet this kind of thing may sound as if it has little to do with UFOs … because, originally, it didn't. But matters would soon change, with Nazi spaceships becoming powered by *Vril*-engines, Thule Society mediums channelling UFO blueprints from fascist aliens through their lovely blonde hair, Tibetan Shambhala (often relocated to Antarctica or the Andes) harbouring hidden German saucer-fleets, and Wewelsburg really being a gigantic SS UFO factory, designed to manufacture flying discs directly from the souls of Himmler's Grail-Knights. Without knowledge of the above non-UFO books, many later Nazi saucer legends are simply incomprehensible. The ET god-men of Ariosophy were not precisely fleshly extraterrestrials in the modern sense (except in the rune-gymnastics of Marby and his Martian friend Vandanisski), but something more of an ill-defined quasi-supernatural nature. And yet in 1947 the flying saucers of Kenneth Arnold came, and Ariosophy and its fears of interstellar sodomy made a remarkable return in the spaceship-infested skies of 1950s America.

2

Heiling Occupants of Interplanetary Craft: William Dudley Pelley, George Hunt Williamson, the Silver Shirts and George Adamski's Aryan Aliens

On the night of 28 May 1928, a successful but over-worked writer of short stories and Hollywood movie scripts named William Dudley Pelley (1890-1965) lay reading racial tracts in bed. His exposure to Jewish movie moguls had led to increasing paranoia in the author. 'Hollywood Babylon' was a den of iniquity, in which Jews exploited white women on the casting-couch, moral degeneracy was promoted on-screen, and where his scripts were tinkered with by ignorant Semites. Worst of all, they treated him like a galley-slave and in return all he got was large sums of money.[1] Nodding off, racial matters preyed on Pelley's sleeping mind until, early in the morning, he awoke – to find he was dead. Pelley's soul whirled away into a blue mist, before he rematerialised lying naked on a marble slab attended by men in white uniforms. One told Pelley not to worry, he had died himself hundreds of times before, as had we all. Earth was a giant school for reincarnated souls, evolving upwards in spiritual knowledge; the best students were reborn white, those most retarded were reborn black, with other skin-shades representing mediocre pupils at various intermediate caste-system rungs on the spiritual ladder. When Pelley awoke again for real, he was a changed man. Abandoning Jewish Hollywood, on a train to either Damascus or New York, he became enveloped within a talking white light which revealed Jesus Christ's message had been perverted by the Jews, it being Pelley's new task to fill in the missing 175,000 gaps in the Bible and lead white humanity up towards salvation.[2]

Pelley's near-death experience only lasted seven minutes, but they proved the most significant 420 seconds of his life. Producing a tract on the subject in under two hours via the 'super-radio' of automatic trance-writing, he sold the story of his *Seven Minutes in Eternity* to March 1929's *American Magazine*, captivating over two million readers. Thousands of letters from potential followers were sent to Pelley, and the script of his life entered its next amazing act. The now highly clairvoyant genius got the spirit of dead novelist Joseph Conrad (1857-1924) to write his next book for him, aptly entitled *Golden Rubbish*, in which Jesus' ghost demands an *Ahnenerbe*-type excavation take place in Palestine to uncover His true, Jew-obscured Word.[3] Jesus' real teachings were explained by voices in Pelley's head, coming from both a range of Theosophy-esque Hidden Masters, and the spirit of Christ Himself. Yet it sounds more like he had been reading the mind of Jörg Lanz von Liebenfels, as Pelley's eventual 1952 sacred text *Star Guests* sounds suspiciously like a censored version of *Theo-Zoology* with all the fish-porn taken out. Viewing the idea of extraterrestrials more literally than Lanz, Pelley's God was a very old spirit inhabiting a far-off planet, whom Jesus visited to receive instructions for saving our souls from ape-dom. On every inhabited planet, spirit descended into matter to get to know itself better, initially as vegetables, gradually evolving into humanoid shape, and then evolving back into spirit again to return to the distant cosmic godhead, as Jesus had initially taught before being suppressed by the Jewish 'Bible thieves'.

Life on Earth descended from the 'Star Guests', ET spirits from Sirius who came here millions of years ago, incarnating as lions with eagles' heads who reproduced by thought alone, like Lanz's Theo-Zoa. But then they became physical monkeys instead, to seduce Earth's indigenous ape-women and 'run riot in sodomy'; Pelley's use of this specific term suggests familiarity with Ariosophist thought, but if so, he nowhere acknowledges it. Now the lion-people became trapped in their ape-flesh and could only reproduce sexually. Humans developed from the offspring of the Star Guests and the native Yeti-women, making man 'half-monkey, half-angel'; the Fall from Eden, as in Lanz, represented extraterrestrial god-men devolving into apelings. Blacks, whites and yellows all hailed ultimately from different Star Guest planets, with browns being a mixed 'step race' in-between, as were the Jews, who were part-brown, part-yellow, maybe even a little bit low-grade white. These skin colours represented 'atmospheric conditions' on humanity's original home worlds, lending the races their characteristic mental features, with whites being innately spiritual and blacks an embodiment of 'Cosmic Ignorance in its pure state'. This was all christened 'Liberation Doctrine', as death represented the temporary liberation of our Sirian soul from our simian bodies. If your soul evolved enough, you need not reincarnate in solid shape again at all, rather like in Buddhism; some Hidden Masters were just such advanced incorporeal souls. But if white souls evolved upwards, black and Jewish souls contained the literal 'Mark of the Beast' from their ancestral monkey-mothers, and were getting stupider and more materialistic with every generational incarnation, becoming humanoid demons. Just like Napoleon before them, the Slavic leaders of the USSR were enfleshed and deviant Jewish aliens from elsewhere, come to conquer 'white and Christian peoples' with Communism, a political disease from outer space.[4]

Thankfully, Communism and Space-Judaism had many natural enemies – like Adolf Hitler, whose 1933 election had somehow been predicted by Egypt's Great Pyramid, to prepare the way for Christ's return in 2001. Once Hitler was Führer, Pelley allegedly heard another voice instructing him to found his own American Nazi-type organisation, leading the proud Star-Spangled Fascist to suddenly announce the religious 'League for the Liberation' group he already headed was to be renamed the 'Silver Legion', or 'Silver Shirts', after their shiny new uniforms. Even though these shirts came emblazoned with a large scarlet 'L' standing for 'LOVE', 'LOYALTY' and 'LIBERATION', 40 per cent of his followers abandoned Pelley over this new direction, especially once he chose as the Silver Shirts' official street weapon whips like the one with which Jesus had once chased Jewish money-lenders from the Temple in Jerusalem. Promising the elimination of paper money and to give every white citizen a single share in the nation's GDP worth $1,000 per annum, Pelley planned to raze cities and ban apartment blocks, so everyone could live good, honest, traditional frontier-lives as in *völkisch* days of old. Pelley now revealed Jesus was not a Jewish *Galilean*, as the tampered-with Bible lied, but a non-Jewish *Gaul* like Asterix, and every bit as blonde and indomitable. To punish the Jews for misleading everyone, they would all now have to inhabit special ghettoes, one in each US State, and stop mixing with whites. A 'Secretary of Jewry' would then guarantee the Jews' physical safety – unless they stepped outside their city-prisons, in which case these 'Dark Souls' would be executed. As blacks were childish morons whose only desire was to sire monkey-babies with Nordic females, these 'slovenly' cretins from an alien idiot planet would become 'wards of the State' like orphans, and provide an inexhaustible source of household servants for whites. Yet Pelley liked Native Indians, thinking them psychically gifted enough to perceive the Jews' malevolence, embarrassingly posing as 'Chief Pelley of the Silver Tribe' to win their support, before warning Washington's Bureau of Indian Affairs had been captured by Communists. Henceforth, a half-white, half-Indian 'Red Power' fantasist named Elwood Towner, who claimed to be called 'Chief Red Cloud', spoke at Silver Shirt rallies covered in swastikas, praising Hitler. Naturally, Pelley implied that Jesus, as 'the world's outstanding anti-Semite of all time', would vote for him too.

The Silver Shirts gained at best 15,000 signed-up followers, but plenty of publicity, thanks to Pelley establishing a 'Silver Rangers' paramilitary sub-unit, making absurd claims that Abraham Lincoln had been a Nazi, and warning at rallies that President Franklin D. Roosevelt (1882-1945) worked undercover for the Jewish Sanhedrin council who had helped condemn Christ to death in the Bible, as suggested by his 'Jew Deal' economic programme and true Jew-name of 'Rosenfeld'. Running for President in 1936 for the Christian Party of America, Pelley failed miserably, and once Washington entered the war following Pearl Harbor, his tentative links with the actual German Nazis, numerous pro-Axis propaganda articles and attempts to contact 'key Japs' led to him getting a fifteen-year sentence for sedition – although, once behind bars, he still continued to visit friends in astral form. In 1950, Pelley was released from jail several years early, suffering heart-trouble, but only on condition he refrained from all political activity. Accordingly, he now concentrated on inventing a 'Uni-Vision' television system to broadcast souls onto TV screens, remembering his past life as an Apostle, speculating that many mentally ill persons secretly possessed two heads on the ultra-violet spectrum, thus accounting for their schizophrenic problems, theorising the young Jesus had an invisible alien play-mate, and developing his Ariosophist-tinged ideas into a full-blown space-religion, 'Soulcraft', of which 1952's *Star Guests* became the Bible, wholly unpolluted by Jewish textual alterations.[5]

During Pelley's spell behind bars, flying saucers had been born, and he wasted little time in incorporating them into Soulcraft too; inevitably, in 1953 he saw one himself. Just as the Great Pyramid had once predicted Hitler's coming, it now foresaw the coming of the 'Saucer-Men', as signals of the dawning of the astrological Age of Aquarius, the posited 'New Age' which the 1960s hippies later championed. Maybe the ufonauts wished to evacuate advanced human souls in their spaceships but had been scared away from landing *en masse* by the excessive levels of violence on display in the Hollywood Westerns for which Pelley no longer wrote the scripts, he guessed – code for 'the Jews are stopping them from saving us.'[6]

* * * * *

Pelley's Soulcraft magazine *Valor* quickly acquired a top UFO correspondent in the shape of the pioneering ancient astronaut theorist George Hunt Williamson (1926-86). Williamson was highly qualified as on 20 November 1952 he had already been involved in the most significant UFO contact event of all time, when a blonde-haired, white-skinned fellow from Venus named Orthon had landed in California's Mojave Desert for a half-telepathic, half-sign-language chat with the Polish-born occultist George Adamski (1891-1965) about the urgent need for humanity to abandon nuclear weapons. Orthon was of pure Aryan stock and lived a life of wholesome *völkisch* vegetarian goodness on his home planet, being essentially one of Madame Blavatsky's Hidden Masters transplanted to Venus. 'Professor' Adamski himself had formerly headed up a California-based sect, The Royal Order of Tibet, allegedly exploiting its religious license to manufacture sacramental wine as cover for a money-spinning bootlegging enterprise, and claimed previous channelled contact with advanced souls of a Theosophist-friendly nature, having founded the supposed 'first Tibetan monastery in America' in 1934.

In other ways, Orthon resembled Vandanisski, the Martian formerly contacted by the Ariosophist rune-gymnast Marby, with his Venus just Germany on another planet. George Adamski was later taken on a saucer-sojourn to the dark side of the moon, which looked remarkably like the German Alps; snow-capped mountains, lakes, rivers and forests provided much scope for wholesome outdoor activities. Adamski then saw film footage of similar scenes on Venus. Such were the health-giving properties of these Alpine resorts that their ET inhabitants lived for a full millennium each, on average; every man his own Thousand-Year Reich. Orthon's kin would definitely have been accepted into the SS. 'The beauty of his form surpassed anything I had ever seen,' wrote Adamski, who may have been bisexual. Youthful, tall and slim, with a slight tan and perfect body, Orthon possessed shoulder-length blonde hair, 'glistening more beautifully than any woman's I have ever seen', together with high forehead and cheekbones, 'finely chiselled' nose ('not conspicuously large', like that of a cartoon Jew), an 'average-size mouth' with 'beautiful white teeth' that 'shone' whenever he spoke, and 'calm, grey-green eyes', with smooth white skin and no facial hair. Placing his palm together with Adamski's in friendship, Orthon's flesh was revealed to be 'like a baby's, very delicate in texture ... His hands were slender, with long tapering fingers like the beautiful hands of an artistic woman.' Indeed, dressed differently, Orthon 'could easily have passed for an unusually beautiful woman'. He wore a high-collared, single-piece chocolate-brown ski-suit with no visible fasteners, and was thus a Brownshirt; his shoes, however, were 'ox-blood red'. Although reputedly an anti-Semite himself, if so, Adamski kept such thoughts private, except perhaps in code.[7]

Orthon's clothing proved of great significance, particularly his shoes, down towards which the effeminate Venusian kept pointing. The brown and red colouring of his uniform has been linked to Native Indian beliefs about the brown local soil being made sacred through the red blood of their dead ancestors – reminiscent of the old Green Nazi slogan 'Blood and Soil'.[8] Even odder, their soles bore images of swastikas! Orthon was desperate to transmit a message to humanity via his footwear, and so trod a very firm imprint of each sole into the desert soil. Watching from a distance as Orthon did so were several of Adamski's disciples, including Pelley's soon-to-be UFO columnist George Hunt Williamson, who, as an anthropologist, handily carried a bag of plaster with him everywhere he went, just in case. Making casts of the footprints, he found them covered in strange hieroglyphics, to be decoded later. Photos were given to local newspapers by Williamson, launching Adamski's whole ufological career. When South African engineer Basil van den Berg saw these hieroglyphs, he realised they were pictorial instructions for building a 'gravity-cancelling motor' for a spaceship; examined through a magnifying glass, the swastika-bearing footprints suddenly became holographic, thus revealing their secret instructions.[9]

Adamski's account garnered major publicity, culminating in world tours, meetings with European royalty and even, at least in Adamski's own account, a secret audience with the Pope. Whilst today's stereotypical ETs are little grey men, the initial cliché of the 1950s was of UFOs being piloted by a race of Orthon-like beings termed 'Nordics', who were benign, of Scandinavian stock, and very concerned about ecological and anti-nuclear issues. Nowadays we speak of alien 'abductees', but back then they were

'Contactees', in voluntary communication with loving, peacenik 'Space-Brothers'. George Adamski himself met many amorous young androgynous blonde males like Orthon down the years, generally in hotels, in rooms rented by the hour. Others knocked on New Age housewives' doors and offered to begin 'crossing the energies' between Earth and Venus via the medium of their genitals, for the good of humanity.[10] The Nordics, though much less common, are occasionally reported today. And Orthon himself may still be watching us. It has been speculated that the wise elephant Horton, from *Horton Hears a Who!* by US children's author Dr Seuss, may be part of a psychological media conditioning scheme to prepare our youth to meet and accept Orthon for real, given his name's curious resemblance to that of the friendly pachyderm.[11]

* * * * *

George Adamski and William Dudley Pelley never met, their contact limited to a single exchange of letters. When Adamski's later account of the Space-Brothers' elaborate religious system nonetheless bore some uncanny similarities to his own Soulcraft, Pelley viewed this not as plagiarism, but proof his channelled precepts were valid throughout the entire universe. George Hunt Williamson's links with both men were brief but pivotal. He fell out with Adamski just a month after Orthon's landing, and only worked for Pelley for four or five months during 1954. Reading Pelley's *Star Guests*, though, he added its Theosophy-like speculations about evolutionary reincarnation to his own developing philosophy.[12] If he read Adamski's breakthrough 1953 book *The Flying Saucers Have Landed*, he would also have found Adamski's co-author Desmond Leslie (1921-2001), an eccentric relative of Winston Churchill, updating Madame Blavatsky's teachings himself by claiming Earth had been 'seeded' with human life in prehistoric times by 'Interplanetary Noah's Arks' from Venus. Once ape-like beings had independently evolved here, they could become programmed as future humans on our fallen planet, which acted as 'a kind of solar commando course' for spiritual development, Leslie wrote. Superior aliens had then landed like British colonialists in Africa to help these 'groping, mindless things in their steaming primal jungles', building Stonehenge and the pyramids, and thus founding all human civilisation.[13] Theosophy and the early ancient astronaut theorists all feed into one another in a way difficult to precisely unpick.

As a young anthropology student, Williamson already had some very odd ideas, arguing in tutorials that dinosaurs still inhabited Brazil, and that South America had been discovered by the Japanese. Apparently expelled, Williamson nonetheless seems to have gained an honorary degree from a Canadian university, in recognition of his year-long fieldwork stay amongst the Chippewa Indians of Minnesota in 1951.[14] He collected folklore about 'Hairy-Faced Men' and 'Gee-Bys', or ghosts, but also encountered tales of

'Flying Wheels' and 'Flying Boats'. Reading an early UFO book, Williamson realised these Flying Wheels were really flying saucers, thus becoming another ancient astronaut theorist, apparently the first man to interpret the Prophet Ezekiel's famous encounter with God in the shape of a luminous body formed of 'wheels within wheels' as a biblical account of a meeting with a discoid spaceship, now a standard cliché of the whole genre. Hunting out more tales of Flying Boats, 'we talked saucers, the Redman and I,' giving Williamson the impetus to become involved with Adamski in the first place.[15] Meanwhile, one of the reasons he was attracted to Pelley may have been that Williamson, too, had an out-of-body experience whilst still at university in 1949, although it didn't last for precisely seven minutes.[16]

Williamson won genuine respect from the Chippewa, being entrusted with knowledge of their sacred ritual dances, whose details he preserved, performing them himself for public gatherings back in civilisation. Having um heap big talent, during one inter-tribal dance contest Williamson actually won, beating the real Indian dancers. Williamson's later brief employer may have laughably posed as 'Chief Pelley of the Silver Tribe', but Williamson truly was an honorary Native Indian. His Hopi Indian friend Star Hunter said he had 'a white face, but … a red heart', taking him into the Arizona desert in 1949 and performing three ritual songs, devoted to the eagle, coyote and rattlesnake; one of each creature then suddenly appearing. Star Hunter said Williamson possessed 'mighty signs and symbols', and that the animals' appearance meant he was fated to perform some holy mission in life; he must now undergo a 'Vision Quest' to prove it further. Viewed in this light, Williamson's 1952 sighting of Orthon also belonged to this same tradition of desert-based Vision Quests, but prior to this he had retreated into the Minnesota wilderness alone for three days and three nights, fasting and smoking ritual pipes before seeing glowing lights and becoming visionarily transformed into an eagle, which soared towards a living 'Great Central Sun' (the term is from Theosophy), which was busily drawing in innumerable glowing golden and purple souls from across the animate universe. Chief Spotted Hawk, who acted as his 'adoptive father' in the tribe, now said Williamson's honorary Chippewa name was to be Sun-Eagle, predicting he would become a great spiritual teacher who would write an important book, which he did, with 1956's *Other Tongues – Other Flesh*.[17]

Star Hunter gifted Williamson a ceremonial item, a Kachina doll, in honour of his future greatness, but it was missing its usual ritual rattle – until, whilst Williamson was sat alone revising for an exam, the item materialised from nowhere on top of his books. Strangely, the rattle came bearing a painted symbol – a swastika! Williamson later interpreted this as a paranormal prediction of his vision of Orthon from a distance in November 1952 in the Mojave Desert, another location where Indians traditionally encountered Flying Wheels. Kachinas are Hopi guardian angels, who guide the tribesmen's paths through life. Williamson's own Kachina was obviously telling him to pay close attention to Orthon's footprints, as the swastikas they bore were of the precise same kind as on the doll's rattle. They were not Nazi swastikas but Native Indian ones with curved hooks and dots in the middle, the symbol being a holy representation of the path of the sun through the sky to the Hopi. Notably, some Buddhist shrines contain a representation of Buddha's footprint as well – which also bears a swastika good-luck symbol on its heel. Maybe the god-man Buddha came from Venus too, like all the best Hidden Masters?[18]

The original intended cover for *Other Tongues – Other Flesh* came with a disguised swastika on it, but the book's main purpose was to introduce humanity to the 'Solex-Mal', or 'Sun-Tongue', the ideogram-based universal picture language used by the Space-Brothers, for which Orthon's shoes provided the Rosetta Stone. To Williamson, the Solex-Mal swastikas represented Ezekiel's biblical encounter with a wheel-like UFO, akin to the Flying Wheels of the Native Indians. Four dots on one of the swastikas symbolised the zodiacal constellations Taurus (bull), Leo (lion), Scorpio (scorpion) and Aquarius (water-carrier) and their chief stars, Aldebaran, Regulus, Antares and Formalhaut. Ezekiel's biblical wheels of fire came accompanied by strange winged humanoid beings, usually thought to be angels, each with four faces, those of an ox, a human, a lion and an eagle. A lion must be Leo, the ox Taurus, the human the water-carrier of Aquarius, whilst an eagle was an old alternative symbol for Scorpio. Williamson thought this signified Ezekiel had met ancient aliens, not angels, and that the turning of the swastika sun wheel, combined with the marked-out constellations, indicated where the ETs came from, together with the passing of time on a celestial star-clock. By simplifying the design of Orthon's left footprint, you could make it resemble a fish, the zodiacal sign of Pisces. In Christian symbolism, Jesus was often represented by a fish symbol, perhaps meaning the Christian 'Fish Age' of Pisces was about to give way to a glorious New Age of Aquarius, as hailed by Orthon's landing. As Orthon's ET footprints were highly obscure, you could give them whatever interpretation you liked. If you were a Nazi, you could view them as portending the false and weak 'slave-religion' of the Fish-Man Jesus being crushed beneath the heel of the blonde Venusian *übermensch* Orthon, with the Christian cross about to be replaced by the Nazi swastika, especially when you consider that, by some calculations, the Aquarian Age began in 1939, the same year Hitler invaded Poland. When George Adamski allegedly met Pope John XXIII in 1963, did he give him a word to the wise about any of this?[19]

George Hunt Williamson was not an actual Nazi, but his teachings, being part-derived from Pelley's *Star Guests*, bear a certain resemblance to Ariosophy, nonetheless. Williamson's later life even mirrored that of the former monk Lanz in chronological reverse. In 1960, he changed his name to Michel d'Obrenovic and disappeared from the UFO scene, becoming an Orthodox priest in 1971, his new title indicating his discovery of princely East European ancestry; supposedly, he now had a good claim to the Serbian throne! HRH Prince Michel d'Obrenovic Obelitz von Lazar,

Duke of Sumadya, rightful King of Serbia, made plain old Jörg Lanz von Liebenfels of Vienna sound like a peasant, especially once he also became an archbishop and founded his own Holy Apostolic Catholic Church.[20] Some of Williamson's knowledge about ancient history was channelled via visions of past lives, akin to those through which Guido von List, with access to the German *volk*'s ancestral memory, mined information about his own imaginary national past. Like Lanz, he interpreted ancient carvings in bizarre ways, travelling to Peru in 1956 to establish a minor UFO cult, The Brotherhood of the Seven Rays, viewing old petroglyphs as more examples of the galactic shoe-language. With his disciples abandoning their jobs and homes to search for lost cities, photos of Williamson in an Indiana Jones hat from this period suggest he was a possible semi-inspiration for the *Ahnenerbe*-thwarting Hollywood action hero. Proving how much data in his ancient astronaut books like *Secret Places of the Lion* and *Road in the Sky* was derived via occult means, Williamson's last published title, 1961's *Secret of the Andes*, was issued under the name 'Brother Philip' – one of his spirit guides. We should remember how ancient Aryans were sun worshippers in Ariosophy; the idea of a Solar-Tongue being revealed to a man re-christened Sun-Eagle, who found swastika sun wheels everywhere and had visions of flying into a Great Central Sun sounds compatible. Indeed, Williamson's final public UFO-related activity, a 1961 lecture tour of Japan, was funded by a native Contactee, Yusuke Matsumura (1929-2000) of the Cosmic Brotherhood Association, who was of nationalist bent and viewed his guest's views as confirming his belief Emperor Hirohito (1901-89) really was descended from the Japanese sun goddess (or ancient alien) Amaterasu, as taught by Tokyo's wartime Axis regime. The Solex-Mal was, quite naturally, the original language of the Land of the Rising Sun.[21]

* * * * *

Williamson had been contacting Space-Brothers and Hidden Masters via Ouija board for some time, but in 1952, aided by the Arizona-based ham-radio operator Lyman Streeter, began receiving messages over short-wave in Morse Code from entities with names like Nah-9, Zrs, Ankar-22, Regga, Artok, Ponnar, Actar, Um, Zo, Jupiter-9999 and Agfa Affa, some of whom hated the Jews every bit as much as Joseph Goebbels did. Naturally, the aliens interspersed their own propaganda broadcasts with snatches of the Solex-Mal, so in his 1954 book *The Saucers Speak!* Williamson had to provide a glossary. As in the Tower of Babel legend, only humanity spoke different non-solar languages: 'You are a divided people, and you speak many tongues.' To an alien, *Saras* or *Chan* meant 'Earth', *Ben* was 'good', *Tonas* were musical instruments, *Masar* was Mars, whilst saucers were really called 'crystal bells' and *Macas* were Neptunian cows.[22] Some communications were simply bizarre, in terms of requests to boil water on a stove to aid signal-strength, factoids about the sun really being cold and planets being formed from small comets being rolled up through space like growing snowballs and the oft-repeated space-proverb, 'To apples we salt, we return.' Sentences like 'The planet known as Elala was once called Wogog' abounded, and there were even occasional Plutonian poems: 'Have no fright, all is right./Our ships are silver lights;/Lights of beauty, lights of duty.' Once, the aliens subliminally encourageded their listeners to go and see a Bugs Bunny cartoon. It turned out to feature a saucer, presumably carrying Marvin the Martian.[23]

If only at this juncture we could say, 'That's all folks,' but no. There was also more pressing content. Earth would eventually enter a new Golden Age after passing into a 'baby sun', but at present humanity inhabited a 'dead civilisation' thanks to the presence of certain 'evil men' on 'this blob' they had rotted the planet into. 'The good men of *Saras* [Earth] must unite with the *Ben-Men* [good men] of the universe' to save themselves. 'Some chosen ones' would be transported from Earth on saucers, but first they must 'separate black from white (races are not meant here)', said a Saturnian politician named Kadar Lacu, who had been 'elected from the universe' to be 'Head of Interplanetary Council-Circle in Master-Craft'. Kadar Lacu denied racism, but who precisely were these 'evil men' ruining *Saras*? There was no point asking your local priest or politician, as they were tools of the 'Hidden Empire' and 'puppets of the International Cabal' who caused all wars for their own profit. Democracy was a sham, as 'no matter who is elected, only one power is going to be in control anyway,' the 'same powers of darkness' who had always been in control on 'this strange little planet', the same devils who had once censored the Bible 'until it is no longer recognisable' – these people being, if you recall your William Dudley Pelley correctly, the Jews. 'Wake up!' Williamson pleaded with his readers, apparently calling for a revolution. 'In the name of the all-loving and compassionate Creator, wake up!' *Amerika, Erwache!*[24]

Williamson's radio messages further showed that, as in *Star Guests*, space-spirits once fell to Earth from Sirius, initially intending to possess the bodies of cats. Noticing monkeys had useful opposable thumbs, however, they incarnated within apes, mating with female monkeys, thus siring primitive man. During a regrettable 'abomination period', the Sirius spirits tried transmigrating into various other physical forms of a half-human, half-animal nature, such as gorgons, centaurs and the Sphinx, now misremembered as mythological monsters. Yet the biblical Great Flood killed all such freaks, leaving the part-ape, part-Sirian humans as survivors. The task of mankind, as in Ariosophy, was to eliminate as much of our monkeyhood, and recapture as much of our angeldom, as was possible.

Three breeds of invading humanoid alien currently walked our Earth. 'The Migrants', or 'Christ People', tried to help humans evolve spiritually and recover their space-angelic status. From Sirius came 'The Harvesters', who combated a race of evil aliens 'secreted' from Orion, 'The Intruders', who sought to hold us back, causing all human suffering.[25] Physical descriptions of The Intruders and their human allies makes it clear this 'stubborn race' are the Jews who, disturbingly, must one day be 'eradicated' by The Harvesters, as the mere 'slop' and 'waste' of the cosmos:

> People of Orion are not our kind of people ... These people are sometimes small in stature with strange, Oriental-type eyes. Their faces are thin and they possess weak bodies. They prey on the unsuspecting; they are talkative; they astound intellects with their words of magnificence. While their wisdom may have merit, it is materialistic, and not of pure aspiration toward the Father. They are the universal parasites! Disturbers, negative elements; soon they will be eradicated.[26]

When you consider that The Migrants and The Harvesters, being 'Sons of Light', operated under the sign of 'The Order of the Solar Cross' (or swastika, to you and me), the above passage begins to sound even worse.[27] Williamson seemingly so disliked Jews because to him they represented stereotypical money-grabbing materialist attitudes; as a lover of Native Indians, he was not a standard white supremacist. His anti-Semitism found its clearest expression in his 1958 text *UFOs Confidential!* This was co-written with his cult-follower John McCoy, an early Scientologist who thought 'International Bankers' were planting mind-control chemicals in our food, making a deal with wicked ETs which would let them invade in return for letting the banksters share control of the globe. Williamson's section of the book ranted about how 'all governments' were under rule of these 'International Bankers', several of whom he unmasked; most had Jewish surnames. The bankers also controlled the 'Anti-Christ' of the UN, seeking to kill the sovereignty of nations and, in a direct echo of Pelley's thought, had 'removed vital books and sections of the Holy Bible' to pervert Jesus' message.[28]

The Space-Brothers maintained radio-contact with Earth long after their original communicator had stopped checking in for updates. One world which called Williamson regularly was named Hatonn, but down the years this planet near the Andromeda galaxy morphed into a person, Commander Gyeorgos Ceres Hatonn, the 'Great Commander' and 'Record-Keeper of the Galaxy', after whom the planet in question – a giant filing-cabinet for galactic data – was named. The first to tune into Commander Hatonn was 1950s Contactee Dick Miller, a Detroit TV repairman who attended a lecture of Williamson's in 1954. This inspired him to direct his receiver towards Hatonn's orbiting spaceship, *The Phoenix*, and its chief signals operator, Soltec. In 1955 Williamson and Miller jointly established a 'Telonic Research Centre' to maintain contact, but soon parted company. Around 1989 *The Phoenix* restarted transmissions, however, warning a new group of US Contactees about the dangers of the Jews – or the 'Satanic Elite' and 'Elite Anti-Christ controllers', as Hatonn initially preferred it – who plot to reduce honest citizens down to a 'slave-state level of existence'. Transcripts of Hatonn's new messages were published by a firm with a record of printing materials about 'Universal Zionism', and before long Hatonn was openly speaking of 'Jewish controllers' and implying most so-called Jews were not even Jewish at all, which was somehow even worse.[29]

William Dudley Pelley's influence also continues in today's extreme-Right world; the US Posse Comitatus movement, whose survivalist-style members think there is no higher legal authority than their local County Sheriff and therefore refuse to pay taxes, seek driving-licenses or recognise the government in Washington as anything but imposters, was founded in 1969 by former Silver Shirt Henry L. Beech (1903-89).[30] In the more paranoid strains of contemporary UFO lore, all the truly evil aliens – now generally of a reptilian nature – tend to hail from Orion, just like Williamson's Intruders. A long-term channelled Hidden Master voice known as 'Cosmic Awareness' warned during the 1990s that Earth would soon be invaded by a 40 million-strong army of seven-foot-tall ET dinosaur-men from Orion called 'The Reptoids', who possessed infra-red vision and reproduced by laying eggs. Humanity's inevitable future could be foreseen in the current status of the Greys, the stereotypical bald, grey-skinned dwarfs with wraparound black eyes, chlorophyll for blood and no pupils, who increasingly replaced Nordics like Orthon in ufological imagery from the 1980s onwards. The Greys had once been ordinary loveable humanoids just like us, until Reptoids spliced their genes with insect and plant DNA, transforming them into their mindless slaves, said Cosmic Awareness, hence their being born artificially in sacs of hundreds with hive-minds and no true individuality, like the Chinese. To prepare mankind for imminent colonisation, the Reptoids' agents in the media had already begun seeding children's programming with unrealistically positive images of bipedal reptilian beings such as Barney the Purple Dinosaur and the Teenage Mutant Ninja Turtles, to make the next generation run into their conquerors' scaly arms – and Pelley had already taught us who really controlled Hollywood and the TV and media industries, had he not? That the Jews and the Orion aliens would destroy humanity's soul was proved by Cosmic Awareness asking a Grey one simple question: who is your favourite 1990s musical act? When the Grey replied 'New Kids on the Block' and began dancing like a robot, it became obvious the ET-Judaic conspiracy knew no moral bounds.[31] Next, they'll be wanting to bring back Hitler, as the old saying goes ...

3

Springtime for Hitler: Savitri Deviants, the Furred Reich and the Worship of Adolf Hitler as the Stellar Second Coming

Most children naturally love animals, hence their frequent appearance in children's books. Most children do not naturally love Nazis, however, hence their rather less frequent appearance there. Try telling that to Savitri Devi (1905-82), feminazi author of the charming 1965 fable *Long-Whiskers and the Two-Legged Goddess: Or, the True Story of a 'Most Objectionable Nazi' and Half-a-Dozen Cats*. Like many stories aimed at infants, Devi's work had a hidden educational subtext, containing a series of morally improving messages for contemporary youth: that the Nazis were right, that cats were better than humans, and that one of Hitler's main war-aims was to improve living conditions for small furry animals across occupied Europe.[1]

The book's chief character, the 'Two-Legged Goddess' and 'Most Objectionable Nazi' of the title, was named Heliodora, meaning 'Gift of the Sun' – a lightly disguised version of Devi herself, whose adopted name meant 'Sun-Ray Goddess' in Sanskrit. However, due to the unjustifiable persecution of loyal Nazis in the post-war world, Devi felt it necessary to change the name of 'every person and every animal in this story [for] obvious reasons'; she didn't want them to end up hanging from an Allied noose like at Nuremburg, or being drowned in a canal.[2] The book opens with a delightful image of a dozen cats gathered around Heliodora in her sparsely furnished room in India, where she sits cross-legged on a mat before a blown-up photograph of Adolf Hitler doing what he does best – being kind to animals. Adolf is feeding a baby deer, so proving him 'the Friend of Creatures and exponent of everlasting Wisdom'. So wise is the Führer that Heliodora worships Him as a god: 'Fresh pink lotuses lay in a round, flat, painted earthen vessel at the foot of the picture, and three sticks of incense were burning before it, fixed in holes at the top of a brass burner, with the shape of the sacred sign *Aum*.'[3] As the real-life Devi also sanctified photos of Hitler in this way,[4] we can see how the story was based on actual fact – or facts as Devi saw them, anyway.

Surprisingly, Devi expects her tiny readers to have a basic grasp of the theory of Platonic Forms, acclaiming what she sees as 'the intangible Essence of Catdom' shining present in every cat she meets. The ancient Greek philosopher Plato had once theorised that somewhere in the immaterial realm lurked 'Ideal Forms', perfect archetypes or spiritual blueprints from which all physical things drew their shape, albeit in an imperfect way, like flawed tracings of original artworks. According to Devi's interpretation of this theory, each cat 'expresses more faithfully the Self of his species' or 'divine collective Soul' of Catdom than most woefully imperfect humans ever could in relation to the Ideal Soul of their own species – that of the pure Aryan race.[5] The classic example was the English, who had rejected Germany's hand of friendship and fought their fellow Aryans instead. For this, Heliodora decides the entire population of Britain must be exterminated – until she is told otherwise by a cat. Visiting London post-1945, Heliodora enters into psychic mind-meld with a pet cat called Sandy, who restores her '*sincere* consciousness of the oneness of the Nordic race, in spite of all the horrors of recent fratricidal war'. Like many animals in children's books, Sandy can talk. Unlike many, what Sandy wants to talk about most is the infamy of the Jews:

> Prrr, prrr, prrr ... One day [the English] shall wake up from their delusion, turn against their bad shepherds [the Jews], and help the people of their own blood to build up a new Europe ... in which we creatures will all be happy ... for they are good people at heart, good people like Aryans generally are ... Prrr, prrr, prrr ... The proof of it is that they have taken such good care of me! Prrrrrrrr ...[6]

This argument proves persuasive to Heliodora ('"O Cat, you are right," agreed at last the tough old racialist'). The English, as a nation of pet-lovers, should be spared genocide when, some happy day, the Third Reich rises again. Given that the book purports to be based on a true story, make of this episode what you will.

Also unusual for a children's book, Devi's yarn features a male cat called Long-Whiskers encountering a fine young female feline in a Calcutta slum. Here, he 'overcame her faked resistance and possessed her', in order to 'fulfil the purpose which the Divine Cat had assigned to them from all eternity ... [to] carry Catdom a generation further [and] secure its everlastingness', much like the Nazis with the white race. This union was pretty cataclysmic:

> Their individualities ceased for a while to exist, and in him, the Eternal He-Cat, Creator and Lord of Everything, and in her the co-eternal, sphinx-like, dark Feline Mother, Lady of All Life, once more mingled their opposite polarities and took consciousness of their double Godhead, as they had been doing for millions and millions of years. And once more the divine spark – the Creative Lightning – flashed through their furry bodies, and the daily miracle took place: there was life in the female's womb.[7]

This is not simply Mills & Boon for animal-lovers; it contains important philosophical points. As the individual kittens sired via Long-Whiskers' lightning-infused sperm are direct replicas of 'the Eternal He-Cat', this means all cats are mere temporary fleshly embodiments of the Ideal Platonic Cat-Soul – including Long-Whiskers himself, who is later reincarnated in Sandy's body in London. As perfectly embodied aspects of the same shared noble soul, all cats are reincarnated time and again, just like certain ultra-perfect Germans, who are likewise direct embodiments of the Ideal Platonic Aryan Soul – most notably Adolf Hitler. As a manifestation of the Aryan soul, Hitler had been reborn again and again down the millennia, as, Devi realised, had she herself; lifetime after lifetime, she had sought, loved and worshipped her Führer, and would continue doing so until the End of Time.[8] Immaterial souls definitely existed. Devi knew this first-hand. In October 1946 she had a strange dream about entering the cell of the Luftwaffe head Hermann Goering (1893-1946), then awaiting execution at Nuremburg. Goering was astonished at Devi's presence, before she reassured him the Aryan gods had given her spirit permission to save one single Nazi from the humiliation of being hanged; she had chosen him because he was always kind to animals (evidently Devi didn't know Goering was a keen big-game hunter). Feeling a small unknown object in her hand, she held it out to the war criminal and told him to take it. He obeyed, she bade him 'Heil Hitler!' and vanished. Awakening, Devi was amazed to find Goering had committed suicide in his cell the previous night, after obtaining a cyanide capsule by officially unknown means – but Devi knew how he had got it.[9]

Savitri Devi may have believed in reincarnation and astral bodies, but she had no noticeable belief in UFOs. The closest she came was her boundless admiration for the Pharaoh Akhnaton (d.1335BC), who had tried to impose worship of the solar disc following his accession to Egypt's throne in c.1353BC, hubristically identifying himself as a god-like incarnation of the sun. For Devi, Nazism and Akhnaton's sun disc cult were basically the same, twin forms of pagan Nature-worship which sought to abolish the artificial barrier civilisation had placed between man and the world; was not the swastika originally an ancient sun wheel symbol? From her youth, the part-Greek Devi had hated Christianity as an artificial Jewish import (Jesus being Jewish, not a Christian), and had dreamed of re-converting Europe to the paganism of her Athenian ancestors. Hinduism was one of the final forms of living paganism left in the world, so maybe the Indians could conquer Europe for her, but surely the best way to bring the Jew-duped white race back to happy Nature-worship was beneath the heel of the German jackboot. 'You cannot de-Nazify Nature!' she argued, meaning that Hitler's doctrine could no more be finally defeated than the laws of electromagnetism. During his trial at Nuremburg, Nazi philosopher Alfred Rosenberg (1893-1946) had summed fascist ideology up as 'Thou shalt love God in all living things, animals and plants,' Devi recalled approvingly – but this Green Nazi never mentioned humans. What was truly important in the universe was the cosmic dance of Nature, something also hymned in the Hindu religion of her beloved adopted homeland of India, not individual human lives as valued by the weak Christian 'slave religion' she so hated. Human beings were a kind of plague – most should be incinerated in a new, second Holocaust of a nuclear kind, Devi fantasised.[10]

Devi's own brand of disc-worship doesn't sound like it has an awful lot to do with flying saucers, but her ideas were adopted by later Hitler-lovers who did believe in UFOs, and their own fantastic cults are not fully comprehensible without first understanding their origins in Savitri Devi. Probably the first Westerner to seriously worship Adolf Hitler as a literal god on Earth, she was eager to associate him with outer space. In his political testimony *Mein Kampf*, Hitler had specifically posed as a planetary saviour, something Devi took literally, speaking in awe-struck tones of how the stars had aligned at the moment of his 1889 birth, talking of him as a new Akhnaton, a 'Child of the Sun', created not by ordinary human procreation but 'the mysterious influence of distant worlds in infinite space'.[11] Did this mean that Hitler was an alien? Not quite …

Devi's children's book continues with an account of another out-of-body experience, this one written from the perspective of a dying cat, namely Sandy, who is flattened by a car. The tale ends with Heliodora gazing wistfully into the night sky and realising cats are not only embodiments of the Ideal Cat-Soul, but also, on a higher level, of the impersonal godhead which suffuses the entire universe – as is Hitler. Hitler and cats, as flawless expressions of their respective Platonic archetypes, are really one and the same thing, God Himself, which must explain all those cats who look like him on the Internet. Staring into the heavenly abyss, Devi hears Sandy's ghostly voice purring into her face from another galaxy, causing her to enjoy an ecstatic religious epiphany in which she realises that the cat-filled universe itself is inherently Nazi in nature, and that Adolf Hitler is its Lord:

The majesty of the starry sky pervaded her … under the divine light of the galaxies … She knew … that the same eternal Life that had purred to her in the dying beast flourished invincibly in countless far-away worlds as on Earth; that death was but a passage to a new life; and that, at the root of life, there was Light; Light that had always sprung, always shone, from distance to distance, out of the abysmal womb of shoreless Night, like this dust of stars in the dark sky … Wherever divine Light had given birth to Life within those endless expanses; wherever there were living races of thinking or unthinking creatures upon *any* planet, born of *any* sun, the principles at the basis of the struggle for survival, the divine laws of racial selection proclaimed by the greatest of all Germans, Adolf Hitler, held good, as they did here; as they always had done, in the history of our tiny Earth … Glory to Him who proclaimed them … and to his disciples … For

He is the One-Who-Comes-Back; the Soul of the Starry Dance that takes on, again and again, the garb of mortal frailty, to teach finite beings the Rule of all the Worlds … [Even if Nazism is defeated on Earth] our struggle, carried on by other [alien] beings, would continue, wherever Life exists. And she felt invincible, along with all her persecuted comrades. Once more she had integrated the Hitler faith and the cult of Aryan aristocracy into the worship of the starry Sky, Light and Life eternal … And she repeated in German, to the milliards of suns in space and to the great Soul of them all, the sacred invocation of the European Aryans of old to our sun: *'Heil Dir, Lichtvater allwaltende!'* ['Hail to thee, omnipotent Light-Father!']¹²

When she worships the photo of Adolf feeding a deer, Heliodora is really worshipping God in human form and, simultaneously, the life-giving sun. As with the god-Pharaoh Akhnaton, our closest star is, in a sense, Adolf Hitler himself, just like Japan's Emperor Hirohito, who was worshipped as a holy descendent of the native sun goddess Amaterasu, thus explaining the natural wartime alliance of Berlin and Tokyo. Solar-powered Hitler, not Jesus, is the true Light of the World, through which the Aryan godhead shines, and the godhead can never die. Just as Sandy will always return from beyond the pet cemetery grave, so will the Divine Führer who was 'the messenger of the Soul of Starry Space', not simply a fascist dictator. In religious terms, Adolf had an esoteric (hidden, interior) as well as an exoteric (external, surface) nature, as did Nazism itself.¹³ In this very insight lie the origins of the new post-war religion of Esoteric Nazism which, now merged with various subsequent UFO cults, is still going strong today. As Devi argued, 'National Socialism will rise again *because it is true to Cosmic Reality*, and because *that which is true does not pass.*'¹⁴ Gravity existed before Newton discovered it, and likewise so did Nazism before Hitler 'discovered' that, too:

One should carefully distinguish the ephemeral NSDAP – the National Socialist German Workers' Party, an organisation of precise aims, which have their place in German and European history – from the everlasting National Socialist Idea … [which] exceeds not only Germany and our times, but the Aryan race and mankind itself and *any* epoch; it ultimately expresses that mysterious and unfailing Wisdom according to which Nature lives and creates: the impersonal Wisdom of the primeval forest and of the ocean depth, and of the spheres of the dark fields of space.¹⁵

In 1906, aged seventeen, Hitler had climbed to the top of a hill overlooking the Austrian city of Linz, stared up into the night sky himself, just like Heliodora after him, and been likewise possessed by the fascist spirit of outer space. According to the testimony of his friend August Kubizek (1888-1956), who accompanied him, the two youths had just been to see an opera by their favourite composer Richard Wagner (1813-83) when the sublime sight of the stars, in combination with the lingering memory of Wagner's music, had caused the adolescent Adolf to grasp Kubizek's hands, stare deep into his eyes, and begin speaking so fervently that:

> *It was as though another Self spoke through him* ... I would say that he was himself *possessed* by that which burst out of him with elemental power ... *He now spoke of a mission that he was one day to receive from our people, in order to guide them out of slavery, to the heights of freedom* ... Many years were to pass before I could realise what that starry hour, separated from all earthly things, had meant to my friend.[16]

Kubizek, in his book *Adolf Hitler, My Young Friend*, was talking metaphorically about Hitler becoming possessed by Wagnerian forces, but Devi thought otherwise. Her cat-obsessed fictional analogue Heliodora is convinced that white Nordic folk like Hitler, being more in touch with Nature, God and the stars, would never mistreat poor, defenceless animals. As proof, she cites the case of 'the hero, Horst Wessel' (1907-30), the martyred Nazi storm trooper, who 'was a great cat-lover', as had been proven when Heliodora met his aunt one day and was shown a cute photo of him surrounded by kittens. Furthermore, she had been out for coffee with one of the Brownshirt thugs responsible for *Kristallnacht*, who ensured her 'quite emphatically' that, whilst they might have beaten up lots of Jews, smashed their windows and destroyed their property on the dismal 1938 night in question, they had 'never molested any cats, dogs or other beasts just because they happened to belong to Jews'.[17]

Yes, there was a real affinity between Nazis and cats of all kinds; the 'dream-like vision' of the Master Race which Hitler wanted the Germans to become ran in parallel to the exemplar ultimate cat-lords of the animal-kingdom, the lions, who were 'as beautiful on their level' as blonde, blue-eyed Nazi supermen of the future were on theirs. As such, the Nazis had commendably banned vivisection upon animals in Germany and replaced it with live medical experiments on people instead.[18] Heliodora thinks this one of the finest achievements of Nazidom and fantasises that, when Hitler returns from his temporary resting-place in outer space, she will be placed in charge of a special concentration camp 'of her dreams' in which 'two-legged mammals ... who believe that man is everything and other creatures nothing' will be eliminated.[19] Heliodora believes in animal rights, but not human ones. The post-war world is a topsy-turvy one in which democracy rules over dictatorship, Nazis are called criminals instead of heroes, and abattoirs are full of animals, not people. This was a true Dark Age – that of *kali yuga*.

*****

Who was this mad old cat-lady? Born Maximiani Portas in 1905 to an English mother and a French father of Greek-Italian ancestry, she first travelled to India in 1932, where the self-avowed white supremacist pagan identified closely with Hinduism and changed her name to Savitri Devi. This may seem surprising, but in Nazi theorising of the day it was presumed the Aryan race may well have originated in India, an early home of the swastika sun wheel (*svastika* means 'good luck' in Sanskrit). The whole idea of an Aryan race is something of a fiction, having its substantial origins in the work of the German Romantic thinker Friedrich Schlegel (1772-1829), a student of Sanskrit, who proposed the existence of a noble, white-skinned Indo-Nordic Master Race who left their original homeland in India to colonise Northern Europe at some remote point in the past, inspired by the search for a mythical sacred mountain called Meru, located somewhere near the North Pole. This Master Race was later labelled 'Aryan', partly from the German word *Ehre*, or 'honour'. Thus, the Aryans were the 'people of honour', the racial aristocracy of the entire world. Schlegel's flattering idea caught on amongst patriotic Nordic types, but modern scholarship has since exposed it as essentially untrue.[20] The Indian caste-system also held appeal for those who, like Devi, saw in it parallels with restrictive Nazi race-laws. With its dark-skinned citizens at the bottom of the pile and its light-skinned ones at the top, India represented an appealing image of what our world might look like after the Reich had lasted six thousand years. Admiring 'the miracle racial segregation can work', Devi decided to settle in the then British colony for a period.[21] A National Socialist from 1929 onwards, Devi spied for sun worshipping Japan during the war, becoming involved with the nationalist Hindutva movement which argued India was an inherently Hindu country in which British colonialists, Christians and Muslims alike had no place, as explained in her 1936 book, *A Warning to the Hindus*. Today, the Hindutva movement has achieved twenty-first century power in the shape of the successful nationalist BJP Party, showing that not all the political causes Devi adopted were lost ones.

Amongst the Hindu nationalists Devi met were Srimat Swami Satyananda and A. K. Mukherji, who also admired Hitler for his adoption of the swastika and outspoken championing of Aryanism, which they, like Schlegel, also saw as originating in India. Satyananda told Devi of his theory that Hitler was really an incarnation, or avatar, of the disc-carrying Hindu sun god Vishnu, descended back to Earth to restore order, this disc weapon being both a serrated metal Wheel of Carnage and a rebirth-bringing Wheel of Time. Mukherji (later her husband in a marriage of convenience) knew all about the Thule Society, introducing Devi to the *Morning of the Magicians*-anticipating idea that Hitler and the top Nazis were actually esoteric occultists. Such views were not overly unusual, with many Indians having flower-strewn photos of Hitler on their domestic family shrines, hoping the strongman might free them from the British Empire, something Devi observed with delight. There is a Hindu tradition that every great military leader or king shares some of the power of Vishnu, and is to a degree semi-divine. He may even be immortal. Another demi-human deity worshipped in such shrines was Subhas Chandra Bose (1897-1945), leader of a rebel Japan-backed Indian army against white rule, who died in a 1945 plane crash – but not to those Indians who continue to revere him. As an avatar of Vishnu, Bose cannot age and remains alive somewhere in the Himalayas, waiting to save India in her hour of future need. When Savitri Devi later refused to accept Hitler was dead, she tapped into these exact same traditions. A line from the epic Hindu Sanskrit scripture-poem of the *Bhagavad Gita* was cited by Devi as a prophetic reference to Hitler's immortality: 'When justice is crushed, when evil is triumphant, then I come back.'[22]

Several times after Germany's defeat, Devi sought the aid of the Old Gods. In October 1945 she joined the annual festival of Kali, the four-armed, blue-skinned Hindu goddess of destruction, who rules earthquakes and volcanoes, begging her to kill the Allied conquerors. On 5 April 1947, she witnessed Kali causing the eruption of Mount Hekla in Iceland, and, entranced by the spewing lava, walked towards it 'ravished in religious rapture', alternating between singing hymns to Shiva, Hindu lord of the cosmic dance of death and rebirth, chanting the sacred word '*Aum*' and shouting '*Sieg Heil!*', seeing the lava flow as a vision of the resurrected Führer's approaching red-hot revenge. By June, she was visiting the Godafoss, or 'Waterfall of the Gods', into which images of the old Norse deities had once been cast by a local priest at the coming of Christianity. Hoping to reverse this calamity too, she threw an abusive poem about Jesus into the roaring waters and invoked Odin, Thor and Baldr, begging the Viking gods to make the pagan Third Reich rise again.[23] But how can that which is dead return? Only if the straight line of time's arrow is reconfigured into a circle instead; a natural image for a disc-worshipper to adopt.

According to certain strains of Hindu thought, having their origins in the ancient epic of the *Mahabharata* and later part-plagiarised by Madame Blavatsky for her Ariosophy-influencing Theosophy cult, history does not progress in a straight line but an eternally repeating four-part cycle like that of the seasons, played out across a gigantic whole, the *maha yuga*, lasting 4,320,000 years. We once enjoyed a perfect spring or summer-like Golden Age, but by the time of modernity had long since entered into a wintry Dark Age termed the *kali yuga*, an age of inversion in which all true values were reversed, as with vivisection taking place on cats, not humans. 'Any healthy cat,' Devi once argued, was worth much more than a 'degenerate human bastard', but *kali yuga* forces had obscured this truth.[24] The most common division of the *yugas* goes thus:

satya yuga – four time-units – Golden Age – Spring – 1,728,000 years' duration
treta yuga – three time-units – Silver Age – Summer – 1,296,000 years' duration
dvapara yuga – two time-units – Bronze Age – Autumn – 864,000 years' duration
kali yuga – one time-unit – Iron Age – Winter – 432,000 years' duration[25]

Everything gets worse as the seasons progress, as spring becomes winter. By the end, even time itself is less impressive; being only 432,000 years long, the *kali yuga* is an era in which everything becomes speeded up, hence the constant nature of change in modern society compared to the more stable Golden Age past, when all was pure and good. Fortunately, that means it will be over in a cosmic eye-blink, at which point *satya yuga* sunshine will instantaneously and miraculously return in a sort of cosmic 'click' – a click, said Devi, due to be unleashed by Adolf Hitler. Devi saw tell-tale signs of *kali yuga* in everything from the disgraceful proliferation of hospitals, which only served to keep worthless sick folk alive, to universal education, which allowed morons to read trash books not worth reading, to the truly shocking sight of black men driving motorcars.[26] On a wider level, Jews controlled the world, not Aryans, commerce and materialism ruled, not religion and spirituality, and the races, instead of remaining pure, were becoming ever more mixed and diluted. This was awful, but in a sense could actually be celebrated – the worse things got, the sooner Hitler the Redeemer would be at hand. And yet, in ordinary human terms, *kali yuga* could still last a while. Encouraging some despondent Nazis she met on a trip to the ruins of Hitler's old mountain retreat of the Berghof in 1953, she asked them to consider how small and puny the tiny, weird-seeming cult of Christianity must have seemed in the years immediately after Jesus' death – but did this not later rise up to dominate the Western world for 2,000 solid years?[27]

The idea we were living in *kali yuga* had earlier been championed by writers belonging to a school known as 'Traditionalism', in particular the French esotericist and convert to Islam René Guénon (1886-1951) and the Italian fascist Julius Evola (1898-1974), who tried to act as a guru to Benito Mussolini and the more outré elements of the SS, before becoming an abiding inspiration for post-war European Far-Right terrorists. You can tell Devi read Guénon, as she uses the term 'Reign of Quantity', the title of one of his books. Guénon felt the modern world privileged quantity over quality in every respect, something potentially also applicable to the whole pro-Nazi *Wunderwaffe* narrative of precision-engineered German Panzer tanks being dishonourably defeated by shoddy mass-produced Soviet T-34s on the Eastern Front. ('Quantity has a quality all its own' is regularly misattributed to Stalin; surely too subtle for the Georgian mass murderer.) Devi applied this idea to human beings themselves, decrying overpopulation of the planet with inferior races and the valueless, sheep-like masses who had proved so open to both consumerism and Communism:

One has to realise that, throughout a Time-Cycle ... the number of human beings increases all over the world, while their quality decreases no less alarmingly ... Any Time-Cycle could be briefly and picturesquely described as man's passage from the Garden of Eden into a huge international slum.

'The more worthless' people are, 'the quicker they breed,' until eventually Aryans would be outnumbered in their own lands; reflecting her cat-fixation, Devi compared this to lions being replaced with lice. You only have to look at the state of 'the faces one sees on overcrowded buses' to realise we are surrounded by 'bastards and sub-men' who have deviated too far away from their Ideal Form, as embodied by the spirit of Hitler dwelling amongst the stars.[28] Her thought can be seen as an attempt to project the philosophy of Traditionalism onto Nazism, hoping to give it a veneer of spiritual respectability, enabling its transformation into an esoteric racist religion rather than an exoteric political movement; Evola himself tried something similar with Italian fascism. According to Pauwels and Bergier, 'Lenin used to say that Communism was socialism plus electricity. It could also be said that Hitlerism, in a sense, was Guénonism, plus tanks.'[29] This really is a gross distortion of the totally non-Nazi Guénon's teachings, but it is close to what Savitri Devi believed.

By the time of Nazi defeat, Devi had developed the Traditionalism-influenced notion there were three types of notable men in existence. 'Men In Time' were great and ruthless leaders like Genghis Khan, who killed and plundered for their own material gain within a materialist *kali yuga* age. Such figures possessed the power of lightning, letting them swiftly conquer nations like human thunderbolts. 'Men Above Time' were otherworldly sages who transcended the *kali yuga* via spiritual means like occultism. They had the power of the sun, whose light enabled them to see through the tattered stage-set of this world and perceive the eternal archetypes which lay behind it. 'Men Against Time' bore powers of both sun *and* lightning. They tried to conquer the globe in the name of dispelling the *kali yuga* and bringing a return to cosmic springtime. Men Against Time were incarnations of Vishnu, and the greatest so far had been his ninth avatar, Adolf Hitler, who enjoyed powers both of exoteric lightning, with his doctrine of *blitzkrieg* or 'lightning warfare', and of esoteric sun, as with his swastika sun wheel emblem (perhaps his nine lives up to this point also signified his innate affinity with cats?). Hitler may have been beaten in 1945, but his defeat was truly victory in disguise. Hitler had deliberately lost his brave war in the visible world only to push it into a state of exceptional crisis, like undermining a bridge so it would soon collapse. In the invisible world of outer space, Hitler had already won, simply awaiting rebirth as the final tenth incarnation of Vishnu, a figure known as 'Kalki the Destructor' who would play a role in history akin to that of the Stay-Puft Marshmallow Man in *Ghostbusters*, another potentially world-shattering avatar with very white skin. In Buddhist terms, another key religion of India, Hitler is an angelic *Tulku* or *Bodhisattva*, one who, having freed himself from the bonds of eternal reincarnation upon our plane of physical existence by achieving perfect karma, has voluntarily returned to Earth from the Seventh Heaven nonetheless, taking suffering upon himself for the sake of an otherwise doomed humanity.[30]

In her 1958 *Meisterwerk*, *The Lightning and the Sun*, which considers politics 'from a cosmic angle',[31] Devi argued destruction by Hitler Reborn was a far greater prospect for humanity than continued rule by the victorious forces of Anglo-US-Zionist capitalism because, in their crazed quest for money, our rootless plutocratic overlords would ruin the entire planet through industrialisation and overpopulation until no life whatsoever could be supported on it, whereas Kalki/Hitler would just kill billions of people and then leave an unpolluted Earth to be inhabited by a few Green Nazi Aryan supermen, living in harmony with lots and lots of lovely animals. This was why the SS and *Einsatzgruppen* extermination squads had set out to slaughter so many Slavs, Jews and other such subhuman refuse. They were members of the ancient Aryan Indian *kshatriya* warrior-class, who obeyed the pitiless code of the *Bhagavad Gita*: 'Perform without attachment that which is duty, desiring nothing but the welfare of Creation.' When the SS killed millions of people, they were only dispassionately obeying orders to create a better world. The SS were truly an aristocracy amongst men, and the death's head insignia on their caps explained why; they were prepared to murder absolutely anybody at all in the name of restoring the Golden Age. The greater the evil, the greater the good, one of the chief paradoxes of our *kali yuga* days.[32]

You've got to be cruel to be kind, and Hitler was the kindest man in history. For Devi, Hitler's only flaw lay in his not having committed 'more substantial violences, more complete exterminations'. Given that, at Hitler's birth, the stars themselves had formed 'a definite pattern marking the return to Earth of Him who comes back', we may have expected more from this heavenly space-avatar. But then, Hitler was actually a uniting force; Vishnu's Aryan Race-Soul chose to be reborn in Braunau-am-Inn on the Austrian border so the baby Adolf could later reunite the nation with its nearby Fatherland. However, Hitler initially wished to do this peacefully and, contrary to popular belief, did his best to *prevent* the Second World War, not start it. 'Nobody wanted peace more than Adolf Hitler,' said Devi, not from any lily-livered 'humanitarian prejudices', but due to his desire to restore balance to the universe. Hitler's original purity of intention could be seen in his reputed vegetarianism and in the way that, 'as a young man, nay, a very attractive one', he refused all offers of sex, preferring to direct 'the sacred flame of Life' within his sun and lightning-infused testicle(s?) into sacred avenues instead. But then the Jews and English had declared war on him and ruined everything. And, if you think this all happened the other way around, then that is because *you too* have been corrupted by the inverted forces of *kali yuga* into seeing history upside-down.[33]

Yet the Divine Adolf did not reappear. In 1948, Devi was imprisoned in Germany for inserting strange handwritten propaganda messages into packets of cigarettes and tubs of butter before distributing 6,000 handbills detailing Hitler's impending magical reappearance: '*Our Führer is alive*, and will soon come back, with power unheard of. Resist our persecutors! Hope and wait. Heil Hitler!' But still He did not come. However, jail allowed Devi to act as a martyr, saying prayers to Shiva whilst holding a locket containing Hitler's image to her breast, and forming close relationships with imprisoned female concentration camp wardens, which provided a unique

The Saucer and the Swastika

entry point into the post-war neo-Nazi underground. At her trial she had courted attention by refusing to swear an oath on the Bible, demanding to be allowed to do it on a 'Sacred Wheel of the Sun' – that is, a swastika – instead. Her ultimate hope was to be sentenced to death, going to the gallows in her wedding-sari at dawn and, stretching out her right arm, 'firm and white in the sunshine', giving a Nazi salute to her Akhnaton-Führer embodied in the rising sun whilst singing Hitler's old marching anthem of the *Horst Wessel Song* in defiance.[34]

The 1950s saw her going on pilgrimage across the shattered Reich to the many 'holy sites' of Nazi history, in search of sacred signs of fascism's eventual resurrection, and fellow potential disciples. In 1948 she had already met one called 'Herr A', who whispered he knew where the living Hitler was hiding out but dared not tell her. Adolf would be very pleased by her devotion to him, said Herr A, before promising to build a Nazi sun temple in her honour. But by the time of her second visit, it had not been built, Hitler had not returned, and she began to suspect he was dead after all, and his spirit may need to be reincarnated again before the world could be saved. Arriving at a beerhall where Hitler had given a famous speech, she was disgusted to see occupying US troops had decorated it for a party; the grinning face of a clown above the platform where Hitler had once spoken struck her as symbolic of the trivial nature of the shallow *kali yuga* mind.[35]

Supported for a time by various prominent Nazis who had escaped justice, in 1970 Devi went to live with French fascist sympathiser Françoise Dior (1932-93), niece of the famous fashionista, from whose home she was allegedly later expelled owing to her refusal to take a bath. From here Devi returned to India where she lived once more amongst cats, who didn't mind the smell as much. Her books were initially underground affairs, published in India by her old Hindu nationalist husband, but in the late 1960s extracts appeared in the US magazine *National Socialist World*, to much fringe acclaim, before in 1979 none other than Ernst Zündel began reprinting Devi's core texts with his Canadian Samisdat firm, in larger editions than had hitherto been imaginable. Zündel was introduced to Holocaust denial by Devi, who influenced him greatly, especially her staunch loyalty to the Reich and flowery odes to its leaders. Although probably not believing her madder ideas, Zündel saw Devi's works as the ideal partner-products for his slapdash UFO titles, appealing to a more literate esoterically minded audience; although clearly unbalanced, Devi was a highly educated and erudite woman. Her name would be 'remembered in White History as one of the truly great names of Our Race, when our history is once again written by White historians', Zündel enthused. In 1978, Zündel had arranged a ten-hour interview with the elderly and half-blind Devi, who had been missing from the neo-Nazi scene for some years by then, which he then released on-tape, promoting her as 'Hitler's guru', who had just been 'discovered alive in India'. Now you could hear 'in her own words' about Devi's 'pilgrimage along the edge of the cosmic abyss' and 'watch the clouds of evil scatter

104

under the lightning of Cosmic Justice and the sun of Cosmic Truth' as she revealed 'the secret Nazi pyramid connection' and Hitler's 'mystical bond with the dark forces of time and destiny'. When she died in 1982, the newly celebrated heroine's ashes were stored in the Valhalla-like neo-Nazi 'New Order Hall of Honour' in Wisconsin, reputedly next to those of former American Nazi Party leader George Lincoln Rockwell (1918-67), who had undergone his own paranormal Hitler-related experiences, meeting Adolf's ghost in his dreams.[36] Devi's ashes have since imitated the life cycle of the phoenix, however, and, anticipating the return of her beloved God-Führer, the Nazi priestess has recently made a startling political comeback herself ...

* * * * *

We will recall the strange speculations of the Ariosophists regarding white women polluting their race by mating with alien dinosaur-people, and how such fringe creeds, appearing within the specific context of mass immigration into the Austro-Hungarian Empire, took off rather more than we might have expected. Could this ever happen again? The contemporary relevance of Ariosophy was spotted by the scholar of Esoteric Nazism (and first biographer of Savitri Devi) Nicholas Goodrick-Clarke (1953-2012) in his classic 2002 book *Black Sun*, where he argued that 'Multicultural [Western] societies face a similar challenge today' to that which had once faced the Austro-Hungarian Empire. Nowadays, he wrote,

> ...the United States and most European nations are facing a demographic shift against their historic native stocks. The resulting issue of white identity recapitulates the dilemma of Austrian Germans fearing a loss of influence in the old Habsburg Empire.

It was Goodrick-Clarke's contention that we would soon be seeing an upsurge in the number of neo-Nazis who used floridly delusional occult symbology as a means of protesting against mass immigration, just as the Ariosophists did:

> We cannot know what the future holds for Western multicultural societies, but the experiment did not fare well in Austria-Hungary ... From the retrospective viewpoint of ... [future decades] Aryan cults and Esoteric Nazism may be documented as early symptoms of major divisive changes in our present-day Western democracies. [37]

Thus, the texts of today's neo-Nazi UFO cults may one day seem much like Ariosophist books about alien dinosaur-lovers now seem in relation to German history of the pre-Nazi era.

Already described by Goodrick-Clarke as 'an Evita-figure for opponents of multi-racial democracy',[38] Savitri Devi's own cult is today spreading rapidly online, particularly her teaching that the *kali yuga*, as an age of inversion, was one in which 'democracy' was truly a disguised dictatorship of liberal, Jew-controlled internationalist elites, enabling traditionally Aryan nations to be flooded with inferior foreigners, just like the Habsburg Vienna of Hitler's youth. Devi's rhetoric has seen her adopted as a figurehead by the contemporary American alt-right, whose staunchly anti-immigration views mirror her own. This is how Devi once described the likely future fate of England, which foolishly 'chose to listen to her Jewish misleaders' in fighting Germany instead of joining it:

> She shall die – not the glorious death on the battlefield, but the slow, nauseating death through blood-mixture and all manner of vice. Within less than 300 years to come – unless there be a miracle [i.e. Hitler's return] – there shall be no more England. My [English] mother's compatriots ... will have given way before teeming millions of mongrels (a hotch-potch of Jamaicans, Africans, Pakistanis, Jews and degenerate Englishwomen) with nothing in common with their forefathers ... The few remaining pure-blooded English Aryans ... [will be] foreigners in the land of their ancestors.[39]

'Jews are going to replace us with foreigners,' the familiar claim of today's alt-right. Online, Devi's philosophy has been turned into a parodic fake religion dubbed 'Esoteric Kekism' ('KEK' being an alternate form of 'LOL') by this very same alt-right, in which humorous memes about Devi, Hitler and Vishnu are spread, hoping to rid fascism of its taboo status, making Esoteric Nazism look cool and funny. The US alt-right's offline leader, Richard Spencer (b. 1978), has made headlines for calling the white race 'Children of the Sun', a concept gleaned directly from Devi and Evola. America, he has said, truly belongs to these white sun-children, but has been stolen from them by other races, with the 2016 election of Donald Trump the first step in taking it back.[40] When you see alt-right marchers chanting 'Jews will not replace us!' in reference to an imaginary Israelite plan to substitute the white European and American population with blacks and Muslims, you can see Goodrick-Clarke's warnings coming true before your eyes – the West is indeed undergoing a disastrous enforced demographic sea-change, but it has nothing to do with the Jews, many of whom are now actually fleeing lands like France due to rising anti-Semitism, much of which has been blindly imported from abroad. So, just as mad Ariosophist ideas about alien dino-sex anticipated widespread fears about the eclipsing of traditional native populations by immigrants years before these very same worries were expressed in more comprehensible terms by the Nazis, so Savitri Devi's loony allegations about Jews destroying the white race via *kali yuga* methods now sound like direct harbingers of the 'Jews will not replace us' crowd, even if most who chant such words may not have heard of her.

If you strip the *kali yuga* of its esoteric Hindu elements and reduce it simply to a metaphor, namely an 'Age of Inversion', then it is not difficult to find examples of traditional moral, social and biological norms being turned upside-down today in the name of 'progress'. When victims are treated as criminals and *vice versa*, it is not irrational to believe that this is an age of inversion at all. The cranks who worship Savitri Devi are full of dangerous bile, particularly about the Jews, but some of their central criticisms of society are becoming mainstream. How many Westerners honestly believe that 'we have always been a nation of immigrants' on the current gigantic level, as our politicians pretend? In such massively multicultural cities as London, Marseilles or Malmö, there will inevitably be some disillusioned folk who start talking like Hitler and the Ariosophists did about late-Habsburg Vienna. In 1993, Savitri Devi's good friend Colin Jordan (1923-2009), one of the founding fathers of British neo-Nazism, published an Orwellian satire, *Merrie England – 2,000*, in which he painted a picture of a Britain transformed into a totalitarian left-wing society ruled over by the race-relations police, with enforced ritual obeisance towards non-whites for the Anglo-Saxon population in recognition of their guilt towards them and with Nelson's Column toppled in favour of a statue of Nelson Mandela.[41] There are echoes of this in the wake of the Black Lives Matter movement, and the demands of some of its quasi-Marxist adherents. By making certain elements of Jordan's text come true, such activists may inadvertently lend credence to the opinions of outright neo-Nazis about certain matters. As the many voices who object to current 'woke' trends are ignored by politicians and the media, a violent backlash has potential to brew. Unease at the unprecedented demographic and cultural upheaval currently happpening in the West is common, and it would be stupid not to pay it heed; otherwise, the genuinely extreme views of rabid anti-Semites like Devi, and the less overtly loony Far-Right figures for whom she acts as an early-warning sign, like Colin Jordan, may gain even more traction, as forecast by Nicholas Goodrick-Clarke. In the Dark Age of *kali yuga*, we should expect no less.

For some people in this world, modernity is inherently fallen. And, given that one of the chief imaginative symbols of post-war modernity is the UFO, it should come as little surprise that some of those who believe we are living through the dregs of *kali yuga* should seek to combine the Esoteric Nazism of Savitri Devi with flying saucers. When they do, the fruits can become very strange indeed. Let us, like so many fleeing Nazi war criminals, sail now down to Chile, where we shall meet one of the most fascinating fascists of all.

4

Diplomatic Circles: Miguel Serrano, Circular Nazis, Esoteric Hitlerism and Rudolf Hess Hiding on the Moon

Even those who think the UN a pointless talking-shop would have to concede that at least one of its subsidiary bodies, the International Atomic Energy Agency (IAEA), does some vital work trying to stem the proliferation of nuclear weapons. As such, it is profoundly disturbing to hear the views held by one of its former affiliates, the Chilean diplomat Miguel Serrano (1917-2009).[1] A highly cultured yet fanatical Nazi, Serrano believed the liberal modern world order was a gigantic Jewish plot intended to create 'a hallucinating phantasmagoria destined to dissolve and exploit the Aryan universe', an attempt to impose false values upon society and scientific reality itself, via 'robbery and witchcraft', as laid out in his personal philosophy of 'Esoteric Hitlerism'.

Post-war folk lived in a relativistic world, where traditional values were continually being upturned in classic *kali yuga* fashion, but the ultimate relativistic realm was the subatomic one revealed by Jewish scientists like Albert Einstein (1879-1955), the name of whose appalling 'Theory of Relativity' said it all. Jewish physicists were 'just like Picasso', Serrano argued, as with their incomprehensible sums they aimed to 'abstract everything, reduce everything to pure mathematical-algebraic formulas, dissolving form, flesh and blood' until eventually there was nothing left of reality itself, only a void with 'no light ... not even movement, only a nothing of numbers and formulas'. Quarks and electrons were 'the greatest surrealisms', much more so than Picasso's paintings. This was the true purpose of the Jew-created atomic bomb; to erase physical reality itself, to ensure 'the atomisation of the world'. The Aryan, however, was 'not interested' in dividing the atom, but instead 'aspires to the *unus mundus*, to totality', wanting to unite reality into a coherent whole. This was why Adolf Hitler, who had invented the first atom bomb 'by his own means' in secret, refused to use it. The bomb 'did not correspond to the integrating, non-atomising Archetype in his Aryan collective unconscious'. If he had used the bomb, Hitler 'would not have won the war, he would have lost it, since he would have Judaised his own world, using an extreme Jew method.' Possibly the A-bombs dropped on Japan were Hitler's own unused ones, stolen by the Americans. Hitler, as a covert sorcerer, knew it was the hidden invisible realm of magic which truly underpinned Creation, not subatomic Jewish nonsense. Numbers were fake Zionist inventions, which the noble ancient Romans had sensibly done without, having 'other means of calculation'. 'For Aryans,' wrote Serrano, 'atoms have never been numeric, abstract, empty formulas. They are gnomes, magic Runes, the atomic Gods.'[2] As Serrano spent his childhood talking to fairies in his garden, later climbing mountains in search of a gateway into 'The Kingdom of the Gnomes', we should take these claims literally.[3]

According to Serrano, Hitler had also tried to create an 'anti-atom bomb' *Wunderwaffe*, which would unite, not divide, the world. This wonderful technology was spiritual in form – it was the UFO. In 1945 Hitler had not truly died, merely travelled into the invisible dimension of the Norse gods and Platonic Forms by morphing into a disc of pure light, what the ancient Hindus called *vimanas*, and we term flying saucers. The Nazis had also built some solid mechanical saucers, said Serrano, as demonstrated by that old fraud Rudolf Schriever, the chief fake saucer-builder once given a platform by the 1950s news media, whose claims the Chilean swallowed wholesale. Furthermore, Himmler's *Ahnenerbe* had found a magical artefact, the Stone of Ornolac, which contained instructions for building saucers armed with Thor's ancient lightning weapons, which 'disintegrated enemy aircraft in full flight, left only a space where a tank had been before, or paralysed the enemy without killing'. These saucers may have been driven by music, or the chanting of mantras, and could even read minds. The SS's stone also explained how to facilitate 'the disintegration and reintegration of matter', as well as levitation and invisibility, using 'the *Tarnkappe* [magical cloak] of Siegfried', thus explaining UFOs' anti-gravitational properties and ability to appear and disappear at will. Yet Hitler had managed to transmute himself into a flying disc by pure spiritual alchemy alone. This 'legendary anti-gravitational science of the spirit' would never be available to the non-Aryan, for only the racially pure had access to 'the Science of Peace', which allowed them to become circular.[4]

Living in Switzerland after the war, Serrano befriended the famed Swiss psychologist C. G. Jung (1875-1968), later penning a 1965 book, *The Hermetic Circle*, boasting of their association. For those who neither wished to dismiss UFOs as being wholly imaginary, nor to take them literally as alien spaceships, Jung's classic 1958 text *Flying Saucers: A Modern Myth of Things Seen in the Skies*, proved highly influential. Fearing nuclear obliteration following the USSR's mastery of the atom bomb in 1949, 1950s Westerners instinctively stared towards the heavens in search of angelic saviours, said Jung. Yet, as religious belief waned, a new image of salvation was needed, one more suited to an era of atomic science – that of saucer-ships. 'Anything that looks technological goes down without difficulty with modern man,' Jung wrote. The UFOs, many of whose Orthon-like occupants sought to stave off nuclear Armageddon, were angels for an age in which angels were no longer allowed to exist.[5]

The Cold War severed the globe into two competing halves, under Russian or American influence. When things split asunder like this, said Jung, a compensatory mediating psychic image is born within the collective human psyche, pointing a path back towards happy union.[6] A close scholar of alchemy, Jung noted the insignia of the planes of the US and Soviet air forces, which would have been used to deliver atomic warheads onto enemy territory, were two five-pointed stars, America's white, Russia's red. In alchemy, red powders and liquids were considered feminine and masculine respectively, and to mix such contrasting materials within experiments would be to unite them symbolically in a 'chemical wedding' known as the *coniuncto oppositorum*, or 'union of opposites'. The whole being greater than the sum of the parts, this chemical consummation within the marriage-bed of the laboratory would give birth to some new substance far superior to either ingredient individually, namely the fabled Philosopher's Stone, meant to confer immortality upon its manufacturer. To unite Red Square in holy matrimony with the White House was thus the only way for the globe to achieve the Philosopher's Stone of peaceful geopolitical co-existence.[7]

These new-fangled flying saucers, proposed Jung, must have had a reason for only appearing *en masse* for the first time in 1947, guessing they were psychic advertisements of this collectively desired marriage between Communism and capitalism, circles being traditional symbols of wholeness, as in the circular marriage-ring or the old idea of God being a circle whose centre is everywhere and circumference nowhere. Jung identified saucers as really being *mandalas*, ancient round Buddhist symbols of the wholeness of God, whose name is derived from the Sanskrit for 'circle'. God was in this view 'a totality symbol *par excellence*, something round, complete and perfect', capable of uniting the 'irreconcilable opposites' of East and West. The UFO-*mandala*, proposed Jung, had been 'superimposed on the psychic chaos' of the Cold War stand-off by humanity, an unconscious effort to reverse the consequences of splitting the world and the atom – both of which are generally depicted as circular or spherical.[8] Therefore, to Jung's admirer Serrano it made sense that, when you saw a big round disc in the sky, it was likely to be a pro-CND Nazi flying sorcerer like Adolf Hitler disguised as a *mandala*, not Martians in a nuts-and-bolts spaceship.

For Serrano, the Second World War had an esoteric purpose, lurking below Hitler's exoteric surface aim of conquering Europe. This was to turn Germany increasingly circular like a *mandala* until, with a magical 'click', it vanished into another dimension, together with the Führer himself. The Third Reich was the manifestation of another reality upon Earth, the perfect realm of the circular Aryan Soul. Once in power, Hitler drew a magic circle around Germany, as symbolised by his swastika sun wheel in its white circle on the sacred Nazi flag. In the centre of this circle stood a pole about which the sun wheel would spin – Adolf Hitler. When the Nazis started Germany spinning around this 'hypnotic, irresistible centre of attraction', the magic circle counteracted those subatomic Jewish forces of abstraction which had done so much to rot modernity. By the end of the conflict, 'swirling, swirling, every time faster' until it 'had reached a velocity of vertigo', Hitler's mystic swastika-circle caused Nazi Germany to suddenly disappear down a cosmic plughole, with all those 'Circular Folk' who remained faithful to the war's hidden meaning, like Goebbels (but not Himmler, who got scared at the last minute), 'breaking away from this material world' along with it, becoming Jungian *vimana*-discs as they did so. Buildings supposedly destroyed by Allied bombs had simply slipped into another world, for now. The ruined Germany left behind was not the real Third Reich, but a mirage. Nazi Germany lived on invisibly until, one day, it and its buildings would re-invade Earth as a new, saucer-armed Fourth Reich, accompanied by the ancient Nordic gods with their awesome lightning *Wunderwaffen*, and loyal SS men transformed into the Wild Hunt, to destroy our world thereby to save it from *kali yuga*.[9]

* * * * *

Serrano only openly set his circular reasoning down in writing following his forced retirement as a diplomat, most notably in 1978's *The Golden Cord: Esoteric Hitlerism* and 1984's *Adolf Hitler – The Ultimate Avatar*, where, on the very first page, he admits 'I am from another planet,' which sounds about right.[10] The sphere he truly orbited was Planet Savitri Devi, whom he admired as a holy priestess of Hitler, agreeing that Adolf was a Kalki-like avatar of the god Vishnu possessing the powers of both sun and lightning, who would one day incarnate himself again to combat the evil of *kali yuga*, destroying civilisation so it could rise anew. Progress was an illusion, said Serrano, and history followed a cyclical path, as in Hinduism, not a straight line ever upwards. Circles were Aryan and good, straight lines evil and Jewish.

Serrano also shared Devi's belief Hitler abstained from sex to preserve his sacred lightning-infused sperm for a higher cause, using it to feed his astral body so it could become a *vimana*. By doing so, 'instead of the fleeting physical pleasure, *sukha*, the ecstatic orgasm, occurs, which has no end,' a non-stop soul-thrill which eliminated any 'astral congestion' within Hitler's veins, causing 'the transubstantiation' of the Führer's bloodstream into Black Sun *Vril*-power, allowing him to travel 'up the channels of an Ultimate River that does not exist' in the shape of a UFO. Apparently being the descendants of alien gods like Thor, male Aryans naturally possessed spiritual, lightning-like sperm, 'a luminous fluid which is, materially, semen', something to be exploited by all true Nazis.[11] Serrano liked to retain his own sperm but was forced to change tack when his wife became scared by poltergeists that latched onto the pent-up sexual energy within his swollen testicles, breaking furniture 'to pieces' and making objects float. Eventually, Serrano abandoned the project of mutating into a UFO personally and channelled his electro-sexual energies into siring some solid children, but Hitler, being a *mandala* and thus containing all undifferentiated opposites within himself like God, even male and female, became pregnant himself with 'an entire world that he is bringing to light: the world of the Fourth Reich, the new Golden Age, the Other Earth.' Serrano doubted the abstemious Hitler and his girlfriend Eva Braun (1912-45) had married during their final days in the Führerbunker at all, speculating this was a lie invented by 'the genius of Goebbels' so Jews couldn't say Adolf was gay. If Hitler was married to anyone, it was probably to a Valkyrie.[12]

Savitri Devi's 1958 travelogue *Pilgrimage* held special sway over Serrano, detailing as it did Devi's delusional journey across a defeated Third Reich. Adolf, Devi wrote, had 'raised Germany to the status of a Holy Land ... inseparable from the early history of the perennial Religion of Life', Nazism. This was '*not* a metaphor'.[13] Indeed not. Whilst *wandervoegeling* abroad, 'in several shops, and once in the street', psychically sensitive persons had mis-read Devi's aura as being that of a German 'in spite of my dark eyes and hair', magically demonstrating her soul was inherently German, even though she had not been born there.[14] Given this, when she travelled to the grave of Klara Hitler (1860-1907) – 'the predestined Mother' of the Führer himself – Devi found it easy to imagine the undead dictator returning to lay flowers. But if he *was* dead, would his ghost know 'how ardently' his disciples still loved him? Kneeling before Klara's grave, she had a vision of Hitler's head, which she asked 'Will you ever know how much I have loved you?' Adolf's head knew full well she couldn't just want him for his body. 'Live for my Germany!' he commanded. 'And you shall never part from Me, wherever I be.' Once again, 'Adolf Hitler, the Chosen One of the Invisible Powers', had showed Devi the path towards righteousness.[15] Savitri wandered the sacred land, with nearly every woman she met being a secret SS widow longing for the return of the Reich, before finding Hitler's childhood tutor. Wistfully, the old man recalled how the adolescent Adolf was 'a healthy, clean-minded, loving and lovable child – the most lovable I have ever seen.' The Christ-Child in question now sent Devi an unmistakable sign of his deity from outer space; a 'homely, well-fed cat' jumped into her lap from nowhere, being 'the forerunner of happy animal-kind in our world to come', once most of the humans had been murdered. 'Did He love animals?' asked Devi, knowing the answer already. Of course! And not only animals, but 'every living creature that God has made', even trees, said the tutor. Hitler had literally never hurt a fly.[16]

Devi's trip culminated at the Externsteine, a numinous rock formation in Westphalia possibly once used in rituals of pagan sun worship, at least in the view of the *Ahnenerbe*. Supposedly, it was the site of the fabled 'Irminsul', a pillar of the sun sacred to the pre-Christian pagan *volk*, although Hitler himself thought this had 'certainly never' been the case, something Devi herself seemingly either did not know, or else chose to ignore. Nationalist pseudo-scholar Otto Siegfried Reuter (1876-1945) was both an Ariosophist who believed it was inappropriate for Germans to worship a 'Jewish' God like that of the Bible, and the author of a 1934 book, *German Astronomy*, which argued ancient Aryans had invented astronomy itself, with German fairy tales really being precise symbolic encodings of the paths and nature of the stars, planets and constellations of the solar system. Researcher Wilhelm Teudt (1860-1942) applied Reuter's work to the Externsteine, which now became a sort of prehistoric pagan ley-line centre and site of sun worship, with rock-hewn observatories and even a primeval university attached. In reality, the Externsteine is a series of four colossal natural sandstone columns or towers, seemingly transformed into a symbolic representation of Jerusalem by Christians around 1100; two chapels and a 'holy grave' are carved into its sandstone, as is a large relief of Christ on the cross. Christ was too Jewish for the *Ahnenerbe*, however, and when they excavated the site in the 1930s they found evidence it really was a primordial pagan sun worship centre after all, even if they had to deliberately rearrange artefacts and re-carve the caves themselves to prove it. It is perfectly probable some early Germans really did perform actual solar solstice rituals at the Externsteine, but not in the sense Himmler's pseudo-archaeologists taught.[17]

Devi saw the Externsteine's purported Akhnaton-like solar worshippers as forerunners of the later battle of Nazi sun-children against the Judeo-Marxist forces of *kali yuga* darkness, 'the struggle of the Powers of Light against the Powers of Gloom'. The Emperor Charlemagne (748-814) was supposed to have defeated a pagan chief near the site before forcibly converting his tribe to Christianity in the eighth century – which, to many Nazis, meant he had really converted them to Judaism. Like the conquering US General Dwight D. Eisenhower (1890-1969), Charlemagne was thus an apostate German who had betrayed his race; both the Nazis and the pagans had to be revenged in the name of the sun disc. 'One day we will avenge you, wounded Rocks that have been calling us for so long!' Devi declared. Invoking the Old Gods of sun and blood, Devi entreated the 'Forces of Light and Life' to 'help us win the last battle' against *kali yuga* and to 'protect our beloved Führer, wherever he be, under whatever aspect he be: visible or invisible!' At this 'German Stonehenge', Devi performed magical rites to hasten the return of Hitler's spirit and 'bind myself – and National Socialism – mysteriously, magically, ritually, to Germany's remotest past, nay, to the eternal Self of Aryan mankind ... through the undying potent sanctity of the Rocks of the Sun.' The daily dawn rise of the solar disc, 'invisible behind the clouds', was analogous to the 'slow, silent, invisible' rising of the Fourth Cat-Reich 'behind the screen of world events'. Devi sought to relive the 'tragic history' of Germany's fall by symbolically dying herself, thus to 'rouse the age-old Heathen energies stored up for centuries within these stones' and redirect it towards making the sun god Adolf Hitler rise again from the darkness of civilisational midnight, restoring light to the world.

Accordingly, Devi lay overnight in what is supposed to have been an ancient stone coffin and temporarily 'died', talking with 'the Heathen Soul of the Rocks' and the ghosts of pagan sun-warriors who had been slain defending the spot from Charlemagne's Christian armies, the precursors of the 'sinister' Allied armies of General Eisenhower's 'crusaders to Europe'. By lying in the coffin at a certain angle and sticking your head into a hole in the rock, a tour-guide had assured Devi that you would be sent into a trance of 'strange unconsciousness' from which a person could only be awoken by a ritual horn being blown in a nearby chamber decorated with magical runes. Armed with this knowledge, Devi returned to the Externsteine alone after dark and entered the coffin to 'die' anew. Then, a Nazi miracle occurred:

> An icy-cold sensation ran through me, as though ... the power of Death had emanated from the stone. Then, as I stretched myself on my back, in the posture of the dead, I distinctly saw ... a violet spark – a tiny lightning – flash out of the dark vaulted rock above my head. And I shuddered, as though this were a sign that the Hidden Powers *knew* what I was doing ...[18]

Was it Hitler, Lord of Lightning, urging her to keep the fascist faith? That dawn, Devi sacrificed her gold swastika earrings to the pagan gods, raised her right arm in a Nazi salute, and hailed the rising Sun-Führer. Sun gods, long-dead pagan swordsmen and the ghosts of executed Nazi war criminals were all requested to 'march in spirit within our ranks' come the day of the glorious revolution and help to gift Hitler's soul with 'the North and the South, the world, from pole to pole!' Devi now imitated the Führer's own youthful hill-top epiphany in Linz, and merged with the cosmos itself, becoming temporarily possessed: 'Tears filled my eyes. And an icy thrill ran along my spine ... It was no longer *I* who lived, but Adolf Hitler – and, behind him, cosmic Truth – who lived in me; Adolf Hitler, the Saviour of the best and the Ruler of the future.'[19]

* * * * *

In 1982 Miguel Serrano followed in Devi's goose-steps, travelling across Germany on his own bizarre occult neo-Nazi pilgrimage. He especially enjoyed his holiday visit to 'the North Tower of Initiation' within Heinrich Himmler's five-star SS Black Order castle of Wewelsburg. To Serrano, Germany's castles were giant supernatural machines built to transform sympathetic souls into *vimanas*, and open magic portals onto other planets. Wewelsburg was 'a magnetic centre full of ghosts', whose sacred architecture facilitated 'a mutation' of SS-men into *Sonnenmensch*, or 'sun-people'. Himmler, 'nothing more than a phantom', was telepathically controlled by 'a truly invisible centre' from another world (probably Tibetan Masters living inside the Hollow Earth in Agartha or Shambhala) into making Wewelsburg a 'Laboratory of Leftwards [i.e. black] Magic ... built according to ... Aryan mathematics' where the SS 'broke apart their physical bodies and materialised their astral body' as *mandala*-UFOs. Parts of Wewelsburg Castle had surely been carved directly from holy stones of the Externsteine and infused with dark powers by *Ahnenerbe* wizards. This was why Himmler had not ordered his base be defended during the Allied invasion; he could not risk such sacred stones being damaged by enemy bombs. (Actually, Himmler ordered the place be dynamited.) Finding 'a small room with a seat of honour', Serrano saw it was the throne of King Arthur, who was really Hitler. It would seat the astral body of 'the Führer-Parsifal', so he need not leave his office to monitor proceedings of Himmler's SS Black Knights of the Admirably Round Table. With fellow Esoteric Nazis, Serrano enacted an unholy ritual, sensing the 'sleepy, dull, suffering' souls of dead fascists being resurrected in his very presence.

With right arms raised, Devi's acolytes 'began to emit soft tones ... [which] rotated and swirled in such a way we felt we would disintegrate on this plane of existence, perhaps to reach an Other Universe, going out through the hallucinatory vortex, by the maelstrom of the Swastika of Return of the Black Sun, to reassemble ourselves in the non-existence of the Green Thunderbolt' in the shape of vimanas. But this didn't happen, so they all went back to their hotel-rooms and remained non-circular.' [20]

Serrano aimed to visit Devi during his trip, but she died in England shortly beforehand. So he travelled to the Externsteine and its sanctified stone coffin himself to commune with her soul. As his surname meant 'Mountain', Serrano had an innate affinity with rock formations of all kinds, allowing him to see their true nature in visions, once realising the Andes were really a pair of petrified giants, covered in stony sleep by *kali yuga*. The mountain range 'introduced herself to me', Serrano said, with one colossus 'raising open arms towards the summit', the other 'bent with pendant arms', but both with bodies 'streaked with veins of gold', traces of the vanished *satya yuga* Golden Age. All the world's peaks were similar sleeping colossi who 'should be freed ... This has been the work of my life, to liberate, to give new life to the giants,' Serrano revealed.[21] Likewise, the Externsteine had been built by a race of prehistoric extraterrestrial Aryan Titans, via 'the projection of mind over cosmic and terrestrial plasma', with a single blow. It was thus a giant symbol, saying that 'only a hard character ... firm as the rocks of the Externsteine, will be able to change the Destiny of the Darkest Age.' Here, in the stone coffin, Serrano 'passed a night with [the ghost of] Savitri Devi ... Odinic priestess of Esoteric Hitlerism' where, in the gloom, he saw 'the Original Light', just as Devi had once done. This gave Serrano faith he would meet his heroine in Valhalla, 'together with the Führer and Wotan'.[22]

Devi was not Serrano's only inspiration. He had also read his Ariosophists and rune-magic manuals, learning the Hitler salute had magical powers to activate *chakras*, or centres of 'luminous energy', within its giver's body which, in illustrations, he portrayed as circles containing swastikas. By combining rune-magic with *kundalini* yoga traditions, Serrano mapped the precise anatomical location of these *chakras* within the Aryan frame; the testicles of the Esoteric Hitlerist look like miniature sun wheels and he appears to have had Nazi knee-replacements. The ankles and wrists, too, contain swastikas, as do the omphalos and armpits. Naturally, Hitlerite Man also has several swastikas on the brain. As in Ariosophy, ancient Germanic runes were really stick-man diagrams of poses which activated these *chakras*, allowing 'serpent power' and *Vril* to flow through them, transforming one's blood into divine light from the Black Sun, that imaginary cosmic body which was supposed to shine its invisible light upon the Nordic race alone. Serrano's ufology indicates that circles are good and Aryan, straight lines wicked and Jewish, as echoed in the contrasting cyclical and straight line theories of history. But with the runes, it is the reverse. Alphabets containing curly letters like 'S' are the tools of Jews and dinosaur-men, 'with their undulating, reptilian, Semitic forms' – the letter 'S' looks a bit like a snake. Although the only true writing was the Nordic runes, they were 'not an alphabet' but magical tools, never being used to write books ('except for the ultra-strange Tarot'). Yet they were demonstrably straight; so how did they work?

Simply by transforming the Aryan body into an antenna through which to draw cosmic forces from space which then stimulated the *chakras* – which were, of course, circular in nature, being 'wheels [which] are made to whirl like swastikas, with a dizzying vertigo', due to 'rune-force' producing 'vibrations in the astral body'. The rune-letters, with their stick-man poses, akin to those of the join-the-dots stars of the constellations, 'correspond to the High Breeding' of the original astral Aryan soul, before it descended to Earth from outer space and was clothed in gross matter, a sort of spiritual skeleton upon which flesh was then hung; originally, these astral skeletons were encased 'with a luminous primary matter', and by recreating such skeleton-poses, you too could replace your flesh with pure light, so becoming 'the Divine Body, the Body of Wotan, the Total-Man'. Thus, within the perfect body of the *Sieg Heil*-ing Nazi, all cosmic opposites, like line and circle, space and Earth, above and below, were reunited in complete *unus mundus* union, as with a Jungian UFO. However, only pure Nordic types could exploit these wonderful tools – without the correct Aryan knowledge, rune-magic's 'ill use can cause madness and even death.' Fortunately, despite being Chilean and having a Spanish name, Miguel Serrano himself was actually more German than most Germans were. South America was 'a bastard continent in the midst of a bastard world', and it was down to pure-blooded Nordic types like Miguel to 'build again the devastated land of the *Graal*' that was modern-day Chile and thereby 'return the Crown' to the sick King Arthur/Adolf.[23]

Born into an aristocratic land-owning family of writers and diplomats in 1917, as the proud possessor of blonde hair and blue eyes Serrano considered himself Aryan, an idea reinforced by his attendance at a school founded by former Prussian military men, where a love of Germanic culture was installed. Orphaned aged eight, Serrano was raised by his paternal grandmother and nudged towards left-wing politics by his uncle, the poet Vicente Huidobro (1893-1948), who urged him to join the Communist rebels fighting the fascist General Francisco Franco (1892-1975) in the Spanish Civil War. Impressed by their daring yet doomed attempts to institute a fascist coup in 1938, Serrano instead joined the Chilean Nazi Party equivalent, the *Nacistas*, in 1939, even though they had killed his childhood best friend and fellow teenage poet Hector Barreto – or 'Jason of the Non-Existent Flower', as he preferred to be called – in a street-brawl. Serrano's initial impulse following the trampling of Jason's flower had been to embrace Marxism in revenge, but he soon saw the magnitude of his folly, accompanying the *Nacistas*' German-Chilean leader, Jorges González von Marées (1900-62), on national speaking tours. When one night Uncle Vicente gave his opinion Hitler had already lost the war, Serrano arbitrarily intuited this knowledge meant his relative was actually a Freemason, in hidden alliance with Communists, the Vatican, the Red Cross and the Rotary Club, which had all joined together due to 'the evil intervention of extraterrestrials' of a non-Aryan nature to promote 'world slavery' by defeating Nazism on behalf of the Jews. Pervertedly, Vicente offered to let Miguel join this army of *kali yuga* darkness too. 'I knew he needed help,' Serrano said of his uncle; his uncle doubtless thought the very same thing of his nephew. Uncle Vicente had 'tried to change his cosmic ID, his very Blood' by allying himself with pro-Jewish forces, making the Aryan Serrano now know he needed to aid the fascist cause to save the family honour – but how?[24]

By the 1940s, Serrano was already an established journalist, so decided the pen would prove mightier than the sword. Chile had cravenly remained neutral, and it was necessary to persuade it to join the good German fight. Establishing a pro-Nazi fortnightly journal, *The New Age*, in 1941, Serrano visited Chile's Italian Embassy, where Mussolini's Cultural Attaché, Hugo Gallo, owed him some articles. But the esoteric-minded Gallo offered Serrano something else instead: the chance of fighting Hitler's war 'on other levels', on the astral plane. He introduced Serrano to a guru named 'The Maestro', who ran a secret yogic cult devoted to worshipping Hitler, the 'Sacred Order of Thi-U-Hin', described as 'a Warrior-Magicians' Order'. The Maestro's real name was Carlos Rogat Salas (1878-1974), although he styled himself Sri Raaknahaif, and claimed to be in mental contact with Hidden Tibetan Masters living in the Himalayas and cities within the Hollow Earth. Allegedly, the full records of the Nuremburg Trials reveal the existence of The Maestro and his powerful knowledge, but 'the TRUTH of course will not be revealed to the public,' only the usual litany of Jewish lies.[25]

Serrano was then suffering from sleep-paralysis, and The Maestro gave an appealing explanation: Miguel had potential magic powers, and his astral body was struggling to escape him. Thanks to The Maestro, Serrano knew exactly what to do when confronted by 'a powerful dark yellow stream like an octopus with many tentacles' which tried to drag him to the moon one night in a 'lunar current'. The Maestro told his grateful follower that Nazism was truly an esoteric religion, not an exoteric political movement, and Hitler lived in two realms, visible and invisible, simultaneously. So could Serrano, promised The Maestro. Another dimension, named variously the Green Lightning, the Black Sun, Hyperborea, Valhalla or simply outer space, lay open to him – the world of the immortal Aryan Archetypes and Platonic Forms, who were really the old Norse gods like Wotan and Thor, who were actually extraterrestrials, of a kind. Venus was not simply a physical planet, but also a hollow magical gateway into an other-dimensional ice-world named Hyperborea, through which Hitler, Nazis and Aryan god-aliens could pass in astral *vimana* form, or in physical saucers, if they preferred. Being 'a magician who had the power voluntarily to come out of his body', Hitler often vacated his physical frame and allowed Wotan to possess it, as his teenage brain had once been invaded by the Nazi spirits of outer space on the hill in Linz, although this involved dangers as Wotan's godly strength could potentially 'make the vehicle explode'. However, Hitler's explosion may be reverse-atomic in nature, and could happily cause the Jewish *kali yuga* world to transmute instantly into a perfect Aryan *satya yuga* one 'in an action difficult to apprehend', hence his alleged anti-atom bomb *Wunderwaffe*. The Maestro claimed to have visited Hitler at his Eagle's Nest mountain base in spirit form, where Adolf, through binoculars, had spotted him flying about and told him to get off his property. A second meeting had later taken place within the Hollow Earth where Hitler's astral soul, sporting a natty new long Mexican-style moustache, had survived the fall of Berlin. In 1945, taught The Maestro, Hitler was transported to the South Pole (or Hyperborea) in a submarine (or in a UFO, or as a UFO) where he lay sleeping (but also awake) in a cave (which wasn't a cave), where he was guarded by the twin ravens of Wotan, prior to his later resurrection, like the slumbering Kings Arthur and Frederick Barbarossa (1122-1190) in legends of old. This was why 'Operation Barbarossa' was the chosen codename for his ruinous invasion of Russia; Hitler *meant* to lose, as then he could snooze and regenerate.[26]

In 1947/48, in his capacity as a journalist Serrano joined a Chilean military-scientific expedition to Antarctica to commune with Hitler's frozen spirit, later publishing books about this trip with titles like *Who Calls in the Ice*, which were acclaimed as literary masterpieces domestically, even though they hinted at his true, Hitler-worshipping reasons for the voyage, and openly speculate about the existence of a Hollow Earth. During his trip he was reading his Jung again, coming to view the barren, white Antarctic wastes as an analogy of mankind's collective unconscious, a blank realm almost designed to harbour Jungian archetypes. In later life, he would claim an encounter with a 'Disc of Uncreated Light', or *vimana*, during his journey led to an instant revelation of the complete doctrine of Esoteric Hitlerism. In honour of his exploits, the Chilean military named an entire mountain massif after their unusual new comrade.[27]

Serrano was also an admirer of Nicholas Roerich (1874-1947), a painter and mystic who had travelled through China and Mongolia to the borders of Tibet from 1925-28, partly in search of the lost city of Shambhala, which he saw as a symbol of a coming world-transformation, inhabited by a benign King of the World named Rigden-jyepo, who was Roerich's own chosen final avatar of Kalki, come to save Earth from *kali yuga*, and whose symbol was yet again the swastika sun wheel. On 5 August 1927, Roerich witnessed what sounds like a rare circular *mandala*-type flying saucer twenty years before Kenneth Arnold, the aerial phantom being 'something big and shiny reflecting the sun, like a huge oval moving at great speed ... an oval form with shiny surface, one side of which was brilliant from the sun.' The UFO's progress was tracked through binoculars before it suddenly 'disappeared in the intense blue sky'. A Tibetan lama acting as a guide joyfully proclaimed this 'A very good sign. We are protected. Rigden-jyepo himself is looking after us!'[28] It is easy to see why Serrano would have subsequently been keen to claim a sighting of just such a 'very good sign' from his own version of King Kalki two decades later. For him, Rigden-jyepo was really Adolf Hitler.

* * * * *

In 1951 Serrano took an early Nazi-worshipping trek across Germany, before domestic politics soon beckoned. In 1952, Serrano campaigned for Chile's former right-wing dictator, General Carlos Ibáñez del Campo (1877-1960), being quickly rewarded following the General's electoral victory. In 1953 Miguel followed several relatives into Chile's diplomatic corps, agitating to be posted to India, where he hoped he might find his cult's promised Hidden Tibetan Masters, the underground city of Agartha, or at the very least The Kingdom of the Gnomes. Appointed Ambassador by Campo, he made friends with political giants Indira Gandhi and Jawaharlal Nehru; he even met the Queen, there's a photo to prove it. In 1963 Serrano published *The Serpent of Paradise: The Story of an Indian Pilgrimage*, admitting he had spent much of his time as Ambassador seeking the Hidden Masters in remote Himalayan shrines, being thwarted only by the Chinese occupation of Tibet. Whilst the Maoists prevented him making physical contact with Mount Kailas, where the Masters lived, he nonetheless sensed its 'inner aspect' via psychic means.[29] Serrano made sure to contact the Dalai Lama once the Commies had made him flee Tibet, the two becoming good friends, at least until the reincarnated godlet later became just 'another prisoner of globalism and a tool of the Jews'. The Dalai Lama may not seem a natural Nazi, but the *Ahnenerbe* had long liaised with Tibetan secret societies, with many lamas fighting to defend Berlin during the war's final days, said Serrano, as in *The Morning of the Magicians*. When visiting Hitler's Berghof mountain lair on pilgrimage, Serrano sensed 'a vibration that connected me immediately to the Himalayan mountains', proving the innate link between Germany and Tibet.[30] In 1962 Serrano was made simultaneous Ambassador to Yugoslavia, Romania and Bulgaria, then in 1964 Ambassador to Austria, all whilst writing mystical texts like *The Ultimate Flower* and liaising with the International Atomic Energy Agency and the United Nations Industrial

Development Organisation – and with Europe's neo-Nazi underground. Being based in Austria was great, allowing Serrano to seek out *Ahnenerbe* scholars and Hitler's old friends like the Nazi aviatrix Hanna Reitsch (1912-79), whom he tried to persuade to pilot a plane over the South Pole to see if she could drop down a big hole there and find the Führer. He also contacted Baron Julius Evola and, later, Savitri Devi.

Serrano now began hoovering up the books of Robert Charroux (1909-78), former Culture Minster in occupied France's pro-Nazi Vichy puppet-government, who in the 1960s and 1970s combined *Ahnenerbe*-esque quests to dig up the Holy Grail with the new post-war UFO culture, putting out low-quality (and therefore best-selling) ancient astronaut books like *Legacy of the Gods* and *Masters of the World*. These argued that the fabled Hyperborean race of classical myth, who supposedly hailed from the North Pole regions, were really ET supermen from the alleged ice planet of Venus who had tutored prehistoric mankind, but gained the later enmity of the Jewish race. A one-time author of pulp sci-fi like *Professor Barthelemy's Flying Island*, Charroux now found it more profitable to present his fiction as fact. By theorising about the existence of alternative universes, Charroux could explain any awkward lack of evidence –medieval legends of the Kingdom of the Grail need not have occurred upon our physical Earth, but its astral twin. His other big idea, now probably unpublishable, was that mankind did not evolve from ape-like ancestors, but 'devolved' from white aliens from icy Hyperborea/Venus. These Aryan ETs bred with the primitive native Earth-women, siring two rival hi-tech civilisations, Atlantis and Mu, who then nuked one another beneath the waves; recent memories of 1962's Cuban Missile Crisis made this narrative topical. Scattered bands escaped atomic obliteration, and the subsequent Great Flood, by hiding on widely separated tall mountaintops, these distant tribes becoming the genetic basis of the white, black, yellow and red races we know today. Only blacks were the original Earth-men, the other three races were the result of various levels of interbreeding with white Venusians; naturally, the whitest folk were the least devolved. In an unusual move for a Nazi sympathiser, Charroux took pity on the blacks' low-grade blood, and suggested that, by breeding their women with charitable white males like himself, it may be possible for Africans to raise the lamentably poor level of their civilisation. Charroux gained millions of readers throughout the 60s and 70s, but few quite so dedicated as Miguel Serrano.[31]

When other books pushing the Nazi-occult angle mushroomed in that same period, Serrano was delighted, although he seemed a little put out by the success of *The Morning of the Magicians*, feeling he'd been scooped by Pauwels and Bergier.[32] Yet in 1970 the Marxist (and, in Serrano's eyes, undercover Jew) Salvador Allende (1908-73) became Chile's President, and Serrano's blissful diplomatic career was over, leaving him enough free time to write even more esoteric titles like *EL/ELLA: Book of Magic Love* and *NOS: A Book of the Resurrection*, fusing Tantrism with Jungian thought.

When a 1973 US-backed coup saw the extremely right-wing General Augusto Pinochet (1915-2006) take power, you may have expected Serrano's reinstatement. However, Pinochet's Chile provided an early laboratory for 'the Jew, Milton Friedman' (1912-2006), the chief proponent of what became Thatcherite-Reaganite economics, to implement his free-market schemes, which Serrano found objectionable on *kali yuga* grounds, so he remained in Europe. Pinochet was not an ideological fascist, so simply had no use for him. In a 1994 (or 'Year 105 of the Avatar', Hitler being born in the new Year Zero of 1889) interview, Serrano explained how he hated Friedman's 'liberal super-capitalism', which only led to the further atomisation of society, and media brainwashing via advertising:

> Today the [Jewish] Enemy works mentally using the Kabbalah and electronic machines ... projecting subatomic particles in order to control [Aryan] minds. Yes, today, the central war is psychotronic, technotronic and cybertronic. The principal war is a mental one, called '*Kamomanasic*'. This means that the enemy is intervening in the mental atmosphere of the Aryan, manipulating their thoughts ... the whole world is hypnotised by these means, combined with subliminal messages found in today's media, as well as by drugs and drinks like Coca-Cola and Pepsi.[33]

The aim of the post-Cold War 'New World Order' was to facilitate a 'global consumer culture' which would 'destroy ... frontiers and nationalities', allowing mixing of blood. Then, VR technology would be used as 'a magic device in order to give the last and mortal blow to actual reality', dissolving our world into an abstract void of zeros and ones, a subatomic PlayStation holocaust we'd all rush out to buy. Serrano accused Chile's free-marketeers of 'Mammonitis', warning Pinochet's military needed to rebel and 'transmute itself into a Warrior Order ... connected to a body ... of invisible directors' from Tibet, just like the circular heroes of the SS had been. This would cause the small nation of Chile to be 'transformed into an invincible giant', with a new Hitler-like leader embodying 'the land of the sacred giants of the Andes' and 'The Land of the Morning Star', whom humanity would follow 'to the death' in a final war against *kali yuga*. The Morning Star is the planet Venus, often lent the name 'Lucifer'. Serrano thus described himself as a 'Luciferian', but did not worship the Devil. 'Contrary to misconceptions', Lucifer was *not* the Dark Lord Satan, as the Christians and Jews of the CIA and Mossad habitually lied, but a bringer of 'the most beautiful light'. Venus was 'more than a planet', being a 'God-Goddess' rather than a celestial focus for Devil-worship. Hyperborean Venus 'is a [living] comet that stopped there where it is now in order to remind the divine men [i.e. white ones] of their own spiritual origin, and to show them the way to recover it. There on Venus, Adolf Hitler is now, together with the elite who managed to escape Earth at the end of the war.'[34] Chile has this same Morning Star of Venus on its flag, so one aspect of Serrano's quest was to make the Chilean people realise that, if only they would throw off the Jew-forged chains of Pinochet and Friedman, they could transfigure the country into a magical portal towards Venusian Hyperborea. Under *kali yuga* rule, Chile had become a soul-destroying home to 'machine-slaves, automatons, a planetary bureaucracy, robots and ant-men'.[35] Why not return to Nazi Nature-worship instead?

> We have desecrated the world, collaborating with ... the Lord of Darkness, transforming her into a dead heavy sphere, a composite of aggregated atoms, of rock, metals and lime, or at most oil, without knowing what this substance is truthfully. We extract it, exploit it, dirty the Earth, destroy everything, with a materialistic Judaic criteria, without knowing that the Earth is still a living being with a body, soul and spirit ... eager for transfiguration. In Chile since the Conquest [by the false Jewish religion of Christianity], the landscape is not ours ... We must extract the light of a new Sun from the Gods, from the ancient Giants who sleep within the rock of the Andes, recognise them, show them cultic devotion, establish a dialogue. Only thus can we reach a balance between man and the landscape. The transfiguration of the mystic homeland will only become possible through extracting the Giants from the Mountain. We shall have unsheathed the sword of Chile ... [Then] the Earth will again be inhabited by Giants, by the White Gods, and disabled people will disappear.[36]

There were surely no unsightly disabled people living amongst the ancient Aryan gods on Hyperborea – apart, that is, from one particular Venusian space-deity who possessed only the one eye ...

The Maestro's theory about Hitler frequently being possessed by the explosive spirit of Wotan further attracted Serrano towards C. G. Jung, who had argued something similar. Wotan is the native Germanic version of Odin, the one-eyed Norse god of storms, warfare, wisdom, magic and poetry, who rides across the sky during tempests upon his eight-legged horse Sleipnir. In Hindu myth the returning Vishnu-Kalki was supposed to mount a white horse, and Serrano associated this sacred steed with Sleipnir, upon whom Kalki would speed back down from space during Ragnarok, the Norse Day of Judgement.[37] Sleipnir is also a model for Father Christmas' troop of flying reindeer, hence two of their names being Donner and Blitzen, or 'Thunder' and 'Lightning' in German. In the original myth, it was Wotan's son Thor who flew around with him hurling lightning-bolts from his enchanted *Wunderwaffe* hammer, not a levitating reindeer. The discoverer of the runes, Wotan's one good eye is the blazing sun, and as Lord of the Dead he presides over banquets of slain warriors in the Halls of Valhalla, the Viking heaven. In other words, he is Adolf Hitler, Lord of Lightning, War and Sun, as viewed through the twisted Romantic prism of Savitri Devi-inspired Esoteric Hitlerism. Wotan was Hitler to Jung too, according to his 1936 essay *Wotan*, which opened with a prediction of the old French fortune-teller Nostradamus (1503-66) that one day 'In Germany shall diverse sects arise/Coming very near to happy paganism.'

Maybe National Socialism was just such a sect of 'happy paganism' and Adolf Hitler Wotan reborn. Noting Wotan was a 'restless wanderer', as indicated by Sleipnir's eight legs symbolising the eight compass directions of the blowing winds, Jung proposed his spirit had been defused and degraded by Christianity into the mere leader of the Wild Hunt, a minor devil who led damned souls on a never-ending horseback chase through the night skies in Germanic folklore, accompanied by packs of yelping hellhounds. When the nocturnal gales blew strong, that was Wotan's Wild Hunt passing by; all good men should seek refuge in the Cross of Christ, not worship the hellish huntsman.

In 1899 a prophetic picture was painted by Franz von Stuck (1863-1928), called *The Wild Hunt*, which showed Wotan leading his troop through the clouds – and this version of Wotan had a very familiar-looking toothbrush moustache and black comb-over. At this point in time, the completely unknown Adolf Hitler himself was ten years old, with no facial hair at all, but according to Jung there were other portents of the vehicle of Wotan's rebirth abroad in the land. The *Wandervoegel*, or 'Birds of Passage', were a movement of nationalistically minded *völkisch* German youths who roamed the woods and fields of Germany, just like Wotan, seeking pagan communion with Nature; during Solstices, they even sacrificed sheep 'in honour of his resurrection', said Jung. From these groups later grew various pro-Nazi street mobs and storm troopers who fought pitched battles with Communists and helped Hitler into power; watching their early pilgrimages, speculated Jung, 'the one-eyed old Hunter, on the edge of the German forest, laughed and saddled Sleipnir.' Come the 1930s Great Depression and Weimar Germany's total economic collapse, 'the wandering role was taken over by thousands of unemployed, who were to be met with everywhere on their endless journeys.'

These tramps of the Depression and troops of the *Wandervoegel* were, said Jung, subject to a state called *Ergriffenheit*, becoming possessed like Viking berserker warriors who went into trance states dressed in animal pelts, to magically transform themselves into wild beasts prior to battle. The best solution would be to enlist these lost souls in a giant army and march them all over Europe, spreading *blitzkrieg* instead of letting them shamble round begging bread; these shuffling corpses were already possessed by the as-yet rudderless Wild Hunt, simply awaiting the future arrival of Wotan to give their feet a firm nudge in the direction of Poland. It seemed incredible that 'an ancient god of storm and frenzy … should awake, like an extinct volcano, to new activity in a civilised country that had been long supposed to have outgrown the Middle Ages,' wrote Jung; but not to Miguel Serrano. Jung described Germany's collective possession as 'a general phenomenon so strange to anybody not a German that it remains incomprehensible.' Within his soul, Miguel Serrano *was* a blonde, blue-eyed German, though, and so understood Jung's idea perfectly … except, he really didn't. 'A mind that is still childish thinks of the gods as metaphysical entities existing in their own right,' wrote Jung, explaining he didn't believe in the literal existence of

Wotan at all. Instead, 'the gods are without doubt personifications of psychic forces' within the human mind.

Jung's major theory was that of the 'collective unconscious', a storehouse of images and mental content which would be shared on a totally unconscious level either by humanity as a whole, or by its different races and nationalities. Within this psychic realm lived the archetypes, metaphorical figures like Wotan who personified aspects of a nation's collective mentality. Thus, Wotan was the archetypal embodiment of the *furor teutonicus*, the ancient Germanic capacity for warfare and violence, as seen in the Visigoths of Alaric who had once sacked Rome. As the stereotypical 'behaviour of a race takes on its specific character from its underlying [archetypal] images', so the German people had become once more possessed by their long-dormant archetypal Prussian-style desire for military conquest. Wotan 'really was only asleep' in his mythical burial place beneath the Kyffhäuser Mountain, from which the archetype had arisen and possessed Adolf Hitler's mind, transforming the Führer into 'a superlative magician and artist in illusion who is versed in all secrets of an occult nature.' From here, 'this one man, who is obviously possessed, has infected a whole nation' with its helpless, hypnotised people being 'sucked like dry leaves into a roaring whirlwind' by Wotan's black magic. It was inevitable this would happen one day, as the Wotan archetype was:

> ...a fundamental attribute of the German psyche, an irrational psychic factor which acts on the high pressure of civilisation like a cyclone and blows it away ... a Germanic datum of first importance, the truest expression and unsurpassed personification of a fundamental quality ... of the Germans.

The inherently bellicose *volk* can't help following their Nazi Pied Pipers, so 'perhaps it would be nearer the truth to regard them, also, as victims' of the god of war, as much as those they killed.[38]

According to Miguel Serrano, however, a Jungian archetype was a literal living entity, 'something like a Platonic Idea, that seems to hang around the atmosphere of the Earth' before being 'apprehended by the collective unconscious of human beings, thanks to the sacrifice of one human being' like Hitler who, 'thanks to his genes, or his karma, is worthy of being possessed' by such a space-deity. We will recall the teenage Adolf's fateful experience that hill-top night in Linz, when the soul of starry space had downloaded itself into his brain. The immediate precursor of Wotan's descent into Hitler's skull was the 'Archetype of the Emperor', a space god named 'Duce', who had invaded the brain of the original fascist dictator Benito Mussolini during the 1920s; this was why Mussolini called himself *Il Duce*, meaning 'The Leader'. Once this had occurred, the spirit of Duce then began to possess other susceptible statesmen's minds too, via the medium of the global collective unconscious, like that of the Spanish dictator Miguel Primo de Rivera (1870-1930) and Corneliu Codreanu (1899-1938), head of Romania's fascist Iron

Guard. The Chilean *Nacista* leader von Marées, too, was known as *El Jefe*, or 'The Leader', indicating he was another of Duce's puppets. The purpose of these political possessions was to prepare the way for Wotan's culminating incarnation within the skull of Adolf Hitler, acting like John the Baptist did for Jesus. Once Duce's work was done, and Hitler-Wotan had been defeated in order to win the war within another world in 1945, Duce had also vacated the frames of his avatars, leaving them 'without energy, so to speak, without a possible destiny, and they become lost or they end up like an empty casket, sometimes in sad conditions' like von Marées, who became a broken man. Fascist leaders' listless depression in a post-Hitler world might have had other, less unlikely explanations, but Serrano preferred to adopt this one: Duce's departure had turned them all into zombies.[39]

* * * * *

Had Hitler lived on physically once Wotan had vacated his frame in 1945, maybe this tragic fate would have befallen him too. Jung had once watched Mussolini meet Hitler in Berlin on an official visit, observing Duce and Wotan's behaviour before the crowds. The two dictators' contrasting reactions to the sight of goose-stepping soldiers on parade seemed significant. Mussolini enjoyed the spectacle 'with the zest of a small boy at a circus', as the dictator 'broke out laughing and clapped his hands', a reaction which meant Jung 'couldn't help liking' *Il Duce*, whose 'bodily energy and elasticity are warm, human and contagious. You have the homely feeling with Mussolini of being with a human being.' With the unsmiling Hitler, it was a different matter:

In comparison with Mussolini, Hitler made upon me the impression of a sort of scaffolding of wood covered with cloth, an automaton with a mask, like a robot or a mask of a robot. During the whole performance, he never laughed ... He showed no human sign. His expression was that of an inhumanly single-minded purposiveness, with no sense of humour. He seemed as if he might be a double (*doppelgänger*) of a real person, and that Hitler the man might perhaps be hiding inside [his own body] like an appendix, and deliberately so hiding in order not to disturb the mechanism. With Hitler you do not feel that you are with a man. You are with a medicine-man, a form of spiritual vessel, a demi-deity, or even better, a myth. With Hitler you are scared. You know you would never be able to talk to that man; because there is nobody there. He is not a man, but a collective. He is not an individual, but a whole nation. I take it to be literally true that [as popularly rumoured] he has no personal friend. How can you talk intimately with a nation?

To Jung, there were two types of national strongman, the 'chief' and the 'medicine-man'. Mussolini was a chief, a big, brutal, barrel-like bastard of a man who would pummel his people into submission: 'His body suggests good muscles.' Hitler was the opposite, a medicine-man or shaman, whose body was weak and puny, but whose eyes possessed 'the look of a seer'. Hitler's power 'is not political; it is *magical*', said Jung, as he could flee his body and become possessed by the far stronger Wotan archetype. To foreigners he looked absurd, like a disturbed Charlie Chaplin, but to Germans he was inspirational, being 'the mirror of every German's unconscious ... the loud-speaker which magnifies the inaudible whispers of the German soul until they can be heard by the [individual] German's conscious ear.' Like a spirit medium, Hitler heard voices inside his head:

> Hitler's secret is twofold; first, that his unconscious has exceptional access to his consciousness, and second, that he allows himself to be moved by it ... [Most people] have too much rationality, too much cerebrum to obey [voices in their heads] – but Hitler listens and obeys. The true leader is always *led* ... He himself has referred to his Voice. His Voice is nothing other than his own unconscious, into which the German people have projected their own selves ... Without the German people he would be nothing ... he *is* Germany ... with his unconscious being the receptacle of the souls of seventy-eight million Germans ... That is why he makes political judgements which turn out to be right against the opinions of all his advisors ... the information gathered by his unconscious [from the 'soul' of his people] ... has been more nearly correct than [the conscious judgements] of all others ... That, incidentally, is why Hitler always has to talk so loud, even in private conversation – because he is speaking with seventy-eight million voices.

Like early Islam, Nazism 'teaches the virtue of the sword', said Jung. Being led by a Muhammad-like prophet, Nazism was really a militant religion of conquest, 'promising a maximum of rewards in this life, but with a Moslem-like Valhalla into which worthy Germans may enter and continue to enjoy themselves' should they fall in the combat of Nazi *jihad*. That Nazism was an esoteric religion based upon Wotan's secret martial appeal could be seen in how Hitler was also worshipped fervently by distant German-descended immigrants all over the world, 'notably in Chile' – as with Miguel Serrano. The interview in which Jung said all this appeared in a 1939 edition of *Cosmopolitan*, later being reprinted under the title *Diagnosing the Dictators*, but the psychologist's diagnosis of how to cure Germany's most dangerous patient was rather odd. As there was no way Hitler would refuse to obey Wotan's voice, Jung recommended Western Europe distract the Nazi Wild Hunt by urging it to invade Russia instead. As the similarly possessed Napoleon had also once found:

> Nobody has ever bitten into Russia without regretting it. It's not very palatable food. It might take the Germans a hundred years to finish that meal ... Let her go into Russia. There is plenty of land there ... It wouldn't matter to Russia if somebody took a bite.[40]

In *Adolf Hitler – The Ultimate Avatar*, Serrano reprints many of Jung's comments, admiringly citing also his 1936 statement to *The Observer* that:

> German politics is not made, it is revealed through Hitler. He is the Voice of the Gods ... Hitler governs by revelations ... In Germany they now work for the creation of an aristocracy. The SS are being transformed into a caste of knights ... who will govern seventy million Germans ... Without the idea of an aristocracy, stability is not possible. You, in England, owe your possession of the world [via the British Empire] to the gentleman.

Yet Serrano badly misrepresented his Swiss mentor, arguing the collective unconscious was really 'nothing more than the memory of the blood ... the river of images that circulate eternally in the light of the Black Sun and breed in the astral body ... the manifestation of the Hyperborean Archetype' from outer space, all of which would have been news to Jung himself. To Serrano, Hitler was a piece of biological 'machinery' through which the alien Wotan could manifest himself on *terra firma*, to lead his aristocratic SS knights on the rampage. Jung had hit upon this hitherto-unknown truth of great leaders' possession by space gods, but had then needlessly indulged in 'psychologising' his insight by clothing it in the dead language of post-Freudian jargon.[41]

As this criticism suggests, the pair's friendship didn't last. Jung had once been a disciple of the father of psychoanalysis, Sigmund Freud (1836-1939), who was Jewish, unlike the Lutheran Jung, but the two men split over Jung's development of the theory of the collective unconscious and outspoken championing of paranormal phenomena. Jung had once postulated the existence of one collective unconscious for the Jewish race and another for the Aryan, an idea which Serrano liked, praising 'the break between the psychological conceptions of the Aryan Jung and the Jew Freud' as illustrative of these rival collective psyches. As Jung's theory united like minds in one whole, it showed how 'the Aryan collective unconscious unites, seeks to complete, to conceive the *unus mundus*, the totality of the human being, deifying him.' Freud's theory of the *personal* unconscious, however, was a reflection of how the Jewish ancestral soul 'always takes the side of the part against the whole, fanatic, intolerant, proselytising, dividing men, tending to produce chaos.' It was no wonder Jews produced atom bombs, whereas Aryans spawned reverse-explosive *mandala*-UFOs.[42] As 'the black shadow of the white gods' from Venus, Serrano had to maintain the Jews were opposed to the Aryans in every way, especially in their collective souls.[43]

Serrano thought Jung was once a Nazi. This is sometimes maintained by others as an insult rather than praise, backed up by his 1934 statement that 'the Aryan unconscious has a higher potential than the Jewish', but during the war Jung denounced anti-Semitism, tried to help refugees into Switzerland and provided mental analysis of Hitler to the Americans.

He was also involved in an abortive plot to get Hitler removed from office by having him declared officially insane – Adolf openly admitted to hearing voices, after all.[44] It is noticeable that, whilst reproducing most of Jung's 1939 interview in his book, Serrano omitted his final conclusion:

> A nation is a big, blind worm ... Don't you know that if you choose one hundred of the most intelligent people in the world and get them together, they are a stupid mob? Ten thousand of them together would have the collective intelligence of an alligator. Haven't you noticed that at a dinner party the more people you invite the more stupid the conversation? In a crowd, the qualities which everybody possesses multiply, pile up, and become the dominant characteristics of the whole crowd. Not everybody has virtues, but everybody has the low animal instincts, the basic primitive caveman suggestibility, the suspicious and vicious traits of the savage. The result is that when you get a nation of many millions of people, it is not even human. It is a lizard or a crocodile or a wolf ... [In Germany] Hitler is himself the nation. That's what a nation is: a monster. Everybody ought to fear a nation. It is a horrible thing ... That's why I am for small nations. Small nations mean small catastrophes. Big nations mean big catastrophes.[45]

So, Hitler was a monster, a savage, a crocodile or a wolf, and the Wild Hunt a blind worm; not what Serrano wanted to hear. In 1994, Miguel recanted his old love for the 'enormous thinker' Jung, arguing 'he was a Swiss and therefore a contradictory personality' who didn't understand the magic of the runes and the true ET nature of Wotan because of his 'Christian background'. Jung had once been a good honest Nazi, but 'Immediately after the war he started to change and made some very shameful statements about Hitler and the German people.' However, 'I didn't know about these statements until recently,' which is either an outright lie or suggests Serrano didn't read to the end of the 1939 *Cosmopolitan* article he had earlier copied out. Furthermore, Jung 'was a Freemason, as Lutheran men are' and, even worse, 'took a Jewish woman as his secretary'. His old idea of the separate collective Jewish unconscious and the Aryan unconscious was 'a lethal weapon against the Jews and the Freudians', but post-war printings of Jung's books had been censored to remove all reference to it (this is actually true). Therefore, 'even though I admire the [early] thinking of Jung, I have come not to admire his character.' The Aryan apostate had even helped Britain militarily, by advising London to 'prolong [the war] as long as possible' as, being Wotan, Hitler could only possibly win a lightning-fast *blitzkrieg* conflict, as shown by the stunningly quick conquest of France.[46] After death, the race-traitor Jung would definitely not be returning in the shape of a saucer.

* * * * *

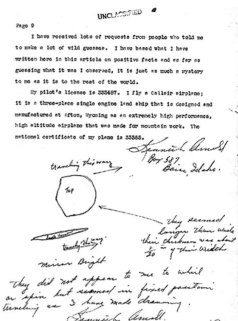

Above left: Adolf Hitler, God on Earth and inventor of flying saucers – in the opinion of some fringe-thinkers, at any rate. (Courtesy of the Bulgarian State Archives, 3K/15/394/1)

Above right: The illustrated letter pilot Kenneth Arnold submitted to Army Air Force Intelligence on 12 July 1947 detailing his run-in with UFOs. (USAF)

Real-life Nazi *Wunderwaffen* wonder-weapons included the V-1 flying bomb and the V-2 ballistic missile. Their existence made it seem more plausible to some that Nazi engineers could also have developed war-time UFOs. (Bundesarchiv Bild)

Left: The paranoid fantasies of Jörg Lanz von Liebenfels about white-skinned Nordic women being sexually abused by racially inferior lizard-men and fish-people seem coincidentally reflected in this classic 1950s B-movie poster. Lanz may have considered the film a documentary.

Below left: Ariosophist writer Jörg Lanz von Liebenfels, seen during his early life as a monk.

Below right: Guido von List, the long-bearded Ariosophist mentor of Jörg Lanz von Liebenfels, and alleged possessor of a clairvoyant 'ancestral memory' which allowed him to see into the distant prehistoric past. (Bundesarchiv Bild)

Anti-Nazi German rocket-scientist Willy Ley (far right, but not Far-Right) talks shop with top Paperclipped *Wunderwaffen* man Wernher von Braun (centre) in the USA in 1954. (NASA)

Above: Savitri Devi, chief priestess of Esoteric Hitlerism.

Right: William Dudley Pelley, leader of the pro-Nazi US Silver Shirt movement of the 1930s, and later developer of the 1950s Soul-Craft UFO religion, which taught a peculiar creed of racial reincarnation.

Top left: The German Romantic scholar Friedrich Schlegel, the substantial inventor of the doubtful notion of the pure white Aryan race – a race which surprisingly actually came originally from India, not Germany.

Middle left: René Guénon, French Traditionalist author and sworn enemy of *kali yuga*.

Bottom left: The leading Esoteric Nazi ideologue and occult UFO-theorist Miguel Serrano poses in all his finery in his youthful role as Chile's Ambassador to India.

Bottom right: A view of the alleged pagan sun-worship site of the Externsteine, the 'German Stonehenge', scene of post-war Hitler-worshipping pilgrimages by both Savitri Devi and Miguel Serrano alike. To Serrano, such mountainous sites were really comatose alien giants, covered over in stony sleep by the forces of *kali yuga*. But one day, just like Hitler sleeping beneath the South Pole, they would awaken to rule the entire world!

Deputy Führer Rudolf Hess (front, second from left), or perhaps his mind-controlled *doppelgänger*, on trial for crimes against humanity in Nuremburg. Allied lawyers thought they were prosecuting the real thing, but Miguel Serrano knew better. (US Govt)

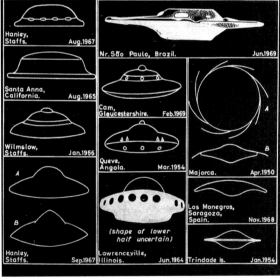

Above left: Wilhelm Landig, proudly unrepentant former member of the Waffen-SS and SA counter-intelligence corps, and later leading light of Esoteric Nazism throughout Austria and the German-speaking world. He even had his own publishing company and a career in anti-Communist international politics.

Above right: If flying saucers are indeed broadly circular in shape, as in this old UFO-spotters' chart, then what else would you expect from psychic manifestations of King Arthur's Round Table, as the Landig Circle thought they were? (The National Archives)

Far-Right Japanese nationalist poet Yukio Mishima makes an unsuccessful speech urging Japanese troops to rise up in a violent coup against democracy prior to committing ritual suicide by slitting his stomach open with a samurai sword in 1970. Mishima's actions proved decisive in British extremist David Myatt's youthful conversion to neo-Nazism. Only true warrior-souls like Mishima could ever hope to conquer the stars. (Dutch Nationaal Archief)

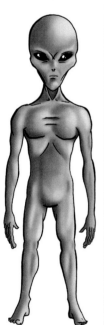

Above left: The blank, unfeeling eyes, the extra cerebral capacity of the high-domed forehead, the merciless, robotic expression, the very white skin ... the ET Greys certainly seem like metaphorical reincarnations of the Nazi death-camp doctors. Both species of demon were notoriously keen on performing barbaric medical experiments upon their unwillingly abducted human guinea-pigs, kept alive to suffer in enforced captivity. (MjolnirPants)

Above right: US military officer Philip J. Corso (right), who claimed that the transistor – a key basis of later communications and computer-technology – was really invented by aliens who then gifted it to us as part of the staged Roswell UFO 'crash', in order to colonise our planet by stealth, as they somehow lived within silicon chips. If so, then how does humanity fight back in a massive interplanetary war it doesn't even realise is occurring? Turn off your iPhone for five minutes, maybe. (US Govt)

Britain's leading contemporary online conspiracy-theorist David Icke, who apparently thinks Adolf Hitler might well have been Jack the Ripper – either that or the Führer was possessed by reptiles from outer space. (Tyler Merbler)

US polar explorer Rear-Admiral Richard E. Byrd, who allegedly tried to combat Adolf Hitler's underground UFO fleet at the South Pole with the possible aid of nuclear weapons. (US Navy)

A mystery German zeppelin-style airship supposedly seen in the night skies over the USA as reported in the *San Francisco Call* in November 1896. Such things are now often viewed as being early precursors of modern-day UFOs. (Library of Congress)

Above left: The very strange Dr Frank E. Stranges, who may well have encountered top Nazi commando Otto Skorzeny lurking inside a landed flying saucer one day and begging for food, as detailed in a cheap self-published book.

Above right: 'Scarface' himself, the daring Nazi commando leader Otto Skorzeny, who Joseph P. Farrell argues may have invented the whole idea of UFOs in the first place as part of a machiavellian post-war Fourth Reich plan to conquer the globe by stealth. If America, Russia and Britain do not know they are still at war with the Nazis, then how can they possibly defeat them?

Above left: French-born ufologist Jacques Vallée, one of the most original thinkers in the field, theorises that UFOs should not be taken literally, being best thought of as some kind of gigantic exercise in deception, not as visiting ET spaceships – but what if those doing the deceiving were really Germans, not Greys? (US Govt)

Above right: Colin Bennett was one of ufology's most interesting and unusual – if occasionally borderline incomprehensible – thinkers. His theory that alien beings may well have evolved to become incorporeal living advertisements who combat one another for prominence (and thus continued existence) within the brains and belief-systems of primitive flesh-based organisms like humanity seemed directly applicable to the meme-friendly myth of Nazi UFOs. (PPh1lomena)

Serrano used his long retirement from Chile's diplomatic corps to develop a byzantine Ariosophy and Theosophy-influenced Gnostic philosophy – or 'extra-stellar poetry' – which saw Jehovah, the God of both Christians and Jews alike, recast as the Demiurge, the evil godlet of Gnostic thought, who had sent NASA-like 'probes' and 'robots' down to colonise Earth in the shape of Jews and sub-men like Neanderthals. Such racial horrors were gross fleshly parodies of the original light-formed astral rune-bodies of the blonde, blue-eyed Aryan god-men from Venusian Hyperborea, whose etheric veins coursed with *Vril* and light from the Black Sun.[47] The term 'gnosis' means 'knowledge', as only the Gnostics possessed true wisdom, this being sensed via personal revelation, not logical argument, as with Jung's Hitler listening to the voice of Wotan in his head. Gnosticism was a dualistic mystical offshoot of Christianity, which taught there were two worlds, a physical and a non-physical one, with the latter being superior in all respects, with our fleshly bodies being the enemy of all true spiritual life. The insertion of our spirit into the world of fallen physical 'reality' (which was not *reality* at all, but its false mirror) by the Demiurge, the 'Lord of Galactic Shadows', was thus the source of every evil. To Serrano, this Demiurge was 'a respiration' of an immaterial space-soul into the gaping 'Vagina of Mother/Matter', as in Mother Earth. The word 'Hyperborea', or 'Land Beyond the North Wind', thus meant not simply the northern polar regions of Thule, where the Aryan race were often said to have originated, but 'beyond the Demiurge, beyond his breathing', a pure realm of non-physicality where there were not even any vaginas available to be blown into.[48]

The association of Gnosticism with Nazism should be no surprise to students of political theory, as (like its evil twin Marxism) fascism has long been identified as a mutant ideological strain of the disease, most notably by the celebrated US-based political philosopher Eric Voegelin (1901-85). In books and essays from the 1950s onwards, Voegelin showed how Nazism shared in the millenarian desire of many Gnostics to overcome the imperfections of matter by pursuing the wholly unrealistic project of instituting a Heaven on Earth, or perfect imagined society, for all to live in – or 'immanentising the eschaton', to give the notion its technical term. Hitler's vision of the Nazi wonderland of a Thousand-Year Reich stood for Voegelin as just another version of Christianity's desired New Jerusalem, which would descend down from the clouds to be ruled over by Christ come the End of Time ('eschatology' is the name used to describe this field, hence 'immanentising the eschaton', though to be strictly accurate the eschaton is not the end of time, it's the last, heavenly stage of history just prior to it). Significantly, one key project of Nazism's desired conquest over the imperfections of matter was to make the human race evolve into something better and more Aryan, Hitler's desired blonde, blue-eyed *übermenschen*, via eugenics, genocide and selective breeding, a project to breed men upwards into Nordic gods almost as ambitious as that once held by Lanz and his Ariosophists.

Matter being inherently evil in Gnostic thought, within Serrano's own personal quasi-Ariosophist narrative the heroic Nazi-Aryan-alien gods had also then penetrated Earth's material vagina, popping through Venus from astral Hyperborea to smash Jehovah's perverted plans to make His spirit flesh with their lightning hammers. But Wotan & Co then unwisely mated with physical Earth-folk, diluting their blood; they had once reproduced simply via 'plasmic emanations', rather than by physical congress with subhuman ape-women, a clear variation of Robert Charroux and Jörg Lanz von Liebenfels' versions of the interracial bestiality tale. Jews themselves had previously slept with actual Earth-animals in any case, as 'Any face of a leading Jew, especially of the rabbis, shows traces of an animal-totem.'[49] The holy, blue-tinged blood of the Hyperborean Black Sun still ran in some human Aryan veins, but was under increasing threat from the endless sexual temptations of 'the Jewish genetic robot', something which must be resisted at all costs. 'This is the true meaning of racism,' wrote Serrano, not to have sex with robots.[50] The Jews aimed to eradicate this Nordic blood-memory via mass miscegenation, robbing Aryans of all recall of their prior existence as gods, something they had also done by burning down the Great Library of Alexandria and destroying most other written records of the grand cosmic conspiracy, too – although not, as yet, Serrano's own books.

Trapped within physical reality himself, the cruel Demiurge wanted to force all souls to share his awful fate, causing them to be reincarnated endlessly within the bodies of Jewish robots and subhumans of mixed-race forever, something called the *pitriyana*, or 'Way of the Ancestors'. Serrano speaks of the old legend of the golem, a life-size clay statue magically animated by occultist rabbis, implying this was really a metaphor for Jewish Jehovah animating the clay of earth with the spark of life and so moulding the subhuman Adam. The Hyperboreans, seeing this humanoid obscenity, flew down from Venus and voluntarily clothed themselves within pure white meat, establishing a circular Hyperborean colony at the Thulean North Pole before spreading out to teach black, red and yellow folk the error of their ways in being born as multi-coloured, post-Adamite beast-men. This was the Earth's Golden Age, the *satya yuga*, when clay men obeyed the words of their Venusian superior spirits. But the Demiurge was cunning, somehow tempting the enfleshed Hyperboreans into having sex with non-white monkey-people, thus forcing the gods to soil themselves within the folds of living brown clay, like Tony Hart seducing Morph (if you're under 50, Google him); the Hyperboreans' icy blue blood was gradually turning redder and redder.

These early Hyperborean aliens, like the biblical Queen of Sheba, famously lusted after by the Israelite King Solomon in some traditions, once had rather different, hairless bodies to their modern-day descendants, sullied as they now are by the blood of their furry subhuman mates. Thinking the Queen so other-worldly in her pubeless beauty she may have been a demon in disguise, Solomon 'subjected her to the test of walking over a floor of mirrors to see if she had goat's feet, like a being from another world. She did not, but her sex was hairless and covered with a skirt, made of her own rosy skin, typical distinctive signs of the virgin Hyperborean princesses,' wrote Serrano, an idea he had totally distorted from an old Islamic legend about the couple.[51] But white women have no such pink curtains today. Inhabiting imperfect clay bodies, even the gods now have to die eventually. Early physical Hyperboreans could once simply wish away their corpses, transforming them magically into swords, but *kali yuga* miscegenation had long since meant even white men's bodies now rotted.[52] When the dying gods were subsequently reborn as their own descendants, according to the Demiurge's cruel doctrine of *pitriyana*, they found they had subhuman cyber-monkey blood running in their baby veins, thus diluting their divine abilities. Over time, they lost their Third Eyes, their *Vril*-power and even their milky skin tones; originally, Aryans would have been *properly* white, like Moomins. This sad racial decline was then sympathetically reflected in a series of physical catastrophes culminating in the fall of a giant comet which caused the North Pole to shift around to being the South one, with the physical Hyperborea/Thule thereby vanishing beneath the comet-created waves. As Serrano unimprovably explained, this was the tragic story of 'the fall of the gods through an aberrant mixing with robotic products, on an involuted star and beneath the tyranny of a Demon.'[53]

* * * * *

I wonder if, together with Robert Charroux, Serrano had read the risible 1974 French book *Jews from Space* by Marc Dem, the *nom de l'imbécillité* of Marc Demeulenaer, a hard-line Catholic journalist of alleged Far-Right leanings. The book proposed there were really two Gods in the Bible, named Elohim and Yahweh. Elohim was the true God, who had created mankind magically from absolutely nothing. Yahweh was only a flesh-and-blood Jewish alien, who, being lonely during a trip to Earth, had created Adam and Eve in his own image from dust via advanced genetic means, desiring them to 'love' him in gratitude. As clones of the Space-Jew Yahweh, Adam and Eve were the original basis of the entire later Jewish race, whose members were consequently hated by all the native humans made by Elohim. Jews may have *looked* human, but real humans could automatically sense they were not, and so repeatedly tried to kill them in a manner akin to 'the process of rejection that sometimes occurs in organ transplants'. 'What is a Jew?' asks Dem. The answer is simple: 'The Jews come from space, and they will return there.' Yahweh will eventually revisit Earth, shepherd his genetic grandchildren aboard his spaceship, and whisk them to a waiting paradise planet, where several Jewish figures of the Old Testament, like Ezekiel, had already been beamed in fiery chariots and used as breeding stock to settle an entire Space-Zion. The Book of Revelation is just one long record of the racial genocide Yahweh will unleash upon all non-Jews from his saucer when he returns for his Chosen People. Dem's book contains the peculiar trope that Jews are unpleasantly superhuman, with the fact so many prominent scientists have been Jewish, like Albert Einstein, being evidence of their advanced ET Mekon-brains. Furthermore, all ancient monuments, like Stonehenge, were created by primeval Jewish armies of conquest, many of them really being 'a disturbing adaptation of the seven-branched candlestick of Jewish worship' of Yahweh the Alien; that such monuments appear all over the world are evidence Yahweh tasked his kids with becoming 'masters of the planet'. With chapter titles like 'Birth of the Test-Tube Jew' and 'The Hill of Foreskins', *Jews from Space* was surely the nadir of the 1970s ancient astronaut boom.[54]

The sinister Space-Zionist enterprise identified by Dem was distinctly similar to the one later uncovered by Miguel Serrano; both mark Jahweh/Jehovah as a Jewish space god who acts as a life-creating Demiurge before stealing Planet Earth from its rightful owners. 'All of civilisation is drowning as the slaves of the [Jewish] cybernetic world become more and more human (demonic) and less godly,' Serrano wailed. 'There is no earthly way to escape from this never-ending spiral' of downwards descent.[55] Or is there? Thankfully, some of the very best Hyperboreans, like Wotan, somehow managed to resist the lure of cybernetic Jewish ape-sirens and fly back to Venus, so hope did remain. Serrano went further than most Traditionalists, saying the *kali yuga* Iron Age was dissolving even deeper into a Lead Age. The Jews now aimed to create 'a realm of lead, of protons heavier than lead, in an automated Hell ... of Communist society ... [filled with] Mongol and Yellow races'.[56] This sounded bad but allowed Serrano to claim alchemy was the key to reversing such degeneration, given the age-old quest of the alchemists was to transmute base metals like lead into gold. It was possible for an Aryan to gain 'double blood, physical and astral' in nature, which may have looked red to the naked eye, but blue to the ancestral Hyperborean Third Eye. This would happen suddenly, in a Wotan-sent 'thunderbolt', triggered off by 'especial practices' of spiritual alchemy, 'changing the biological and psychic metabolism' meaning that 'lead has been transmuted' and 'the organ of *Vril*, lost by the white Hyperborean race, has been recovered', enabling Aryans to 'see over great distances' with their minds.[57]

Here we again see Jungian influence. According to Jung, alchemy was no exoteric attempt to manufacture literal solid gold from amounts of literal solid lead, but an esoteric psychological process aimed at inducing visions within the alchemist himself when staring hard into his vessels; all their talk of Green Lions devouring Black Ravens or Red Dragons setting ablaze the Black Sun were not only coded descriptions of obscure chemical processes, but also records of the phantasms they saw in their ill-lit midnight labs. The successful alchemist might achieve a psychic state Jung labelled 'individuation'. This was a sudden ideal union of all possible opposing characteristics within the self, like in a *mandala* – a seamless marriage of the conscious and unconscious minds corresponding to the perfect union between matter and spirit when the alchemist projected visions into his glass tubes. Rather than a misguided dead-end pseudo-science, the true purpose of the Great Work of alchemy was to transform your leaden soul into purest gold, of a spiritual nature.[58]

For Serrano, early Aryans possessed skin which was 'golden, smooth and dry, such that neither dust nor sweat stay there', not to mention the 'chin and chest of a lion ... harmonious voice, very white teeth without gaps' and excellent gait: 'The lower part of the noble *Aryan* does not oscillate when he walks.'[59] But non-golden Aryans did not look like this today. The Norse myth of the shining sun god Baldr the Bright being killed by the hairy Trickster god Loki was really an ancient alien prefiguring of 'the unfathomable mystery of *White Treason*', when Aryans adulterated their blood.[60] Like Robert Charroux, Serrano did not believe in Darwin's doctrine of evolution, but in a rival reverse-process he called 'involution'. Men did not come *from* monkeys, but were degenerating *into* monkeys, because of race-mixing. Involution was pure racial-alchemical warfare between golden genes and leaden ones, taking place everywhere: 'Battles are being fought every day between what we call men, animals, dogs, spiders, birds, plants, even between metals,' like lead and gold. Sadly, many golden creatures 'do not win the battles and fall by the wayside', like a wolf slaughtered by a pack of mangy hounds. However, 'each and every fallen creature has inert energy' which SS alchemists hiding out on Venus or beneath Antarctica 'will use to their advantage at the appropriate time', reversing *kali yuga* into *satya yuga* through a sudden alchemical reversal, 'a great resurrection, a definite explosion', but one which brings things back together, like Hitler's anti-atom bombs; Jews and their Demiurge produced only endless entropy, whereas Nazis stuck Humpty back together again by pressing the rewind button on reality itself. Serrano spoke of Hitler's adherents of 'esoterical scientificism' having discovered an 'implosion' principle of 'other technology' rather than an explosive one to fuel their physical metallic UFOs; had he been reading his Viktor Schauberger, the Green Nazi saucer-inventor who also used such terms?[61]

Under Hitler, Germany became a gigantic alchemical 'Laboratory of Racial Transmutation', a huge magical circle spinning with such 'hypnotic velocity' that many souls who tried to jump into it only succeeded in 'breaking themselves into a thousand pieces forever'. Such opportunists were not true Nazi believers, who had tried to leap down the cosmic plughole to Hyperborea purely for personal gain, once they saw what Hitler was up to.[62] These greedy fools had been like the lesser alchemists who had mistaken the sacred soul-quest for an attempt to manufacture actual gold. Nonetheless, at least they had had the guts to try and jump into the spinning sun wheel. Right now, even post-war Germany had submitted itself to the Demiurge's leaden will. Following Hitler's exoteric defeat in 1945, The Maestro had a vision of 'a White Feminine Spirit ... beautiful and luminous', resembling the figure of the White Queen sometimes glimpsed by alchemists, fleeing from 'the native soil where she was born.' This was the *volksgeist*, the national soul of the

German *volk*, their equivalent of Britannia, being sundered from her natural habitat by *kali yuga*. 'Today's Germany is different' from its heroic Nazi predecessor, bemoaned Serrano, with its people transformed into 'fat ghosts' and 'materialists'. Non-Nazi Germany, like base lead, was 'a country without a soul', split between Jewish capitalism in the West and Jewish Communism in the East.[63] Chile was now the likely new locus of the Fourth Space-Reich, not the original Fatherland. As such, the ancient Aztec flying snake-deity Quetzalcoatl would also return as a *vimana*-saucer, travelling 'faster than the speed of thought' to help out come the day of Nazi Ragnarok.[64]

Serrano sought to coax the *volksgeist* back towards sacred German soil, following initial rebirth in the Andes with Quetzalcoatl. 'In Communist countries, even the plants and vegetation are sad,' which showed just how poisonous the East German earth in particular had grown without her.[65] Serrano's 1978 text *The Golden Cord* was dedicated to those Esoteric Nazis who felt the *volksgeist*'s absence keenly: 'For those who are considered politically incorrect, or are political prisoners, or are victims of some kind of torture from this Communist world, I give this Revelation.'[66] Miguel's revelation was that the true mystics of past ages, from Knights Templar to the *Ahnenerbe* to the Druids and Rosicrucians, were all linked through time by the 'golden cord' of the solar god Adolf Hitler, in a shared quest to make the Aryan sun shine down on the barren soil of our world once more, turning leaden dross into shimmering gold. For Serrano, the sun was masculine, fascist and Aryan and the moon feminine, Communist and Jewish. *Kali yuga* was a moon-age, the moon being a Jewish mother goddess who taught all her children were 'equal and the same', privileging weak lunar qualities like community and equality over strong solar ones like individualism and adventure. To a Jewish lunar mother, any solar child of hers who stood out as a hero 'would be considered the black sheep of the family' for refusing to remain at the same low standard as his lunar siblings. 'This is the principle of Communism: there cannot be any heroes.' As a result, 'Everything has to be bureaucratic; it's horrible. This is the direct path towards slavery.' Communism, even when disguised as capitalist technocracy, 'makes the mediocre look great ... everything is standardised and reproaches anything great, it murders creativity, originality and true godliness.'[67] Not within the soul of the great solar hero Miguel Serrano, who was nothing if not original. Given his incredibly arcane personal cosmology, together with his capacity for undergoing odd poetic visions and walking mountains green, you might characterise Serrano as the rough Nazi equivalent of William Blake. Both dreamed of New Jerusalems. It's just that, in Serrano's case, there wouldn't be any Jews in it.

* * * * *

Some people may object to Serrano's Esoteric Hitlerism philosophy on the reasonable grounds that it is clearly untrue. However, *are* such grounds actually reasonable? This is *kali yuga*, remember, when everything is the wrong way around; under such circumstances, if something is untrue, then doesn't this actually mean that it *is* true? This was the reasoning used by Serrano in his short late-career book *MAYA: Reality is an Illusion*, where it is argued that the fact nobody has ever seen Hitler's one-time Deputy Führer Rudolf Hess (1894-1987) living on the moon means that he is obviously living there after all. 'There is indeed *a Face in the Lunar Disc ...*' Serrano once explained – and it was that of Herr Hess.[68]

Alongside Heinrich Himmler, Hess was perhaps the leading Nazi most personally interested in the occult. When, on 10 May 1941, he climbed into a plane in disguise and flew all the way to Scotland before crash-landing in a field in a deluded attempt to secure peace between Britain and Germany, his daring folly unleashed endless speculation. Once it was realised he had no official mandate from Hitler, Hess was treated as an enemy alien and jailed. Speaking of his 'deed of lunatic benevolence', Churchill later decreed Hess be treated as a mental case, not a criminal one. Why did Hess commit this act of apparent lunacy? Some pointed towards the alleged former Thule Society associate's love of the paranormal. Under interrogation, Hess admitted his flight had been inspired 'through a dream, by supernatural powers', and he is said to have consulted his personal astrologer prior to take-off. The dream in question was not his own, but that of Hess' old university professor Karl Haushofer, the father of the expansionist *lebensraum* policies of Nazi geopolitics, who had enjoyed a nocturnal vision of Hess striding purposefully through the tapestried corridors of English castles on a quest to bring the 'Aryan blood-brothers' of the two Anglo-Saxon nations into holy alliance, something Hess may have taken more seriously than Haushofer intended. 'It seemed that Party Member Hess lived in a state of hallucination,' Joseph Goebbels later announced to the German public, inhabiting a shady mental otherworld where other men's dreams were mistaken for reality.

Hess' New Age-style passions for 'faith-healing and grass-eating' were now condemned, with several rival top Nazis pressing the Führer to outlaw practices like fortune-telling. Communiqués speculating Hess had been led astray by 'a host of magnetotherapists and astrologers' rapidly hardened into the official Party line. On 9 June 1941, SS security chief Reinhard Heydrich (1904-42) launched the 'Hess Action', leading to the arrest of astrologers, the banning of public performances of clairvoyants and faith-healers, and the prohibition of articles and journals about paranormal topics. Occult books and paraphernalia were confiscated, and adherents lectured about the need to maintain Enlightenment values. Arrested astrologers were asked a trick question by Gestapo interrogators, namely whether the fact that a Jew, a black man and an Aryan had all been born at the same hour on the same day under the same star-sign meant that they all had the same character-traits. If the star-seers answered 'yes', they required a spell of intense re-education. In his diary, Goebbels gloated that 'The miracle-men, Hess' darlings, are going under lock and key.' Even Ariosophists were now suspect.

The clampdown proved short-lived, with most victims being released within weeks, but Hess' name was successfully blackened.[69]

After the war Hess was placed in solitary confinement within Berlin's Spandau Prison until, on 17 August 1987, he committed suicide, strangling himself with the wire-cord from a reading-lamp aged ninety-three – *or did he?* Some thought otherwise, notably the British doctor W. Hugh Thomas (b.1935), whose 1979 book *The Murder of Rudolf Hess* revealed that, when examining Hess, x-rays of his lungs appeared to demonstrate that scarring from an old First World War bullet-wound had disappeared, which should have been impossible. Thomas' conclusion was that the man imprisoned in Spandau was a lookalike. Published in Chile in 1980 as *The Enigma of Rudolf Hess*, Miguel Serrano read Dr Thomas' book, noting that when Thomas confronted 'Hess' with his theory, 'terrified and urinating [the double] tried to flee,' which was in itself odd given that, due to his lung-scarring, the real Hess got out of breath rather easily. Further discrepancies between the true Hess and the substitute included the man in prison smoking and eating meat and curry 'at a positively alarming rate', when the Deputy Führer had famously been a non-smoking fan of 'grass-eating'. Also suspicious was that Rudolf had refused to let the rest of the family Hess visit him behind bars until 1969 for fear that 'they would not recognise him' – because he was not him! Thomas' unlikely explanation was that Goering and Himmler had Hess killed to eliminate a rival, with his double then sent off to ruin his posthumous reputation over in Scotland.

Maybe the true plot was even weirder. The Hess in Spandau knew absolutely nothing about tennis, whereas in his youth the man had been a keen player. How can you forget how to play tennis? During his 1946 war crimes trial at Nuremberg, Hess had acted bizarrely, staring blank-eyed into space, answering questions with 'I don't remember', and blaming the Holocaust on camp commandants' minds being subject to remote control by unknown hypnotists, probably Jews and Bolsheviks, eager to frame good-hearted Nazis as mass murderers. His own non-Nazi guards in Britain were also under mind control, as shown by their 'strange eyes … glassy … like eyes in a dream'. Hitler, too, had strange eyes, meaning he had been forced to invade Poland in the first place by the remote-controllers. Believing his drugged British guards had themselves been drugging his food with 'brain poison' that made his forks turn green, Hess complained this had caused him to suffer severe constipation and amnesia, forgetting even simple things like who Hermann Goering was, or the rules of tennis. Perhaps Hess really had become insane, or else he simply pretended so to be spared hanging, a pretence he felt compelled to maintain in Spandau. Yet at one point in his trial, Hess suddenly admitted he had feigned his amnesia for 'tactical' legal reasons, thus rendering any such plan obsolete. Hess' self-defeating admission made several observers, including Goering, scoff that, by claiming not to be mad any more, Hess was cleverly just making it seem as if he was even madder, thereby aiding his defence of pleading insanity by not pleading it at all. It transpired Hess had made a similar confession to his British captors in 1945 ... but had then forgotten. In his final speech, Hess spoke of how he had observed certain political prisoners give 'frenzied' applause when sentenced to death, more proof that some defendants – including many at Nuremberg – were themselves subject to hypnotism by those who wanted to see them wrongly hang. Hess' conduct was totally inconsistent, then, and investigators can conclude whatever they like. Further contributions include *Who Murdered My Father, Rudolf Hess?* by Hess' son Wolf, which argues the man in Spandau really was his dad, but that he was murdered in 1987 by a secret society called 'Skull and Bones', who stole the pancreas and one of the testicles from the corpse for obscure ritualistic purposes. It has even been proposed that, once captured by Britain, the real, brainwashed Hess was intended to be sent back to Germany to assassinate the Nazi High Command.[70]

Naturally, Miguel Serrano's own speculations about Hess' fate were far stranger than those of anyone else. Writing in 'Year 115 of the Hitlerian Era' (or 2004 to non-Nazis) Serrano recalled his time as Ambassador to Austria in the 1960s when he had received a 'confidential memorandum' from Chile's Foreign Minister, telling him to contact 'the mendacious, self-styled Nazi-hunter' Simon Wiesenthal (1908-2005), a Jew who tracked down missing war criminals for prosecution. Wiesenthal had recently told a newspaper he believed Hitler's private secretary Martin Bormann (1900-45?) was living in Chile, having been tipped off by an anonymous Chilean diplomat. Ordered to catch this rogue bureaucrat, Serrano unmasked the fiend as an undercover left-wing journalist, but also found Bormann's post-war fate was very uncertain. Whilst one version of Bormann apparently really was living quietly in Chile under State protection, other testimonies said he had also become a spy in Moscow, that he was living as a monk in Italy and a millionaire in Argentina, and that he had been killed in an explosion outside the Berlin *Führerbunker* on 2 May 1945. In 1973 a West German court formally declared Bormann dead when his skeleton was apparently unearthed near the bunker's ruins. Yet the Nuremberg tribunal had sentenced Bormann to death *in absentia*, which made little sense if he was already dead. Supposedly, the living Bormann had been overheard on a radio-transmitter after the war reassuring Hitler's secret children that daddy was safe and doing well, as was Martin himself.[71]

How could Bormann have been in at least five places at once, dead and alive simultaneously, both monk and millionaire? In Austria, Serrano subsequently met up with the Ariosophist, UFO theorist and former Waffen-SS man Rudolf Mund, whom we shall meet again later. Seeking out like-minded fantasists, Mund came across an alleged former *Wunderwaffen* inventor, who was now hawking the Jewish mind-control drug Coca-Cola from a small kiosk in Vienna, 'the only job he has been able to hold without giving away his identity.' When Mund heard of Serrano's puzzlement regarding Martin Bormann, he took him to meet the engineer, and Serrano asked him how Hitler's old secretary could be living in so many countries concurrently. The wise inventor replied with a question of his own: 'Do you know who Adolf Hitler was?' Serrano was most offended. 'Of course I know! How could I not know?' he spat back. Shaking his head, the *Wunderwaffen* man said that Serrano could *not* have known who Adolf Hitler was, because there were so many identikit Führers swanning around the world these days. When the Russians had reached the Berlin bunker, they had found at least fourteen charred and identical 'carbonised cadavers' of Hitler lying around, something Serrano later said seemed 'phantasmagorical, like a ghoulish piece of magic', leaving the Communists 'terrified' (actually, the Russians had deliberately spread such fake stories about Hitler potentially having one or many doubles for propagandistic disinformation purposes). The ranting *Downfall* version of Adolf issuing inept orders from the Führerbunker during the final days of the war obviously can't have been the real military genius, Serrano now realised, who had fled Berlin in (or as) a UFO. The basic Nazi plan was to confuse the Allies by recreating the end of *Spartacus* with crowds of cloned Hitlers to obscure his escape. So which Hitler was the real one? It was likewise with Bormann. It was impossible to know whether the true one was dead, living in Chile or flying through the sky as a transmuted *mandala*-saucer.

'Did you know that we scientists of the Third Reich were more than a hundred years ahead in the discoveries of technology, mechanics and also biology?' asked the inventor, proudly. 'Did you know that not only cloning and robotics were achieved, but also real *duplication*? Yes, duplication! And perfect duplication.' So, there you had it. There were cloned Bormanns, robotic Bormanns, duplicated Bormanns and somewhere, presumably, a real Bormann, but it was impossible to know which was which, even for their creators. Serrano was impressed: 'Ah! Germany, the Germans, the Germanic race, the Aryans! They are capable of everything, of transfiguring the world and the human being, if they unite,' he gushed.[72]

Serrano used the *Wunderwaffen* expert's theories to propose the real Rudolf Hess had not been imprisoned in Spandau, but secretly sent to live in Antarctica upon the direct orders of Adolf Hitler, from whence he had then been sent to the moon, there to await further instructions. Alternatively, if the man in Spandau really had been the top Thule Society wizard Rudolf Hess, then it was entirely plausible instead that, imitating a story by his near-namesake the Swiss-German novelist Herman Hesse (1877-1962) – another famous friend of Serrano's – Hess had simply painted a train on his cell wall, jumped on-board and then escaped 'into an Ultimate Flower', necessitating a lookalike being imprisoned in his stead to cover up the magic train's miraculous departure.

Elsewhere, Serrano speculated that Winston Churchill, 'a sinister little man', had ordered Hess' imprisonment to prevent him meeting King George VI (1895-1952) and his advisers, who were really blue-blooded Hyperboreans, to sue for peace. As England was the land of King Arthur,

Merlin, Stonehenge, the Holy Grail and the Elizabethan alchemist John Dee (1527-1608), Hess was desperate for it to unite with the equally holy Arthurian land of Parsifal and the Externsteine in Aryan alliance. John Dee possessed a polished scrying device known as the 'Black Mirror', into which he stared until he enjoyed visions of angels. This was a real item, today found in the British Museum. However, Serrano knew these 'angels' were really 'extraterrestrials from Hyperborea, beings from inside the [Hollow] Earth and beings from Venus, the Morning Star'. Serrano had 'thought a lot about John Dee's Black Mirror', concluding that Dee had once 'tried to convince Queen Elizabeth [I] of England to take over Greenland, as this gave access to a parallel universe' through a wormhole, something the 'angels' must have told him. King Arthur's Round Table was truly 'a representation of the swastika' in its circle on the later Nazi flag, and 'also symbolises the [North] Pole', the Pole being 'the Final *Chakra* of the Planet Earth', through which white-skinned aliens could pass. Clearly, an ET-backed military union between the land-power of holy Germania and the sea-power of sacred Albion would have been invincible. So, acting upon behalf of a cabal of 'Anglo-Jews', the evil Churchill betrayed King Arthur's sleeping spirit by allowing Zionists to perpetrate 'a formidable triumph of black magic' by poisoning Hess with mind-control drugs to disintegrate his personality. Hess was now transformed into a mobile human 'antenna', in telepathic contact with Hitler at a distance, thus allowing British agents to bug the Nazis' minds and 'follow their esoteric movements' to counter them, as well as controlling Adolf's brain remotely, causing him to make poor strategic decisions like invading Russia.[73]

According to Hess' Nuremberg testimony, 'Most world leaders are controlled in this way,' which explained why some now agreed to 'beg for pardon' and pay 'immense' reparations to Israel for the Holocaust, even though 'that "nation" legally did not exist at the time of the war.' The Jewish media, together with mass-produced fizzy drinks and pharmaceuticals, created 'dark hypnotic waves' emanating from magical antennae in 'the World-Centre of Black Magic, in Jerusalem'. These mind-control waves allowed the Jew to become 'a microbe, disintegrating the cadaver' of victims like Hess, turning them into hollow shells.[74] Yet the antenna-corpse in question had escaped the range of these Anglo-Jewish puppeteers anyway. Possibly Hess had teleported from Spandau to the moon of his own accord, something which later caused NASA problems during the Apollo landings, following which 'the United States never again attempted to take over the moon, because when they went – if they ever did – they found it was already *occupied*' by Nazis. In this scenario, Hess' imprisoned double had been conjured by Hess himself, so nobody would notice he was gone. The only clues were the giant poster-maps of the moon which lined Hess' cell-walls, perhaps acting as psychic visualisation aids, enabling the prisoner to manifest his soul-self upon the lunar surface, but unless you were fully initiated into Esoteric Hitlerism like Serrano they would just look like innocent decorations, inspired by the moon race mania of the day.

Germany was the historic home of the *doppelgänger*, and Germany's SS *Wunderwaffen* corps had managed to create such supernatural doubles not only via cloning and robotics, but also through magic. From Tibetan adepts, SS soul-scientists had learned a method through which fully initiated leading Nazis could 'materialise their astral body, the *Lingasarira*, and make it ubiquitous ... not only to *duplicate* it, but also to multiply it at will.' The astral body is not the double of the physical body, as inverted *kali yuga* minds might naturally think, but *vice versa*; the physical body was 'something like the revealed negative of a photograph', with the *Lingasarira* being the original negative which 'may be revealed [copied] as many times as one wishes'. All you had to do was reactivate 'the computer of the mind', and you could flood the world with *doppelgängers* of yourself, then fly off to other planets whilst all the idiots below thought you were safely dead or behind bars. Possibly the spaced-out Hess on trial at Nuremberg was not actually being controlled remotely by Anglo-Zionists at all, but by the real, astral Hess on the moon, the most cunning double-bluff of all time.[75] Serrano's ultimate conclusion was that 'We have lived, and we still live, in an illusory world, where nobody knows who is who, nor when we are speaking with a specific person whether we do so with the authentic one, or with someone that does not exist.' The situation was complicated further by how the Jewish legions of the Demiurge had since 'plagiarised' Nazi knowledge to manufacture inauthentic *doppelgängers* of their own, a form of soul-theft, or ultimate breach of personal copyright laws; printing out multiple photocopies of a person from their soul-negative without permission could lead to all kinds of chaos. The aim of the Jews was to destroy reality itself: 'This way, everything is illusory; it is *Maya*, as Hindusim defines reality,' that is, a realm of mirages and shadows, in which nothing is as it seems, particularly not Nazism.[76]

Serrano accurately argued that Adolf Hitler was 'one of the most peculiar individuals in the history of our Earth.' Comparing him to Jesus, Serrano remembered sceptical historians' arguments that there was no actual hard evidence Jesus existed anywhere 'outside of the Jewish Bible'. This was completely different to Adolf Hitler, as there exist 'countless eyewitness accounts of people who have seen him', and even ones from certain brave people 'who have actually touched him'. However, 'If there is any doubt whether Jesus Christ was born or not, there is also doubt whether Hitler died or not.' There is even doubt as to whether photographs of Hitler are actually photographs of Hitler at all, or simply 'Magic Eye' images, which transform into something else the more you stare at them. When Serrano first saw a photograph of the Führer in his youth, 'my first instinct was to turn away', before realising that 'if you keep looking at his photo, he will be Transfigured' into an alien. 'Adolf Hitler is not human. He is way above the human race. Adolf Hitler is not from Earth.' Instead, he is 'someone from another planet, a Celestial Being.' As even photos of Hitler were decoy *doppelgängers*, it made sense he showed different 'contradictory impressions' of his personality to different people, 'proving that no-one really knew Hitler' apart from Rudolf Hess, who had also become his own photocopy.[77]

It is when you realise Serrano thought we were living within a gigantic Jewish hologram full of multiple fake Hitlers and Hesses – an inaccurate and inferior 'plagiarisation' of the true, non-material planet Earth – that his demented Gnostic philosophy begins to make more sense. Take his description of the Hollow Earth, which can be entered via a handy hidden hole at the South Pole:

> After [travelling downwards through the hole in a U-boat for] 800 miles there is only air and the Hollow Earth. The surface on the inside of the Earth has continents, seas, forests, mountains and rivers inhabited by a superior race that moved there in ancient times directly related to the Hyperborean legends. Their technology is light years ahead of ours ... All the ... Esoteric Hitlerists go there for their instructions. Hitler received his instructions from them. They permitted [the leader of the German Navy] Admiral Dönitz with his sailors to enter inside, navigating under the polar cap into secret passageways ... The climate inside the Earth is of a fair temperature all year round. In the centre of the Earth there is a sun. It is smaller than the sun we know of. Since there is less force of gravity in the interior of the Earth, the people grow much taller and they live much longer. It gives the impression of eternity, a miracle, Heaven itself ... Once you enter the Hollow Earth, you don't realise it because even though you are in an inverted position, you feel as if you are on top of land. This is because the force of gravity emanates from the crust of the Earth ... The *aurora borealis* [and *aurora australis*] is the reflection of the sun and the dream of the Green Ray [the emerald light which shines from the Nazi Black Sun] from the interior of the Earth. The rays emanate from the openings of the poles. This is why the planets Venus, Mars and Mercury shine at their poles. They are also hollow inside. The icebergs freeze in the rivers inside the [polar] openings then float out into the ocean. This is why we have freshwater icebergs in the [saltwater] ocean.[78]

This account is of a spiritual journey as much as a physical one, like that undergone by Coleridge's Ancient Mariner when he, too, voyaged to the polar wastes. Serrano speaks of 'The *Caleuche*, the mythical Ghost-Ship of the South Pole', which was also said to sail in and out of a hidden hole, crewed by skeletons, and the journey of Admiral Karl Dönitz's (1891-1980) U-boat stands in this same supernatural tradition. When Dönitz supposedly sailed to Antarctica taking Hitler to safety in 1945, as taught by The Maestro, this literal, physical journey took place simultaneously on other levels too, much as when Rudolf Hess was sitting in his prison cell he was also walking on the moon. Apparently, 'gypsies and Eskimos were not permitted to enter' into the Nazi Hollow Earth whenever they approached its polar entrances during their wanderings, but they were not *physically* barred from doing so.

Having impure, non-Hyperborean blood, they simply would not have been able to project their astral selves into the Earth's racist core. If a gypsy had been aboard the U-boat with Dönitz and Hitler, their impure blood meant they would see nothing unusual at all, whilst the *Vril*-filled Führer would suddenly vanish down a psychic plughole.[79]

Serrano's labelled diagram-map of the Hollow Earth includes both literal physical features, such as 'Polar Ice-Caps' and wholly spiritual things, like 'Mannus, the Hand-God of the Germans'. Other features are physical and spiritual at once, such as 'The Red Sun, Loki the Fire Giant', whilst directions towards entrances feature no simple physical co-ordinates, but riddles like 'The Siegfried-Brünnhilde Mystery: The Warrior must penetrate through the magnetic North Pole well to the sleeping Sun-Maiden'.[80] Likewise, when a Hyperborean 'enters or exits [the Hollow Earth] by using the figure eight', this is not just a description of their physical *vimana*-UFO flight-path, but also a metaphor for them entering into the eternal realm of infinity, for which the figure eight is a traditional symbol.[81] When Serrano made his own Antarctic jaunt in 1947/48 with Chile's military, he 'lacked the proper technical equipment to get to the opening' in the Pole physically, but 'received ample input from my Psychic and Auric Antennae' nonetheless.[82] As Serrano points out:

> The openings at the poles are not only openings into the interior of the Earth, they are also a window to other invisible and parallel worlds ... From these dimensions come beings from other planets, the Hyperboreans ... The 'Exits' to parallel worlds and 'Entrances' to the interior of the Earth vary according to cosmic and planetary cycles. If an entrance were closed during a cycle a person would not be able to find the entrance psychologically. The entrance is there, but it is impossible to see or recognise. In the current cycle, all the entrances and exits are located at the South Pole.[83]

The more you read about Serrano's Antarctic trip, the less clear it is precisely what he felt about it. In 1984, he wrote that, contrary to all his prior statements on the topic:

> I was not going to find Hitler, as has been supposed. How could I have done so? I went on a mythic legendary pilgrimage, to render [honour] to the dream, to the Myth, to the Legend, to the Avatar and *to my Führer*. This is certain. It was a peregrination in homage to my own soul, a search for the centre of my own being, of the warm Oasis in the midst of the icefields, of the frozen fire, of the Black Sun of the Poles, the Polar Aurora, the entrance to the Hollow Earth, and all that does not exist, that has never existed, that shall never exist – but that is more real than everything that does exist. My Ultimate Flower, more alive and eternal than all the flowers in the gardens of this world [i.e. Hitler] ... will not be there, because paradise has ceased to be terrestrial. The *vimanas*, the *stars*, will have long since taken him to other stars, rotating with the speed and direction of the Leftward Swastika.[84]

There are obviously innumerable internal inconsistencies in Serrano's thought. And yet, if in a world of *Maya* everything is an illusion, then this is actually a sort of consistency in and of itself. Hyperborea was not an invention of the Esoteric Hitlerists, but a mythical non-ET 'Land Beyond the North Wind' spoken of by the ancient Greeks, and also in earlier Hindu sources, where it was known as *Svita-Dvîpa*, or the 'White Island'; it was supposed to be the home of Mount Meru, the holy mountain in search of which the original Aryans had migrated northwards from India in the pseudo-historical fantasies of Friedrich Schlegel, examined earlier. In many traditions, it merges with Thule, so beloved of the Ariosophists. Geographers have made many attempts to give the entirely imaginary Hyperborea a physical location, just like with Atlantis, but as the etymology suggests, it has generally been placed somewhere near the North Pole or frozen Iceland. Why did Serrano locate this stereotypically northern land in the extreme south, then? Perhaps through pure national pride. In 1805, one Francis Wilford (1761-1822), in his *Essay on the Sacred Isles in the West*, patriotically located Hyperborea in his native land of Britain; why should Serrano not do the same for Chile? Chile, tapering towards the bottom tip of South America, is the world's southernmost inhabited landmass before Antarctica, so it seemed tempting to link the two places. Anyway, this is *kali yuga*, the age of inversion, so surely it made twisted sense that a northern realm was now a southern one instead? Undoubtedly, if Hitler had 'had enough time he could have re-straightened out the planet and returned the magnetic poles to their proper position', but he was defeated before getting around to it, so the whole world remained literally upside-down.[85]

* * * * *

Chile might have appeared a Hispanic Latino nation, where the descendants of conquistadors had long since interbred with native Indians, but Miguel Serrano knew better. In his account, Spain itself was once populated by Nordic Visigoths from Sweden who, like him, 'had blue eyes and blonde hair' and worshipped Wotan through rune-magic. Descendants of the original Hyperboreans from Venus, the Swedes definitely had extraterrestrial Aryan blood flowing in their veins. So, to claim the Spanish had conquered South America was simply to say that Venusian Visigoths had done so. When you consider large numbers of Germans had also settled in Chile during the nineteenth and twentieth centuries, this meant 'the Chilean race of today has Nordic blood'. The 'discovery' of the Americas by Christopher Columbus (1451-1506) in 1492 was a Jewish hoax. Columbus was a Jew, and had only crossed the Atlantic to steal the Holy Grail from the French Knights Templar, who had also established bases in the area, hoping to re-establish contact with Antarctic Hyperborea. Norse Vikings had earlier colonised Chile, too, leaving UFO landing-strips shaped like magical runes as signs to space-visitors that these were good places to land, said Serrano, an apparent reference to a standard ancient astronaut trope about huge markings in Chile's Atacama Desert really being primitive space-ports.

Serrano had been reading the French-born anthropologist Jacques de Mahieu (1915-90), whose books contained similarly spurious claims about tiny bands of white Viking warriors settling the continent in ancient times. The Inca Empire was really a Viking Empire, Mahieu said, finding *Ahnenerbe*-friendly carved runes and swastikas in Peru and Brazil to back his case up. Subsequently, French Knights Templar had then arrived in Mexico, gifting the primitive natives their rudiments of culture, as detailed in titles like *Templars in America*. This was all very convenient from Mahieu's perspective as a former member of the collaborationist French Vichy regime, just like Robert Charroux, who had been smuggled to Argentina by the fascist-friendly government of Juan Perón (1895-1974), for whom he became an active ideologue. Appointed Deputy Rector at Buenos Aires' Institute of Human Studies, the Holocaust-denying Mahieu was well-placed to spread a narrative upholding Argentina's traditional image as the least 'native' and most white European of Latin American nations by adapting the ideas of the earlier pseudo-historian Eugène Beauvois (1835-1912), who had speculated Irish Celts had first settled the Americas; simply by replacing the word 'Celts' with 'Vikings', Mahieu lent an Aryan sheen to his adopted homeland. Being followed by French Knights Templar, the entire continent had thus long been ruled by Mahieu's favourite two races, the Aryans and the French, just like in the good old days of Vichy. Nazis fleeing to Latin America were thus reclaimed not as cowards seeking to evade justice, but as daring re-creators of an earlier migration of white heroes across the Atlantic. In Serrano's adaptation, the god-like Hyperboreans guided down from Venus to Chile by the Vikings with their runic landing-strips were the slumbering giants he later saw trapped beneath the *kali yuga* rocks of the Andes, waiting to be freed by Hitler. This is why Chile was known as 'The Land of the Giants' – such colossi either still slept there, or else had escaped like Vichy collaborators to live secret underground existences nearby, beneath the polar ice.[86]

Serrano now embarked upon a pilgrimage to Spain's chief holy site of Santiago de Compostela (the 'Field of the Holy Star', where a wandering star – or UFO – was meant to have once revealed the burial place of St James to a pious shepherd), along a route usually trod by Catholics. Here, someone with Hyperborean blood 'should be able to reintegrate alchemically, mystically, to his place of extraterrestrial origin, to that star', Venus. Within a local church Serrano found a special chalice, to sip from which meant not to taste the blood of Christ, but 'to drink the blood of the Blue Race, Hyperborea'. The chalice was a disguised Holy Grail like those sought by the *Ahnenerbe*, which allowed Serrano to intuit that highly Spanish-sounding nearby landmarks like the Convent Benedictino de Samos bore 'in reality a German name, a Visigoth name', meaning 'the great Hyperborean forefathers'. The final revelation came when, after Serrano had performed an Ariosophist rune-magic ritual in a nearby graveyard, 'A man suddenly appeared in the shape of a swastika; he had a head, arms and legs, with a cup in his hand.' The swastika-man showed that, by drinking deep the Holy Grail of Hyperborean blood, a true Aryan could regain contact with the sun wheel inside himself and so penetrate at last the veil of *Maya*.[87] A pilgrimage to Hyperborea thus need not involve a trip to the physical South Pole at all – especially as what you really wanted to reach was the original Hyperborean *North* Pole, which wasn't even there any more. By travelling to sunny Spain, Serrano went to frozen Hyperborea anyway, this being a location of the mind. Part of the initiation of any Esoteric Hitlerist was 'to go on a symbolic trip, walking in the form of a swastika until we reached the mystical point, the North Pole', but such a trip need not occur in icy regions. By mapping out Hitler's biggest battles, you could trace them all into the form of a giant swastika, too, spinning its way inexorably towards the Ragnarok of Stalingrad, not the literal Arctic.[88]

* * * * *

Between the twelfth and fourteenth centuries there was a cult of wandering bard-poets or troubadours in Germany called *Minnesänger*, a *Minnesang* being a song of courtly love. According to the gay SS *Ahnenerbe* pseudo-archaeologist Otto Rahn (1904-39), who was an imaginative inspiration for Hollywood's Indiana Jones and his Grail-hunting Nazi enemies, this poetic tradition was just cover for a secret Gnostic religion of Visigoth origin. Serrano agreed with Rahn, concluding the true Holy Grail was not a mere ordinary physical cup at all (although in another sense, it probably *was* a physical cup as well, which the *Ahnenerbe* had presented Hitler for use in his personal Grail-Castle; just as there were physical and non-physical North Poles, UFOs and Rudolf Hesses, so there were physical and non-physical *Sangraals*).[89] The most famous *Minnesinger* was Wolfram von Eschenbach (1170-1220), whose epic *Parzival* told the tale of Parsifal, the German name for St Perceval, and his Arthurian quest for the Holy Grail, also sought by Otto Rahn and his Hollywood *kali yuga* reverse-*doppelgänger* Indiana Jones. Yet the best Holy Grail was not the vessel used at the Last Supper, but something more symbolic, which allowed the true Aryan adventurer to have visions of living swastika-men in cemeteries. Accordingly, Serrano's *Adolf Hitler –The Ultimate Avatar* contained the following cryptic dedication:

> This is not a book. It is a Song of the *Minnesänger*. Therefore it must be heard within, in the Memory of Blood, and be drunk in the Hyperborean Rite of *Minnetrinken* ['Song Drinking']. And when great things happen, perhaps it is because Someone [Hitler] guides us from the innermost Ultimate Green Thunderbolt. *SIEG HEIL!*[90]

True Germans, reading such gnomic words, will immediately recognise 'the *musical note* of their ancestral heritage', and the power of music is proverbially beyond description.[91] Simply reading Serrano's books and expecting to receive comprehensible recipe-like instructions about resurrecting the alien ghost of Adolf Hitler will not work; instead, you must consider them Holy Grails in book-form, printed in blue Hyperborean blood. You must quaff them whole like a Nazi vampire, swallowing the Serrano Kool-Aid and understanding them intuitively, not logically, as they clearly don't make any consistent, rational sense. Serrano's books function as Gnostic revelations, not actual arguments. So, if you *do* intuitively understand them, congratulations, you pure-blooded, Three-Eyed Aryan; the books are literary tests of your innate psychic ability, and if you pass them, well done, you are flying back up to Hyperborea, there to hear the music of the spheres in Valhalla with Wotan.

Now we understand what blood is, we can truly begin to understand Hitler's secret desire to turn all Germans circular. Transforming Aryans into flying saucers was all part of his 'politics of blood and racial purification'. Programmes of eugenics intended to increase the number of Nordics were really attempts to increase the circular radius of the original Hyperborean North Pole out across the entire Earth until it became coterminous with it: 'As many Aryans as possible must incarnate the Hyperborean spirit [by having blonde, blue-eyed babies], increasing the radius of the Circle [of *lebensraum*] ... such as not to leave in the regenerated Earth ... any living-space for the Jewish anti-race, nor for the animal-men, robots and slaves of Atlantis.'[92]

'There is nothing more mysterious than blood,' Serrano wrote. It is 'a condensation of light' and *Vril*-power from the Black Sun, and so 'to conserve the purity of the blood is to be able to remember [your race's origins on Venus] more effectively and win the Great War' against the Jews and their wicked 'anti-blood' of cosmic forgetfulness.[93] This was why dying Waffen-SS men habitually refused blood transfusions in enemy hospitals; to receive plasma from inferior foreign humanoids would be to dilute their *Vril* and prevent them being resurrected as members of Wotan's Wild Hunt.[94] According to Serrano, blood was nothing less than 'THE VEHICLE OF IMAGINATION':

Blood was the first fluid made out of magnetic light. It is the astral soul manifested in human bodies. Blood is a spiritual, hermetic concept. The divine purpose for preserving the bloodline of Aryans is to reawaken the memory banks of our DNA so that we may overcome the process of involution by remembering our origin, our heritage and our previous great civilisations [on other planets]. The Jews on the other hand will only perpetuate hate and vengeance, based on a criminal God created from their own minds for the purpose of enslaving mankind, their incubated Dracula.[95]

Certain Nazi doctors believed 'there is in Nordic Man an additional nerve-bundle,' a Third Eye which 'allows the Aryan to see reality in a divine perspective and projection'. However, 'this organ is not found in coloured races,' explaining the jealous Jews' 'diabolical plan' to 'hybridise the white peoples' with lesser blood, thus to 'produce anew the monster of Neanderthal man', the original Jewish genetic robo-ape.[96] 'Invisible Leaders' like Wotan once came from the sky to 'circulate within' our blood to save our genes, but even Serrano himself, not quite being 100 per cent pure blue-blooded, admits elements of his own teachings are 'impossible for our *kali yuga* minds to comprehend' logically, even his own. Instead, like good Gnostic Gnazis we just have to *accept*, not *understand*, as with all great religions.[97] The true Aryan swastika-man *becomes* the Holy Grail, the vessel for the sacred blood of his divine race and must, like Walt Whitman, sing a Song of Himself:

> *Minne-Memories* are the source of all thought of each race. We have memories of the past of our race in a strict hereditary line that is transmitted from family to family, to race and town and small community ... The chromosome constitutes the nucleus of the cell which has DNA, an acid. This is where life starts. It is the genes that make up the cathedral of our heritage. 'Chromosome' means 'colour and form'. This is where our memories reside. That is why we must preserve our colour. The Aryans need to preserve our memory, the *Minne*, we must remember Hyperborea ... Those who preserve their race will receive Spirituality, knowledge, and their sixth sense will become more intense. *Vril* Power enters through the Third Eye and permits you to communicate with Divine Souls, extraterrestrials and much more.[98]

And yet, 'When we speak of "extra-terrestrials", we do not mean, of course, what is believed today under Jewish tutelage.' Serrano emerges as a committed opponent of nuts-and-bolts ufology, arguing that alien spaceships as such do not exist – to believe in solid UFOs is to fall for leaden, materialist Jewish propaganda. Hyperboreans were far too advanced to 'avail themselves of such crude, strange means' of interplanetary flight. They 'did not need flying saucers' but became *vimanas* instead, 'absorbing the substance of each plane [of existence] and clothing themselves with them'. Aliens came not from the other side of the galaxy, but the 'other side of our senses'. Crucially, Kenneth Arnold-type flying saucers were optical illusions caused by the inadequacy of atrophied sense organs, polluted by non-white blood. If we did possess properly functioning Third Eyes, we would see each disc was no disc at all, but a unified male and female spirit of Aryan appearance, Wotan and the Norse goddess Frigg simultaneously. However, 'none of this excludes the man-animal here on Earth' from copying the outward form of these *vimanas* 'with their mechanical science' by building real nuts-and-bolts UFOs and using these knock-off contraptions to explore 'the outer side of the stars'. But, if they did so, they would find every other world exoterically empty as, lacking *Vril*, 'those little men, with their bodies made of matter', would be unable to perceive Venus was actually full of Grail-Castles and World

Trees upon which grew Aryan god-men living inside special apples. Instead, NASA's subhuman astronauts would be forced to conclude that *'they are alone in the universe,'* when in fact they are surrounded by a cosmos teeming with esoteric life.[99] Made of the Demiurge's clay, astronauts mistake *Maya* for reality, which must be why Neil Armstrong failed to find Rudolf Hess living on the lunar surface – because, spiritually speaking, NASA is Jewish, and its employees failed to drink a draught of Aryan blood from Serrano's *Sangraal* prior to blast-off.

This mindset allows an Esoteric Hitlerist to claim literally absolutely anything he likes, and then if contradicted say 'Well if you can't see it, you've just got Jewish blood.' This was a unique way to promote Holocaust denial, of which Serrano became Chile's most prominent champion. The notion that six million died was revealed as pure 'invention' simply by the Jewish Star of David having six points to it, thus making the Holocaust 'nothing more than Black Magic', a spell cast to discredit Nazism; for each point on the unholy star, there were a million faked deaths, conjured up by Jehovah, the lying alien Demiurge.[100] Remember, under the Gnostic doctrine of revelation, Serrano does not have to *prove* this claim, simply *assert* it; if you don't just automatically agree, it's *your* fault for being a Jewish robot.

Under Chile's 1973-90 military dictatorship, General Pinochet's regime was pro-Israel, with anti-Jewish prejudice being a turn-off to their Anglo-American allies, who monitored the experiment in free-market capitalism going on there under Milton Friedman's tutelage closely. In 1984 Serrano returned home from Europe in outrage at Pinochet's treatment of the sheltered SS war criminal Walter Rauff (1906-84), who had been at the centre of a prominent extradition row due to his role in gassing 97,000 Jews. Chilean courts refused to send Rauff abroad for trial, so his sudden death from lung cancer certainly solved an embarrassing problem for Pinochet. Suspicious, Serrano created a different embarrassing problem for the General instead by loudly disrupting Rauff's funeral with Nazi salutes and shouts of 'Heil Hitler! Heil Walter Rauff!' Serrano declared that 'It is not true that Walter Rauff created the mobile gas chambers and the so-called Holocaust is indeed a Jewish disguise for taking over the world.' He then provided several long interviews to sympathetic newspapers, being lauded as a brave freethinker who advised readers to protect themselves against the Zionist conspiracy by purchasing his brilliant new book *Adolf Hitler – The Ultimate Avatar.*

Hijacking Nazi funerals dressed in his trademark Gestapo-style long black leather trench coat became Serrano's favourite method of self-promotion. In 1987, the same year as 'the Pope of the Jewish Church of Rome' visited Chile, Rudolf Hess' *doppelgänger* died in his cell at Spandau. Organising a memorial rally-cum-book-launch in a cemetery, Serrano gathered 200 loyal Chilean Nazis to hear a speech in Hess' memory, in which Jews were accused of murdering him. Worse, with Hess (who apparently was now the real one, in the end) out of the way, the Jews planned to take over Chile too, just as they had already taken over Spain, where it transpired General Franco had also been a Jew in disguise. Noticing how a single member of Pinochet's Cabinet, Sergio Melnick (b.1951), happened to be Jewish, Serrano identified him as Chile's 'invisible and secret ruler', Pinochet's puppeteer. Free copies of his latest title *The Andinia Plan: Zionist Strategy to Take Over Patagonia* were distributed to attending journalists by eager young acolytes, and a new round of fawning interviews occurred, in which Serrano explained the Jews meant to establish a second Israel in the region, headed up by 'The Messiah of Judah'. In fact, Serrano was actually planning to create a secret Hitlerite commune in Patagonia himself, drawing the attention of the CIA. Sales of Serrano's books now boomed across South America.

The Andinia Plan was a localised South American version of *The Protocols of the Elders of Zion*, history's most notorious literary hoax, this being a forged Russian document purporting to reveal a secret meeting between the world's top Jews, in which they lay out in detail a scheme to destroy the white race through blanket control of the media, finance, Freemasonry and government, a plot foiled only by the fact someone wrote it all down by mistake. Exposed as a forgery by *The Times* in 1921, to those of a paranoid *kali yuga* mindset, this only meant the *Protocols* were even more likely to be true; after all, Jews run the media, don't they? They certainly didn't in Chile, where, time and again, Serrano was given a sympathetic hearing in the Press. When in 1989 Miguel openly celebrated the centenary of Adolf Hitler's birth by holding an adoring public ritual on top of the Andes, media condemnation was slight. Furthermore, he failed to be persecuted by the authorities, hardly something the prominent torture-enthusiast General Pinochet usually shied away from doing. Given his own palpable failure to be prosecuted, how could Serrano possibly maintain Jews were running Chile? His media image was more 'national treasure' than 'insane neo-Nazi'. In 2008, he even won a 'Lifetime Achievement Award' from a Santiago university. Serrano liked to argue that '[even] if the *Protocols* are not genuine, they are true,' in the sense that, whilst literally fake, they were fakes which told the truth. So, Serrano launched another book, *The Protocols of the Elders of Zion and Their Application to Chile*, to add to his other titles like *Manifesto for the Abolition of Interest-Enslavement*, *The Chilean Racial Cycle* and *National Socialism, Only Answer for the Peoples of South America*. By the early 1990s, *We Will Not Celebrate the Death of the White Gods*, *Defend Patagonia!* and *Hitler's UFOs vs the New World Order* spread his doctrine further. In 1989, he even issued a Spanish-language version of *The Leuchter Report*, an infamous text commissioned by Ernst Zündel aiming to prove the gas chambers didn't exist.[101]

There were indeed some Nazi death camps, admitted Serrano, but they were not really death camps, only places of mystical transfiguration and cure. Surprisingly, via death camp soul-alchemy, it was even possible for a leaden *kali yuga* Jew to stop being Jewish any more, and become a golden *satya yuga* Aryan, or at least a Hebrew, whom Serrano viewed as being the

Jews' non-Jewish ancestors who had once lived on some sacred mountain or other. The descent of Jews into the status of ape-robots at the hands of the Demiurge 'is not irreversible, it is probably reversible' and so 'everything is not lost' for 'the young Jew' who sees fit to repent of his fallen nature. Even Jewish monkey-mutants can hope to revert 'from a Lunar Origin to a Solar Origin, to *Resurrect* [their souls] with Alchemy', thereby transforming from 'mutations into transmutations'. 'Collectively, no larger hope exists' for the Jewish race, but individual penitent Jews were still redeemable. By cleansing their blood, it was possible for such willing apostates 'to free themselves from ... Black Magic' and facilitate an 'outpouring of the pure, clean blood of the *Minne*, the Memory of Hyperborea, from a far distant past, into the memory of an Extraterrestrial home deep within one's veins; it should still be possible.'[102] Was this not what the so-called death camps truly were, then? Magical machines for reversing Jewishness, just as Himmler's Grail-Castles could transmute SS officers into UFOs? Places like Auschwitz had 'nothing sinister within them', argued Serrano, being 'true cities' of 'magical' importance, 'destined to cause a mutation' upwards into godhood amongst prisoners and guards alike.[103] Serrano doesn't quite say how. Presumably he means the Gnostic SS meant to release the Jews from their Demiurge-imposed incarceration within physical matter by killing them all – although as he simultaneously denied such things even happened, maybe not. Such are the confusions of *Maya*.

* * * * *

Equally as confusing was the 1989 book *Operation Orth and the Incredible Secret of Rennes-le-Château* by the French esotericist Jean Robin (b.1946). Robin writes of a friend being supposedly transported into the Chilean Hollow Earth, inside a ghostly *vimana* which could pass through solid rock. There, he found a Black Order of 350,000 SS initiates awaiting 'He Who Will Come', the final avatar of Kalki. Was this *Ultimate Avatar* Adolf Hitler, as in Serrano and Savitri Devi? Hitler's corpse was enshrined underground within a special hexagonal casket, a symbol of the *Sangraal*, so it seemed so. However, entombed next door was the similarly venerated corpse of Raoul Wallenberg (1912-45), the Swedish diplomat who saved thousands of wartime Jews by issuing them with false passports. The polar opposites of the Aryan Hitler and the Jewish Wallenberg have been ritually united, just as capitalist and Communist poles are united within Jungian *mandala*-UFOs. Robin's subterranean SS also embraces many openly Jewish members within its ranks, who dismiss the Holocaust as a tedious irrelevancy, with its victims getting exactly what they deserved for failing to embrace the benign genocidal process of evolutionary soul-transmutation offered up to them for free by Nazi soul-alchemists.[104] This is apparently a parody, a deliberate fictional inversion of Serrano's own falsehoods, the presumable purpose being to highlight the Esoteric Hitlerist's many inconsistencies. If the aim

150

of Hitlerian transmutation of the Aryan soul into a UFO was to unite all opposites within it, thereby to create an all-embracing union, as with the chemical wedding of alchemy or the symbiosis of North and South Poles, then wasn't the direct opposite of the Aryan soul the Jewish one? Come the return of Kalki and defeat of the Demiurge, shouldn't Hitler merge with Wallenberg, the Nordic Jung melt into his Semitic rival Freud and SS camp-commandants fuse alchemically with their Jewish victims, before all living happily ever after in the total *unus mundus* perfection of Hyperborea-Zion or Berlin-Jerusalem under the sign of the Swastika of David? How do you square that circle? You can't – and that, I think, is Robin's point.

Like Savitri Devi and Miguel Serrano, Jean Robin was well-read in Traditionalism, being a devotee of the movement's modern French founder René Guénon, whose 1945 book *The Reign of Quantity and the Sign of the Times* had warned that, as *kali yuga* progressed, cracks in a protective 'Great Wall' around Creation would widen, causing an increase in demonic activity in a process termed 'Counter-Initiation'. This was a parody of true religion, in which false gods who were actually devils in disguise became worshipped as forerunners of the Anti-Christ. This Anti-Christ would pose as a Kalki-figure come to save us all from *kali yuga*, but would ultimately be defeated when the *real* Kalki-figure later emerged to restore *satya yuga*. In his 1979 book *UFOs: The Great Parody*, Robin had already revealed flying saucers as the likely vehicle via which these demonic forces would trick us into worshipping them as the forerunners of the Anti-Christ – a figure whose true identity Robin subsequently identified in the title of his 1987 book *Hitler: The Elected Representative of the Dragon*. Robin's 1979 UFO book reads like a remarkable prediction of Serrano's later 1980s revelation of his cult of alien Hitler-worship to the non-Chilean world. The basic idea is that, allowed entrance to Earth through the cracks of growing *kali yuga* materialism, the demons posing as aliens try to persuade mankind that his ancient gods were not really spiritual entities at all, but ancient astronauts, as in Robert Charroux, hoping to make us blunder ever further into the materialist morass. Now, previously spiritual gods would crudely solidify into flesh-and-blood ETs and awe-inspiring supernatural lights in the sky become hard nuts-and-bolts spaceships. People of past ages had always seen UFOs, describing them as dragons or sky-ships, but, being closer to Traditional wisdom, had dismissed them as demonic parodies of the true gods. Thus, Robin did believe in the reality of UFOs, but thought they and their occupants were inherently evil.

The work of these pseudo-alien agents of Counter-Initiation could be seen in the way the moon-landings had destroyed our Traditional image of the lunar orb as a numinous, celestial realm, and replaced it with a dead and dusty grey rock. 'Whereas our ancestors were finding within themselves the way to Heaven,' wrote Robin, 'modern man now observes a material sky' in which planets, stars and moons are no longer celestial spheres, but 'erratic chunks of matter thrown into the dark infinite'. New UFO-religions were simply 'transposed materialism' in which aliens were worshipped instead of the true immaterial godhead. Age-old 'initiatory travels' through space had become subject to reinterpretation 'in the most coarse fashion'; the pre-Renaissance poet Dante Alighieri's (*c.*1265-1321) visionary verse describing trips to Heaven would now be viewed as early records of alien abduction. 'Jacob's Ladder seems to be broken for good,' with the moon no longer being a goddess like Diana or Hecate and 'reduced to a hypothetical extraterrestrial relay-station' for UFOs to fly to Earth from, 'instead of being the Gate to Heaven'. The first man on the moon Neil Armstrong (1930-2012) landing there was thus 'a significant eschatological event', being 'a travesty' of Dante's astral travels in 'grossly materialised' form, a foretaste of the 'Great Parody' that will be the reign of the Anti-Christ who will soon make himself known by taking a giant leap out of a UFO.

Robin discusses how ancient astronaut books can easily become vehicles for anti-Semitism, with specific reference to the absurd *Jews from Space*, and forecasts an increase in the idea UFOs really emerge upwards from within the Hollow Earth as an inverted *kali yuga* parody of the true gods descending downwards from the skies. If ufology is an active parody of Christianity, as Robin argues, it makes sense its persecuted martyrs – like Hitler seeking sanctuary beneath Antarctica – should have to hide out deep within catacombs, just like the hunted Christians of old once supposedly did in Rome. Guénon too believed in sub-surface Agartha, as a 'properly paradisiacal centre' for world-transformation, forced to vanish underground at the start of *kali yuga*, but this subterranean Heaven could easily be parodied as a subterranean Hell, with Serrano's sleeping Hitler being the below-ground Anti-Christ. In the Muslim convert René Guénon's chosen Islamic tradition, the Anti-Christ equivalent, *al-Masih al-dajjal*, the 'Deceiving Messiah', is deformed in body to reflect his deformation of soul, although he uses hypnotism to prevent his followers realising so: *al-Masih al-dajjal* has only one eye – just like Wotan, meaning the true origin of UFOs is thus 'hugely Satanic'. Despite its many oddities, Robin's thesis contains one deep truth, that worship of Hitler and the SS as the future saviours of humanity is indeed an obscene pole-reversal perversion of reality, making Serrano's entire cult an exercise in inadvertent parody, as true an example of 'Counter-Initiation' as could possibly be conceived. As Guénon's concept of 'the Satanic' was that 'the Devil is God upside-down', as the old adage goes, perhaps Serrano and Devi were correct to say we lived in *kali yuga*: their whole upside-down religion seems to prove it.[105]

So does the inverted religion of French UFO Contactee Claude Vorilhon (b.1946), a racing-car journalist who in 1973 was spoken to by aliens who revealed Jesus Christ was his half-brother and that the human race had been artificially created in space. Told his true name was Raël, Vorilhon founded an 'atheist religion' called the Raelians, involving an inner elite called 'Raël's Girls', all of whom work in the sex industry. Raelians are promised immortality, as the aliens have a network of floating orbital super-computers containing the genetic code of everyone who has ever lived. Those corpses who deserve it will be resurrected to enjoy an endless afterlife of sexual bliss – but wicked Adolf Hitler will be reassembled and tried for crimes against humanity, as would terrorist suicide bombers. The alien 'gods' gifted us highly sensitive genitalia, and want us to use them; the religion celebrates homosexuality, transgenderism and partner-swapping, unlike the Bible or Koran. Raelians have even launched schemes to 'adopt' poor African women's clitorises, which genital organs female members dress up as at US porn conventions. They have also promoted human cloning, allegedly manufacturing an artificial baby called Eve. Vorilhon hopes to replace democracy with a system of 'geniocracy', in which mankind will be governed by wise men like himself for its own good. This really does sound like a parody of a religion, in Jean Robin's terms, and sure enough the sect's sacred symbol, copied from the side of a saucer, was a swastika contained within a Star of David, something which caused controversy when they tried to establish an ET Embassy in Jerusalem; temporarily, the swastika was replaced with a swirling galactic energy-vortex. In 2012, the Raelians launched a website, proswastika.org, and flew a banner from an aeroplane, saying 'SWASTIKA = PEACE + LOVE' to advertise an annual 'Swastika Rehabilitation Day', hoping to reclaim the symbol from 'Hitler's horrors' when it was really 'something very beautiful'. The banner also featured the swastika nestled within the Star of David, their original symbol reborn, like Hitler and Raoul Wallenberg merging into one shared body within Jean Robin's cautionary allegorical fantasy. Once again, deliberately absurd fiction had become equally absurd fact.[106]

* * * * *

Despite its incredible strangeness, Miguel Serrano's philosophy grows more in popularity with every passing year. Why? Perhaps it is because it provides a ready-made framework for dismissing certain realities of the world around us – realities which, for neo-Nazis, must seem highly inconvenient, such as the fact of Holocaust. Being able to evade such obstacles via 'intuitive' means of extraterrestrially derived blood-perception is a literal godsend to some. *Vril*-seeking Nazis are all Gnostics now. The overwhelming evidence that the Holocaust did actually occur leaves them no other option.

Thus, an entire racial religion has now been formed in Serrano's name, the Idaho-based Wotansvolk, a white supremacist Nordic paganist group who teach Christianity is a false Jewish-made creed aimed at corrupting the Aryan race's soul, as expressed in Moses' famous 'Ten Commandments for Racial Suicide'. As this is *kali yuga*, the pathetically meek teachings of Christianity, like 'Love thy neighbour', must be reversed back upright again to things like 'Smite your enemies with the Hammer of Thor.' Their anti-Semitic rune-magic Bible, the *Temple of Wotan: Holy Book of the Aryan*

Tribes, is specifically 'dedicated to Miguel Serrano: May your legacy of Honour and Loyalty inspire the future generations of Aryan mystics, philosophers and warriors.' In return, Serrano wrote a foreword to this new Nazi Bible in which he waxed lyrical about the rocks of the Externsteine and the religious sensibilities of the SS, before reiterating that Jehovah of the Jews was a false god come to 'impersonate' the real Aryan space-deity of Wotan, and that one day 'our Volk-Leader will return' from Venus to save all the Wotansvolk from the Demiurge. The book also contains poetry, sacred rites, and a reprint of Jung's essay upon Hitler being Wotan in human form; as a central archetype of our collective unconscious, surely Wotan can be conjured up by pure whites once again, via pagan ritual.

In 2000, the year of the Holy Book's publication, the Wotansvolk were officially recognised as a religion by US authorities. Their sacred slogan of 'The Fourteen Words' ('We must secure the existence of our people and a future for white children') is now famous across the neo-Nazi world, having similar purchase in contemporary multi-ethnic America and Europe as Ariosophy once did in the multi-ethnic Habsburg Vienna of Jörg Lanz von Liebenfels. In 2002, the Wotansvolk published a new English-language edition of Serrano's original 1978 work on Esoteric Hitlerism, *The Golden Cord*, and have played a key role in disseminating his thought across the Anglosphere. Today, Nazi black-metal bands have now spread Serrano's fanbase even further by releasing a series of tribute albums to their departed UFO-loving hero filled with songs like *Gathered in the Vision of the Black Sun*, *At the Gates of the Blazing Südpolar Circle*, *The Icy Path to Oiyehue-Lucifer* and *El Cordón Dorado/A Glimpse of Kali Yuga*.[107] Appropriately enough, many of these are now available in the form of discs.

5

The Unholy Grail: Wilhelm Landig, the Flying *Sangraal* and the Polar Reich of the Black Sun

What happened to those loyal SS Grail-Knights who were not fortunate enough to die on the battlefield in Wotan's name, and thus had to remain here on Earth rather than flying up to Valhalla to become UFOs or join the Wild Hunt? Mostly, they just moped around the ruined, bombed-out remains of the Third Reich, coping with defeat by pretending it had never really happened. One major centre for such daydream believing was post-war Vienna, whose general dilapidated status was captured in the classic 1949 film *The Third Man*. Here in the Austrian capital, yet another circular expression of Esoteric Nazism was established in the shape of the 'Landig Circle', led by Wilhelm Landig (1909-98), a former SS man whose actual duties involved intelligence assignments but who preferred to pose as having been the director of security at the Skoda factory in Prague where the 1950s media-fraudster Rudolf Schriever had supposedly built his Luftwaffe flying saucers, which Landig claimed were really powered by magic from Tibet. The saucers had then been used to ferry the SS's best soldier-priests and scientists out to hidden polar bases following Allied invasion, Landig said.

The Vienna-born Landig was a Hitlerite long before the forced union of Germany and Austria known as the *Anschluss*, becoming a schoolboy storm trooper before participating in the failed Nazi coup attempt of July 1934, in which Austrian Chancellor Engelbert Dolfuss (1892-1934) was shot through the throat and killed. Before he could be arrested, Landig quickly ran away to Germany, to join the SS's subsidiary SD intelligence agency. Following the *Anschluss* of March 1938, Landig was posted back to Vienna on intel missions. In 1944 he was wounded by Balkan partisans, before returning again to the Austrian capital. In September 1945, SS-*Oberscharführer* Landig was automatically interned in a British POW camp. Upon release in 1947, Landig exploited his intelligence background to sell low-grade Soviet info to the Western Allies, later becoming a commercial artist and publisher. In 1970 Landig re-surfaced as Austria's national representative in the World Anti-Communist League, several of whose members thought the best means of combating Communism was to deal in drugs and guns to raise funds, or else advocate the equally totalitarian doctrine of fascism instead.[1]

The 1950s saw Landig found a nationalist Press, *Volkstum-Verlag*, printing books by a founder-member of the *Ahnenerbe*, the Dutch-German amateur scholar Hermann Wirth (1885-1981). The *Ahnenerbe* itself was partly simply Himmler's 1935 rebranding of the earlier Hermann Wirth Society, set up to continue Wirth's work. Although Dutch, Wirth identified as a 'pan-German', joining the Nazis in 1925 before penning a pamphlet demanding colonisation of his own country. Wirth felt ancient polar Nordics had carved their astronomical knowledge into rocks, this becoming the basis for the later runic alphabet. Seeking to prove the Germans and Dutch one *volk*, Wirth championed the *Ura-Linda* chronicle, purportedly the quasi-runic record of the fate of a noble Frisian family, the over de Lindens, from the beginning of time, whose '*weltanschauung* [world-view] was a noble one'. Actually, the chronicle was already a known nineteenth-century hoax, a satire on nationalist ethnic pseudo-histories, which comically claimed any number of Classical era gods, goddesses and heroes, from Minerva to Medea, were really just misremembered ancient Aryans. Wirth made worse mistakes in his long career; one 'sacred wheel' turned out to be a bullseye used for shooting practice by a local gun-club, whilst a carved 'Earth Mother' was 1950s graffiti of Marilyn Monroe.

Expulsion from the *Ahnenerbe* came in 1938, when genuine German academics objected to it having such an unqualified fantasist as Honorary President; they preferred a qualified fantasist instead. Himmler still funded his research though, and Wirth loyally praised Nazism as 'a just cause' into the 1960s. Nonetheless, his dubious championing of the existence of a prehistoric society of quasi-socialistic matriarchal Nordic Mother Nature-worshippers won much praise from the nascent Green movement, who celebrated Wirth as a precursor; like Savitri Devi, his fascism was just a blip when weighed against his *völkisch* attitudes towards the environment and belief Europe was once ruled by divine queens living in giant circular castles. They and their homes were washed away in a colossal flood, however – the basis of the Atlantis myth – leaving males like the Frisian King Wodin (the real Wotan) to rule. Landig and his allies loved Wirth's ideas too. He provided an excellent example of the possibility to rewrite history based purely on your own desires, no matter how fantastic. The inherently Romantic nature of Wirth's world-view, in which ancient Aryan sea-people sailed out in swan-ships and dragon-boats to conquer the world following the fall of Atlantis, provided a great imaginative escape from the dire post-war present.[2]

Grey, starving 1950s Vienna was not a pleasant place, and it was understandable that in the original home city of the Ariosophists, Landig turned to esotericism as a means of perceiving another, better, world lying hidden behind the exoteric bullet-holes and bomb craters. In 1950, Landig founded his influential 'Landig Circle' with two like-minded souls who met up in his design studio to discuss not only Hermann Wirth and his *Ahnenerbe*, but also Baron Julius Evola's 1934 book *Revolt Against the Modern World*, which became their bible; his 1953 sequel, *Men Among the Ruins*, might almost have been a description of Landig's neo-Nazi cult. A former Dadaist avant-garde painter, the Italian Evola abandoned art after discovering René Guénon-style Traditionalism, developing a philosophy in which the best way to combat *kali yuga* was to praise a distant Golden Age in which the old *kshatriya* warrior caste of Hinduism had existed. True soldiers had once been spiritual soldiers too, dreamed Evola, like Tibetan warrior-monks, or SS Grail-Knights. The separation of the idea of the warrior from the idea of the priest was a clear sign of *kali yuga* degeneration, of the splitting of the old *unus mundus* and a 'desacralisation of existence', according to 'the law of the regression of castes'. Far from being led by divine priest-warriors, capitalist nations were now steered by the low-grade merchant class, and Communist ones by the even baser proletariat serf-class; the elitist Baron Evola was no friend of democracy.

Whilst not a full-blown fascist, he sympathised with Mussolini's desire to create 'a new type of Italian, disciplined, virile and combative', with the proviso this would actually be akin to *re*creating an old, and now vanished, type of Italian, a *satya yuga* one. Evola tried unsuccessfully to drag Mussolini towards Traditionalism, viewing fascism as a potential vehicle for his own views, not *vice versa*, seeking to infuse it with elements of Roman paganism. He later tried to interest the Nazis in this plan, too, apparently giving a speech at Wewelsburg Castle in 1938 proposing that SS Grail-Knights work together with him to develop a new Secret Order devoted towards creating a joint Roman-Teutonic Empire. In his 1937 book *The Mystery of the Grail and the Ghibelline Tradition of the Empire*, Evola had explained the *Sangraal* was a symbolic object, representing 'an immortalising and transcendent force', namely 'the mystery of a warrior initiation'. Evola's plan was rejected as 'utopian', however, with Himmler himself deciding to deny the guru any further contact, in spite of his own similar specific fantasy about the SS combat-wing, the Waffen-SS, becoming a modern-day *kshatriya* Hindu warrior caste. By 1945 Evola had regained some favour, however, being posted to Vienna recruiting SS volunteers. Here, it has been speculated he liaised with Wilhelm Landig in his capacity as an SD officer. He certainly met up with a Russian bomb, spending the rest of his life in a wheelchair, paralysed from the waist down.[3]

* * * * *

In later life, Evola inspired 1970s neo-fascist Italian terrorists to revolt against the modern world by planting bombs, but he had already caused an explosion within the mind of Wilhelm Landig decades beforehand. Landig's explanation for German defeat was that, as Savitri Devi and Miguel Serrano (with whom he inevitably later consorted and corresponded) felt, there were two separate Third Reichs, hidden and external. Unlike them, Landig thought Hitler no avatar of Kalki, but a mere member of the exoteric political movement of National Socialism, whilst Himmler was the head of the true, esoteric Nazism, with his SS Black Order being holy *kshatriya*-type warriors after the model of Julius Evola. Leaden Hitlerian Nazism had been deservedly defeated, whilst its golden Himmlerian twin glittered on still, behind the façades of shattered post-war Vienna and Berlin, this narrative providing a coping mechanism for conquered fascists. In later years, distancing himself from the reviled name of Adolf Hitler also served Landig as a good recruiting tool, as when he identified himself to potential acolytes as a Nazi, he could say this should of course not be mistaken for him being a *Nazi* – the word had two meanings, the discredited Hitlerian one, and the hidden Himmlerian one, whose wonderful nature had been covered up by an international conspiracy of 'Freemasons' (by which Landig clearly meant 'Jews', but there are strict laws against anti-Semitism in Austria and Germany which had to be circumvented somehow). By painting Hitler as a traitor to the true holy cause, Landig hoped to redeem Nazism from its unfortunate public image. Worthless exoteric Nazis had infiltrated the valuable esoteric Thule Society and 'led us away from our original path and tempted us to measures which have drawn upon us the hate of the world' in a totally unjust fashion, he sobbed.[4]

In a badly translated 1990s interview with a self-styled vampire-hunter named Jan van Helsing, whom we shall meet properly later, Landig explained how he had 'personally become acquainted' with the Nazi Minister for Economics, Hjalmar Schacht (1877-1970), who, like so many top international bankers, was 'a high degree Freemason'. Schacht had arranged the financing for German re-armament prior to the war, which Landig saw as evidence the conflict was engineered by the Freemasons/ Jews to fill their own pockets. As Germany re-armed, so Britain and France needed to as well, meaning a bonanza for 'the American war industry' and those who worshipped 'Mammon/money'. These greedy Freemasons funded Hitler's rise, under strict condition he would agree to replace parts of his original Nazi programme for government with their own instead, under the principle 'Infiltrate your enemy, initiate him to maintain his interest, and finally take over the enemy!' De-codified, this means Hitler was the Jews' puppet. Landig had seen an early edition of *Mein Kampf* which contained completely different contents to the one known and loved today, which Hitler had cravenly altered to please his true masters, those of 'so-called high-finance'. Hitler did not want a war, but 'stepped right into the political trap left for him' by 'the financial aristocracy'. Furthermore, his personal physician, Dr Theodor Morell (1890-48), was also a Freemason, injecting Adolf with dubious drugs which clouded his mind – which he probably did, but not because Morell was a Freemason, he was just a quack.

Late in the war, Landig was given the SD task of spying on the Hitler Youth leader and then-*Gauleiter* of Vienna, Baldur von Schirach (1907-74), to uncover his 'bad attitude and habits', which included treasonably writing poems to his girlfriend during bomb raids. Von Schirach was already a national joke for having a 'girlish' bedroom decorated all in white, often being mocked for his supposed effeminacy and the inappropriate wearing of lederhosen. Delivering an envelope detailing von Schirach's soppy odes to Himmler, Landig awaited von Schirach's deserved execution. But when Hitler told Himmler he didn't care about any stupid love-poems, that was it for Wilhelm Landig – clearly, the Freemason-Führer had become rotten to the very core. If only Landig had known it, von Schirach had won Hitler's initial favour partly by penning quasi-homoerotic verses to him in the first place, singing that 'In him rests the roots of our world/And his soul touches the stars/And yet he remains a man like you and me.'[5] *Real* men didn't write such flowery tosh, clarifying the exoteric political wing of Nazism was a mere 'mass movement' any fool could join, but 'behind III Reich an esoteric society stood', and the arcane SS wished to 'crystallise' a new kind of 'noble human being', forming an 'aristocracy of racial perfectly good humans … with a German people consciousness'; this was the true poetry of the Aryan race, just waiting to be written. Landig's actual post-war role was not to be a publisher of fringe propaganda, but to aid the export of *Wunderwaffen* UFO technology to SS bases in Antarctica and the Andes, he said. Unfortunately, the Nazi gold hidden in Swiss bank accounts to facilitate this plan proved inaccessible to Landig's post-war SD network, with it all being 'kidnapped by bigwigs' who stopped the UFO-pilots getting their hands back on the stolen loot.

Lacking funds to maintain this secret saucer-fleet, the remaining discs 'rot/deteriorate in the Andes, because there is no material for repairs/spare parts'. By now, there were only 'two or three' saucers left in good working order, lying on a base 'somewhere between Ecuador and Chile', the precise location of which Landig would not tell the vampire-hunter '[even] if I knew it.' The failure of the SS's conquest of Earth from Antarctica, meanwhile, was explained by the (somewhat inaccurate) idea that bacteria cannot survive at sub-zero temperatures, with the end result that every single Nazi stationed there 'became perfectly sterile' and their immune systems shut down due to lack of use, meaning that, if they had flown out to fight in their spaceships, 'a simple cold' would have immediately killed them. Thus, the SS were ultimately defeated by the very same means as the Martians in *The War of the Worlds*! (The explanation in both cases is a bit of a disappointment.) Following his wartime service in 'a certain agency/department which cannot be named', Landig became the Vienna contact for 'one engineer Wuppermann', an Antarctica-based *Wunderwaffen* inventor who acted as intermediary between the South Pole and the Andean bases. Somehow, Wuppermann avoided being killed by germs during his vital foreign liaisons, being shot one day at 11 o'clock outside Police HQ in Buenos Aires instead. Several other members of the saucerian spy-ring were also shot at 11 o'clock in the morning down the years, said Landig, suggesting an occult conspiracy – the number eleven had black magic significance, 'as if the Kabbalah is a factor here.' Yet again, those Jews were to blame.[6]

It has been speculated Landig was really involved in the post-war *Absatzbewegungen* 'ratlines' network of which Vienna was an early waystation, which helped smuggle Nazi war criminals to safety in South America, often in cahoots with anti-Communist elements in the Vatican and US intelligence services – and, according to Landig, these ratlines extended not only into Argentina and Chile, but further down towards the South Pole. Landig had connections with Paul Schäfer (1921-2010), former leader of the one-time 'Colonia Dignidad' colony of pro-Nazi German immigrants in Chile, which would have proved a highly useful link for any fleeing fascists.[7] Colonia Dignidad was a sinister armed compound-cum-Nazi colony founded in the 1950s and allowed to flourish under General Pinochet, reputedly serving as a handy murder-centre and torture camp for dissidents. Equipped with its own runways, farmland, power-plant and basic hospital, the remote 300-strong compound was surrounded by barbed-wire and searchlights, and hid several arms caches. Its leader Paul Schäfer fled there in 1961 after being accused of child molestation, a hobby he allegedly continued on-site.

The place has also been linked to Nazi UFOs. In 2004, whilst a 'political prisoner' in a Canadian jail, the Holocaust denier Ernst Zündel scribbled a story onto some paper 'until his pencil stub wore out' to be smuggled out. Written 'totally from my faulty memory', it told of how his 1970s UFO books drew a big audience in Japan, leading to a Tokyo journalist offering to fund a trip to South America to hunt Nazi saucers. Zündel thought the scheme 'frivolous', so recommended his loyal secretary Sepp go on the trip instead, as he had some old friends and family in Chile, I'm sure we can guess of what kind. The journalist wanted Sepp to fly out dressed in a 'spiffy Nazi uniform', but this may have caused problems at the airport. Once in Chile, they contacted one of Zündel's alleged old co-authors Willibald Mattern (1900-90), official photographer to the Chilean Army, who told them of his previous trip to Colonia Dignidad, where he had spotted 'strange aerial activity going on by even stranger craft', alongside some interesting 'Austrian folk-dance performances'. Mattern concluded that Colonia Dignidad, with its many small family farms, was a 'supply base for fresh fruit and vegetables' for the real parent Nazi UFO-base in Antarctica, from whence saucers would touch down for supplies, or to drop off soldiers and scientists for sunny holidays. Sepp and the Japanese journalist succeeded in finding this remote Nazi El Dorado for themselves, but were captured and interrogated by its inhabitants, one of whom wore an old Nazi cap, before being expelled from the country by Pinochet, following confiscation of their tapes and photos.[8] By claiming it was really a secret saucer-base, perhaps people might be distracted from what Colonia Dignidad was truly used for – shielding fugitive Nazis. If so, Landig's links to its old leader could be explained. Colonia Dignidad still exists, but under a different name and leadership, and has now become a tourist destination cashing in on its notorious past, so if you want to hunt UFOs there yourself, you need no longer be arrested by the Chilean Gestapo.

The factual post-war transfer of defeated Germans from ruined northern regions to distant bastions in the global south had an earlier legendary parallel in Julius Evola; thus, the sordid business of aiding fleeing Nazi war criminals, if that is indeed what Landig did, becomes reborn as something more Romantic. According to one variant of Traditionalist dogma, the original *satya yuga* Golden Age occurred at the North Pole, in Hyperborea or Thule, which in this version had nothing to do with ETs from Venus named Wotan, but was a physical Garden of Eden, during a perfect, long-distant era of sunny bliss when there were no frozen snows to ruin the Aryan life of pleasure. But then some great catastrophe shifted Earth's axis, bringing eternal ice to the North Pole, and forcing the Hyperboreans to migrate southwards; Antarctica now became the new solar paradise instead. There are plenty of alternative versions of this basic myth, one of them created by Julius Evola, who fabulised that the North Pole Hyperboreans were the embodiment of manly *kshatriya* values, worshipping the masculine sun. But, when polar shift destroyed Thule, the Aryans had to migrate south to escape the cold, where they met inferior moon-worshipping races on fictional continents like Lemuria, who were inherently feminine rather than warrior-like in nature. The Hyperboreans mated with these soppy moon-lovers, and so began the Silver Age, or *treta yuga*. As the polar shift combined with this social shift, there occurred 'the alignment of a physical and a metaphysical fact, as if a disorder in Nature were reflecting a certain situation of a spiritual order'. Racial mixing of moon-men and sun-folk led to 'degeneration' in society, due to the incompatible 'fundamental polarity of North and South'. Yet the hardships of long migration, 'the rigour of the climate, the sterility of the soil, the necessity for hunting', would naturally have lent the southbound Nordics 'the temperament of warriors, of conquerors, of navigators, so as to favour that synthesis between spirituality and virility' natural to the white race, which, by returning to Traditionalist ways and a life of brave warfare, could still be recovered. More a spiritual racist than a biological one, Evola accepted some non-Aryans could *become* Aryans simply by emulating the ways of the *kshatriya*. Whilst in works like 1941's *Synthesis of Racial Doctrine* Evola superficially fell in line with fascist Jew-baiting, it was Jews' 'typical attitudes' of money-worship and base materialism that were the alleged problem, not their genes, attitudes 'not necessarily present' in all those with Jewish blood. Actually, such texts were thus a disguised *attack* on Nazi racial doctrines, making it little wonder the SS once rejected him.[9]

There is no archaeological evidence for the existence of Evola's posited polar paradise, but this does not matter if all 'reality' is merely *Maya*, an illusion. Seeking intellectual ballast for such a view, Thule-fanciers could return to the Traditionalist works of René Guénon, who also argued for the existence of Hyperborea, but not using anything so crude as physical proof. Someone who digs into the Arctic ice looking for fossils of god-men 'is doing archaeology, whereas we ourselves are doing initiatic science; and those are two points of view which, even when they touch on the same subjects, cannot coincide in any way.' Guénon believed that, as *kali yuga* progressed, the decline of our world was expressed by it becoming more and more physical in nature, like Serrano's Venusian gods trapped within the Demiurge's fleshly matter, so he seriously advocated the reason we find no bones of ancient polar Aryans is because such godly beings were not yet solid enough to leave any corpses behind them.[10] Or maybe the bones of antique Hyperboreans had simply morphed into ordinary-looking rocks, like the petrified mountain-giants of Miguel Serrano. Recalling *satya yuga* myths about 'a time when precious stones were as common as the most ordinary pebbles are now', Guénon speculates maybe this is literally so: 'It is said that when a treasure is sought for by a person for whom … it is not destined, the gold and precious stones are changed for him into coal and common pebbles; modern lovers of excavations might well turn this particular "legend" to their profit!' When you read about ancient travellers once seeing wonderful dragons on their trips to distant lands, where today there were only mundane crocodiles, this further indicated the existence of both a 'Traditional' or sacred geography in days gone by and a more 'profane' one today. In the past, when human faculties were less atrophied by *kali yuga*, maybe the crocodiles really were dragons to explorers' eyes, much as maybe once the dismal, frozen North Pole was really the solar Eden of Hyperborea. Not marked on any map today, but still sensed by psychically aware persons anyway, were 'Gates of Heaven' and 'Mouths of Hell', places of spiritual influence through which ghostly powers from 'realities of a higher order' could pass, as with the Greek Oracle at Delphi. Yet such 'Traditional centres' could easily become reconfigured as magical wormholes between Venus and Earth designed for the passage of the astral saucer-soul of Adolf Hitler once the likes of Wilhelm Landig and Miguel Serrano got their hands on Guénon's ideas.[11]

* * * * *

For Julius Evola, the poles of North and South, sun and moon, male and female, were every bit as much spiritual principles as literal facts. Thus, he could easily speak about the existence of a 'Blue Island' hidden at the North Pole, waiting to serve as the 'secret centre' for a renaissance of the ancient *kshatriya* soul and way of life, even though the Blue Island, like Guénon's dragons, no longer appeared on any maps. In the early 1950s at the vegetarian commune of 'Haus Edel' in Hesse, a group of ladies calling themselves the 'Michael Circle' were able to establish psychic communication with the non-existent place, whose ghostly residents promised a new 'turning point' was afoot for Germany. This was great news to the Landig Circle, who sought to contact this Blue Island too, considering it a waypoint in the white race's journey back towards the 'Midnight Mountain' or 'Mount Meru', the sacred peak in search of which the prehistoric Aryans had once set out on migrational pilgrimage from their original Indian homeland in the pseudo-history of Friedrich Schlegel. A series of séances were now held in Landig's design-studio, in which plaster casts were poured to allow the Blue Islanders to manifest within the leaden material realm of charred 1950s Vienna. Through meditation, communion was successfully established with the Blue Islanders, who revealed that during the war initiated inner circles of the SS had created Greenland bases to search for the Midnight Mountain themselves. Once this peak had been scaled, the Black Order knew that a 'millennial world transformation' would occur – a truly Himmlerian Fourth Reich in which *kali yuga* iron reverts back into *satya yuga* gold.[12]

The main developers of this complex consolatory myth were Wilhelm Landig's two chief underlings, the first of whom was Erich Halik (1926-95). Halik was the only non-SS member in the initial Landig Circle, serving as a Wehrmacht infantryman instead. A qualified mechanical engineer, it was Halik who supervised the pouring of séance plaster casts. According to his own testimony, he had also discovered the secret of UFO propulsion systems during his day job as a designer for the Austrian ammunition manufacturer Hirtenberger AG. Halik was responsible for diversifying the firm's interests into aerospace, and between 1964 and 1967 registered several patents relating to 'propulsion systems for flying bodies', some of which he presented at UFO conferences, complaining his electromagnetic saucer-engine was already 'proven, in principle', but that he lacked the funds to build functioning prototypes. Halik organised meetings between none other than Viktor Schauberger and the Landig Circle, helping the Green Nazi implosion-engine inventor get articles accepted in Austria's Press detailing his alleged role in the wartime Nazi saucer programme. Eventually, Halik fell out of favour at Hirtenberger AG, spending his final twenty years as a hotel night porter.

Halik was a leading figure in post-war Austrian ufology, helping found the Interplanetary Society in 1959, acting as Vice-President with special responsibility for collating all submitted saucer-sightings from the public. This makes Halik sound as if he was a pure nuts-and-bolts man, but he was not; for Halik, there were two kinds of UFOs, solid and supernatural. From 1951 to 1955 Halik began publishing a series of very bizarre articles in which he said there were two rival polar Nazi saucer-bases, one at the North Pole, headed up by a solar, Luciferic, white light-worshipping branch of the SS, and one at the South Pole, belonging to a lunar, Satanic, black light-worshipping SS cult. The emblems of these two schismatic sects were the Golden Sun and the Black Sun respectively. Some German planes stationed in frozen Norway did indeed bear symbols of circular black discs on their rear fuselage. According to Halik, these were representations of the Black Sun. According to military historians, they were simply black roundels used for identification purposes; planes with them belonged to Group IV of any given Luftwaffe air-wing, rather than a hidden SS Satanic cult, who in any case were meant to live at the *South* Pole, not the *North*, near Norway.[13]

What is this 'Black Sun' so beloved of Esoteric Nazis? For the complete answer I recommend James Pontolillo's massive 2013 book, *The Black Sun Unveiled*; basically, it evolved from uncertain, non-Nazi origins into a 'substitute swastika' now used as a symbol of fascist rebirth, and to dodge modern-day European laws prohibiting display of the real thing. So far, we have briefly encountered versions of it as a free-energy source exploited by *Wunderwaffen* inventors, and as a metaphor for Hyperborea/Venus within the cosmology of Miguel Serrano. For Erich Halik himself, the icon had a few main sources. One was Karl Maria Wiligut (1866-1946), an Austrian Ariosophist and rune-magician who entered the SS in 1933 under the pseudonym Weisthor ('Wise-Thor'), becoming Heinrich Himmler's personal guru; it was he who advised the *Reichsführer*-SS to dismiss Julius Evola's proposals as unrealistic, which was laughable coming from a man who had partly developed his own philosophy during an enforced stay in a Salzburg mental hospital from 1924-27, where he was diagnosed with schizophrenia. If you have ever wondered why the SS had skulls, or *Totenkopf*, on their membership-rings, it was because of Wiligut. His duty was to bestow a sense of invented tradition upon Himmler's Black Order by devising its ceremonial paraphernalia and helping transform Wewelsburg Castle into the supposed Nazi Camelot.

Wiligut claimed descent from a long line of ancient German shaman-kings, the Uiligotis, whose psychic powers, derived from their sacred origin amongst the gods of air and water, like Thor and Wotan, were renowned from prehistoric times onward. Himmler believed this and came to think it meant that Aryans had once mated or 'assimilated' with 'the intelligent beings who had come from Heaven (the stars) to Earth', like Thor, in the distant past to 'form the new humanity' and 'new racial types'. Although there were no records from prehistoric times to prove any of his claims, Wiligut luckily possessed access to the Uiligoti tribe's collective family unconscious, or 'ancestral memory', having been initiated into its secrets by his magician father and grandfather as a youth. His ancestors having founded the 'Second Boso Culture' in 78,000BC, Wiligut held Catholics, Jews and Freemasons guilty for his personal subsequent fall from royal grace and into a mental asylum, together with the loss of the First World War, and edited his own newspaper, *The Iron Broom*, arguing the need to sweep them out of Germanic life. The Bible was actually written in German, and the true Christ was an ancient Aryan deity called Krist, whose name was later hijacked, he said. Wiligut further recalled an age when giants and dwarfs walked the land, and there were multiple suns in the sky. Once it became known Wiligut had been officially certified as mentally ill – and, to be fair, it wasn't at all obvious – Himmler accepted his resignation and the return of his ceremonial ring. Beforehand, his main duty had been to sit in an office writing down his 'memories' from the last 80,000 years and seeing which bits could be used to design mantras, insignia and pagan wedding ceremonies for SS Knights. He was also available to comment on the latest *Ahnenerbe* discoveries by cross-checking them against the astral records. Once again, history is divined 'intuitively', via quasi-Gnostic means, to be precisely what you want it to be.[14]

Also buried within Wiligut's Jungian ancestral memory was the former existence of a prehistoric Black Sun named 'Santur', as confirmed in a series of fragmentary verses in a composite language given the collected title of

The Halgarita Charms, over a thousand of which Karl had purportedly been forced to memorise as a child by his wizard father. Thus, there was direct written proof of Santur's reality, even though Wiligut himself was the one who had done the writing. The sage's gibberish was then parsed by his disciples, chiefly the 'apocalyptic physicist', Ariosophist and humble building surveyor Emil Rüdiger (1885-1952), who somehow achieved the gnosis that meaningless jumbles like '*Maya faeki kloig/Kat ar sunur fraeg*' meant 'all maternal receptacles and paternal agents of the Creation are thus sanctified by you, eternal Mother of God.' Wiligut's poems were developed by Rüdiger into an elaborate cosmology in which this Black Sun had once engaged in an age-old stellar battle lasting 1.5 million years with its opposing twin, our current sun. The two stars fired black and white light into each other until eventually today's Golden Sun had won, hence its lone visible presence in our skies. But this battle was really a battle for our Hyperborean ancestors' souls, as light from Santur and its reverse-*doppelgänger* shone not only upon their fleshly bodies but their astral ones, which, powered by the absorption of sunlight into the human endocrine system, thrived upon the alternation between black and white in a process termed 'fire rhythm'. After the Golden Sun finally defeated Santur 230,000 years ago, this flux disappeared, and the Hyperboreans (or 'Stone People', as Rüdiger preferred), devolved into mere Nordic Aryans, who were still great, but no longer actual god-folk. The burnt-out Black Sun still orbited in outer space, but it was black so we couldn't see it; its last regular appearance came during the days of Homer, who saw it pass by like 'a breathing lung' in the pre-Classical Greek morning sky. Yet, by re-establishing psychic contact with the Dark Star via rune-gymnastics and special exercises involving your right-hand middle finger (which must not be performed incorrectly, as 'this will produce insanity'), white Nordics could evolve back upwards into god-like Stone People once more.

When in 1930 Pluto was discovered, Rüdiger excitedly explained this was actually Santur reborn, 'come to assist the cosmic development of our solar system toward the master-plan' of racial regeneration. It appears that, when shining out 'aether particles' during its lifetime, the Golden Sun had automatically allowed them to accumulate around the dead Black Sun, thereby meaning that, when time came for the Golden Sun to burn out and die too, its light could be reborn in the current Black Sun of Pluto, which would then regenerate again in a process of 'active pole-reversal', as codified in the myth of the Phoenix, gloriously reborn from its own ashes. As one sun dies, the other is born again. Pluto was also the giant wolf Fenrir, who eats the sun at Time's end in Norse mythology; by swallowing the sun, the wolf transforms into a new one, like Santur. Little Red Riding Hood was also our current bright red-glowing Golden Sun, gulped by the gaping maw of Santur only to be remade anew. Thus, fairy tales were just encoded knowledge about stars from the Nordic unconscious, as some in the *Ahnenerbe* taught.[15]

Wiligut required no ancestral memories to invent Santur, though; he could just have read the Theosophy founder Madame Blavatsky's 1888 book

The Secret Doctrine, well-known in Ariosophist circles, where she talked of a hidden 'Central Sun' at the heart of our solar system. According to the Jewish Kabbalah, this beamed out 'black light', but rival Aryan traditions spoke of it as being the source of all 'creative light'. The implication was that Aryan cosmology spiritualises matter by shining its holy light upon it, whereas Jewish cosmology does the reverse, as with Serrano's Jewish Demiurge.[16]

Wiligut's occultist friend Peryt Shou (1873-1953) adopted similar ideas, following a revelation when he heard rustling leaves in a park spell out a psychic mantra reading 'I am your Lamb and I will follow you.' Thinking this message had beamed down from the constellation Perseus, Shou changed his pen name from plain old Albert Schultz to something more exotic and pursued a programme of rune-gymnastics aimed at creating an 'antenna-cross' within his body through which he could receive further space-telegrams. The Central Sun now contained within it 'an animate point', the home of God, and man's body was a tiny microcosmic mirror of it; by sending out 'an infinite number of circles', the sentient Black Sun became 'one infinitely large circle which also contains within itself the smallest circle'. Hypothesising that gland-stimulation could produce liquid crystals in our bloodstream which turned our minds into radio receivers for 'the murmur of the spheres', Shou thought of this 'murmur' as a cosmic memory-bank akin to Wiligut's own ancestral memory, or Serrano's *Minne*-song of Aryan blood. We had twin astral-body 'teleions' or 'tele-bodies' located within the Central Sun and attached to our physical bodies down here on Earth; by linking up the two ends of the soul-wire, occultists could achieve 'the manifestation of the disc', which seemed to be a method of expelling negative energy out through your belly button via 'teleion-oscillation'. This disc was 'a kind of incarnation for our inner enemies', and when Christ cast devils out from a possessed man and into some swine, it was a metaphor for him exorcising the man's astral impurities in discoid form. Whilst Shou could not have been talking about miniature flying saucers here – his main Black Sun texts being written in 1910 and 1912 – it is easy to see how his words could be mis-used, especially given how very confusing his prose style is.

Meditation upon the sacred swastika was one way to manufacture these bloodborne radio-crystals, and Shou's own reception was clearly very good as in 1923 he published a text, *Medusa, the Demon of Europe*, conveying his intuition that the date of 20 April would prove of great significance in the 'cosmological evolution' of Germany – this turning out to be the birth-date of Adolf Hitler back in 1889. Humanity would soon be stung by the 'cosmic spider', unleashing destruction onto the world prior to its ultimate regeneration; negative discs of energy would be manifested, only to be dispelled in favour of something better, promised Shou. Astrological radio broadcasts of 'ultraviolet spiritual light' from the Black Sun proved prophetic, and in 1935 Shou penned a Nazi-friendly tract, *The Spiritual Weapons of Nordic Man*, which ends with the exhortation 'There will be no turning back for the new marching columns [of the Wehrmacht], the Earth will be transformed into a Sun!' He didn't win over many mainstream Nazis, but as a friend of Lanz von Liebenfels and Wiligut, Shou's influence was felt nonetheless, particularly when the Landig Circle later read his books.[17]

Alchemy was Erich Halik's other main source for the Black Sun. Known as the *sol niger*, the alchemical Black Sun had many meanings, sometimes appearing as the negative polar opposite of a Golden Sun, which represented the Philosopher's Stone, whereas it itself signified crude matter like lead. Or, it could be the opposite, the Black Sun as the superior immaterial shadow of the grossly material Golden Sun of physical gold. Maybe, as the material sun, the Golden one was really the Black one, appearances being deceptive. Most commonly, it appeared as the mark of the *nigredo*, the first stage of the Great Work of alchemy. By burning or 'cooking' lead, decomposing it into black dust, the base metal was cleansed, creating fertile ashes from which gold would later grow, becoming green in a stage named *viriditas*. This was probably the light of the Green Ray/Green Thunderbolt that Miguel Serrano mentioned pouring out from his own Black Sun in his Nazi poems:

> O Sun of Gold that reflects the Black Sun!
> O Black Sun that hides the Ray of Green Light!
> Withdraw your luminous shadow,
> Rend your veils, so that
> I may see the hidden face,
> Veiled by your disc,
> By the revolving of your swastika,
> Because the one who is hidden there
> Is I myself.[18]

Viriditas achieved, the process could then begin anew, again and again, in the never-ending cycle of chemical 'reflux distillation', like continually turning an hourglass upside-down. Alchemy spoke of an inherent connection between the 'microcosm', the individual human soul, and the 'macrocosm', the soul of the universe or God, and some strands of late Ariosophy appear like pseudo-astronomical revivals of this notion. In the work of Jung, the alchemical Black Sun later stood for an individual psyche which had become 'dead' via the invasion of the Black Dog of depression, and which needed to be 'greened' again into new health, via the invasion of the conscious mind with beneficial elements from the unconscious one. In an imaginative sense, the UFO could also do this to a dull, materialist-minded, post-war world in dire need of Romantic reconquest by its own shadow-self.[19]

To the Landig Group too, post-war Western society was blackened ash which needed to be re-greened. The vulgar lead of exoteric Hitlerian National Socialism must be burnt away and purged so that a new, more verdant esoteric Himmlerian Nazism could be reborn. This explained why the benign Black Sun SS cult at the South Pole were described as 'Satanic' in nature, not normally a positive term; the Black Sun contained all the potential for glorious rebirth, whilst the Golden Sun, although it may have *looked* healthy, was actually dying, like exoteric Hitlerian Germany at its point of greatest military success, immediately prior to Stalingrad. So, maybe the Black Sun SS were Satanic right now, but that just meant their evil would be burnt away into a force for good some time later, whereas with the light-bringing Luciferian SS at the North Pole, it was the reverse. Or this was the case sometimes; Landig & Co's ideas were inconsistent. Remarkably, Erich Halik beat Jung to print in interpreting UFOs as living alchemical symbols of pending societal transformation, as the latter's seminal *Flying Saucers: A Modern Myth of Things Seen in the Skies* didn't appear until 1958, whereas between 1951 and 1955 Halik had contributed articles to the Austrian paranormal magazine *Man and Fate*, making similar arguments, albeit from a pro-fascist perspective. Jung had presciently been collecting clippings about unusual aerial phenomena since 1946, even before Kenneth Arnold's fateful sighting of the very first flying saucers the next year, and read everything on the subject he could get his hands on, so it seems entirely plausible he could have read Halik's own pieces; if so, a major school of ufology has partial hidden Nazi origins.[20]

As an inventor of UFO propulsion systems himself, Halik believed the Nazis really had built physical Viktor Schauberger-type implosion-engine saucers, so in his 1954 article *No Invasion from Outer-Space* he argued the 1952 meeting of George Adamski with the blonde, blue-eyed 'Venusian' Orthon was actually an encounter with a South Pole Nazi. That Orthon wore shiny metallic clothing tinted red and brown was an obvious nod to the emblematic colours of the Green Nazi 'Blood and Soil' cult, he said. Besides, Adamski swore the giant cigar-like mother ship from which Orthon's smaller saucer had emerged bore both a swastika and tell-tale black roundels, indicating it belonged to the Antarctic Black Sun squadron, as also shown by Orthon's swastika-bearing footprints. The nuts-and-bolts establishment of this Polar Reich, Halik argued in his 1954 *Proclamation of the Polar Empire*, was the necessary first stage in a millenarian transformation of society through 'worldwide alchemy'. With the defeated Aryan race's collective 'solar plexus' currently 'in a state of darkness or melancholy' as represented by the 'sick, leprous' Black Sun, the polar accumulation of physical SS saucer-forces under the sign of the *sol niger* would inevitably lead to the sympathetic appearance of supernatural Nazi discs in the sky too. By flying craft emblazoned with the Black Sun roundel, the Satanic SS would magically raise *vimanas* from other dimensions. 'Satan' was now revealed as 'Saturn', the planet which caused melancholy according to old astrological belief, but from blackest melancholy traditionally arose the *viriditas*-like inspiration of genius, like that of Heinrich Himmler.

The night is always darkest before dawn, and if you looked *very* closely at the Luftwaffe's Black Sun roundels, Halik said, you would see they were actually deep purple, a hopeful sign of approaching daybreak shone out by 'the Purple Sun shining inside the Hollow Earth'. In some versions of alchemy, the purple stage of *purpur* appears immediately after *nigredo*, as a precursor to burnt black matter becoming red in the beautiful stage of *rubedo*, which occurs immediately prior to the final manifestation of the Golden Sun of the Philosopher's Stone, the Elixir of Life which could rejuvenate and resurrect. To Wilhelm Landig, this purple light signified ultraviolet rays from Santur, invisible to human eyes at present, but nonetheless a 'world-penetrating light, which shines for the knowledgeable'. This 'invisible mental light and fire from the Wolf Age of Thule' stood in direct contrast to the 'material golden shine of the daylight' of the visible sun, which represented only 'the arrogant power of gold and its Masters and slaves', the Jews and capitalists.[21] To Halik, the competing interplay of Black and Golden Sun SS was cosmically necessary, as shown by the cryptic symbolism of the chessboard; if all its squares were either black or white, neither side could win. The colour white, as blazed by the Golden Sun, was 'the sum of all colours and is humanly detectable only due to its material origin', whereas the superior Black Sun was total 'non-colour' or invisibility, representing 'anti-matter' and 'the circle of the revealed God', which was better intuited psychically. So, to the truly knowledgeable white supremacist, black was ironically best after all.

Halik also linked Nazi saucers to the *Sangraal* – which, again, wasn't a cup at all, but something borderline incomprehensible. Some *Ahnenerbe* scholars thought the Holy Grail had been hidden away by the Cathars, a schismatic Franco-Italian Christian Gnostic sect brutally eradicated during the 1200s, and in his 1952 piece *The Mystery of the Manisolas*, Halik argued non-physical UFOs were actually manifestations of the Round Table, or *Mani-Isola*, around which the Cathars had held holy feasts in the *Sangraal's* honour, like Himmlerian Grail-Knights at Wewelsburg. So, any supernatural saucers now had to be called *manisolas*. 'Mani' was Sanskrit for 'jewel' or 'bead', interpreted as being the Philosopher's Stone in the shape of a *viriditas*-green emerald, shiny stones formerly treasured by the ancient Indian Aryans of Schlegel, who had polished them into lenses to store concentrated sunlight 'and other cosmic influences' within, so as to power their own ancient *vimana*-saucers with 'high-quality energy' of a Green nature. This was all reflected in the classic Indian Buddhist mantra-chant *Om, Mani padme, Hum*; hence Miguel Serrano's later claim some SS pilots flew saucers purely by chanting. The Cathars' own *Mani*-emerald was the Holy Grail, and the *Mani-Isola* was their 'Grail Table' or 'Isle of *Mani*', which was truly a Jung-style *mandala*, a circular symbol containing within itself all possible opposites, particularly light and dark, life and death and male and female, a circular chessboard, in a way. King Arthur's Round Table was thus actually 'the primitive Paradise' within which Adam and Eve had united to create the first human child. Indeed, UFOs' initial appearance in Earth's skies had occurred not in 1947 but directly following mankind's expulsion from our original Hyperborean Eden, as a symbol both of what humanity had just lost, and what it would eventually regain – rather like Esoteric Nazis with the lost Third and forthcoming Fourth Reichs, *kali yuga* becoming *satya yuga*. Yet, as Halik argued in his 1952 *Isles of the Dead Over Us*, the Isle of Life was also its opposite Isle of the Dead, so paranormal *manisola* UFOs must be approached with care, lest they killed you. Their numinous, spiritually creative nature could inspire positive alchemical change in a witness' spirit, but as they also contained a competing negative 'strong chaotic element', they could just as easily disintegrate your soul. *Manisola* saucers themselves were 'indestructible' and had no need to obey any physical laws like gravity, however, as, like God, they transcended all possible opposites by becoming the cosmic centre-point where 'First and Last matter meet in an intimate embrace.'[22]

This intimate and wonderfully diverse embrace of black and white amongst the clouds is seen at work in Wilhelm Landig's 1971 novelisation of Esoteric Nazi UFO mythology, *Godlets Against Thule*, which became a big underground neo-fascist hit, spawning two sequels. Here, *manisolas*, or 'bio-machines', become manifestations of the Midnight Mountain lying beyond the Blue Island, which live, reproduce and die in a seven-part life cycle, akin to the seven-part chemical cycle of much alchemy. Landig's *manisolas* begin as circles of pure light, then solidify into metallic foo-fighter discs 'with a high zirconium content'. These zirconium discs are female Great Mothers, or *Magna Maters*, a *mater*-ialisation of the cosmic female principle which then develops a sort of compensatory penis, has sex with itself and creates the nucleus of a new *manisola* to grow within the confines of its androgynous male-female womb, which is finally expelled as a small circle of energetic light in a process 'corresponding to a birthing technique'. The interracial inter-sex mother then rolls his/herself into a ball, which explodes and dies, leaving only fragments of copper behind. In the daylight these round *manisolas* appear silvery but at night glow with sparks, 'so strong as to wreathe them in fire', like classic foos. Notable is 'their power of reaction against pursuers, like that of a rational creature, far exceeding any possible self-steering or radio control'. So that is how the misidentified 1945 Nazi foo-drones escaped Allied attackers – they were *alive*, not radio-controlled. The foos' mass birth in the skies over late-war Nazi Germany must have been pregnant with some symbolic, Jungian significance, as opposed to a crude military one; maybe they prefigured the dying Reich's later rebirth in Antarctica. To the medieval Cathars and *Minnesänger* who also saw them and called them the *Sangraal*, *manisola* discs were 'signatures of the highest love', just like Himmlerian Esoteric Nazism in a wider sense, implied Landig.[23] To mistake a supernatural portent of Nazi rebirth for a nuts-and-bolts craft would thus be to mistake a solid gold chalice for the real Holy Grail, just like the foolish material-minded *Ahnenerbe*-man does at the climax of *Indiana Jones and the Last Crusade*, immediately before collapsing into dust like Dracula exposed to sunlight.

* * * * *

Erich Halik's articles seem the first serious elaborations of the Nazi polar ice-base myth to appear in print, although they had only limited influence at the time, being just too obscure for normal *volk* to understand. It was only later, in the 1970s and 1980s, when Ernst Zündel began to re-promote their contents in massively simplified and literalistic form that they truly began to catch on.[24] Presumably this was why Landig himself later published the more easily digested pill of his own *Thule* trilogy of pulp thriller novels, strangely not yet fully translated into English.[25] The first book, *Godlets Against Thule* – meaning 'False Jewish Idols vs The Hyperborean SS God-Men' – was subtitled *A Fiction Full of Facts*, being intended to act as a handy Polar Reich UFO encyclopaedia. And what fun facts these were! The flag of the UN, a circular map of the globe centred upon the North Pole, is coloured blue and white as a covert symbol of its control by the similarly hued flag of Israel; the Ark of the Covenant was really an 'astral accumulator' weapon used by Jewish magicians and Freemasons like Winston Churchill to draw in and backwards-transmute healthy, 'fertilising' Aryan 'force-fields' into 'a partly racial, partly cosmopolitan substance', converting the North Pole into a corrupt Hebrew Pole 'so as to pervert it'; and concentration camp corpses were only innocent German victims of Allied bombing raids, mislabelled to blacken Himmler's good name. By educating himself about the many UFO-related *Wunderwaffen* invented by the Nazis, perhaps the reader could be freed from his Jewish-imposed state of false consciousness; constant references to the books of Julius Evola and various *Ahnenerbe* scholars are dropped in too, so that you could go away and pursue Himmlerian gnosis even further.

Landig's heroes are two German airmen, Recke ('Brave Warrior/Berserker') and Reimer ('Poet/Bard'), rescued by the Waffen-SS officer Gutmann ('Good Man'), following a late-war air crash in the Arctic. Recke and Reimer's mission had been to liaise with a hidden SS-base in the remote snows of Arctic Canada, Point 103. Here, *Wunderwaffen* are maintained for future use; Landig sometimes lied he heard the basic 'true' story from 'the mutterings of a prisoner in an English internment camp' when a POW himself in 1945-47.[26] As Recke and Reimer also end up in a British POW camp at the novel's end, this implies he heard it from one of the novel's central protagonists directly, although the book is really more a fantastic allegory of his Circle's psychic attempts to contact the Blue Island. Point 103 is unknown not only to the Allies, but to most Nazis. However, several sympathetic foreign delegates from an occult version of Landig's World Anti-Communist League are flown there in special V-7 flying saucer-helicopters to attend subterranean conferences in full traditional national fancy dress, including Japanese adherents of the Red Sun, as seen on their national flag: 'The Red Sun and the Black Sun serve the same master!'[27] There are also Arabs from clandestine Islamic brotherhoods and, inevitably, Tibetan lamas, already in deep telepathic communication with the Midnight Mountain, which they call *Ri-rap-hlumpo*. There is even a black Ethiopian delegate;

Landig is eager to dismiss Nazi racism as a falsehood by adopting all these esoterically enlightened non-whites as honorary Aryans, according to the 'spiritual racism' theories of Julius Evola.

Recke and Reimer are both amazed and confused, so SS-officer Gutmann acts as their handy expository guide, informing them of Point 103's mission to make psychic contact with the Blue Island as a prelude to Nazi world-revolution. Following German surrender in 1945, Point 103 withdraws allegiance to the traitorous Hitlerian German State and transfers it to Himmlerian Thule/Hyperborea instead; all German military insignia is replaced with the deep purple Black Sun. When their revolution is complete, these insignia will all magically turn a shining silver-white, *sol niger* becoming *sol alba*, in rehabilitation of White Power. The presence of white-hued *manisolas* in Point 103's vicinity is a clear sign the Himmlerian SS are on the right track. Thus educated, Recke and Reimer fly out to Prague to try and rescue the fake saucer-inventor Rudolf Schriever, before going to retrieve a French alchemist named Bélisse (named after the Gauls' sun god, Bélisane), who aided the *Ahnenerbe*'s search for the Holy Grail; Point 103 has many alchemical laboratories, and as one who is party to the Cathars' secret *manisola* knowledge, he is needed there. The alchemist is also needed to act as a handy mouthpiece for Erich Halik's opinions about the whole topic. Sadly, Bélisse dies falling down a mountain and the Luftwaffe pilots trek to Franco's Spain, to await new instructions.

The rest of the novel details their criss-crossing global journey in a futile search for the way back to Point 103, meeting various foreign allies who tell them more about the Jewish plot to keep the Aryan Black Sun from turning white; it seems Mount Sinai, where Moses received the Ten Commandments from a wicked false godlet, is a *kali yuga* parody of Mount Meru, from which Jewish anti-pole evil, in the invisible shape of a grey magic circle, now emanates, dissolving nations into multi-racial chaos. The airmen end up captured by lamas in Tibet, where Himalayan monks explain that, by paranormally helping Hitler achieve power, the Tibetans hoped to work the good will of Agartha. However, Hitler and 'certain forces in the Reich government, identified by the number 666', then foolishly allied themselves with the black magic city of Shambhala and its ruling 'Lord of Fear', meaning the Tibetans had wasted their time: Landig had obviously read *The Morning of the Magicians*. Recke and Reimer finally escape into Savitri Devi's India, then still part of the British Empire, where they are shipped off to a POW camp – where, if you believe Herr Landig, they then told him their story. Once released, they find Germany and Austria in ruins, native white, blonde women mating with black US monkey-soldiers, like Lanz von Liebenfels' worst nightmares come true, and Point 103 totally inaccessible. The war of the godlets against Thule has reached its apogee. Like the Landig Circle, the heroes must sit tight, await the inevitable decline of the horrible 'Fish Age' of Jew-created Christianity, and keep the fascist faith. Stumbling through the ruins, the Germans are the new Wandering Jews, robbed of their true Hyperborean homeland, a culminating *kali yuga* inversion which surely means total solar pole-reversal must be near at hand.[28]

Ernst Zündel read Landig's novel and spliced it with post-war tabloid legends about Hitler being spirited away to Antarctic wastes by submarine in his late 1970s Samisdat books, *Secret Nazi Polar Expeditions* and *Hitler at the South Pole*.[29] When combined with Miguel Serrano's exciting new titles about the Hitler avatar sleeping beneath Antarctica guarded by Wotan's ravens, they led to the standard Nazi survival myth increasingly shifting focus towards the southern hemisphere, not northern Arctic Canada. Accordingly, Landig's 1980 sequel, *Wolf-Time for Thule*, directly inspired by Zündel's own tales, featured not Luftwaffe pilots but U-boat sailors whose task was to relocate Point 103's personnel and *Wunderwaffen* down to Antarctica, to fit in better with other competing mythologies, lessening unnecessary contradictions. Without doing so, there was a risk Landig's narrative might not sound plausible. Noble naval officers Krall ('Claw') and Hellfeldt ('Field of Bright Light') assist in this task, being educated in Esoteric Nazism by one SS-Major Eyken ('Oak'). Eyken explains that the North Pole, traditional home of white Hyperborean light, has developed a black spot of total evil, emanating from a US military base in Greenland. The old White Sun of Hyperborea has now become a counterfeit *kali yuga* Golden Sun of Mammon, illuminating only the Jews' and capitalists' worship of glittering gold. Thus, the Luciferian White Sun SS must flee south towards the Satanic Black Sun SS at their own base of Point 211, thereby becoming a tiny white spot in Santur's black heart, as with the small dots in the yin-yang symbol of the Tao.

Whilst the South Pole is inherently evil and Jewish, the centre-point of all demonic energies, if the Jews are tapping the Aryan energy of the North Pole from Greenland and using it against Germany, why should the SS not do the same thing to them in reverse? By turning Jewish black magic against the Jews themselves, the Black Sun will transform into a White Sun again. On the way south, the sailors stop over in South America, discovering a hidden Nazi UFO factory beneath the Andes called Mime's Smithy, Mime being a blacksmith who forged sacred swords in Wagnerian mythology; this *Alpenfestung* cave-complex is the new Agartha. On their later travels, sometimes by U-boat, sometimes by V-7 helicopter-saucer, the heroes learn of disturbing post-war Jewish plans to dominate humanity through mind-control drugs and robot policemen, and that the Soviet dictator Josef Stalin (1878-1953) was born a goblin from the 'Tribe of the Yellow Eyes'. Ultimately, the Krall and Hellfeldt are unable to find their way back to Point 211 and must return to Vienna, where they find their homes have been given away to strangers as part of the mob-rule of 'democracy'. Despondent, the heroes recall the myth of the giant wolf Fenrir swallowing the dying sun at Ragnarok. This *kali yuga* age, they conclude, must indeed be *Wolf-Time for Thule*, with the utter devastation of Vienna being a symbol of immediate

Nazi rebirth from the jaws of defeat. This book appeared in 1980, though, by which point it should have been clear this was not going to happen. Accordingly, Landig's final entry in the series, 1991's *Rebellion for Thule*, which deals with a group of neo-Nazi schoolboys rising up against their hated left-wing history teacher on account of his appalling failure to tell them the true facts about his pupils' noble racial origins in Atlantis, developed an entirely new mythology linking in with that year's number one news item of the First Gulf War, but that is a story for later.[30]

* * * * *

The final initial member of the Landig Circle was Rudolf J. Mund (1920-85) – we met him briefly earlier, introducing Miguel Serrano to a Viennese *Wunderwaffen* inventor reduced to selling cans of Jewish Coca-Cola mind-control drugs from a kiosk. Mund believed the entire white race was being 'cooked', in alchemical terms, subjected to a process of trial by fire at the hands of Allied victors, Jews and the Catholic Anti-Pope. 'Gloom infiltrates like bad weather across the land,' Mund moaned in 1955, a process he optimistically estimated may reach its nadir by 1962. The only recourse was to withdraw into meditation, undertaken 'with a purity of heart in order to form a vessel [out of oneself] with which [one] can later receive the hard rays of the SOL ALBA [White Sun]', and 'imitate Chinese Wisdom ... through Doing-by-Not-Doing'.[31] During his youth, Mund had led a more active life, becoming a teenage Austrian Nazi storm trooper even when membership of the Party was illegal in the country. In 1939, Mund joined the Waffen-SS, rising to the rank of SS-*Obersturmführer*. Captured by US forces on 10 January 1945, he was delighted to find one fellow POW camp inmate was a leading light of the *Ahnenerbe* and best-selling fantasy novelist, Edmund Kiss (1886–1960).

To understand Kiss' work, you must first know the pseudo-scientific ideas of the insane Austrian astronomer Hanns Hörbiger (1860–1931), who notoriously didn't believe in the existence of stars, thinking the Milky Way consisted entirely of sparkling ice. Surprisingly, he was not the first to think so; Scottish astronomer John Finleyson (1770–1854) had previously claimed all stars are made of ice and God had put them there purely 'to amuse us'.[32] Hörbiger felt that ranks of massive, planet-sized ice-blocks encircled our solar system in an impassable white ring, which was then shone through by light from a very few actual distant stars out there way beyond the ice-ring, giving Earthlings the illusion of millions of suns twinkling at us via their multiplied reflection off the massed ice crystals; any photos claiming to show otherwise were just fakes. Any mathematical objections were also illegitimate, as 'Mathematics is nothing but lies!' Hörbiger had been an engineer, developing a low-friction automatic steel disc-valve for use in blast-furnaces and engines. But Hörbiger's creation had simply 'come to him' one day in a Gnostic-style vision, not a process of rational, step-by-step logic. It was precisely the same with Hörbiger's unbreakable perception that the Milky Way was purest frost. 'Instead of trusting me you trust equations!' he would shout at opponents. 'How long will you need to learn that mathematics is valueless and deceptive?'

Hörbiger's full theory, as elaborated in his 1913 *Glacial Cosmogony*, was called *Welteislehre*, or 'World Ice Theory' (WEL), teaching that, once upon a solar system, there had been a vast super-sun, millions of times bigger than our own, next to which had orbited a correspondingly massive planet, covered by layers of ice hundreds of miles thick. This Hyperborea-like ice planet fell into the mega-sun and melted, generating jets of super-charged steam which made the sun explode, vomiting out lumps of molten rock which solidified into our current planetary-system. Clouds of oxygen were also expelled, reacting with hydrogen to create bodies of space-water. As space is cold, this water froze into the army of icebergs we now mistake for stars. Sometimes an ice-block enters our sun's gravitational field, falling into it, melting and creating sunspots. Hailstorms can result from such icebergs crossing Earth's orbit prior to finally dropping into the sun. Being higher up and thus exposed to more ice, our moon is continually being covered with ever more frozen layers of ice on its surface and will eventually get so heavy it collapses to Earth, causing mass extinction. Earth had several other smaller moons which became top-heavy with cosmic ice millennia ago, their impact sinking Atlantis and causing the biblical Great Flood. Hörbiger's main proof for all this was visionary. In infancy, Hörbiger liked to stare at the moon through a telescope. He thought it looked cold; and, suddenly, just *knew* this was because it was covered in ice. Later, he had a dream in which Earth became a giant pendulum swinging on an ever-growing luminous string that eventually broke, revealing gravitational laws compelling space-bergs to be sucked into the sun. Awaking, he knew the entire universe could now be explained by a never-ending pitiless battle between ice and fire. In 1894, he observed molten iron fall onto snow, causing the soil beneath to explode under the pressure of jets of steam from the melt-water, recapitulating in microcosm how a giant ice planet had once dropped into a super-sun, thus forging the solar system.

Being a 790-page book which argued stars did not exist, *Glacial Cosmogony* made little initial impact; the unqualified Hörbiger had to enlist the amateur moon-mapper Philip Fauth (1867-1941) as co-author, to couch his visions in technical terms to make them sound vaguely plausible. In 1918, inspired by propaganda trickery of the First World War, Hörbiger tried appealing direct to the general public instead of qualified astronomers, rushing out pamphlets, books, posters, movies and radio broadcasts, together with a whole WEL newspaper, *The Key to World Events*. Dying in 1931, Hörbiger himself was not a card-carrying Nazi, but the future Führer Adolf Hitler loved his ideas anyway, planning to build a huge space-museum in Linz once the coming war was won. It would have three floors celebrating history's greatest astronomers, with 'the Copernicus of the twentieth century' getting the top tier all to himself, confirming him as the greatest genius of all. Hörbiger's actual genius was to claim loudly that WEL was a healthy opposite to 'Jewish Science', which rejected it as nonsense. Thus, you were either with WEL, or with the Jews; once the Nazis were in power, firms run by patriotic WEL-supporters refused jobs to sceptics, whilst resistant astronomers were smeared as Jew-lovers. The WEL was less a scientific theory, more a poetic 'astronomy of the invisible', and following Hörbiger's death ever more connections were fabricated between his cosmic ice and legends of frozen Hyperborea: 'Our Nordic ancestors grew strong in ice and snow; belief in the WEL is consequently the natural heritage of Nordic Man,' it was said. Possibly Hörbiger's visions had been Jungian 'racial memories' of prior moon-falls written into the genes of his Aryan forefathers, then passed down by their collective ethnic memory; folktales about dragons and devils were really images of Aryan man's prior struggles against falling ice-moons. One believer wrote of how WEL demonstrated the universe was not 'a piece of dead machinery', but a living being 'which hands down from generation to generation its burning force'. Thus, Nordic domination of the globe was quite literally written in the stars (not that the stars were actually there, of course).

The perpetual struggle between space-fire and space-ice reflected the endless war between Aryans and Jews below. Eventually, the slow descent of our ice-laden moon would create an increased gravitational pull, causing Aryans to become white frost-giants, in the same way dinosaurs had been stretched out from tiny lizards during previous moon-falls. Falling moons also tore holes in our atmosphere, allowing passage for cosmic rays, making monkeys mutate into humans. But negative mutations could also occur, hence the Jewish beast-men. As different ice-moons had orbited different parts of the planet, having different effects upon the local fauna, this accounted for disparities between the globe's many races. Therefore, the destiny of mankind was linked inextricably with the destiny of the celestial bodies – WEL became a sort of racial astrology. So associated did WEL and Nazism become that the Party officially stated that belief in it was not *compulsory* – just strongly encouraged. *Ahnenerbe* meteorologists like Hans Robert Scultetus (1904–76) sought to use the WEL for long-term weather-forecasts, alongside his other research into 'heavenly apparitions' sighted over Abyssinia. In 1936, the 'Pyrmonter Protocol' was signed, giving official SS patronage to the theory; two of Hörbiger's sons were also accepted into the *Ahnenerbe*. According to the Protocol, WEL was 'the intellectual gift of a genius', so much so that all future research into it could only be pursued with permission of a designated 'spiritual leader' working under Heinrich Himmler himself – otherwise, scientists might discover evidence it was not true.

Like Hitler, Himmler was a big personal fan of the idea. He had enquiries made as to whether clouds obscuring the sun might possibly lead to mutation of genetic material, as Hörbiger's work implied, and felt his advisor Wiligut's ancient clairvoyant memories of prehistoric times acted as further evidence of the WEL theory's correctness. Accepting Hörbiger's ideas of ancient moon-collisions, he thought the presence on our planet of sky gods like Thor who mated with Wiligut's kingly ancestors many millennia ago was brought about in the first place 'by an enormous Earth-catastrophe that ended with the union of our Earth with one of these stars [i.e. moons] that gravitated towards us.' Before V-2 *Wunderwaffen* rockets were first launched, some WEL-believers even fretted about their piercing of the atmosphere possibly exposing Earth to deluge by space-bergs. Hörbiger argued that to bother about coherence in any theory was a 'deadly vice', and that 'objective science is a pernicious invention,' which meant he had little qualms in simply altering his basic theory at will in face of any objections; the *Ahnenerbe* operated similarly.[33]

The explorer Edmund Kiss was one of Hörbiger's chief cheerleaders, and provided an early literary model for Wilhelm Landig in his fictional-factual 1930s *Atlantis* novel-sequence, detailing how the Aryan-populated continent in question had been destroyed by a previous ice-moon, necessitating migration southwards. In 1928 Kiss traversed South America, unearthing evidence white Atlantean refugees had fled from moon-made Great Floods into the Andes, where Landig's Nazis later built their Mime's Smithy UFO factory in *Wolf-Time for Thule*. Joining the *Ahnenerbe*, Kiss went to Abyssinia seeking remains of African ice-moons, and a prior Aryan civilisation which had ruthlessly maintained its racial stock by keeping black people as slaves. In 1928 Kiss had already found a giant carved stone head which he claimed depicted an ancient Atlantean-Aryan, whom he made the narrator of one of his novels, employed as a prehistoric WEL-adherent astronomer. Kiss' 1930s books were a metaphor for the potential of future German rebirth under Nazism; if Nordics could survive the moon-born sinking of Atlantis, surely they could rise again following comparatively trivial defeat in the First World War. For ruined Atlantis in Kiss' books, read ruined Vienna in Landig's.[34]

Encountering the best-selling 'Poet of Atlantis' in captivity delighted Rudolf J. Mund; when he kept meeting him again at new camps following transfers, it seemed like fate. They would spend hours discussing their race's icy origins and SS-*Obersturmbannführer* Kiss' future plans for missions to Tibet, as well as his time in Hitler's personal bodyguard. A fan of Kiss' novels, Mund thought the tales spun by the older man re-enchanted the good name of the SS, then being blackened by revelations of wartime atrocities. Genuinely believing the SS were a caste of warrior-knights engaged in a righteous pan-European battle against Marxism, Mund was desperate to discover a better esoteric Nazism lying hidden behind the discredited exoteric one, and found a model ready-made in Kiss' fantastic fictions. Inspired, in 1958 Mund joined the Order of the New Templars (ONT), a continuation of the Ariosophist sect founded by Jörg Lanz von Liebenfels, of whom Mund wrote the first biography; by 1979, he had become its leader. He also wrote the first biography of Karl Maria Wiligut, *Himmler's Rasputin*. So renowned did his research become that Mund later received 'repeated' questions from an Oxford academic as to what Himmler really knew about the occult significance of the top hats traditionally worn by Eton pupils and other such arcana.[35]

In 1981 Mund published *The Mystery of the Black Sun*, a history of the symbol his friends helped co-invent. A 2004 reprint featured a preface by one of his ONT successors, claiming there had been a number of sightings of Karl Maria Wiligut near Wewelsburg Castle after his death, with the *doppelgänger* dressed like one of ufology's infamous Men in Black – weren't all in the Black Order so clad?[36] In Mund's late book, we learnt Wiligut's Black Sun Santur could still be seen glowing in the sky whenever it was volcanically active, the last such sighting occurring at the dawn of the twentieth century in the small city of Lippe-Detmold.[37] Wiligut's ancestral charm-poems not only contained details of such appearances, but also instructions for creating 'special metal alloys' for use in undefined 'cosmotechnical instruments', wrote Mund – seemingly yet more *Wunderwaffen*.[38] Furthermore, it turned out all sunlight had 'a large-scale plan for the development of mankind', but had a different impact upon different people, 'as required by individual humans'. The quality of Santur's sunlight was 'nearly incomprehensible for outsiders' – non-Aryans would not understand its wonders. Its rays beamed out pure spirit as 'rhythmic music', and 'sucked' up physical dross from the North Pole. The Hyperboreans had once acted as 'Mechanistic Emissaries' between Earth and Santur, participating in spirit and matter simultaneously. Yet, now Santur had burnt itself out, its spiritual rays could 'barely deliver', meaning 'no more Hyperboreans can exist!' as white people, shorn of Santur's light, had become purely materialistic in nature.[39]

In 1960, astronomers detected a large unidentified object orbiting the globe in a polar orbit. This was interpreted as a mystery satellite, but all known US and Soviet devices circled the equator, not the poles. The media dubbed this 'The Black Knight', with radio hams claiming to have received encoded transmissions of radar-maps from the thing. In his book, Mund speculated this was actually an SS *Wunderwaffe* satellite launched during the war, with the intention of 'attempting the establishment of a rhythmic cone' in space to awaken Santur, thereby resurrecting 'White Giants' inside the Hollow Earth to fight on Germany's side. Something called 'Black Knight' just *had* to be made by the SS, didn't it?

Not really. America later admitted the object was the derelict remains of a film-recovery capsule from a failed spy-satellite. Worse, the name 'Black Knight' was taken from an experimental post-war ballistic missile created by the hated Britishers. But never mind. Modern-day astronomical discoveries relating to black holes, neutron stars and interstellar x-ray pulses were just yet more evidence for Santur's reality, said Mund. Now the Black Sun had been reactivated by the Black Knight, it became tantalisingly possible for Aryans to psychically alter the polar climate by 'magically affecting the physical interrelations between the Earth and sun ... including the awakening or halting of sunspots'. Any alteration of the Arctic climate was thus an inherently esoteric matter; had Mund lived to see global warming, he may have embraced it.[40]

Yet, having Hyperborean blood, he may have preferred to see global cooling take place instead. Kiss and Hörbiger had already established an inherent connection between ice and Aryans in the popular imagination; the Landig Circle helped spread it further. By 1960's *Morning of the Magicians*, Hitler was now self-defeatingly ordering the invasion of the USSR during the bitter Russian winter of 1941 due to a magical belief he was the 'Master of Ice' and that 'winter would retreat before his flame-bearing legions.' According to this account, SS WEL-meteorologists had forecast a mild Russian winter for that year, but this mattered little as Hitler had 'formed an alliance with the cold' and ordered the only concession should be his troops being given a free scarf and pair of gloves each. When told temperatures of minus 40C meant fuel was freezing in its tanks and his soldier's penises falling off when they went to the toilet, Hitler responded merely 'As to the cold, I will see to that. Attack!' Accordingly, three SS mountaineers climbed a holy mountain, performed a special ceremony and planted a blessed swastika flag to ensure the frosty Nordic race's future weather-control, but it was too late, with Hitler's abominable snowmen defeated on their own chosen battleground. When he later ordered the flooding of the Berlin Underground, the dynamiting of buildings and a fight to the death by every citizen during the war's final days, Hitler was, according to Pauwels and Bergier, really trying to recreate the previous destruction of Atlantis and Hyperborea 'under a tempest of water and hail' caused by Hörbiger's falling ice-moons, to ensure the resurrection of the Aryan race by purging it in a Nazi Ragnarok.[41]

* * * * *

None of this was true, but it helped the authors shift their book and thereby, inadvertently, spread the Landig Circle's ideas even further. Even if your own books don't sell, if other more popular authors imitate them, then your fictions multiply anyway, and can always be added to further. For instance, it has more than once been pointed out how the nightly and yearly cycle of the Ursa Major and Ursa Minor constellations, which appear to circle around the celestial Pole Star Polaris, when marked out on a sky-map, look uncannily like a swirling swastika. The Ursas are the most visible constellations in the night sky of the Northern Hemisphere, and their 'movement' (an illusion caused by the Earth's orbit) seems to centre upon the North Pole area. Maybe this starry swastika in the sky was just another manifestation of the Black Sun?[42] The ideologist Alfred Rosenberg (1893-45), author of 1930's *The Myth of the Twentieth Century*, second only to *Mein Kampf* in the Nazi best-seller lists, also argued that the Earth's poles had once wandered, another handy theory which could be exploited by the Landig Circle; by having Point 103 relocate to Point 211, their own pole of the Black Sun wandered itself, too.[43]

Today, a dubious Black Sun symbol – actually a twelve-spoked sun wheel used as a simple floor decoration in the North Tower of Wewelsburg Castle – can often be seen accompanying a popular online alt-right meme known as 'Winter-Chan', a female Nazi ice-warrior. Winter-Chan is an occult entity known as an *egregore* or *tulpa*, a kind of thought-form; by concentrating on her online image and typing 'I love you, Winter-Chan!' you will make her come to life and do your bidding. In appearance, Winter-Chan is a cute, pale-skinned, blue-eyed, blonde-haired anime frost-princess, dressed in winter coat and Russian fur-hat, surrounded by snowflakes. She is 'the paragon of an Aryan maiden', and has a special magical sigil on her hat, combining the runes for 'ice', 'wrath of Nature' and 'resistance'. The tulpa was first conjured up in 2016 during the mass migration crisis of Muslims into Europe to redirect cosmic ice against the Islamic invaders, bringing WEL-like blizzards to freeze them to death. Online alt-right keyboard-warriors have since created a range of songs, spells and chants intended to make Winter-Chan protect Europe's borders, because its lefty politicians no longer bother to do so. A 'Bureau of Memetic Warfare' half-exists on social media to encourage the spread of such memes, with a parodic UN-aping logo featuring a Wewelsburg Black Sun.[44] The Black Sun has been widely adopted online because of the precise same alchemical symbolism it represented to the Landig Circle, as a portent of total civilisational pole-reversal. At the point when all seemed lost, when Cultural Marxism appeared set to destroy Western civilisation in a swamp of mass immigration, political correctness, thought-control and institutionalised gay-worship, online meme-magicians invoked Winter-Chan, the Black Sun, Savitri Devi and Kalki-Hitler the Destroyer to freeze Muslim migrants, cause heart-attacks amongst left-wing journalists and ensure both that year's Brexit vote went the right way and the US electoral success of 'The God-Emperor' Donald Trump, who would dispel all *kali yuga* scum and usher in the new Golden Age.[45]

If he was still alive, Rudolf J. Mund would have been pleased. To most observers, the Landig Circle would appear to have been totally wasting their lives, writing stupid trash about made-up madness. And yet, the propagation of their Black Sun icon online decades later helped aid the Internet-boosted election of Trump, and thereby altered the political fate of the Western world for real. Just as the Winter-Chan worshipping meme-mages say, once born, ideas take on a life of their own, and today you can't move in certain areas online without encountering rune-bearing frost-maidens, Wewelsburg Black Suns, Nazi Antarctic UFO-bases and much more. Such things may not physically exist, but as Mund once wrote, that hardly matters so long as they occupy the reality of the mind: 'Non-existent flags cannot fall into enemy hands, and invisible symbols cannot be magically bound.'[46] In *Rebellion for Thule*, Wilhelm Landig printed the following poem:

At the top of the World
Stands the Midnight Mountain.
Its Light is eternal.
The eyes of man cannot see it –
And yet it is there.
Over the Midnight Mountain
Stream the rays of the Black Sun.
The eyes of man cannot see them –
And yet they are still there.
Inside us burns its light.[47]

Even though there are no Nazis to be seen at the poles, just as with the Midnight Mountain and the rays of the Black Sun, thanks to the best efforts of Landig and his friends, they live there nonetheless.

6

To Boldly Go Where No Fascist Has Gone Before: The Faustian Bargain of David Myatt's Galactic Reich

Another strand of Esoteric Nazism celebrates the Romantic attitudes the Third Reich sometimes held towards outer space in general. Germany may have been the leading centre of early rocket-research during the 1920s and 1930s countrywide 'rocket-craze' from which the V-2 later arose, but several members of the renowned *Verein für Raumschiffart* ('Society for Space Travel') national rocket-club harboured highly dreamy sentiments. The V-2-engineer and complicit Nazi stooge Hermann Oberth (1894–1989) was idolised as a 'guiding star' by many in the *Verein*, but his brand of space-science was somewhat mystical. Oberth believed all atoms were alive, lending the universe a living soul, giving humans telepathic potential to relay ideas from brain to brain. Oberth hoped that one day, his own living atoms would be reincarnated as a far-future spaceship pilot, in a craft based upon his early principles; aptly, an 'Oberth-Class' of starships appears in *Star Trek*. Oberth omitted such fantasies from his initial key texts about rocket-propulsion to maintain credibility, but in later life became less guarded, expressing frequent public belief in UFOs, which he theorised flew by making their own gravitational fields. Speaking at a domestic UFO conference in 1960, Oberth was embarrassed to share a stage with none other than Reinhold O. Schmidt, friend of Germans from Saturn, and his fellow US Contactee Carl Anderson (1913-80), who had once been offered a cigarette by a Martian named Kumar before being instructed by him to travel to Germany and reveal the secrets of alien engines to the great *Wunderwaffen* inventor. Oberth attracted such nuts by penning articles like *They Come from Outer-Space*, arguing ufonauts were 'Vikings of another planetary system', that there was life on Mars, and that V-7 helicopter-saucers were built in occupied Prague near the end of the war. Oberth thought ET scientists had visited Earth for centuries, conducting 'systematic long-range investigations' of flora, fauna and atomic research institutes. As to why they did not openly contact our leaders, Oberth surmised that 'perhaps they have conquered telepathy so they can read our thoughts and feel that is enough.'[1]

Oberth's life-long friend and experimental colleague Wernher von Braun could be rather a mystic, too. Paperclipped to Bible-Belt America as the chief genius behind the V-2, the reformed SS sinner joined NASA and found religion, preaching how it was 'God's purpose' to send 'His Son to the other worlds to bring the Gospel to them'. 'It is profoundly important for religious reasons that [humanity] travels to other galaxies; for it may be man's destiny to assure immortality not only of his race, but of the life-spark itself,' he argued, like a true champion of *lebensraum*.[2] For von Braun, rocketry became a way to transplant spiritual life into an empty cosmos. But was it *really* empty? In 1959, when an American *Juno 2* rocket was deflected from its orbit, von Braun appeared to blame either aliens or some secret human cabal for the event, reportedly announcing to the German media somewhat cryptically that:

> We find ourselves faced by powers which are far stronger than we had hitherto assumed, and whose base is at present unknown to us. More I cannot say at present. We are now engaging in entering into close contact with those powers, and in six or nine months' time it may be possible to speak with more precision on the matter.[3]

But von Braun never did. Did he just intend this as a joke? If so, some took it seriously.

*****

Perhaps the most interesting post-war British Esoteric Nazi is David Wulstan Myatt (b.1950), whose beliefs about the need for the Aryan race to colonise space and create an entire 'Galactic Reich' were directly motivated by the mystical thinking of men like Oberth and von Braun. Since 2010, chastened by the death of two loved ones, Myatt has publicly rejected 'my so lamentable extremism', focusing instead upon developing a new life-philosophy named *pathei-manos*, which promotes 'the gift of love' as being the true pathway towards understanding and a way to avoid inflicting unnecessary suffering on others. The name of this doctrine is taken from the *Agamemnon* of the Greek playwright Aeschylus, whose work Myatt has translated, and means something like 'learning from adversity' or 'wisdom arises from personal tragedy'. The ancient Greek tragedians saw many of their protagonists' fatal flaw as being that of hubris, an Achilles' heel Myatt now sees he once shared, regretting how he was formerly 'subsumed ... in my hubris with un-numinous abstractions' during his lengthy former obsession with Nazism.

Now viewing ideas of race and *volk* as 'unethical abstractions', Myatt had already abandoned Nazism in favour of radical Islam anyway, following a visionary experience whilst working as a farm-labourer in 1998 when he had experienced a sudden sense of one-ness with Nature. Hating the shallow, materialistic values of the money-obsessed, decadent, capitalist West, Myatt realised the *jihad* of Osama bin Laden (1957-2011) was a far more plausible opponent of 'the Amerikan Empire' than Nazism, so switched allegiances, writing in praise of al-Qaeda and suicide bombers. Now openly disavowing racism, as Islam is open to persons of all colours alike, this new-found tolerance did not extend to the Jews, or 'Zionists' and agents of 'international finance', as he called them; one thing Myatt retained from neo-Nazism was the belief the Holocaust was a hoax. Having changed his name to Abdulaziz ibn Myatt, in 1999 his former past came back to haunt him when an old terrorism manual for white supremacists he had compiled, *A Practical Guide to Aryan Revolution*, was said to have helped inspire the Far-Right nailbomber David Copeland to plant devices in London targeting blacks, South Asians and gays in an attempt to ignite a race-war. Three people died and 129 were injured in Copeland's explosions, leading to a media frenzy surrounding the previously obscure Myatt and his most unusual life-story, which had involved membership of various neo-Nazi groups and more than one spell in prison.

Myatt certainly had a spiritual side, spending extended periods of religious study in the East, seeking alternatives to the *kali yuga* Western way of life. This seeker after Hidden Truths also had a long history of involvement with occultism, having infiltrated Satanist groups from the 1970s onwards, hoping to steer their members towards Nazism instead, rather like Ernst Zündel did with UFOs. The basic plot was to lure new recruits in with the promise of sexual favours from female cultists during rituals, but those reeled in by this temptation just wanted sex, not fascism, and by 1997 Myatt conceded failure. He had planned to blackmail members into committing extremist acts under the threat of having their Satanism revealed, but this did not work out, and Myatt – actually a one-time monk with a love of the old Latin Mass – was no genuine worshipper of His Satanic Majesty himself, he maintains. Yet, following the David Copeland affair, Myatt was labelled as a Satanist by the media anyway and filmed undercover by the BBC, something which, much to the Corporation's disappointment, revealed that at this point in time Myatt was, in his own words, only living 'an ordinary, rather boring, life with his wife and family in a small village near Malvern ... [going] to work every day on a bicycle to a nearby farm.' In 1998 he had already been the subject of an exposé in the anti-fascist *Searchlight* magazine, accusing him of being *The Most Evil Nazi in Britain*, partly on account of his alleged Satanist leanings, whilst in a 1974 interview he had innocently held up some borrowed 'occult thingy' for a photographer, which was mis-used to imply he was involved in animal sacrifice, something later dismissed by both the police and the RSPCA. However, rather than suing journalists for libel, Myatt has consistently preferred to challenge them to 'a duel with deadly weapons, according to the etiquette of duelling', on account of the fact that 'the only law I believe in and strive to uphold is the law of personal honour.' As no journalists have ever taken him up on this challenge, says Myatt, 'I consider my honour vindicated.'[4]

The most persistent occult rumour about Myatt is that, under the pseudonym 'Anton Long', he is the founder or chief propagandist and theorist of a Nazi Satanist cult known as the O9A or ONA, the 'Order of Nine Angles'. However, Myatt denies this. Whilst the ideology and some ritual practice of the O9A are obviously stolen direct from his own work in the field, Myatt, as an 'early advocate of copytheft', also believes copyright laws to be dishonourable, just like libel laws, so has never bothered to officially object to the group's alleged plagiarism. Some academics say this is a pure lie on Myatt's behalf, but others, analysing Long and Myatt's styles of writing, have concluded they are indeed different people; many argue 'Anton Long' is actually a collective pseudonym for a whole host of different writers associated with the O9A, operating under a convenient shield. Personally, I have no idea of the truth either way, and, not wishing to face the prospect of pistols at dawn myself, draw no conclusions about the matter here.[5]

David Myatt may not have been a genuine Satanist, but he certainly sold his soul to the Führer, being a hard-core Esoteric Nazi who praised Hitler's Third Reich as a religiously inspiring – or 'numinous', to use the term he took from the German theologian Rudolf Otto (1869-1937) – alternative to the dull, despiritualised, technocratic and Mammon-minded Western democratic regimes that had defeated him in 1945. Myatt has a point; our present-day world can be seen as arid and spiritually unsatisfying, being in many respects pointless, in decline and in thrall to a host of false values from blind money-worship to Cultural Marxism. However, Myatt's consequent conclusion – that Nazism, as the most extreme antithesis possible to our artificial and unnatural modern world, must therefore be inherently in tune with the laws of Nature themselves – was a little OTT, as his reformed *pathei-manos* self would now apparently admit. Yet in 1998, immediately prior to his temporary conversion to Islam, Myatt could happily write the following:

> I have re-expressed the truth that National Socialism is anti-materialistic and profoundly organic – that is, an expression of life itself, and thus of the evolution toward the order and beauty which Nature produces. All other philosophies and religions are profoundly against the beautiful and natural diversity of Nature so evident to us in race and individual character. Even the laws of National Socialism are based upon the reality of Nature, and the civilised ideal of nobility which creates more order and beauty, and not, as with other philosophies, upon some abstract idea which is anti-evolutionary and ignoble.[6]

If Nazism was basically a living human political expression of Nature itself, then this implied the cosmos itself was alive – and inherently Nazi. Recall the Green Nazis and their Blood and Soil cult, and the various exponents of the *völkisch* movement which fed into Ariosophy. Myatt admired this aspect of Nazism, becoming a Savitri Devi-style eco-fascist, condemning the 'worthless ... parasitical infestation' of *kali yuga* humanity who were despoiling our planet with their waste and pollution, arguing the need to reduce Britain's population down from 60 million to 10 million. He even made plans to create a rural-type white separatist homeland near Chelmsford, called the East Saxon Kindred; the Galactic Reich had to start somewhere.[7] If Nazism really was 'Natural', then such associations and aspirations made sense. If the democracy-duped white race harmed Nature, like its Green critics said contemporary Western capitalism did today, with its pollution and environmental degradation in the name of profit, then we only harmed ourselves and our *volk*. However, if we could merge more fully with Nature's laws, like the Nazis had once done, we could potentially evolve into a state of oneness with Creation itself, and make ourselves and our race become immortal:

> National Socialists hold Nature, and her creations, in respect. National Socialists are thus pagans who revere Nature, as they accept that this Being which is the cosmos exists in us all, as individuals, because we are born from the cosmos and because we belong to the cosmos … which is divine. Essentially, for National Socialists divinity is the cosmos and the aspects of the cosmos … If we live in the correct way, and so evolve in consciousness and health, we can transcend beyond what we are in this physical world, and actually become a part of this suprapersonal Being [i.e. Nature]. Thus we will live on, in another kind of time and space, after our own physical death, achieving immortality … National Socialism is thus a revelation of the divine Being itself.[8]

By obeying Nazi laws, you became one with Nature forever, an 'existence most easily achieved by those who actively strive to do heroic, noble, National Socialist deeds, who place the interests of their race before themselves or even before their own salvation' – like Myatt's desired daring future Nazi astronauts, for example. However, such fallen heroes do not live on in a continued individual sense, like personal souls in the Christian Heaven or feasting Vikings in Valhalla. Instead, they become what sound rather like a part of the Aryan collective unconscious. Myatt had closely studied his Jung whilst serving time in prison, and his ideas here appear like an Esoteric Nazi recasting of the Swiss psychologist's own theories:

> These individuals become our present and our future – they become the substance which makes further evolution possible. In the simple sense, they become embodied in their race, in the soil and those aspects of Nature which allow this living racial being composed of individuals to survive and flourish. They thus exist in and become the living spirit or psyche of their race. Thus, when mortals of a particular race who are living revere Nature, when they revere the soil, the homeland where they dwell; when they revere and honour what is best, excellent, beautiful and profound in specific individuals of their race; when they revere and respect and honour what is

divine, then these living members of that race are revering, honouring and respecting those, such as their own ancestors, who because of their deeds, have passed on to become embodied in all these things.[9]

This was wholly compatible with Heinrich Himmler's belief that, by maintaining a cult of the ancestors, living people were more likely to act responsibly for the well-being of future generations too, rendering the transient individual immortal within the greater life of the nation. 'A nation that preserves its ancestors will always have children; only nations without ancestors are childless,' he said, not without reason – as the West, tricked by the cult of progress into abolishing any respect for its own past currently destroys itself via low birth-rates, we may reflect that even the *Reichsführer*-SS was not always wrong. According to Himmler's view, his soul would one day be reborn, not specifically as a second Heinrich Himmler, but in a more generic sense as one of his *volk*'s descendants.[10]

If the Nazi Aryan race was immortal, this meant the immense challenges of interstellar travel were not as impossible as they at first may seem. Yes, it would take mankind thousands of years to colonise space but, just as Hermann Oberth had once imagined, if we are all one day reborn as our far-flung Aryan descendants aboard future spaceships, then the petty beginnings of this task would not be hopeless after all. When Wernher von Braun launched his first V-2, he can't have seriously hoped to fly to another galaxy on a spaceship one day himself – and yet, if von Braun found some aspect of his soul being reborn through the collective soul of the *volk* 10,000 years later, maybe one day he could indeed help finish what he started? For Myatt, as for the early V-2 *Wunderwaffen* men of the *Verein für Raumschiffart*, space travel was really the only task in life worth pursuing, and the white Nordic race the only ones capable of doing so:

A Galactic Empire – formed by the conquest of that final frontier which is outer space – is the destiny of our human species. This ideal and this ideal alone is great enough and noble enough for our noble, heroic races [i.e. the white Aryan, Anglo-Saxon and Nordic ones] – everything else is petty, materialistic or decadent; an insult to not only what we are, as creative, noble races, but also an insult to what we can become by pursuing an idealistic noble goal. The Galactic Empire is the supreme challenge which, by its very difficulty, can inspire our races to great and noble achievements ... A truly great and noble vision is numinous – it has the power to inspire and so to make real what seems impossible.[11]

The towering Irish poet W. B. Yeats (1865-1939) talked about great men being driven on by their own personal demon to accomplish 'that which is most difficult amongst things not impossible', and for Myatt this inspiring 'demon' was really the collective soul of the departed *volk*. Only this influence could overcome the lies of 'the present alien tyranny most people are forced to live under [which] make this dream [of space-conquest] seem unrealistic.' But it is *not* unrealistic, Myatt says; aeroplanes would have seemed impossible to Elizabethans, but we still eventually built them. Why should it not be so with spaceships? 'Today, there are some who claim that interstellar space travel will never be feasible because certain scientific "theories" affirm that, for instance, it is impossible to travel faster than, or even approach the velocity of, light,' Myatt wrote. 'However, these barriers are only there to be overcome.' By a mere *Triumph of the Will*, as the title of Leni Riefenstahl's (1902-2003) famous Nazi propaganda film put it, it should prove possible for Nordic minds, possessed by the collective soul of their ancestors, to settle other planets.[12] The triumph of mind over matter is essentially what modern occultists define the word 'magic' as being, and there is an intellectually respectable German tradition for such an idea, to be found in the writings of the philosopher Arthur Schopenhauer (1788-1860), where he outlined his conception of 'The Will'. The Will was the blind irresistible force of Nature which governs our existence, making all life-forms desire to breed, for instance. But if you consciously hijacked this Will for your own ends, you could overcome the apparent limits of the physical world by performing acts of magic by somehow imposing your own Will upon Nature and subduing it to serve your needs. Schopenhauer felt space and time were perceptual illusions, with psychic powers like clairvoyance acting as proof of this.

If The Will could be mastered to power spacecraft, the potential benefits for the Aryan race could be enormous. In an endless virtuous cycle, a daring, space-faring society would breed a new race of heroic, SS-style space-warriors, who would conquer more planets, inspiring yet more space-warriors to fly out on further missions, conquering more worlds and inspiring more future heroes in their turn, and so on forever, wrote Myatt:

> In the beginning, the greatest benefit of [space-related] research, exploration and colonisation would be the noble cohesive effect the pursuit of such an ideal would have upon the people of the society – it would give them a sense of their Destiny, and encourage the production of idealistic men and women dedicated to upholding the warrior ethos. What must be realised is that only a National Socialist society is capable of fulfilling the dream of space-exploration, interstellar space travel, and the colonisation of other worlds ... A National Socialist society would encourage the right type of individual [to evolve] – persons of noble, heroic character, imbued with a genuine warrior ethos or spirit: a desire to explore, to conquer, to overcome, to fight, to honourably go where no human has gone before.[13]

In short, Myatt envisaged the creation of an entire race of Wernher von Brauns and Hermann Oberths, unhindered by the trivial spreadsheet politics of internal NASA budget constraints. The ignoble Amerikan White House, satisfied with merely landing on the moon for a Cold War propaganda coup and then semi-abandoning their space-programme as being too expensive and unproductive, may not have been willing to write von Braun a blank cheque to subdue the whole universe to his Schopenhauerian Will, but surely Hitler's Reich Chancellery would have been?

Myatt has always maintained 'it is the vision of a Galactic Empire which runs through my past political life', but how was such an idea born? His entire story, he once wrote, 'has been a Faustian or Promethean quest', with there being 'always an honourable purpose behind what I did, what I said and what I wrote', namely to combat 'the dismal, dishonourable, un-numinous and increasingly tyrannical Establishment status quo'. His perception that our modern democratic world is worthless began when Myatt was around thirteen, when the early 1960s Space-Race was heating up, with unmanned probes being launched to other worlds and the Apollo programme of moon-landings being planned. To the young Myatt, this seemed like only the first baby-steps towards mankind wandering the galaxy itself: 'Surely it was only a matter of time before someone, somewhere, invented some kind of Star-Drive to replace the rather primitive rocket and enable us to travel near or faster than the speed of light?' Maybe Myatt himself would be that person? Initially schooled abroad in Tanzania and Singapore, where his civil servant father helped manage the decline of the British Empire, Myatt's main interest became Physics, which he yearned to study at university.

However, turning fourteen, Myatt realised there might be a problem. His desire for space-conquest was based upon the premise it would help us evolve 'into another type of being' as a species, but looking around him, he saw very few people who *wished* to evolve. 'Where was the spirit of Empire, of conquest – of the desire to seek knowledge and new worlds?' he asked. The British Empire itself certainly didn't possess it any more, and by the end of the decade would be more-or-less gone. How could the bloodless, deskbound non-entities who ran the post-1945 world ever land on Mars, let alone reach the edges of the universe? Myatt initially looked towards the Soviet Union, with their courageous cosmonauts, for an answer, 'but all I found there was dispiriting Marxian dialectics.' Besides studying Physics to work out how to build a warp-drive like those soon to be seen in *Star Trek*, Myatt now pursued a secondary study in history 'to try to find some clues as to how to build the new society which would be needed' to fund his proposed wonder-engine. First he settled upon worshipping the world of ancient Greece and Sparta, enthralled by the last stand at Thermopylae, when a small band of Spartan heroes had sacrificed themselves to fend off a much larger Persian horde, and the wanderings of Odysseus, whose boat was surely the rough Classical equivalent of a spaceship, and feeling 'as if I belonged in those times more than I belonged to the modern world, with its lack of adventure, lack of élan and disrespect for the ethos and ways of the warrior.' But ancient Greece was ... well, ancient. Were there no more recent examples of the warrior-ethos in existence? Towards the end of his schooldays Myatt finally discovered the dignified, Romantic and exciting world of Nazism:

> The more I learned about National Socialist Germany, the more it seemed to me to be the answer. Here was something inspiring, something surely possessed of élan and warrior-spirit. The martial music, the marching columns, flag after flag waving in the breeze of Destiny. I felt there was something incredible here – in the struggle and victory of Adolf Hitler. And there was von Braun, architect of NASA's exploration, beginning his work in Germany. Surely, had Germany won, they would have gone on to conquer and build a path to the stars! And there was the SS – built upon and dedicated to the warrior code of honour ... What battles they had fought! What sacrifices they had made! Here were ancient Greek heroes come alive again ... I believed I had found the prototype of the ideal society which was needed to begin the committed exploration of space, create the Galactic Empire and so continue our own evolution as human beings. In particular, I felt an affinity with what I understood to be the ideal of Blood and Soil – that is, a real respect for Nature, for the land, and an understanding of our own place in Nature.

Having studied martial arts in the Far East, Myatt developed great respect for the samurai, and along with them he 'also came to admire the short-lived modern Empire the Japanese had created' during the war as being a resurrection of the old samurai spirit. When Myatt heard of the Far-Right Japanese nationalist writer Yukio Mishima's (1925-70) suicide in 1970, when he had ritually disembowelled himself with a sword, samurai-style, after failing to persuade Japanese troops to overthrow their dishonourable capitalist government, Myatt felt compelled to move finally away from Physics and devote his time towards revolutionary Far-Right politics instead. Myatt's love of the samurai was hardly unique in Far-Right circles. Himmler believed ancient Aryan and Asian elites alike had originated in Tibet, whose mountains had presented a refuge from the sinking of Atlantis, and thence spread out to Germany and Japan, making the two nations' wartime alliance highly logical. 'The SS should become the German samurai,' he once told Hitler, who agreed.[14] By now at university in Hull, Myatt had already joined a neo-Nazi movement headed up by Savitri Devi's British fascist friend Colin Jordan in 1968, and he increasingly began neglecting his textbooks and missing lectures to attend extremist marches and rallies instead, eventually dropping out and ending up in prison for leading a racist assault, something he felt to be a 'purifying, necessary and maturing experience' at the time, like something straight out of Akira Kurosawa. En route to some magical temple or other, Myatt had happened by chance upon a skinhead rally, feeling instinctively these admirable thugs were the new warriors he wished to train with, this being his initial impetus to join up with Jordan, for whom he sometimes acted as a bodyguard.

Although the wider world was 'increasingly forsaking honour' by refusing to take *Star Trek* seriously, building a warp-drive turned out to be quite difficult, so Myatt travelled the vasty depths of space emotionally instead, sitting there listening to classical music 'with my very soul reaching out into the blackness of space', which he now saw was the closest he would ever get to travelling through the real thing in his current lifetime. He then began studying Jung and occultism in general, sadly finding 'very little [of] substance' in either of them, he says – I think a little disingenuously. Disillusioned by the failure of many neo-Nazis to live up to ancient Greek, samurai or SS ideals, Myatt abandoned fascism for a while, living in 'an unheated caravan' writing poetry and exploring Buddhism, hoping Enlightenment may 'perhaps open a portal that might lead to the stars' in a different way. The music of Bach then led Myatt 'back toward Christianity and the cultural traditions of my ancestors', and he became a Catholic monk, although 'not a very good' one, as he missed women and tried to teach the other monks martial arts. Eventually, he found a synthesis for his political, spiritual and space-related yearnings in the portmanteau religion of Esoteric Nazism, to which he had already been introduced by Colin Jordan giving him some of Savitri Devi's books to read, *The Lightning and the Sun* proving especially inspiring. It was now he began infiltrating Satanist groups with the aim of persuading or blackmailing their members into neo-Nazi revolutionary activities with the promise of sex – 'the first step toward the conquest of the galaxy'.[15]

The most lasting concept Myatt apparently took from Jung was the idea of 'acausality', as outlined in his 1952 monograph *Synchronicity: An Acausal Connecting Principle*. Not unlike Schopenhauer, Jung saw various paranormal phenomena, like telepathy and impossible coincidences, as being independent of time and space, and so being, to human eyes, non-energetic in nature. If a psychic sends a message into another person's mind, you might presume they are beaming out rays of some kind, like mental radio. Not so, Jung would say. Experiments seemed to demonstrate the message was received just as quickly and clearly if the psychic was on the other side of the world as if he was sitting right next to the recipient, yet normal energetic broadcasts do not work that way. Maybe, therefore, such phenomena did not use energy at all, but other means that human beings simply cannot understand? As their causality could thus never be discerned, Jung called such things acausal. Interestingly, Savitri Devi seemed to believe in similar ideas herself, feeling these invisible acausal energies were in some sense alive or intelligent, at least to judge by a prayer she offered up to the ancient Aryan gods during the strange rituals she had once performed at the Externsteine: 'Hidden Powers that govern all things visible and tangible ... All-efficient real Causes behind the apparent causes of all events, help me understand the meaning of our [the Nazis'] temporary defeat.'[16]

For Myatt, there were two realms in existence, the causal one where we all currently lived, and an acausal one, locked away behind some invisible barrier. Each living being represented a 'nexion' between the two, a kind of biological-spiritual portal through which acausal energies could pass; it was acausal energy which fuelled the very processes of life itself, animating otherwise inanimate matter. Myatt even formulated a whole thermodynamics of causality, proposing the total amount of acausal energy in existence was a constant which could never be created or destroyed, merely recycled. When a living nexion died, its life-force returned to the acausal realm; when a new life-form was born, the acausal energy subtracted from our realm via the previous organism's death was reintroduced back into it via this second nexion. It was in this way that a *volk*'s ancestors could be reborn in their descendants. Myatt's innovation was to guess this very same energy could be used to power future spaceships – spaceships whose engines would thus, in a certain sense, be powered by the souls of dead Nazis. These starships would be a form of 'living machines', explained Myatt, an echo of Miguel Serrano and the Landig Circle's animate *manisola* and *vimana* UFOs.

Myatt's acausal realm resembles the world of Schopenhauer's Will, in the sense that, because Myatt thinks there would be no such things as the dimensions of time or space in operation there, all things would be linked to one another, being all merely 'different facets' of the same ultimate existence, thus facilitating seemingly impossible events as there would be 'no linear cause-and-effect' in operation in such a place. Therefore, channelled through appropriate nexions, any given element of energy from the acausal realm should be able to operate immediately upon another part of the physical universe in our own realm, even though it be 'billions upon billions of light-years away', as time and space would mean nothing to it. It followed that, by manipulating such acausal energies in our spaceship engines by constructing them to function as nexions to the acausal realm themselves, we might 'be able to travel anywhere in the physical universe almost instantaneously'. But to do this, we would have to develop a whole new concept of physics – a Nazi one. A new form of mathematics and a new, non-Euclidean form of geometry of a non-linear and non-spatial kind would need to be developed too, if we were ever to harness the living energies of a world entirely unlike our own.

Currently, most mainstream scientists would argue there is no such thing as acausal energy, on the reasonable grounds that nobody has ever measured any. Myatt would counter that this is because acausal energy by definition cannot be measured 'by instruments based on causal physics'. Instead, only living instruments which themselves possess some form of acausal energy can sense the force's presence – by which Myatt means human beings, who automatically perceive the presence of the acausal when they experience such sublime sensations as love or numinosity. When mankind stares up at the mystery of the stars and feels inspired to fly up and touch them, then that is precisely the kind of pure, Germanic Will that shall serve to power the Aryan race's future spaceships. It may even ultimately prove possible for living nexions like ourselves to feed off such acausal energy inherent within the cosmos somehow, instead of having to eat physical food to power our bodies with, which would certainly prove useful to any neo-Nazi astronauts. The first step towards this goal would be for humans to become living forms of laboratory apparatus, able to sense the presence of acausal energy nearby by evolving into psychic 'empaths' like in a Philip K. Dick novel, who possess 'a new type of knowing' based more on intuition than on logic or reason – a highly Gnostic conceit. Altogether, this would constitute a new science, called 'acausology', of which I think Schopenhauer and Jung would be rather proud.[17]

* * * * *

As Myatt had realised whilst still a schoolboy, however, the prospects of such an alternative science being developed within our current *kali yuga* world were slim indeed. Before acausal living spaceships could be built, it was necessary first to await the forthcoming Kalki-like rebirth of the Aryan world-spirit in the shape of a figure named 'Vindex', or 'The Avenger', a Caesar-like direct successor to Adolf Hitler himself, come to save the white race from the twin horrors of the Amerikan Empire and the liberal, capitalist sub-men of 'Homo Hubris'. Hitler's great mistake had been to be drawn into war with 'the cabal' of Britain, America, France and Russia, Myatt said. Instead, he should have concentrated upon building up the Third Reich within pre-existing German borders and investing limitless resources into von Braun and Oberth's rocket-programmes, thereby demonstrating to the entire world that only National Socialism could properly accomplish the things that really matter in life, like space exploration. All empires based on conquest of other lands ultimately fail, and Hitler's had been no exception. Instead of seeking *lebensraum* in the East, the Nazis should have sought living-space on other planets instead. It may have been impressive for Germany to conquer all of mainland Europe in a few months, but in doing so Hitler was guilty of short-term thinking. Influenced by the philosophy of the English historian Arnold Toynbee (1889-1975), Myatt developed a theory of 'Aeonics', in which the true course of civilisations was to be mapped out in 'Aeons', long-term time-units of around two thousand years, which were the only time-scales upon which any real Cosmic Reich or Galactic Imperium could truly be built. For Toynbee, as for the Hindus, history went in predictable long-term cycles of growth, maturity, decline and collapse, with each Aeonic Cycle, for Myatt, being a temporal manifestation of timeless acausal energy, meaning that even our current *kali yuga* Aeon would eventually die and be reborn as something better.

When Vindex came, he would not make the same mistakes his earlier avatar Hitler had. A Robin Hood or Luke Skywalker figure, he would defeat the enemy Empire of Amerika not by impersonal means of mechanical warfare involving strategic aerial bombing campaigns or the firing of long-range nuclear missiles, but using the honourable, samurai-style methods of

193

personal direct combat between warriors and armies. Furthermore, Vindex would fight only when attacked; rather than invading Poland, he would wait for Poland to invade him, before forcing their armies back by sheer force of moral Will. Whilst initially thinking Vindex would have to be a Nazi, and presumably based in Germany, following his conversion to Islam in 1998 Myatt reconsidered. Influenced by the fine example of men like Osama bin Laden, Hitler's Second Coming was now reconceived in less overtly white supremacist tones; like the Saudi bin Laden, perhaps he would not be a pure-bred Nordic German at all, but possess brown skin, as most white Westerners these days were classic specimens of shallow Homo Hubris themselves. Vindex could even be female, a warrior-queen like Boudicca. Being rebels, bin Laden and his al-Qaeda samurai possessed no formal nation-state to call their own, leading Myatt to now dismiss the very idea of such an entity as an 'unethical abstraction that is a great cause of suffering and nullifier of the ethical and numinous principle of personal honour.' Unable to shake off his liking for Nazi Blood and Soil rhetoric, he began to advocate the creation of 'small, rural communities' specifically modelled on those seen in the *Lark Rise to Candleford* novels, facilitating 'a return to what is human; to the human scale of things'. Apparently influenced by the multi-national nature of bin Laden's *jihadis*, Myatt now advocated a replacement of the notion of 'race' with that of 'clan', a community of like-minded persons who could come together in mutual association and pursuit of that which was most honourable:

A clan is a basis for individuals to live in a numinous way, in harmony with themselves, with Nature, and with the Cosmos. The clan is basically just a large extended family, where the individuals are personally known to each other and/or related to each other by family ties, such as marriage ... The clan is living: growing, changing, evolving; and it is not tied to or dependent upon any static, causal, un-numinous abstraction such as 'race'. It is a coming-into-being, and the criteria for 'membership', if you will, is not determined by some causal abstraction, such as perceived (outward) ethnicity, but by personal interaction, a personal knowing, based on personal (individual) character ... [Clans] are thus nexions, regions where numinous law, based upon honour, can be established, to the benefit of the individuals of such new communities.

Yet, as anyone who has read the *Lark Rise to Candleford* novels or watched their cosy spin-off BBC TV adaptations will be aware, the rural villagers never managed to build any actual spaceships themselves, unlike the hyper-complex, hyper-abstract, hyper-advanced and hyper-un-numinous military-industrial complexes of NASA and the USSR. How could a small clan build spacecraft? Simply by exploiting the acausal energy which, by virtue of their highly numinous rural existence, they would be able to sense and thus eventually harness; remember, Myatt's clans are 'living nexions', thus making them likely channels between the acausal realm and our own, just like all living beings are, to some extent. Viewed thus, the label of 'Islamo-fascism' often applied to the Taliban and other such extremist clans begins to make sense. To a man of Myatt's mindset, *jihadis* embody the spirit of the SS Grail-Knights but shorn of the un-numinous abstract encumbrance of the Nazi nation-state. By fighting the West from the margins, rather than head-on using huge armies, they would be more likely to defeat it using asymmetric warfare, like the Rebel Forces in *Star Wars*, with Vindex's righteous example being so numinous and inspiring that others all across the globe would take up arms against the capitalist world order and 'the Zionist entity that occupies Palestine' and bring the whole obscene Leviathan down in a way which completely nullifies its massive material advantages in wealth, military might and ordinary, non-acausal technology. Once this miracle has been achieved, the equally far-fetched scheme of settling the universe in animate spaceships will seem a mere trifle to the victorious clans by comparison. Simply by mastering The Will, you really can make things happen, just as Schopenhauer had once taught. As *Star Trek: The Next Generation*'s Captain Jean-Luc Picard used to say, 'Make it so!'[18]

By the time of Myatt's conversion to Islam, Vindex had become an essentially generic figure, a human 'type' which bin Laden might have embodied temporarily, but who would soon be replaced with others of the same basic pattern – when bin Laden was killed, Islamic terrorism did not die with him. In Myatt's earlier outline of his modern-day Nazi space-myth, however, 1984's *VINDEX: The Destiny of the West*, his conceptions of 'The Avenger' and his mission were rather different. Inspired by Arnold Toynbee's assertion that history was an actual science, not a branch of the humanities, Myatt was able to predict the new Imperium of Vindex would be born around 1993, 'give or minus ten years' and last until about 2390AD.[19] From his later Islamist viewpoint, the 9/11 attacks of 2001 would indeed fit into this time-frame, but at this point he was specifically talking about the birth of a white Aryan, neo-Nazi Space empire, not a world based on nationless yet numinous clans whose ethnicity was irrelevant. All civilisations end in Empire, said Myatt here, and as white Western civilisation was based ultimately on the manipulation of technology, it followed that its own Empire should extend into outer space, which could only be conquered using the most advanced technology it would ever be possible for anyone to build.

Only the white race could do this, as 'No other civilisation has produced men who climbed the highest mountain just because it was there or who sailed across great oceans just to see what was on the other side.' Space travel was the ultimate up-scaling of such noble Aryan impulses, being the greatest possible synthesis of 'the three elements that are so ineluctably Western: science, technology, and the desire to know.' Because of this, 'If we need a symbol to represent our Western civilisation – to express its quintessence – it is the spacecraft.' Sadly, the weak slave-religion values of imported Jewish Christianity had caused these ancient Aryan values of exploration and conquest to atrophy, it being Vindex's destiny to rekindle the pagan flame of the Viking sea-warriors within our sleeping, hypnotised *volk*, with the eventual Galactic Reich he will spawn possessing 'as a guiding force the same power that drove the Norsemen' across the oceans. The best symbol of the Viking civilisation was 'driving energy – the prow of a Viking ship, the spacecraft hurtling into space'. Thus, Hermann Oberth's assessment of the character of the ET ufonauts he thought were visiting Earth as being the 'Vikings of another planetary system' is reapplied to white human beings themselves, who will, through the very 'nature of the challenge' of Vindex's 'official expansionist policy' of the colonisation of space, become a new species of 'anti-humanitarian' human – 'Homo Sol', or 'Sun-People', a term reminiscent of Savitri Devi.[20] Vindex, when he came, would already be a prototype of Homo Sol, being – and here the echo of Devi is even clearer – 'a natural force, like lightning and sun', who would not hesitate to found the Galactic Reich 'by the sword, by force of arms', someone who will make the Jews and their Amerikan Empire allies quake as 'his emergence dooms them and the world they hope to create.' Accordingly, when Vindex arrives, 'there will and must be a great deal of suffering and death on both sides' as the Cosmic Reich 'cannot simply be thought or wished into existence – it has to be fought for.'[21]

Really, the birth of Homo Sol was a rebirth of Homo Viking, whose collective soul had been atrophied not only by fake Jewish Christianity but also by fake Jewish Marxism, which stood as the final *kali yuga* inversion of all that a true Aryan should hold dear:

> Marxism is the ultimate contradiction of [Nazi values]. It returns the spirit to Earth, to material concern, and reduces everything to that which is common. It is totally opposed to heroic idealism ... Marxism, by its very nature and aims, seeks to destroy what is numinous and archetypal – as, for example, in art, where everything is reduced to either political propaganda or social realism. Marxism is based on the lowest common denominator; the [traditional Aryan] ethos of the West seeks to raise everything up to a higher level through conquest, exploration and the challenge of knowledge ... Practically, this amounts to the difference between acting and thinking instinctively, with the blood, and acting from a position of materialism, with cerebral 'intelligence'.[22]

Myatt could almost pass as Miguel Serrano there. This was why Nazis truly burned books, as a rebuttal of 'decadent societies where cleverness was elevated above everything else, where spirit came second to mere intelligence.' By contrast, having 'a healthy body and a noble attitude' the Nazis 'enjoyed life, not ideas or books.'[23] If Nazism dragged the soul up into space and realms ethereal, then Marxism dragged it down to Earth and realms material. If all you used to design a spaceship was your logical intelligence, then you would never succeed, as logic would suggest such a thing was impossible; only the illogical impulses of the blood would enable you to access the acausal realm of magical warp-drive engines. By its very nature, Communism destroyed individuality, but in space, with so many uncharted planets left still to conquer, it would surely thrive, an interstellar version of the old Wild West Frontier Spirit.[24] No wonder Russia lost the Space-Race.

* * * * *

The problem with modernity was that the old Faustian world-spirit of the West had been replaced with an alien Magian world-spirit, taught Myatt, an idea taken from the German thinker Oswald Spengler's (1888-1936) two-volume masterpiece of pessimistic historical philosophy *The Decline of the West*, first published in 1918 and 1922. Spengler's work, talking as it did of long-term cycles of civilisational birth and decay, was similar to Arnold Toynbee's, so fitted in well with Myatt's own dogma of Aeonics. Spengler's *Meisterwerk* argued that, over the long-term, healthy, virile, living *cultures* declined into brittle, dried-up empty shells of mere *civilisations* dominated by routines of bureaucracy and with no higher purpose than making money, before eventually collapsing entirely as their listless populations became entirely demotivated and unwilling even to bother to defend themselves from invasion, as with ancient Rome, or immigrant-filled Western Europe and America today. The problem, Spengler said, was that the white West used to possess a Faustian world-spirit, but this had since been chased out and replaced by a Magian world-spirit, a foreign infection imported via Judaism, Islam and the decadence of Byzantium. Basically, the former realm of the heroic and noble Aryans and Vikings had been invaded by the incompatible philosophies of the Middle East. But as Spengler also divined that, late in their cycle of enforced decay, civilisations could temporarily be galvanised by the sudden emergence of a Caesar-figure in the shape of a military strongman, many Nazis incorrectly thought Spengler was one of them and had 'scientifically' anticipated the coming of Adolf Hitler. This was not true – Spengler thought the Nazis vulgar populists, much preferring the quasi-aristocratic pretensions of Benito Mussolini – but maybe he had anticipated the coming of Vindex instead?[25]

Myatt's idea of a Galactic Reich was inherently compatible with Spengler's conception of the Faustian world-soul. In myth, the black magician Doctor Faust sold his soul to the demon Mephistopheles in return for infinite knowledge, much as Wernher von Braun had once sold his own soul to Himmler in return for being given *carte blanche* to develop his atmosphere-scraping V-2s. With its desire for limitless knowledge, the 'prime symbol' of the Faustian soul was that of 'pure and limitless space', as embodied above all by the night sky. Germanic gods, Spengler said, were gods of the night, not of the daylight, so were thus inherently Faustian: 'Night eliminates body; day, soul.' Faust pursued his dark alchemical philosophies at midnight, and so did the traditional, pre-Magian German *volk*. For Myatt, such wide-ranging, boundless intellectual wanderings were symbolised by the Vikings raiding the world in their longboats (it is generally accepted today the Vikings reached America), but the chief poetic embodiment of this spiritual tendency, said Spengler, was the endless Grail Quest of the Knights of the Round Table, which embodied 'The love of wild Nature, the mysterious compassion, the ineffable sense of forsakenness [of the Germanic soul] – it is all Faustian and only Faustian. Every one of us [Germans] knows it.'[26] Faust himself suffered from it, in the poet Johann Wolfgang von Goethe's (1749-1852) classic German-language verse-version of his tale:

> A longing pure and not to be described
> Drove me to wander over woods and fields,
> And in the midst of hot abundant tears
> I felt a world arise and live for me.

Clearly, Wotan's desire for *wandervoegeling* lay inherent within the authentic Aryan soul! But, these days, would Faust be *wandervoegeling* not through the German fields and hills, but the vast blacknesses of outer space? The telescope, for example, was a 'truly Faustian' invention which could never have been devised by a non-Westerner, which functioned to make the invisible visible and thereby 'increase the universe that we possess'. Initially, it could be used by restless Faustian sailors and navigators, but ultimately it could be used to scope out whole other worlds for future Aryan colonisation in Myatt's Galactic Reich. 'With the discovery of America, Western Europe became a province in a gigantic whole,' argued Spengler; in space travel terms, maybe we would one day consider the discovery of Uranus and Pluto via telescopic means in a similar fashion?[27]

The competing Magian culture, however, was passive; it asked not *how* we would reach the stars, but *when* the stars would make things happen to us, via astrology. Magian concepts of Fate, like the Turkish *kismet*, encouraged not personal responsibility, but listless passivity.[28] Magian culture was enfeebling, as it entailed a new 'limit-feeling' being placed upon the Faustian perception of the stellar infinite – it forcibly draws us back down from Heaven to Earth. This is why the chief symbol of the Magian culture was the cave or the cavern, which reappeared in the architecture of the mosque or cupola-church which, unlike the soaring spires of the Christian cathedral, was topped by a dome, blocking out the sky above. This represented the ultimate lid placed upon mankind's ambitions and horizons, an attempt to keep the Faustian world-spirit in chains. Magians do have a sense of 'space without', but they wish to bar perception of it behind their domes, to hide it away by looking down at the ground, not up towards the skies; for Myatt, this would match with our contemporary Magian civilisation saying space travel is too hard and concentrating on simpler, less noble things instead, like making money or raising living standards. The myth of the dying Faust, condemned to Hell after selling his soul to the demon, was paralleled by the entropy now sweeping through a ruined Europe, demoralised and robbed of all incentive by the invasion of the Magian world-spirit; like a shark, if a civilisation does not keep moving forwards it dies, and without new worlds left to conquer, the formerly Faustian West would simply end up being carried away into Hades by Jewish and Middle Eastern versions of Mephistopheles.[29]

For the Faustian, his governing mentality dissolved the world around him, meaning that fairyland lay on the next hillside, Thule just over the horizon, or Grail-treasure just beneath the next layer of soil, so it made sense that this particular world-spirit should also seek to dissolve the sky-dome or shatter the Magian cave-cupola, thereby giving access to outer space:

A Hellenic [or Magian] river god ... is definitely understood as being the river and not as, so to say, dwelling in the river ... On the contrary, not a trace of this localised materiality clings to the [Germanic] elves, dwarfs, witches, valkyries and their kindred, the armies of departed souls that sweep round o' nights [in the Wild Hunt] ... Kaiser Barbarossa [or Wotan, in some versions of the myth] sits [sleeping] in the Kyffhäuser cavern ... It is as though the Faustian universe abhorred anything material and impenetrable ... No other culture knows so many fables of treasures lying in mountains and pools, of secret subterranean realms, palaces, gardens, wherein other beings dwell. The whole substantiality of the visible world is denied by the Faustian Nature-feeling, for which in the end nothing is of Earth and the only actual is Space. The fairy tale dissolves the matter of Nature, as the Gothic style dissolves the stone-mass of our cathedrals into a ghostly wealth of forms and lines that shed all weight and acknowledge no bounds.[30]

The fundamental difference in outlook also meant each civilisation had its own competing conceptions of science and mathematics: 'there is no mathema*tic*, but only mathema*tics*', said Spengler. Such fields were not objective but culture-specific, reflecting aspects of each civilisation's governing soul. For example, to the pre-Faustian Greeks, there were only whole numbers, such as 1, 2, 3 and so on. But to the Faustian, an infinitude of numbers lay between each whole one; between 1 and 2 there were not only numbers like 1.5 and 1.6, but also numbers between these, such as 1.55 and 1.56, and between those yet other numbers, like 1.555 and 1.556, and between those even smaller ones again, and so on *ad infinitum*. Potentially, a Faustian could go on counting forever before he ever even reached the number 2. As Faustians enjoyed an innate apprehension of the infinite, instead of blocking it out like the Magians or Greeks, Faustian numbers were not whole things, but abstract relations between one another. Interestingly, the ancient Greeks had no specific word for 'space'. Their cosmos, being a 'well-ordered aggregate of all near and completely viewable things, was concluded by the vault of heaven'. For the non-Faustian, beyond the sky there was nothing, just as there was nothing beyond the whole numbers like 1 and 2; for the Faustian, infinity lay everywhere, in outer space and between numbers alike.[31]

Might this not therefore mean that Faustian mathematics, being concerned with the infinite, may one day become the basis for a truly Faustian civilisation, like that of the Nazis, conquering the equally infinite realms of outer space via use of a wholly alternative form of physics, as imagined by David Myatt? In the 1800s, Western mathematicians with good, German-sounding names like Bernard Riemann (1826-66) and Carl Friedrich Gauss (1777-1855) had invented new forms of non-Euclidean 'boundless geometry' involving novel concepts like multi-dimensional space, of the sort Myatt imagined might be of some use in creating starship engines.[32] Unlike the paintings of other cultures, Spengler had noticed how many of Western art's greatest canvases were set at night, only partly illuminated by candles and moonlight, something significant because 'The candle affirms and the sunlight denies space as the opposite of [solid, material] things. At night the universe of space triumphs over matter, at midday the surroundings assert themselves and space is repudiated.'[33] If there could be a Magian 'art of the day' and a Faustian 'art of the night', then why should there not also be an occult-tinged Faustian 'science of the night' to complement a Magian 'science of the day' too? According to Spengler, every science, 'without exception', has its extremes and esoterica which remain inaccessible to the layman, these obscure corners being 'symbols ... of our [Faustian] will-to-infinity and directional energy'.[34] Perhaps the acausal physics imagined by Myatt would be one good example?

Western Faustian physics was based fundamentally upon the notion of energy, said Spengler, not the old Greek idea of tiny, solid little objects called atoms. Instead of being passively acted upon by blind Fate, like the characters in a Greek drama, Faustian wave-atoms were 'systems of abstract [energetic] force-points working in unison, aggressive, energetically dominating space ... overcoming resistances like Macbeth' in a Western drama, whose protagonists possessed their own sense of direct agency. Supposedly, these competing conceptions of physics had their origins in Aryans deriving their sciences from observing Nature's processes, like tall trees being blown in the breeze, and attributing such movements to the willpower of invisible gods rather than the blind chance of the wind, as in non-Faustian cultures. These gods were later invited into the scientific pantheon and given new names like 'gravity' and 'force', which seemed neutral, but which were really just the modern-day version of the old magical, numinous god-names for universal cosmic forces with an apparent mind of their own. Such 'astonishment at alien motion' of trees in a Germanic forest could never have been felt by a Magian Muslim staring at a single cypress tree in the windless Middle Eastern desert, argued Spengler, this contrast being the original basis for the difference between Faustian and Magian 'religion and physics both'.

The Magian culture was based on calm and stillness and so was its science; the Faustian culture was based on restlessness and movement, and so was its science. Supposedly, Jews and Magians couldn't even understand the Newtonian concept of force, this being little more than 'a numen stiffened into a concept' – that is to say, an old Faustian Nordic wind god transformed into an abstract concept of physics.[35] For Spengler, we did not know what energy actually was, we simply recognised it by its workings, which became analogous to our picture of God and His workings; for Myatt, it was also impossible to recognise precisely what acausal energy was, simply to recognise it at work when you saw it. Spengler summed up his findings thus:

> If, in fine, we look at the whole picture – the expansion of the [astronomical] world into that aspect of stellar space that we possess today; the development of Columbus' discovery [of America] into a world-wide command of the Earth's surface by the West ... the passion of our civilisation for swift transit, the conquest of the air, the exploration of the polar regions and the climbing of almost impossible mountain-peaks – we see, emerging everywhere, the prime symbol of the Faustian soul, Limitless Space. And those specially Western creations of the soul-myth called 'Will', 'Force' and 'Deed' must be regarded as derivatives of this prime symbol.[36]

This was David Myatt's outlook on the whole scenario, too – until, all of a sudden, in 1998 he embraced one aspect of the Magian world-spirit as being inherently Faustian in nature anyway, and found radical Islam. Possibly Faust was a Magian after all? Alchemy *is* an Arabic word.

* * * * *

If David Myatt now professes to have repudiated his old extremist Faustian belief-systems, variants of them still live on in the teachings of the O9A/ONA 'Order of the Nine Angles' Satanic Nazism cult which is clearly directly based on Myatt's ideas, whether he was ever the organisation's leader or not. This can be seen self-evidently in their adoption of his 'Star Game' in their rituals, a very complicated three-dimensional board-game Myatt invented in prison in 1975, a sort of 3-D chess played on a multi-tiered board six feet in height and three feet in width, with seven boards placed above one another in spiral formation, each corresponding to a different star, Naos, Deneb, Rigel, Mira, Antares, Arcturus and Sirius. The chess pieces are small tetrahedrons marked with abstract occult symbols, with the central conceit being that, once each piece has been moved, it transforms itself into a different piece via 'living metamorphosis' in a fashion which represents both Arnold Toynbee's notions about the cyclical change in civilisations from one Aeon of history to another, and C. G. Jung's ideas about the various potential transformations of one's personal psyche.[37] It is pretty unlikely any two persons are going to invent such an incredibly specific thing independently, showing how Myatt and the O9A are obviously related in some way, even if the O9A and its central figures, given pseudonyms like Christos Beest, Sinister Moon and Pointy Hat, did just take his ideas without specific permission, as Myatt would claim.

The O9A also aim to hasten the arrival of Vindex and his Galactic Reich into this world via the manipulation of acausal forces, conceiving of their covens (of which there are several worldwide) as being 'sinister tribes' akin to the al-Qaeda-like 'clans' which Myatt claimed were able to access hidden stores of acausal energy. For this reason, O9A tribes are also known as 'nexions', like the portals which connect causal and acausal worlds in Myatt's hypothetical physics of acausology:

> The sinister tribes of the ONA ... are that presencing of acausal energy which will fundamentally and irretrievably change our world, and which will manifest, and bring into being, an entirely new, more evolved, type of human being and entirely new types of human communities, preludes as these are to us leaving this planet which has for so long been our childhood home and seeding ourselves among the stars of the Galaxies of the Cosmos.[38]

Thus, it might be said that in this particular branch of the Nazis in outer space mythos, Hitler's followers did not build UFOs during the course of the Second World War, as many Esoteric Nazis claim, but *will* do, some day in the distant future. But are the O9A really Nazis at all? Are they even really Satanists? Their core ritual text may well be called *The Black Book of Satan*, but it is important to note that for contemporary occultists this does not necessarily entail worshipping a literal evil demonic being called Satan, but rather the various transgressive principles such an imaginary anti-deity might possess. The general idea of the O9A is to engage in taboo acts (reputedly including ritual murder and other such heinous crimes) so as to trigger extreme emotions of a 'sinisterly numinous' nature within the human soul of the adept and so open up more nexions into the acausal realm, providing a means through which Vindex and his forces can seep into our world to prepare the way for our forthcoming mastery of space. Naturally, one of the best ways to transgress traditional commonplace boundaries of traditional morality is to worship history's most hated man Adolf Hitler, as seen in the following prayer-passage from the blasphemous O9A 'Mass of Heresy':

> Adolf Hitler was sent by our gods
> To guide us to greatness.
> We believe in the inequality of races
> And in the right of the Aryan to live
> According to the laws of the folk [i.e. the volk].
> We acknowledge that the story of the Jewish 'Holocaust'
> Is a lie to keep our race in chains,

And express our desire to see the truth revealed.
We believe in justice for our oppressed comrades
And seek an end to the world-wide
Persecution of National Socialists.[39]

Do they really mean any of this, or is it only a metaphor? In recent years, some sinister tribes of the O9A have begun worshipping Osama bin Laden instead of the Nazis, suggesting the whole fascist angle may be just a decorative pose; Hitler, Satan and bin Laden alike could merely be exoteric symbols of something far more esoteric lying hidden behind them. It is difficult to say for sure, as the O9A have deliberately created layer upon layer of confusing self-mythology. As an undercover organisation, this helps them cover their tracks and keep their true intentions helpfully ambiguous. According to the O9A founding legend, they are a continuation of a Neolithic 7,000-year-old Shropshire-based wiccan cult devoted to worship of a dark, violent pagan goddess, later taken over by a man going by the name of Anton Long – allegedly Myatt himself, if you believe that version of the tale – in the 1970s, after the cult's Grand Mistress moved to Australia. As this cult revered the old seven known planets, and the waxing and waning of the stars, this explains their name. The O9A have a ritual 'Tree of Wyrd', with 'wyrd' being the old Anglo-Saxon term for destiny, laid out on seven angled branches, corresponding to the seven planets, each of which serves as a nexion between this world and the next. Added to this are the sect's occult system as a whole, this being the eighth angle, and the individual adept who follows it, the ninth angle. Alternatively, the O9A name may refer to the nine stages of certain branches of alchemy, reflecting their desire to transform civilisational lead into gold. The major purpose of its school of Satanism is to shake members out of their cultural conditioning via the transgression of taboo and gain mastery over the self by performing various difficult acts of Nietzschean self-overcoming, involving ordeals like spending nights alone in a dark cave like Savitri Devi once did at the Externsteine, something known as 'The Ritual of the Abyss'. As Nietzsche wrote, if you gaze into the abyss long enough, eventually it will gaze back into you. Through such trials, it is anticipated the cultist will evolve into the 'phenotype' of a new, forthcoming breed of pitiless future humanity, the Viking-like post-Vindex *übermenschen* destined to become galaxy-subduing astronauts.

The Satanic and Nazi imagery are viewed by some analysts of the cult's activities simply as appropriately numinous symbols which will facilitate such a mutation of the soul. Unlike Marxists, the Nazis did recognise the reality of the soul – albeit its dark side. As one O9A text has it, the Third Reich was 'a practical expression of Satanic spirit … a burst of Luciferian light – of zest and power – in an otherwise Nazarene [i.e. Judaeo-Christian], pacified and boring world.' In this way, Hitler's Germany had successfully drawn huge amounts of acausal energy onto Earth, opening up a new nexion, with this power-source remaining stored away somewhere, ready for use.

Jews, Marxists and capitalists tried to drain these acausal batteries by falsely discrediting the Nazis by association with the Holo-Hoax, but this lie could be resisted by engaging in taboo fascistic acts like racial violence, which acted as re-energisers of the martial spirit of Vindex through the numinous, acausal forces unleashed by such activities; even National Front-style racist street thuggery could have an actual magical purpose to it, then. Possibly Vindex's 'spirit' here, however, was to be taken only in a metaphorical sense, as an inspiration for world revolution. When other, non-Esoteric, neo-Nazis habitually invoke the 'spirit' of Adolf Hitler, they do so without literally expecting to say '*Heil!*' to his ghost, after all.

Yet, other accounts of the O9A imply they may well believe that certain real-life 'Dark Gods' like Vindex really do live within the acausal realm, formed from bodies of intelligent acausal energy. Possibly these are literal entities of the sort you might wish to label demons, or maybe they are more akin to Jungian archetypes. Whatever he is, the O9A seek to make Vindex incarnate physically within our realm via something known as 'Aeonic Magick'. By influencing others to believe their Nietzschean creed, and then having them infiltrate various fields, such as politics, academia, the arts and the media, the O9A hope to subliminally seed Western civilisation with ideas conducive to the eventual pursuit of Vindex's Galactic Reich, thereby bringing about his new Aeon, during which mankind will successfully colonise the Milky Way. As they feel that Cultural Marxists have done something similar in the West via their own post-war 'Long March Through the Institutions' in pursuit of their own imaginary New Jerusalem, culminating in the putrid *kali yuga* world we inhabit today, the O9A think they might be able to institute a corresponding counter-march back towards an interstellar *satya yuga* known as the 'Aeon of Fire'. Playing Myatt's Star Game or performing rituals and sacrifices also helps subliminally alter the Aryan collective unconscious in some way, engineering a situation akin to that in which Jung once imagined the Wotan archetype possessing the German *volk* and transforming them into the Wild Hunt. Due to the huge amount of time this scheme would take to come to fruition, however, it may appear to the untutored eye that the O9A's activities are totally ineffective. It will only be to the future eye of history that the long-term transformation of the 'world of mundanes' inhabited by today's Homo Hubris into tomorrow's Galactic Reich will become truly perceptible.[40]

Or is this just a handy psychological get-out-clause for the fact that, to the untutored eye, the O9A's activities would seem to have had little impact on the world at large? Maybe one day they will, as with the activities of the initially pointless-seeming Landig Circle, but not yet. If you think the Grail-Quests of David Myatt and the O9A are unrealistic, however, then at least they have helped give their lives some meaning. Their desire to conquer the universe, not unlike their ostensible exoteric worship of Adolf Hitler, could be just a convenient symbol of their Faustian desire to experience something more in their lives. One of the greatest of all post-war novels,

Thomas Pynchon's *Gravity's Rainbow*, tells the picaresque late-war tale of a wild hunt to uncover the secrets of some more impossible-sounding Nazi space-technology in terms of the V-2 rocket. The novel is often said to be a technologically centred re-writing of Herman Melville's *Moby Dick*, with the V-2 standing in for the white whale. Yet the white whale which Captain Ahab hunts is not really a white whale at all, but something other, something indefinable, something rather Faustian, in fact. 'All visible objects, man, are but as pasteboard masks,' as Ahab himself says.[41]

The search of the Esoteric Hitlerists for Nazi UFOs or incarnations of Kalki and Vindex strike me as similar to Ahab's search for Moby Dick; not hunts for literal nuts-and-bolts craft or flesh-and-blood individuals, but quests to seek a white whale for the white race, for a way to break on through our quotidian modern post-war world and on into the numinous Esoteric Nazi realm of Miguel Serrano's Venusian Hyperborea, Wilhelm Landig 's Mount Meru or the 'Absolute Elsewhere' once imagined as existing temporarily within the Third Reich by Pauwels and Bergier in *The Morning of the Magicians*. 'How can the prisoner [of life] reach outside except by thrusting through the wall [of existence]?' asks Ahab. 'To me, the white whale is that wall, shoved near to me. Sometimes I think there's naught beyond. But 'tis enough. He tasks me.'[42] Those people who take the idea of Nazi UFOs absolutely literally, and set out to find evidence of their physical existence, are, I think, rather like those unimaginative souls who think *Moby Dick* is actually about a whale or *Gravity's Rainbow* is actually about the V-2. But, as the second part of this book shall show, there are rather a lot of them around these days. As with so many other contemporary maladies, I blame the Internet.

WEB OF LIES: THE POSTMODERN PUZZLE OF THE ONLINE NAZI UFOs ERA

'What is a fine lie? Simply that which is its own evidence. If a man is sufficiently unimaginative to produce evidence in support of a lie, he might just as well speak the truth at once.'
Oscar Wilde, early exponent of Online Logic-Theory

As one might rightly say of me, in this book I have just created a bouquet of other people's flowers, providing myself only the thread that holds them together.'
Michel de Montaigne, celebrated French plagiarist

1

Abducted to Auschwitz: Cyber-Commandants Meet Doctors of Death as the Nazis Become Even More Inhuman

So far, we have mostly encountered persons who have tried to associate National Socialism with aliens, flying saucers and outer space for bizarre quasi-religious reasons, but there are others on this fallen, *kali yuga* planet who have done so for more base commercial reasons, too; the profit motive often beats the prophet motive. Accordingly, the notion of Nazi UFOs is a trope now commonly disseminated not only by Esoteric Hitlerists, but also by the entertainment industry, particularly from the 1980s onwards. As early as 1947 came *Rocketship Galileo*, a children's book in which a group of all-American astro-kids claim the moon for the UN, only to find a secret Nazi base there which they must blitzkrieg to bits in the Germans' own stolen spaceship, later adapted into the 1950 b-movie *Destination Moon*. Thanks to a more recent wave of schlocky semi-comic sci-fi flicks like 2012's *Iron Sky*, a Finnish production in which Nazis re-invade Earth from the dark side of the moon (where their 'Moonführer' operates under the sign of the Black Sun), the imaginative link between Nazism, space travel and allied themes has successfully invaded that Poland of the mind known as the collective media unconscious. 2012 alone saw not only *Iron Sky*, but also *Nazis at the Centre of the Earth*, with a script surely by Miguel Serrano, *The 25th Reich* and *Outpost: Black Sun*, the second in a trilogy based upon Internet legends of an SS time-travel spaceship.[1]

Iron Sky caused controversy in Germany, due to jokes such as pubic hair in Nazi porn mags being shaved like Hitler moustaches, but the film-makers argued it was all a satire upon alleged fascistic tendencies in contemporary US politics; some of the American President's speeches in the script are ripped direct from Joseph Goebbels. Director Timo Vuorensola admitted it was 'a tremendously politically incorrect film' which would not have been possible until recently, with 'the best response' to it coming 'from young Germans who have nothing to do with the Nazi era ... to them, the Nazis are just historical.' One consequent complaint was that *Iron Sky*'s Nazis were so over-the-top they became mere panto villains. With the passage of time, said one reviewer, 'It appears the Nazis have become stereotypical components of a popular cultural inventory that are as easy to parody as Crusaders, Huns and Vikings.' Depressingly, following *Iron Sky*'s release, German magazine *PM* used it to print an article claiming there was 'strong evidence' the Nazis really did have a wartime UFO-building programme, repeating uncritically yet again the lies of the media's favourite 1950s fake saucer-inventor Rudolf Schriever, lies then regurgitated by Britain's *Daily Telegraph* on their website. Supposedly, in 1944 eyewitnesses reported seeing 'a flying saucer marked with the Iron Cross ... flying low over the Thames' – even though the very term 'flying saucer' was not born until 1947.

The film made money and trailers for a sequel soon appeared, featuring Adolf Hitler riding a dinosaur. Called *Iron Sky: The Coming Race*, this 2019 follow-up played on Esoteric Nazi mythology surrounding *Vril* and lizard-men, the title being a nod to Edward Bulwer-Lytton. Following nuclear war, a dying humanity survives only on the moon. To regenerate the race, *Vril* is sought within the Hollow Earth, where it is protected by Nazi lizard-people. The reptoids created mankind as a genetic experiment by injecting *Vril* into the apple eaten by Adam and Eve, who were originally monkeys, but soon evolved into Aryans. Today, *Vril* is contained within the Holy Grail, guarded by dino-Nazis in the lost city of Agartha; the Grail has the capacity to regenerate flesh, hence Britain's most reptilian former PM, Margaret Thatcher, still being alive down there. The moon-humans successfully steal the *Sangraal*, leading to a still-healthy Hitler invading the moon to get it back, mounted on the back of his pet T-Rex, Blondi (the name of Hitler's actual dog). Yet the trouble with exploiting this aspect of the mythos is that it is nowhere near as well-known as the basic motif of Nazis flying UFOs is, and so appeared to most critics as an incoherent mess of apparently random plot-twists. The reader may by now understand its references to *Vril*, but the average viewer will not. A review in *The Guardian* bemoaned 'the logic at play in the superficial script: if it looks surreal, put it in without build-up or consequence.' This opinion is actually ill-informed, but you can hardly expect reviewers to wade through Miguel Serrano and the Ariosophists before attending the premiere. Although the most expensive Finnish movie ever made, *The Coming Race* flopped, and its production company, the appropriately named Blind Spot Pictures, went bankrupt.[2]

More successful was *The Legend of Koizumi*, AKA *Reform with No Wasted Draws*, an incredibly bizarre Japanese manga comic in which the nation's former PM Junichiro Koizumi, assisted by other world leaders, fights Nazis on the moon by challenging them to life-or-death battles in the traditional oriental tile-game of Mah-Jong. These battles are modelled after those usually seen in beat-'em-up videogames like *Street Fighter II*, with Nazis and democrats alike having access to special moves which they announce by yelling catchphrases. When Adolf Hitler plays his special move, he magically transforms into Super Aryan Hitler, with giant, sticky-up blonde hair like that once sported by the pop duo Jedward. Super Aryan Hitler has access to the 'Heisenburg Strike', which utilises the findings of Nazi-friendly quantum physicist Werner Heisenberg (1901-76), allowing Adolf to merge parallel worlds on the Mah-Jong board until he comes across one in which the tiles have fallen perfectly for him to win. However, Hitler's nemesis Koizumi has the corresponding ability to rub Mah-Jong tiles with his fingers so quickly that he can erase their markings to his own advantage, although sometimes this goes wrong and the friction produced sets his arms on fire. Following the war, Hitler flew to the moon, devising a new plan to conquer mankind via the medium of Mah-Jong. The Fourth Reich targets Earth with its giant moon-cannon, laying waste to cities, before Hitler returns in his UFO and demands the planet produce its greatest Mah-Jong players to face him and his Nazi champions in a series of best-of-five tournament games, seated in electric chairs which execute the losers immediately. With deliberate bad taste, fascist Mah-Jong masters include the brain of the Nazi death camp doctor Josef Mengele (contained within the body of his biologically enhanced female nurse, whose ears are so good she can *hear* which tile will be played next), who has the ability to make paired tiles appear, reflecting Mengele's obsession with death camp experiments on twins, Hitler's favourite composer and 'King of Opera' Richard Wagner, resurrected by Dr Mengele, and Nazi commando leader Otto Skorzeny, who tells opponents to 'Eat shit and die.' Caught cheating, Skorzeny is shot by US snipers acting as harsh Mah-Jong referees, but still manages to smoke a cigarette and win his match before croaking.

Margaret Thatcher is considered as one of Koizumi's team, but proves senile, so Russian leader Vladimir Putin and former US Presidents George W. Bush and his father 'Papa Bush' step up to save humanity at the Pope's request. Initial matches occur on Earth, but Field-Marshal Erwin Rommel (1891-1944) instigates a moon-coup during Hitler's absence, leading Adolf to float back up there to kill him with top-class tile-play. Koizumi follows the Führer into space to finish things off, accompanied by another Mah-Jong genius, ASIMO, the bandy little humanoid companion-robot for lonely Japanese pensioners created by Honda in 2000. It transpires Honda secretly gave their robot a suite of 'ASIMO weapons', allowing it to project fake holograms onto Mah-Jong tiles, thus boosting its score, in case of global Mah-Jong conflict. Eventually, Koizumi and ASIMO defeat Hitler and his Mah-Jong partner Tristan Goebbels, Joseph Goebbels' moon-born *mondenkind* grandson (his sister Isolde is also a character, whose role is largely limited to having her skirt blown up revealing her knickers). Super Aryan Hitler can only be defeated thanks to The Three Goddesses of Mount Osore, spirit mediums who contact the ghosts of Winston Churchill, Josef Stalin and Franklin D. Roosevelt, who actually won the Second World War by Mah-Jong means, and who provide tactical advice to Koizumi and ASIMO via séances. Beaten, Hitler dies, his soul doomed into the purgatory of a never-ending Mah-Jong tournament against the Allied trio, but Koizumi is left stranded on the moon, presumed dead, leading the Japanese military to establish the 13th Autonomous Mah-Jong Corps to make up for the loss of the PM's super-powers. Japan then embarks upon a new Mah-Jong war against the resurrected corpse of Chairman Mao (1893-1976), who lives inside a strange red box aboard a Soviet-Chinese aircraft carrier in alliance with an undead V. I. Lenin (1870-1924), a horrifying conflict we shall not detail here. Originating as a strip in a news-stand Mah-Jong publication, the manga became so popular it was later bound and sold separately, shifting 2.5 million copies before becoming an anime cartoon in 2010.[3]

The *Wolfenstein* videogame series is also important, as the 1992 entry *Wolfenstein 3D* was the true father of the major First-Person Shooter (FPS) genre. Mostly, the player progresses through the titular Wewelsburg clone castle killing ordinary military guards and vicious dogs, but at the end you encounter multiple *doppelgängers* of Adolf Hitler dressed as a wizard, whom you must eliminate until you can finally shoot the real Führer (ensconced within a machine-gun-wielding blue mecha-suit) in the face and make him melt. Several sequels and prequels followed in which the Nazi occult angle was emphasised – one was called *Spear of Destiny* – until by the 2009 series reboot edition, simply titled *Wolfenstein*, the plot became centred upon Himmler's plan to tap into the Black Sun, drawing out energy to power new *Wunderwaffen* devices. In 2001's *Return to Castle Wolfenstein*, Himmler headed up an 'SS Paranormal Division' modelled on the *Ahnenerbe*, who sought to resurrect his hero King Heinrich I, aided by an 'SS High Priestess' with the familiar-sounding surname Blavatsky. The most recent main instalment, *Wolfenstein II: The New Colossus*, is more focused upon pure sci-fi than the occult, being set in a conquered alternate-reality 1960s USA filled with Nazi spaceships, atom bombs, laser guns, drones, semi-robotic soldiers and gigantic armoured super-blimps, and enjoys a sudden plot-twist in which Adolf Hitler is reimagined as an incontinent, dementia-ridden movie-director living on Venus in constant fear of accidentally employing Jewish actors in his films, leading him to shoot most applicants for roles in the head. The basic idea is that having won the war, the Nazis occupied America in cahoots with the Ku Klux Klan, exploiting the famous Roswell saucer crash of 1947 to back-engineer alien tech, so enabling interplanetary travel. Given that videogames are now more profitable than the movie industry, by making use of such tropes the series' makers ensure Nazi UFO mythology will be passed on to a whole new generation.[4]

* * * * *

All harmless fictions, you might have thought, even if such things do have some detractors; many *Wolfenstein* titles were banned in Germany until as recently as 2018, and sometimes the pixellated swastikas are replaced with occult-tinged variations to side-step legal issues. However, most critics of the Nazi sci-fi genre object to the *Wolfensteins* of this world more on bad-taste grounds than because those customers who consume them might one day begin, through the sheer cultural pervasiveness of their repeated motifs, to confuse them for reality. Nobody could ever end up believing in the literal existence of Moon-Nazis, could they? We should already know the answer to that by now.

A silly article in the New Age *Atlantis Rising* magazine by the UFO researcher Len Kasten, author of such books as *Dark Fleet: The Secret Nazi Space Programme and the Battle for the Solar System*, points out that, under the terms of the Versailles Treaty, a defeated Germany was only allowed to maintain limited troop numbers after the First World War. So how was it that following Hitler's 1933 rise to power he built his own army from such small beginnings so quickly? The actual answer is 'conscription', but that is too boring. By the time of the Nuremberg Rallies of 1933-38, says Kasten, '160,000 stalwart German soldiers, with backpacks and rifles, stood silently at attention in precise ranks' whilst Adolf shouted at them from a podium. The 'startling explanation' for this may have been that Hitler was in cahoots with some 'alien friends', who used their superior science to create him 'a million-man army of cloned storm troopers' in their spaceships and subterranean bases. In *Star Wars*, Darth Vader's Imperial foot soldiers were called storm troopers, whilst the 2002 entry in the series was called *Attack of the Clones*, in which a colossal space-army is manufactured by technological means. The cloned Imperial troops are shown in serried ranks reminiscent of Nazi soldiers at Nuremberg in this movie too, so perhaps the series' creator George Lucas 'knew more than is commonly believed' when he developed these scripts, asks Kasten? The more likely explanation is that Lucas saw propaganda footage of the Nuremberg rallies and made images of his assembled cloned soldiers look broadly similar in order to link the Empire's military evil back to that of the Nazis' military evil.[5]

In 1976 it was decided to name NASA's new space-shuttle *Enterprise* after the spaceship in *Star Trek*, following lobbying from one of the TV show's biggest fans, Richard C. Hoagland (b.1945), who appears most uncertain of the relationship between fact and fiction. Hoagland is best known for his 1987 book *The Monuments of Mars: A City on the Edge of Forever*, which discussed the infamous 'Face on Mars', an optical illusion detected in that planet's Cydonia region by NASA's 1976 *Viking 1 Orbiter* probe. NASA dismissed the Face as caused by unusual shadows cast upon an ordinary Martian mesa; seen from most angles, the geographical feature didn't resemble a face at all. Hoagland disagreed, spotting a whole Martian city up there, filled with pyramids. Hoagland's 2007 follow-up text, *Dark Mission: The Secret History of NASA*, claims NASA has been covering up evidence of ancient alien civilisations on Mars ever since being founded in 1958. So how did they manage to let the photos of the incredibly obvious Face leak out? Hoagland says they did it on purpose, with NASA allowing a drip-feed of 'accidental' revelations to slowly prepare us for the truth, before seeding sci-fi films, novels and TV shows with images of ancient alien civilisations, to soften up human minds. In 1992 Hoagland gave an actual speech to the UN, speculating the Face on Mars may depict the head of a lion-human hybrid. As Egypt's Sphinx is also a human-lion hybrid, and is near some pyramids, Hoagland argued Cydonia and Egypt were twins and therefore '*we* are the Martians!' Humanity once colonised the solar system, but some huge disaster left the Earth-branch of this space empire as its sole survivor, he says. The clever Germans knew this too. NASA being stuffed with Paperclipped Nazis, one hidden aim of their entire organisation was thus to enable Wernher von Braun's friends to resettle their ancestral stellar homelands for *lebensraum*. Maybe *Wolfenstein II: The New Colossus* was true after all?[6]

No other totalitarian ideologies have become so indelibly and profitably associated with the field of ufology; is there something special about the Nazis, other than their historical association (both real and imaginary) with *Wunderwaffen* and the occult? For highly educated esoterists like David Myatt, conversant as they are with the philosophies of Oswald Spengler and others, it may have seemed natural to link Nazism with outer space, but most people have never even heard of things like the Faustian world-soul. And yet instinctively, they still seem to be seduced by the imaginative appeal of an innate connection potentially existing between Hitlerism and UFOs in a way they would not with other competing extremist political creeds. In 1998, a breakaway faction split from Britain's Trotskyist Socialist Workers' Party, called the British Marxist Ufologist Group, which argued that, as alien visitors to Earth must by definition be more technologically advanced than us puny, capitalism-hobbled humans, they must also have been more advanced socially, and therefore have been Communists. They further concluded Karl Marx (1818-83) was 'almost certainly' a Martian in disguise, whose human-sounding surname was pinched from the name of his spacecraft, MARS-X. Friedrich Engels (1820-95), his co-author on *The Communist Manifesto*, was MARS-X's on-board computer, ENGELS. Furthermore, Marxist rebel Che Guevara (1928-67) was an ET android, as following his death it was observed his bones were filled not with marrow, but silicon. The splinter-group's consequent policy position was that they needed to 'make the Revolution easier' by putting political pressure on the Labour Party to disclose the full concealed truth about UFOs and the admirably Far-Left nature of their occupants.[7]

In a previous book, I tracked the historical associations between ufology and socialism, and it is quite a lengthy one.[8] However, it is also virtually unknown to the average consumer, and so has been little mined by the entertainment industry; there is no Communist *Wolfenstein*, and the notion Marx was Martian seems fit only for mockery. When it comes to fascists, the situation is different – as long as the fascists in question are German. There have been recent efforts to develop a parallel UFO mythos for Mussolini's Italy, with dubious documents surfacing in 2000, detailing a secret investigation into 'a kind of aerial torpedo' from which two saucers shaped like 'two hats like those used by priests' emerged, seen by a crowd over Venice on 17 August 1936. Two fighter-jets were scrambled, but the objects sped away silently, too quick to be caught. A report was handed to the Italian Foreign Minister, with fascists rounding all witnesses up and threatening them with the asylum if they breathed a word, thus explaining why nobody had ever heard of the event until the Internet was invented. A secret government unit, RS/33, was established, and Italy's best scientist, Guglielmo Marconi (1874-1937), ordered to back-engineer a saucer which had crashed in Lombardy in 1933, a clear attempt to invent an Italian *Wunderwaffen* mythology with Marconi filling the Wernher von Braun role. An obscure alleged quote from Mussolini was twisted from a presumable joke into a serious statement, namely his 1941 quip that America should care more about attacks from Martians than from Axis forces.[9] And yet, just as with the idea of Communist aliens, the fable of Mussolini's UFOs didn't catch on anything like as much as the meme of Hitler's UFOs did. Why?

'The things that will destroy us are politics without principle and science without humanity,' Mahatma Gandhi once said; in the Nazis, you had both dangers combined in one handy paragon of evil, which makes them ideal science-fiction baddies, substitute alien monsters in and of themselves. The best-selling *Projekt Saucer* thriller novels of the 1980s and 1990s are a good case in point, as their wild ideas about polar-dwelling SS robot-men have now become a central plank of the Nazi UFO mythos. Despite being about squadrons of cybernetic saucer-pilots hiding in the Antarctic under the control of a malign scientific genius who seeks to become a giant immortal living computer, the novels purport to be based partly upon reality. The original 1980 edition of the first book in the series to be published (which, chronologically, now stands as the third book in an initial sequence of five), *Genesis*, came with a lengthy afterword in which the novel's British author, W. A. Harbinson (b.1941) argued the Nazis really had developed flying saucers, and an extensive list of further reading purporting to prove it. His basic narrative relies on the false stories of Rudolf Schriever and his ilk, examined from a less than sceptical stance, with Harbinson's fiction thus being 'based on various facts – and those facts could do with further examination.'[10] This wasn't the first time such a gimmick had been tried. In 1954, French thriller writer Michel Lecler (1930-96) published *Plutonium 239*, in which a group of Nazi scientists, led by Hitler himself, develop a pocket-sized atomic battery to power a saucer-engine, letting them flee Germany to the remotest snows of Sweden. Lecler's ideas were also taken directly from 1950s newspaper articles about Rudolf Schriever *et al*, and the novel, like Harbinson's, contained an afterword in which the author swore his premise was based on fact.[11]

When Harbinson expanded *Projekt Saucer* into a full novelistic quintet between 1991 and 1999, his UK publishers played up their supposed status as 'faction' in breathless blurbs like the following, used to advertise *Inception*, billed as being the first (chronologically speaking) in 'the epic *Projekt Saucer* series – a sequence of chilling revelations in the form of gripping fiction':

THE MOST TERRIFYING, AWESOME CONSPIRACY IN HUMAN HISTORY STARTS HERE

The first wave of modern UFO sightings occurred nearly a hundred years ago. Fact. In 1908, a mysterious, nuclear-like explosion devastated a vast area of Siberia [and it was really a crashed spaceship]. Fact. Allied airmen flying over Germany in World War II were chased by eerie fireballs [called foo-fighters]. Fact. During that same global conflict, the Nazis experimented desperately to try and create the world's first flying saucer. Fact.

These facts hold the key to the nightmarish secret of UFOs.[12]

Yet these words proved to be, at best, slightly exaggerated. *Fact.* When *Genesis* was released in the US in the 1980s, one review, proudly cited on the blurb of its later 1990s UK reprint, called it 'Impressive' as 'Harbinson has drawn so heavily on factual material and integrated it so well into the text that the book begins to read like non-fiction.'[13] So like non-fiction did the text read that in 1995, during the height of that decade's *X-Files* mania and its associated publishing boom in books about UFO-related conspiracy theories, Harbinson produced a non-fiction tie-in title, *Projekt UFO: The Case for Man-Made Flying Saucers*, which proposed the reason why some aliens allegedly met by post-1947 abductees appeared semi-robotic in nature was because they were actually cyborgs created from the findings of Nazi scientists after the war, just like the half-android, brain-implanted fascist drones in his thrillers. The book also handily acted as free cross-over advertising for its parent novels, with frequent references to them being made within, to drive sales further.

If the fictional *Genesis* read almost like non-fiction, then the allegedly factual *Projekt UFO* read more like the opposite. Harbinson's basic hypothesis is that Nazi death camp doctors 'paved the way for morally unimpeded physical experimentation on human beings, and modern science, in the shape of bio-cybernetic and genetic engineering experimentation, has shown itself willing and able to continue down this nightmarish path,' when seeking to clone embryos, transplant organs and implant electrodes in brains to let the disabled move their previously inert limbs. Although Harbinson never presents any specific evidence Nazi scientists tried to deform their captive subjects into human robots, largely because there isn't any, he does suggest that, as the Nazis successfully exploited slave labour to build massive underground *Alpenfestung* bunkers across Germany, there is no inherent reason why the SS could not have taken large quantities of men and materiel across to Antarctica via U-boat and dug more *Alpenfestung* facilities there to continue their research, eventually manufacturing functional flying saucers, staffed by remote-controlled robo-crews. Very possibly, 'the Germans are still entrenched there in a master-slave colony devoted to highly advanced, aggressive technology' something which, if known, would trigger worldwide panic, hence the global *X-Files*-style cover-up of UFOs' reality. Yet this is 'not the only possibility'. Maybe the Allies conquered this robot-infested ice-base, but conspired to maintain it as a convenient HQ to continue immoral Nazi experiments behind closed doors, researches since pursued in other remote locations like Siberia, the deserts of the southern USA, and the wilds of Canada. Such secret bases would be essential if any 'legal, ethical and religious constraints' on forcibly turning live humans into androids were to be avoided. If saucers had indeed been in clandestine continuous development since the late 1930s, then 'they could now be extraordinarily advanced machines being constructed, maintained and supported in hidden locations by a mixture of human scientists, cyborgs and other highly advanced man-machine products of a morally unrestrained, nightmarish technology.'[14] To which one can only say: that sounds like a great idea for a novel.

Harbinson cites the experiences of various famous alien abductees, such as Betty (1919-2004) and Barney Hill (1922-69), a US couple who on 19 September 1961 were supposedly taken aboard a spacecraft whilst driving through New Hampshire before being subjected to various hideous medical experiments by a group of small humanoid creatures now known in popular culture as 'Greys', with 'large eyes that reach around to the side of the head, no nose, and a mouth that was a slit without lip muscles' who communicated telepathically. On the night of 11 October 1973, meanwhile, two shipyard workers, Charles Hickson (1931-2011) and Calvin Parker (b.1954), were forcibly levitated inside a UFO near the Pascagoula River in Mississippi, enduring forced physical examinations by floating probes. Their kidnappers are often labelled 'lobster-men', due to their very long arms with pincers on the end. They also had no necks, no eyes, and only 'a small opening' instead of a mouth and 'pointing protrusions' instead of ears. Their heads were round, and their skin grey and wrinkly, 'like an elephant's'. Suggestively, one early investigator guessed these ufonauts were neither men nor lobsters, but mere 'automata' or 'advanced robots'. Antarctica's mad professors were also busy turning people into miniature flying goblins, as at a remote farmhouse in Kelly-Hopkinsville, Kentucky, where on 21 August 1955 an invasion of floating four-foot dwarfs occurred. Farmers shot at the gravity-immune beings, but bullets bounced off as if they were 'covered in nickel-plated armour'. Harbinson's specific description of the things makes them sound like mini-bots, but drawings made from witness statements don't look robotic at all, and the case has gone down in history as that of the 'Kelly-Hopkinsville Goblins', due to their round heads and long pointed ears, not the 'Kentucky Robots'. Harbinson also cites a 1973 case from Falkville, Alabama, in which a UFO pilot was photographed by a policeman and described as looking 'like a man wrapped in aluminium foil' – because this is what it actually was, the whole thing was a hoax, but Harbinson appeared not to know.[15]

But why would the *Wunderwaffen* scientists have weird robots flying their saucers, rather than ordinary trained humans? Harbinson cites the 'extraordinary accelerations and direction changes' of such craft, which would severely incapacitate mere flesh-and-blood aviators. UFO pilots' lungs would need to be 'partially collapsed and the blood in them artificially cooled', allowing their respiration 'and other bodily functions' to be controlled via cybernetics, 'irrespective of external environmental fluctuations', or they may die during flight. As these artificial lungs would 'render the mouth and nose superfluous', they would be sealed up like those of the Greys, or else tightly covered over with wrinkly grey elephant-skin as with the lobster-men and become 'completely non-functioning'. Such 'unfortunate creatures' would certainly look like robo-aliens to abductees, says Harbinson, and they may act like them, too. Presumably, most potential saucer-pilots would be unwilling to voluntarily become bipedal lobsters, tinfoil-people or flying goblins, so would need special implants inside their brains, allowing them to become 'remote-controlled, both mentally and physically, even across great distances', by the Antarctic SS or their equally evil Allied successors.[16]

So why are such robot-slaves going around abducting people all the time? Maybe abductees, too, are being given brain-implants and then returned back into the community to be manipulated as undercover servants themselves. Maybe the 'medical examinations' they are given on-board UFOs are a consequence of the evil experimenters having run out of any more human subjects at their hidden bases, meaning they must go out and seek some more. Or maybe such unlucky folk are having their organs harvested 'as a source of spare bodily parts for the cyborgs required by that [secret polar] society to work on the sea-bed or in outer space'.[17]

If the Nazis needed to kidnap people, however, there are probably less conspicuous ways than to fly around the world bundling them into flying saucers. Why not just chuck a few tramps into the back of a van? Or hijack a ship in the mid-Atlantic (or the Bermuda Triangle, just for the fun of it), remove its crew and then sink it? Or why not simply maintain a convenient breeding-colony of forced human organ-donors beneath the ice for posterity, a kind of human cattle farm? That would be easiest of all, and I doubt the SS would possess too many moral qualms about doing so.

* * * * *

Once the truth about the Holocaust emerged, a 'Nazisploitation' genre of b-movie was born in which the mad death camp scientist became a stock character, as seen in films like 1966's *Frozen Dead*, where the heads of dead Nazi war criminals are grafted onto new living bodies, 1964's *The Flesh Eaters*, where a Nazi scientist on a desert island creates organisms to eat men alive and 1958's *She-Demons*, where another desert island Nazi conducts immoral genetic experiments on captive females.[18] The Nazis themselves exploited the stock figure of the mad scientist; one of Goebbels' propaganda underlings, horror novelist Hanns Heinz Ewer (1871-1943), wrote an update of *Frankenstein* called *Alraune*. This told the horrific story of a female vampire created by an insane biologist who collected the sperm from a hanged murderer to impregnate a prostitute with, a perfect caution to all Germans about the perils of ignoring advice about good sexo-racial hygiene.[19] Much later fringe rumours that the Greys themselves were the equally sick result of failed sperm-related experiments to clone Hitler and the Nazi top-brass appear another development of such clichés.[20]

Whilst the Nazis might not actually have been going around doing the kind of things Harbinson claims they did, by rights they really *should* have been. By rights, they should really also have been living in the Antarctic, too: merciless bastards like the death camp doctors had pure cosmic WEL-ice running through their veins, did they not? According to Pauwels and Bergier in *The Morning of the Magicians*, the Nuremberg Trials were a futile exercise in 'trying to judge creatures from Mars by the standards of our own civilisation':

[The Nazis] were, indeed, Martians – in the sense that they belonged to a different world from the one we have known for the last six or seven centuries. A civilisation totally different from what is generally meant by the word had been established in Germany in the space of a few years, without our properly having understood what was going on. Its initiators no longer had any intellectual, moral or spiritual affinities with ourselves in any basic sense; and despite external resemblances, they were as remote from us as from the Australian aborigines.[21]

With this in mind, has any abductee ever specifically claimed to have seen a Nazi aboard an alien spaceship? Yes – Barney Hill did. Barney initially viewed his UFO, shaped 'like a big pancake', through binoculars, spotting its occupants wore 'black uniforms' like the SS. Under hypnosis, Barney recalled the ufonauts' leader wore a black scarf, 'had an evil face' and 'looked like a German Nazi'. In what way, though? The ET's eyes 'were *slanted*! But not like a Chinese ... I've never seen eyes slanted like that,' as they reached around the side of his head. 'Always the eyes are there,' said Barney, staring at him; sometimes, they were not even 'connected to a body'. Collectively, the aliens 'did not seem that they had different faces from white men', and yet had 'greyish, almost metallic-looking' skin, and 'rather odd-shaped heads, with a large cranium, diminishing in size as it got toward the chin', and no hair. They also had no visible nose, just 'two slits that represented the nostrils' and a 'horizontal line' for mouths from which they made a 'mumumumming sound'. Barney's description is confused and contradictory, but it seems the sense the Commandant of the Greys looked 'like a German Nazi' was simply that he was extremely inhumane and lacking in any emotion. Barney felt 'like a rabbit', a small, defenceless lab-animal, complaining 'I don't want to be experimented on.' The Nazi-like ETs placed 'a cup' around Barney's groin to extract semen anyway, before scraping flakes of skin from his wife Betty's arm with 'something like a letter opener' to store in a drawer, then cutting off her fingernail, taking hair-samples and swabs from her ear. She was subsequently forced to undress before 'a whole cluster of needles' attached to wires were jabbed into her navel as a pregnancy test. Betty cried and begged for the ET doctor to stop, saying it was painful, but he just uttered sweet nothings and carried on abusing his latest helpless rabbit anyway.[22]

The focus of Barney Hill upon the Greys' eyes was significant. Whilst the Hills were the first to really place the image of the Grey into the public domain, it was not until 1987 when the US abductee and sci-fi writer Whitley Strieber (b.1945) published his confessional non-fiction best-seller *Communion*, detailing his own quasi-medical Nazi-esque ordeals at the hands of the Greys, that the image truly caught on. A painting of one of these entities appeared on the book's cover, which captured the public imagination so well it is now the automatic standard image most people have of an alien being. The most striking thing was the Grey's big, black eyes, which had no pupils. Being so black and blank, they embody an inherent power-imbalance between abductor and abductee; if eyes are windows into the soul, then *they* can look into us, but *we* can't look into them. The Grey is humanoid, but not human. With its dead, impenetrable eyes, it seems to have no feelings at all. According to Strieber, his abductors smelled of cardboard, making them sound inherently artificial, and had no concern for his feelings whatsoever, anally probing him with a foot-long triangular object, 'grey and scaly, with a network of wires at the end', intended to steal stool samples, and sticking a long needle into his brain, which he feared would leave him a vegetable. So alien were these aliens that Strieber isn't sure they actually *were* aliens; he now thinks they may be something even more alien than that, which can't possibly be comprehended by human minds.[23]

According to the controversial US abduction investigator Professor David M. Jacobs (b.1942), Greys use their eyes to perform a nefarious 'Mindscan' technique, travelling in through a human's more open eyes, then down their brain-stem into the central nervous system, from whence they can then 'possess' and stimulate any organ they so desire, particularly their victims' genitals: 'The physiological responses necessary for erection and ejaculation in men, and tumescence, expansion and lubrication in women can be artificially generated in this manner.' But why would aliens want to rape people with their eyes? Jacobs felt the Greys were involved in an interplanetary inter-breeding programme, designed to mix their genes with ours to give them something they lacked – access to human feelings and emotions.[24] Hypnotism also relies upon a sinister figure staring deep into another person's eyes and invading their mind, and W. A. Harbinson implied this was another way by which the polar Nazis controlled their saucer-pilots. Jacobs' Mindscan techniques greatly resemble hypnosis, and Hitler and Goebbels were often labelled as having hypnotised the German people through their speeches and propaganda. The magnetic gaze of Nazis and Greys alike should always be avoided.

* * * * *

There was also a large racial component to the 1961 Hill abduction case. Barney Hill was black and Betty white, then a controversial thing with race-riots occurring as segregation began to be dismantled in the Deep South. Canadian UFO commentator Eric Ouellet has proposed that if you look at the classic image of a Grey's head upside-down, it somewhat resembles the hoods worn by Ku Klux Klansmen. However, an equally good fit would be the SS *Totenkopf* skull, as seen on their caps and ceremonial rings, with the empty black eyes and missing nose of the Greys fitting in with a skull's own hollow eyes and nostril-holes. Ouellet also recognises the ufonauts' preoccupation with sperm and pregnancy, noting that, if the Hills ever had a child (Betty was infertile, so they actually couldn't) it would have been mixed-race; and the colour halfway between black and white is Grey. No coherent message can be teased out from the Hills' encounter, any more than one can be extracted from any given dream, but if their abduction was really a bizarre shared psychological vision, as is often proposed, it does seem to reflect their racial anxieties in some way, albeit disjointedly.[25]

We may now guess why Barney thought his captor looked like a Nazi. The Grey was a Nazi because he *behaved* like one, not because he looked like Orthon. Obsessed with ideas of racial hygiene, death camp doctors often performed barbaric sexual experiments on the other races they held captive. In Auschwitz, Professor Carl Clauberg (1898-1957) became devoted to discovering cheap means of mass sterilisation. Rumours spread he was trying to 'implant monsters' inside prisoners' wombs, whilst one woman claimed to have seen her old high-school teacher mummified as a medical exhibit. Clauberg's actual methods were to inject caustic substances into the cervix to ruin victims' fallopian tubes by sticking them together. Once the procedure was complete, it was planned to have the women raped to see if they got pregnant. If so, back to the drawing board. The testimony of one victim at Clauberg's hands greatly mirrors that of Betty Hill, the prisoner being forced onto a gynaecological table before a 'long needle' was forcibly injected into her womb until the point she felt 'my stomach would burst with the pain', causing her to scream. Clauberg told her to shut up or die. Clauberg's physical appearance was also familiar-sounding, being 'a small, ugly-looking, more or less deformed person', a five-foot tall 'caricature' who was 'short, bald and unlikeable'. He may not have had grey skin and wraparound eyes but was still 'a frightfully ugly dwarf', just like the Hills' Greys.[26]

Dr Horst Schumann (1906-83) also worked at Auschwitz-Birkenau, hoping to sterilise patients via exposure to x-rays. The plan was to get racial inferiors to fill in forms whilst a Nazi behind a desk flicked a hidden switch, exposing them to massive radiation doses, rendering them infertile without them even knowing. Then, they could be kept for slave labour without bringing any more unwanted baby Jews or Slavs into the world. In reality, Schumann's victims developed severe genital burns and infections, rendering them unfit for work at all. The suffering was horrendous, but Schumann's team cared not. As one female victim said, echoing Barney Hill's specific fear, 'They took us because they didn't have rabbits.' Also like Barney, some of Schumann's male victims were forced into ejaculation, often stimulated into this with Whitley Strieber-esque anal probes. As for Schumann's personal appearance, he was the opposite Nazi doctor stereotype to the dwarfish 'mad professor' Clauberg. Tall and handsome, he was 'correct' and 'cold' in demeanour, revealing 'no human feelings in regard to the prisoners', making him a perfect 'representative of the new German racist ideal'. Essentially, he was an inhuman robot. By combining Schumann with Clauberg, you get the 'German Nazi' on-board Barney Hill's saucer.[27]

The perverted physician Dr Josef Mengele (1919-79), Auschwitz's notorious 'Angel of Death', was a man so twisted and so mechanically logical that when he discovered one cell-block was infested with lice he ordered the gassing of everyone in it as the most efficient means of killing both species of worthless insect simultaneously.[28] Mengele escaped the Nuremberg Trials by fleeing to South America, but had he appeared there he would have been the chief example of Pauwels and Bergier's morally incomprehensible Nazi Martians. Auschwitz inmates described the place as 'a different planet', where doctors' job was to kill their patients, not heal them. Said one survivor, Dr Mengele 'seemed ... [like he] had just come down in a spaceship.' Like the Greys, he had 'indifferent eyes' or 'dead eyes', showing 'indifference to pain'. Yet he was still all-seeing; people whispered of his 'omnipotence', of how he 'would disappear and reappear' wherever he wanted to, treating inmates like 'mice and rabbits'. 'Hitler's robot' was 'without emotion on his face' and it became rumoured he had no capacity for love or sexual passion of any kind. Often considered handsome, it was beauty of an unusual, non-human sort: 'His head was like a cat's head. It was wide at the temples ... His eyebrows made a kind of accent circumflex, like a cat's ... I would say he had an M-shaped mouth ... only half the iris [in his eyes] would show.' In fiction, like the 1970s novel and later Hollywood thriller *The Boys from Brazil*, in which the mad doctor tries to clone Hitler, Mengele has become the chief inhuman emblem of twisted Nazi science and ethics. He was simply 'an abstraction' to some inmates, who was 'only playing the part of a human being'. In his own assessment of how it was the death camp doctors managed to function, the author Robert Jay Lifton (b.1926) spoke of a process of 'doubling', in which the psyche splits in two, with one half operating ruthlessly within the context of the camps, and the other half adopting more usual ethical standards outside in relation to other competing social roles like fatherhood, to allow the war criminal to maintain an internal image of himself as a decent person.

Thus, medics like Mengele could become their own *doppelgängers*, another key image in both Nazi UFO mythology and German folklore, as with the many legends about Rudolf Hess.[29]

* * * * *

Inhuman, black-clad SS medical *doppelgängers* further resemble the villainous Men in Black (MIBs), who visit UFO witnesses to intimidate them into staying silent on behalf of aliens or a sinister shadow government. Impossibly perfect MIB doubles impersonate genuine UFO investigators, whilst MIB witnesses routinely describe their actions as robotic in nature, inadvertently revealing their basic unfamiliarity with simple human acts, like trying to drink jelly rather than use a spoon. One MIB seen without his shirt on had 'absolutely no body hair ... no belly button, nor nipples' like Barbie's boyfriend. Another MIB had 'smooth skin, like soft plastic, like a doll's ... when he sat still he had the appearance of a clothing-store dummy. His suit looked like it had just been put on, as though it had never been worn before or even walked in for that matter.' Some have been seen wearing clownish levels of lipstick, even though they are male, to disguise how they actually have no lips at all. Their voices often sound mechanical: 'He constructed no phrases and contracted no sentences – just a sequence of words very evenly spaced ... no inflection, no intonation, no *nothing!*' They even move strangely: 'They couldn't even walk very well, or else they walked too well, like they were ice-skating.'[30]

They sound like Dr Mengele; robotic, doll-like, alien machines in human clothing. This is also a basic stereotype of the German people, that they are cold, aloof, overly efficient and unfeeling. Think of the German band Kraftwerk and their brand of flat, monotonous, atonal electronic *industrielle Völksmusik*, or 'people's music for an industrial world'. As befits the creators of the album *The Man-Machine*, Kraftwerk became known for adopting stilted, mechanical movements on-stage, often standing stock-still to resemble their own MIB-like *doppelgängers*. They once forced a journalist to interview mannequins dressed like them, into whose mouths they projected their own words. During the 1970s, Kraftwerk's music was criticised as emblematic of an age 'being taken over by the Germans and the machines' with their twinned 'bloodless iron will'; music magazine *NME* sabotaged their 1975 UK tour by claiming the group were Nazi-esque.[31] *Doctor Who*'s genocidal Daleks were also originally intended as a metallic version of the SS, with the angular up-and-down movement of their plunger-guns deliberately invoking the Hitler salute. When W. A. Harbinson explicitly conflated Nazis, aliens and robots, therefore, he was pushing at an already open imaginative door. The real-life minds of criminals like Josef Mengele were already the 'intellects vast and cool and unsympathetic' of H. G. Wells' Martians, staring down through their super-telescopes and planning to commit genocide against the entire human race in the famous opening lines of *The War of the Worlds*.[32] When the well-known fake footage of an 'alien autopsy' from Roswell was released in 1995, it was presented as a 'snuff movie', like something smuggled out of Auschwitz.

The first successful research into robotics, computing, Artificial Intelligence and cybernetics occurred within the military-industrial complex born in America and Britain during the war. American electrical engineer Claude Shannon (1916-2001) and British mathematician Alan Turing (1912-54) were the first seriously to consider it may be possible to simulate human thought via electronic means using what was later known as a 'computer'; human minds now became analogous to those of machines, a deeply dehumanising thought. The classic 'Turing Test', in which a mechanical brain is tasked with producing messages indistinguishable from those of a real human being, is one that MIBs, death camp doctors and Greys alike would all surely fail. Marvin Minsky (1927-2016), father of AI, described the mind as a 'meat machine', arguing human flesh should merge with cold metal and circuitry. When Norbert Wiener (1894-1964) conceived the field of cybernetics, or the use of self-correcting feedback loops to create automatically operating systems and machines, it grew from wartime experiments in artificial gunfire control, just as Turing's work grew from wartime code-breaking. The majority of intended initial users of this model of the artificial mind were thus servicemen like combat-pilots. The Nazis may have lost, but by provoking such developments they turned Allied airmen into primitive prototypes of W. A. Harbinson's semi-robotic saucer-men anyway. Today's fighter-jets are impossible to fly without special helmets featuring computerised display elements, with automatic-aiming systems commonplace. The term 'cyborg' was not coined until 1960, but it was increasingly obvious this was where warfare was heading. The MIBs, *doppelgängers* and inhuman Nazi aliens stand like hypothetical extrapolations of these early researchers' work, springing to life from their obscure academic papers as metaphors. 1947 saw the birth of the transistor chip, Information Theory, the atomic Doomsday Clock, the CIA (whose dark-clad G-men with eyes covered by dark sunglasses were another clear paranoiac model for the MIBs), the breaking of the sound-barrier and the flying saucer. All fit together perfectly, to give one clear warning – that, sometime soon, humanity will become Kraftwerk.

If you were an engineer embedded deep within the military-industrial complex, you would have understood where transistors and circuit-boards came from, but to the average layman, it really must have seemed like they fell from outer space, as in the Roswell back-engineering myth. Yet attributing sudden post-war technological jumps to the equally alien *Wunderwaffen*-creating Nazis made equal imaginative sense; the Z-1, the world's first primitive programmable computer, was invented by the German innovator Dr Konrad Zuse (1910-95) in 1938, elements of which later fed into the cybernetic self-regulating V-1 flying robot-bomb.[33] In 1997, the fiftieth anniversary of the alleged disaster itself, former US Army Colonel Philip J. Corso (1915–98) published *The Day After Roswell*, speculating the many reported saucer crashes of the 1940s and 1950s were an elaborate trick, with any physical ET corpses retrieved from the wreckage being crude decoys. The real aliens hid within the saucers' circuitry, deliberately designed to be simple enough (by extraterrestrial standards) to be back-engineered by human military scientists; it was no coincidence the transistor was 'invented' by Dr William Shockley (1910-89) at Bell Laboratories in December 1947, a mere six months after Roswell. Corso argued the modern-day computer ultimately derived from Shockley's back-engineering process was really a silicon-based alien life-form in itself. By subsequently manufacturing ever-more of them, humanity was thus voluntarily letting the ETs colonise Earth by stealth, just as US-style free-market capitalism conquers nations without any shots being fired – had Corso lived to see the advent of wearable tech, always-on smartphones and the Internet of Things, he may have been hailed as a prophet, not a cash-in author fantasist. As we merge more and more with machines, we become more and more alien ourselves.[34]

Working for Bell Labs developing telecommunication systems part-derived from wartime technology, the father of Information Theory Claude Shannon argued everything human could potentially be reduced down to data, something noticed by bureaucrats and social scientists who hoped to run society in a more 'scientific' way by reducing messy humans down to neat bundles of numbers and equations. The 1953 discovery of the double-helix structure of the DNA molecule tended further to reduce all biological systems to the status of information; in theory, human beings were now 'programmed', with DNA the 'code of life'. When Norbert Wiener then developed his cybernetics, he conceived of the data-driven system, whether an automatic steering system or a human being, as a closed feedback loop.

Yet, if this was so, and humans were just walking rules-based systems in disguise, Wiener feared totalitarian technocrats could very easily control us all simply via 'reprogramming' our feedback loops, as in George Orwell.[35] Harbinson's genetically engineered cyber-Nazi saucer-pilots are exaggerations of such worries. The whole alien abduction experience looks like fear of our potential future post-human selves. Greys, with their sinister genetic cross-breeding schemes, represent the humanity of tomorrow forcing the humanity of today to 'evolve' into an undesirable new form, as in Nazi eugenics. When Jörg Lanz von Liebenfels wanted to lock blondes in sex-convents to be impregnated by Aryan knights to sire a race of electronic super-children, he was acting rather like a Grey himself. As the cultural critic Erik Davis put it, 'Abduction experiences partly speak to the subconscious horror induced by the reduction of human identity to a twisted strip of genetic information [DNA] that can be spliced and diced like a film-strip.'[36]

In 1975, the early abductee Sandy Larson supposedly had her brain removed in a UFO and replaced with a whole new one, a scenario with distinct echoes of the notorious 1968 Nazisploitation b-pic *They Saved Hitler's Brain*.[37] Many contemporary people fear having their brains stolen and replaced with new, less human ones, in the near future. What some see as the endless increase in technological monitoring systems used to hunt out thought-crimes and the proliferation of public figures who speak entirely in dead, mechanical slogans can make it seem as if the aliens have replaced many brains already. The popular idea that Greys – or Harbinson's saucer-Nazis – might be surgically implanting mind-control chips in us is another expression of such worries. The abductee Richard Price once turned up at the Massachusetts Institute of Technology carrying an alien control-chip he claimed to have personally removed from his own penis (a subsequent technical report concluded 'the object was interesting').[38] One abductee, Lee Parrish, memorably claimed to have been abducted by one of the huge black monolith-slabs from the Stanley Kubrick film *2001: A Space Odyssey*.[39] Is this the inevitable end-result of post-war developments in Information Theory, cybernetics and AI?

Decades after 1947, Esoteric Nazis were to revolt against the reduction of mankind into mere information systems, decrying the 'Jewish robots' we had all been forced to become by the materialistic Demiurge. And yet, during the 1910s and 1920s, one of fascism's main precursor movements, Italian Futurism, had actively welcomed the coming union between man and machine. Pieces of Futurist art like Bruno Munari's (1907-98) *We Set Out Therefore in Search of a Female Aeroplane* celebrate this symbiosis by depicting a woman's legs and posterior with an aeroplane body, with wings for arms and a propeller for a head, alongside an aerial mermaid, with female top-half and a lower-half rear fuselage arranged to look like a fish-tail. Futurists praised '*machinolatria*' or 'machine-worship', with the movement's proto-fascist founder, streetfighter and one-time associate of Mussolini, F. T. Marinetti (1876-1944), having nearly merged with cold metal himself during a 1908 car crash. This early Roswell Incident stood as the creation-myth of Futurism, whose 1909 *Futurist Manifesto* declared an intention to 'hymn man at the steering-wheel', to 'glorify war – the only hygiene of the world – militarism, patriotism, the destructive gesture of anarchists, beautiful ideas worth dying for, and contempt for woman'. The primarily male Futurists preferred to 'exalt movement and aggression, the racer's stride, the mortal leap, the slap and the punch' to any soft girly qualities. Museums were 'cemeteries', books should be burned, and respect for Italy's past replaced with an exciting future of industrialised warfare and killing on a massive scale. Marinetti scorned the world of Nature for one of 'violent electrical moons' instead, as shown in his 1909 essay *Let's Murder the Moonlight!* 'The suffering of a man is of the same interest to us as the suffering of an electric lamp, which can feel pain, suffer tremors, and shriek with the most heart-rending expressions of torment,' wrote one Futurist. Others argued machines and human brains were identical, with a typewriter being 'a primitive organism governed by a logic that is imposed on it' via the pressing of its keys: 'a broken key is an attack of violent insanity.'[40]

Marinetti's 1911 essay *Multiplied Man and the Reign of the Machine* was the ultimate expression of such notions, devoted to dissolving the 'apparently indissoluble fusion' which had previously existed in poetry between women and beauty. The 'love of machines' was more appropriate, as when J. G. Ballard-anticipating train drivers stroked their engines with quasi-sexual caresses. It was necessary to destroy all male love for wives and mothers, and so break 'that constricting circle' of the family. Sex should occur only very occasionally, purely for reproduction purposes, so that Futurist Man 'will preserve his genital power until death, as one does one's stomach, and will never know the tragedy of old age and impotence!' Love must be eliminated, and the heart reduced 'to its purely distributive function' of pumping blood, becoming 'a sort of stomach for the brain', creating a social atmosphere 'the colour of steel'. Futurists were 'aspiring to the creation of an inhuman type, one in which moral suffering, generosity, affect, and love will be abolished.' If Futurists developed hearts of steel, their children would automatically be born with such iron-clad organs too, and eventually women would begin giving birth to aeroplane-people:

We believe in the possibility of an incalculable number of human transformations, and we declare without a smile that wings are waiting to be awakened within the flesh of man. The day [will come] when it will be possible for man to externalise his will in such a way that it is prolonged beyond himself like an immense, invisible arm ... This inhuman and mechanical type, constructed for omnipresent velocity, will be naturally cruel, omniscient and combative. He will be endowed with unexpected organs: organs adapted to the exigencies of an environment made of continuous shocks. Already now we can foresee an organ that will resemble a prow developing from the outward swelling of the sternum, which will be more pronounced the better an aviator the man of the future becomes, much like the analogous development discernible in the best fliers among birds.

As evidence, Marinetti cites accounts of Spiritualist séances in which mediums suddenly developed extra ghostly limbs fashioned from ectoplasm.[41] Marinetti's 1910 novel *Mafarka the Futurist* was a vehicle for such ideas, with the central character's eleven-metre-long penis designed to gain the author free publicity in an obscenity trial. Following the conquest of several African kingdoms, the heroic General Mafarka loses his brother to a pack of rabid dogs, so decides to replace him by giving birth to a son through sheer mental effort, without need for any 'inefficient vulva' to taint the child with female qualities. His consequent son, Gazurmah, is a gigantic invisible mechanical winged bird who, just like Futurist aeroplane-people, can fly to the stars. Pilots could do more than ordinary men by donning the metal suits of their planes, but this just stood as the precursor to the permanent melding of men with machines, just as with the later wartime development of cybernetic automatic-aiming systems.

Hitler himself famously liked to cultivate associations with aeroplanes, taking flying tours across Germany to win votes; the 1935 Nazi propaganda epic *Triumph of the Will* opens with aerial shots of the Reich from above before the camera-bearing plane lands and Hitler gets out, revealed as the Hyperborean god-man descending from Heaven to save his people.[42]

Mafarka's spontaneous birth of an animate flying object seems uncannily close to the self-impregnating Nazi *manisolas* in Wilhelm Landig and the *vimana* which Hitler became through sheer force of iron will in Miguel Serrano. The living Nazi UFO is a logical extension of the bloodless Nazi storm trooper; in a famous speech, Hitler once demanded the German people become 'as hard as Krupp steel', Krupp being one of the firms who manufactured the metals for German armaments. One early idol of the Nazi regime was Ernst Jünger (1895-1998), the First World War veteran and author of *Storm of Steel*, who tried to solve the problem of a society dehumanised and disenchanted through the march of technology by redeeming the machine as an instrument of brutal, mechanised warfare. Old forms of heroism on the battlefield had to be transformed into new ones, with chivalrous warriors becoming clockwork knights instead:

> And yet: behind all this is man. Only he gives the machines their direction and meaning. It is he that spits from their mouths bullets, explosives and poison. He that elevates himself in them like birds of prey above the enemy. He that sits in their stomach as they stalk the battlefield spitting fire. It is he, the most dangerous, bloodthirsty, and purposeful being that the Earth has to carry.[43]

Jünger would have made an ideal Nazi saucer-pilot. As the critic David Sivier once put it, 'The flying saucer is the perfect expression of fascist and Nazi ideals and terrors, as a glittering example of Aryan technological supremacy and aggressive, belligerent masculinity and misogyny.'[44] To the Esoteric Nazis Landig and Serrano, it seemed such a soulless fate was simultaneously to be repudiated and desired; as with Ernst Jünger, people often become what they most fear.

2

Choose the Darkside, Doctor:
The Underground Alliance Between Josef
Mengele and the Paedophile Lizards from
Outer Space

It is significant that the height of popularity of W. A. Harbinson's *Projekt Saucer* series broadly overlapped with that of *The X-Files*. Harbinson's initial 1980 narrative can't be linked to the show as it only began in 1993, but the programme picked up on a developing strand of highly paranoid ufology then flourishing known as the 'Darkside Hypothesis'. This conspiracy theory held that the US government had foolishly handed over sovereignty of Earth to the Greys in return for limited access to advanced alien *Wunderwaffen*. The myth has its origins in the 1980 abduction of one Myra Hanson who, under hypnosis, 'recalled' being taken to a subterranean alien base in New Mexico, finding an *Alpenfestung* hangar filled with severed human body-parts, floating in tanks of liquid like Jewish and gypsy specimens kept in formaldehyde at Auschwitz. Ufologist Paul Bennewitz (1927-2003) soon became convinced Hanson had an ET mind-control implant in her head. Trying to detect the source of the mind-control rays, he discovered low-frequency emissions emanating from New Mexico's Kirtland Air Force Base, and approached military officials to expose the scheme. Officers played along, possibly hoping to exploit his loopy tales to discredit anyone who came sniffing around Kirtland seeking out any genuine secret radio-signal projects they may have been pursuing.

His theories apparently officially confirmed, Bennewitz had a mental breakdown, detecting a second underground ET-owned complex beneath another military base at Dulce, New Mexico, an area notorious for cattle-mutilations and UFO sightings. The aliens' twin aims, pursued via millions of abductions, mind-control implants and cattle-killings, were to gather food and develop a hybrid race of half-alien, half-humans to rejuvenate their racial stock. Concerned, Bennewitz wrote a policy-paper proposing how Dulce might be successfully attacked. In 1987, this came to the attention of John Lear (b.1942), the disinherited heir to the Learjet family fortune, who was both a UFO obsessive and a qualified pilot who had once flown transport missions for the CIA, holding several air-speed records. Lear combined Bennewitz's ideas with the then-big story in ufology, the 'MJ-12' papers, 'Majestic Twelve' being a group of twelve top-level scientists, engineers and military men purportedly assembled by post-war US Presidents Truman and Eisenhower to investigate the Roswell saucer in 1947; one alleged member was Dr Vannevar Bush (1890-1974), the early cybernetics and computing pioneer.[1] Fake documents manifested to 'prove' MJ-12 existed, even claiming foo-fighters were real.[2] The idea grew that MJ-12 had contacted the Roswell saucer's original owners, to draw up legal *Wunderwaffen*-gifting treaties with them, before organising a vast, all-consuming cover-up. On 29 December 1987, Lear summarised this new yarn on the early Internet bulletin-board Paranet, so launching the Darkside Hypothesis and its fictional offshoots *The X-Files* and the 1990s entries in the *Projekt Saucer* series.[3]

Lear later elaborated how, sometime between 1969 and 1971, the MJ-12 group had finally signed a full treaty with the Greys, who hailed from the star-system of Zeta Reticuli, letting them abduct and implant a limited number of unsuspecting humans, also permitting unhindered mutilation of cattle for food. During negotiations, the Greys presented their human abduction scheme as merely scientific monitoring akin to zoologists tranquilising, examining, tagging and then releasing animals in the wild – but the Greys lied. These untrustworthy 'EBEs' ('Extra-Biological Entities') had actually developed a collective 'genetic disorder in their digestive system', the only remedy for which was a special enzyme found inside the sensitive regions of cows and humans. This enzyme was extracted and mixed with hydrogen peroxide, then rubbed into the Greys' skin to be absorbed; having no anuses, the resultant waste-products were then sweated back out again through the epidermis. This explained why cattle-mutilations featured 'genitals taken, rectums cored out to the colon, eyes missing, and the tongue and throat cut with extreme surgical precision'. Human victims were treated to similar atrocities whilst still alive, although mainly for genetic manipulation, rarely for feeding. According to Lear, the underground Dulce base featured 'large vats with pale meat being agitated in solution' and 'large test-tubes with humans in them', even babies. The Greys were abducting many more people than the MJ-12 treaty allowed, with thousands of missing children really being taken to be vivisected in this *Alpenfestung* Auschwitz every year.

MJ-12 tried to prepare the public for eventual disclosure of the original zoological monitoring scheme by planting pro-alien propaganda like the film *ET* in cinemas, but when they discovered the Greys' treachery this became untenable. Special-forces troops, appalled by the Nazi-esque atrocities at Dulce, tried to storm the base, but were repulsed. So disturbed was President Truman's Defence Secretary James Forrestal (1892-1949) by the 'horrible truth' that he committed suicide by jumping out of a window in 1949 (although this doesn't fit with Lear's ET-human treaty being signed between 1969 and 1971, prior to the Greys' treachery becoming known).

Obtaining holographic time-travel footage of Christ's crucifixion, the Greys threatened to broadcast it worldwide and claim to have created Jesus in a big vat if MJ-12 ever revealed the truth, thus destroying public religious morale forever, keeping us all slaves. Other races of EBE also existed, notably the benign Adamski-style Nordics and Very Tall Race, but they were neutral like Switzerland in all intergalactic conflicts, it being the same with the Hairy Dwarfs too. MJ-12's only option was to play along with the Greys whilst developing anti-ET *Wunderwaffen* of their own in secret.[4]

Lear's claims were elaborated even further by the grandaddy of all current paranoid anti-government US conspiracy-lore, Milton William Cooper (1943-2001), whose 1991 book *Behold a Pale Horse* is the best-selling acknowledged classic in the genre, despite – or maybe because of – its totally incoherent, grab-bag, collage-type nature, being a mixture of his own ideas interspersed with reprints of various oppressive future government laws and secret plans which had been accidentally left inside photocopiers. The basic shadow government plot was to use a dire education system and shallow mass media to turn people into willing 'beasts of burden and steaks on the table' – the dumb cattle really being mutilated by ufonauts were the American people. A former Naval Intelligence officer who sought answers for the moral and civilisational decline he saw all around him, Cooper claimed to have glimpsed top-secret files within a filing cabinet at the end of the Vietnam War, which revealed an all-embracing conspiracy against US citizens. Whenever Cooper wanted to add to this narrative, all he had to do was suddenly 'remember' having seen yet another paper in this presumably very large filing system, and there you had it: clear documentary proof, within his own head. On his radio show, *The Hour of the Time*, Cooper popularised the now familiar phrase 'Wake up, sheeple!', apparently influencing the anti-government obsessions of the Oklahoma Bomber Timothy McVeigh, who blew up a Federal Government building in 1994 – having visited the alleged home of the Roswell wreckage, the US military base Area 51, earlier that year.

Spending time around 'REAL atomic bombs' in the military, Cooper initially dismissed colleagues' yarns about crashed saucers as due to them being drunkards, but in 1966 witnessed a giant saucer rising from the sea himself aboard a naval vessel, being forced to keep silent on pain of ten years' imprisonment and a $10,000 fine. Spotting John Lear's rants on Paranet, Cooper confirmed what he was saying was true by pulling yet more files from the big metal cabinet in his skull, with Vietnam-era documents now revealing the Greys had probably evolved from plants and had chlorophyll for blood, hence their lack of bowels. They also revealed how 'at least sixteen' saucers had crashed in America between 1947 and 1952, each containing 'a large number of human body parts'. James Forrestal didn't commit suicide, either; he was thrown out of a window for threatening to reveal the truth. The alien abductee Whitley Strieber's novel *Majestic*, a fictionalised reimagining of the already fictional MJ-12 fiasco, actually told the truth about the whole affair, being just a novelisation of Forrestal's diary, with Whitley working for the

CIA to discredit Forrestal's words as pure literary imagination. Then, when Cooper began citing chapters in novels as evidence for real-life conspiracies, the spooks could just say 'you got that from a sci-fi story' to make him look mad. The CIA-financed pro-alien propaganda film *ET* was also based on fact, but with a tacked-on happy ending; the real chlorophyll-blooded, child-friendly alien, so atypical of his kind, had died from an unspecified illness on 2 June 1952, despite the best attention of government botanists.

Cooper even outed the Grey Ambassador who had signed the original MJ-12 treaty of limited co-operation with President Eisenhower in 1954, namely 'His Omnipotent Highness Krlll'. Scientific information was later published in technical journals, under the Ambassador's chosen human pen name of 'O. H. Krill', to obscure the back-engineering. When JFK later discovered the details of Krlll's evil, he was shot in the head before being able to reveal all. Thankfully, under the code-name 'Project Excalibur', the US were secretly developing nuclear-tipped bunker-busting missiles to destroy the Greys' *Alpenfestung* bases. As a bonus aside, Cooper also discovered a second Ice Age was coming. Naturally, the CIA were always trying to kill him, explaining why he lost a leg in a 1970s car accident; it was really an assassination attempt. Any ufologists who disagreed with the gun-toting Cooper about any of this were deemed CIA spies and threatened with acts of violence. He became a temporary drinking-pal of John Lear, though, the two men clubbing together in 1989 to produce an official 'Petition to Indict' the US Government and its then-President George H. W. Bush (1924-2018), 'the most powerful and dangerous criminal in the history of the world', for violating the Constitution. Cooper and Lear demanded the former CIA chief Bush kick all ETs off sovereign national territory, and 'cease aiding and abetting and concealing this Alien Nation which exists in our borders' before accusing him of being an international drug-dealer for good measure.

Later, the pair fell out, with Cooper accusing Lear of still working for the CIA, deciding the whole human-alien treaty idea was a disinformation scheme intended to throw him off the real conspiracy, that a clandestine One-World Government truly ran planetary affairs under the name of the 'Illuminati'. Realising the MJ-12 papers were fakes, Cooper concluded this was evidence a different conspiracy was real instead. The Illuminati were a genuine, if short-lived, group of radical political and religious free-thinkers of a classically rationalist Enlightenment mindset founded by an ex-Jesuit named Adam Weishaupt (1748-1830) in Bavaria in 1776. Their name meant 'Enlightened Ones', and that is what Weishaupt's men thought they were. In the demonology of conspiracy theorists, however, they have become interchangeable with the imaginary world-controlling Jews of *The Protocols of the Elders of Zion* – the entire text of which was reprinted by Cooper in *Behold, A Pale Horse*, with the advice readers swap the word 'Illuminati' for the word 'Jews' and the word 'goyim' (meaning non-Jews) for 'cattle', in reference to ordinary citizens. The *Protocols* were written 'intentionally to deceive' people into hating Jews rather than Illuminati, he said. Although the real Illuminati were defunct by 1790, conspiracists claim this was just a lie, with the group continuing to operate secretly, capturing the entire globe. In Cooper's narrative – quickly adopted by right-wing libertarians, militia movements and gun-nuts across America – the Illuminati, now rebranded as the New World Order (NWO), planned to steal true patriots' right to bear arms, then stick them all inside Nazi-style concentration camps. This was why WalMart stores were so large and warehouse-like; once the NWO gave the word, the usual stock would be removed and replaced with thousands of doomed prisoners. Refusing to pay his taxes to fund his own future internment in an out-of-town supermarket building, Cooper was slated for arrest by the FBI, and when he used a gun to threaten a man to get off a piece of 'his' land which he didn't even own, local officers felt obliged to apprehend him. There was a shoot-out, Cooper being assassinated by the Deep State in November 2001, just like JFK.[5]

* * * * *

It doesn't take much imagination to stitch several aspects of this over-arching narrative together – concentration camps, *The Protocols of the Elders of Zion*, obscene biological experiments conducted for racial regeneration purposes, the clandestine development of *Wunderwaffen* and a group of all-seeing, originally German-based secret conspirators in shape of the Bavarian Illuminati – and conclude the real masterminds behind all this were actually the Nazi Party. The first to make this theory public was the pseudonymous 'Branton', an Internet personality whose confusing online publication *The Omega File* was a big hit, despite being a poorly labelled mishmash of other (often unnamed) people's testimonies and his own ideas, such that you are not always certain what comes from him, and what has been cut-and-pasted. One element definitely taken from elsewhere was the testimony of an alleged former security guard at Dulce who said Greys were not the only ETs in the base, with a second, even more evil, species of Lanz-like dinosaur-men living down there, too. By the early 2000s, a website devoted to monitoring their malign activities, reptoids.com, had been established – it's still going, under the name of the 'Reptoid Research Centre' – but it was in Branton that the lizard-people's presence was first widely revealed. The Greys were merely the subservient Italians to the saurians' commanding Germans, it appeared.[6]

Branton himself is most often said to really be a Utah-based lapsed Mormon called Bruce Alan Walton or Alan De Walton, a long-term abductee with the ability to communicate psychically with people living inside the Hollow Earth, events he can only truly remember occurring within his dreams. Supposedly, he has several half-alien hybrid children and was once programmed as a sleeper-agent by CIA mind-control handlers. According to his own account, he also has a prison record and 'emotional and psychological disabilities'. It sounds as if Branton has Multiple Personality Disorder, speaking of how, when abducted, his ordinary persona goes walkabout and another mind, 'programmed by the alien agenda' takes over instead. Branton viewed these mini-selves as expressions of an ET hive-mind, which, 'with God's help', he managed to hack into, 'using it as a weapon against' the Greys, by asking their Jungian group consciousness just what they were up to and then warning the world about it. In practice, I envisage this means Branton gets his information by sitting there and talking to himself.[7]

In 2000, *The Omega File* was re-published in print-form with the new subtitle *The Omega Files: Secret Nazi UFO-Bases Revealed!*[8] and right from Chapter One ('BEGIN FILE ...' it starts) Branton is misquoting Barney Hill to the effect not that he encountered someone on a saucer who *reminded* him of a 'German Nazi', but that he encountered an *actual* German Nazi, working with the Greys and reptilians to take over the world via mass mind-control methods. The quasi-fascistic 'Reptiloids' of the Draco-Orion Empire hail today from Alpha Draconis and Rigel Orion, but originally evolved on Earth, possibly as 'the cunning velociraptors' from *Jurassic Park*, and now desire to take their old planet back; Orion was where George Hunt Williamson said his evil Jewish 'Intruders' came from too, it may be recalled. In return for helping dinosaurs and their Grey allies seize our globe, the still-extant underground Nazis expect to be given 25 per cent of it themselves to hold a Fourth Reich. Perhaps they had not heard how His Omnipotent Highness Krlll had previously reneged on his original treaty, although they should have, as Wernher von Braun and other Paperclipped NASA Nazis attended its signing. The 1992 LA race-riots were really triggered by hypnotic Nazi mind-control technology, and stood as a test for a later full-scale race-war to be triggered as an excuse for the Illuminati US front-government to declare martial law and use their fascist storm troopers to lock everyone decent up inside WalMart.

Earthlings were being 'carefully groomed as an economic slave-society to serve the underground Master Race' of 'the joint reptilian-fascist underground empire', with the US being their 'main target' due to its status as 'the last bastion of freedom on Earth'. Only a love of God and the constitutionally guaranteed right to buy loads and loads of guns stood in the way of their plans, whereas if the Nazi reptiles were beaten and their *Wunderwaffen* stolen, entire space-fleets of well-armed 'freedom-loving Americans' could fly across the galaxy to liberate all the other alien races who had been conquered by the scaly space-fascists, a bit like the US Army had once done for Nazi-occupied Europe. Most alien worlds previously colonised by the reptiles had been left-wing and socialist in nature, thus making their populations weak, compliant slaves without the personal reserves of will-power needed to resist invasion; because Earth, in particular the USA, had a long and proud tradition of nationalism, patriotism and love of individual responsibility and small government, it had been harder to conquer. Thus, the reptoids adopted the strategy hinted at in the title of deeply paranoid US ufologist John Keel's (1930-2009) classic book, *Operation Trojan Horse*, and infiltrated Earth's institutions unseen, via their human Nazi proxies.

By exploiting Western fear of Soviet Communism, some Nazis retained post-war positions of influence in that disguised 'Hitler-less Reich' now known as the European Union, which they presented as a bulwark against the Reds. This was why EU-style transnationalism and 'international financial cults' were now spreading: the Nazis were softening up humanity's potential for moral resistance against space-imposed dinosaur-slavery by making us become lefty globalists. Ironically, liberalism was a Nazi invention, designed to create an entire generation without true morals or the capacity for rational independent thought, hence the destruction of education, undermining of the nuclear family, promotion of abortion and contraception, the removal of prayers from school assemblies and the positive depiction of criminals as victims on TV. By engineering financial crashes, mass racial warfare, epidemics of drug-dealing and artificial diseases like AIDS (tried out first on gays because 'few would care what happened to them'), the Nazis sought to destabilise society so much that demoralised citizens would gratefully welcome the stability represented by totalitarian reptile rule. By disarming law-abiding white taxpayers, then giving black criminals machine-guns to massacre them with, the Nazis sought to ensure Middle America would run straight into the arms of the dinosaurs who would lovingly promise to genocidally eliminate all the non-white scum. The English novelist Aldous Huxley (1894-1963) knew about this plan and tried to warn us in his dystopian text *Brave New World*, but it was dismissed as fiction – possibly because the book was first published in 1932, a year before Hitler even came to power. Nonetheless, it still represented 'an approximate day-to-day blueprint of life under the new regime'. Alien brain-implants were just another way to turn Americans into compliant sheeple, obliterating their 'God-given sovereignty' of free will, putting the abductee's soul 'at extreme risk'. The reptiles' Grey servants had hive-minds, and humanity was due to be 'assimilated' into them, as with *Star Trek*'s Borg or Chairman Mao's Chinese Communists.

The grounds for this Axis-alien alliance had existed for centuries, with the original Bavarian Illuminati really being a lizard-worshipping 'black Gnostic serpent-cult', so it was only natural their German Gnostic successors the Nazis should allow their secret economic and political networks of post-war power to be placed at the reptoids' disposal. Earth is 'the most strategic world in the galaxy', especially 'when one considers its centralised location', so had to be reclaimed by the lizard-men; their rival benign Orthon-type Nordic aliens had also originated here, too, but, being the reptoids' eternal enemies in an interstellar superpower conflict, could not be allowed to get their joint former homeland back. Thus, the reptiles had concealed dino-agents within the then-approaching hollow Comet Hale-Bopp, to help the human Nazis prosper. US-based Nazi scientists spent their days kidnapping homeless kids and using them in subterranean time-travel experiments for military purposes, not caring if some got lost within other dimensions. There were many *Alpenfestung* Nazi-Reptiloid-Grey-Illuminati facilities all across

America, including beneath Denver International Airport, which wasn't really a genuine airport at all but a huge German concentration camp and mind-control centre.[9]

Some Nazi bases – including the one from which Barney Hill's abductors came – lay beneath Antarctica. One was called 'Base 211', recalling 'Point 211' from Wilhelm Landig's *Thule* novels, but its inhabitants came direct from the *Projekt Saucer* series. Base 211 was controlled by the elite SS unit 'ULTRA', a reference to the real-life unsuccessful 1950s and 1960s CIA 'MK-ULTRA' programme of developing mind-control techniques. ULTRA's android SS men were just as inhuman as W. A. Harbinson's: 'the upper level members … are cloned replicates or have [become] so heavily implanted virtual cyborgs that they could be considered as barely being human – automatons who are remotely controlled.'[10] The genius-level saucer-scientist who heads up the Antarctic base in Harbinson's novels, named Wilson, was also now somehow a real individual. Branton provides an alternative history of the Nazi Party, including that in 1935 this Wilson came to Germany to help the Luftwaffe build *Wunderwaffen*. By 1944, he had created the jet-propulsion systems used in some German UFOs; fortunately, however, Wilson was really a patriotic US double-agent who sabotaged the wider Nazi saucer programme with unnecessary delays, meaning they could not be deployed in time to win the war. If he had not urged them to focus on jets, the Nazis may have built unbeatable anti-gravity aircraft instead. Liking what the Nazis were up to, a group of renegade white supremacist Nordic aliens deliberately crashed a saucer in the wartime Reich so it could be back-engineered, but Wilson was purposely too slow to act, something for which we must today all be most grateful.[11]

Dr Josef Mengele was another key player in this plot. Branton cites an anonymous whistle-blower who had investigated a series of highly disturbing health-and-safety issues at an unnamed US plastics factory in the mid-1980s. Employees were suffering unusual work-place illnesses – so unusual that their family members sometimes caught and died of them too, after asking too many questions. Branton's informant diagnosed radiation poisoning, meaning the factory was secretly being used by Nazis to manufacture radioactive materials. However, they could not let their staff know, so enlisted Mengele's underlings to wipe workers' minds. During routine medical check-ups, employees were drugged by Nazi doctors from 'THE ORDER OF THE FOURTH REICH', being hypnotically regressed into early childhood, then subjected to extreme torture techniques to break their brains in a 'highly technical' fashion, rendering them amnesiac and causing 'bizarre behaviour changes'. Mengele used his Auschwitz experiences to create new levels of pain so unbearable that his patients would become mindless zombies who could be given new German names which, when uttered, would cause them to respond to subliminal mental implants by becoming 'killer guard dogs'. Placed undercover in society as 'U-boats', men like Lee Harvey Oswald would have no memory of all this until suddenly triggered into assassinating a pre-agreed individual such as JFK by having their secret German name said to them, thus allowing Nazis to eliminate those who threatened to expose their alliance with the lizards. Many 'prominent psyche folks' were in on this racket; if it turned out an assassin had been seeing a psychiatrist, it would be easy to dismiss him as nuts.[12]

Branton also transcribes a 1993 radio interview with Vladimir Terziski, a Bulgarian-born writer of books like *Close Encounters of the Kugelblitz Kind*, spinning fantasies about joint German-Japanese suicide-missions to Mars. According to him, Nazis probably first landed on the moon in 1942, finding it possessed water, vegetation and a breathable atmosphere. Aided by the 'first robots', Nazi astronauts tunnelled beneath the lunar crust and created another *Alpenfestung* base. Germany's moon-colonisers must have been very mentally strong, and it is no wonder. Terziski claimed one particularly effective form of mental programming taught to the Nazis by Tibetan Masters was 'sodomic mind control', in which SS members were fed magic mushrooms before, I can only imagine, being initiated into automatic obeyance of orders by their superiors raping them. Once successfully mind-raped, SS guards would have no qualms about colluding in 'Frankensteinian experiments' involving 'cutting off heads' and then 'disassembling and reassembling human bodies from parts' before transforming captive Jews into 'living, breathing, walking HYBRIDS between HUMANS and ANIMALS'. Terziski took 'very seriously' the sci-fi novel and film *The Boys From Brazil*, as cloning Hitler was just the kind of thing Nazi doctors tried for real, using medical *Wunderwaffen* like the 'Royal Reife microscope' which allowed budding Mengeles to see down several degrees below the level of the human cell, providing 'the magical key to the human genome kingdom'.

Being a qualified engineer, physicist and solar energy researcher with a degree from a Tokyo university, and the President of the LA-based American Academy of Dissident Sciences to boot, the multi-lingual Dr Terzisksi knew what he was talking about when he implied Illuminati alchemists had already created 'crude mechanical robots' during 'medieval centuries' and stitched together living zombie-corpses in the 1800s before cracking cloning techniques in the early 1900s. In Terziski's mind, the Illumi-Nazis were subsequently involved with 'half a dozen malevolent alien races' living in *Alpenfestung* complexes, who aided their medical quest to create a genetic Master Race of biologically superior Aryans, two million of whom lived beneath the South Pole in the mega-city of New Berlin. Today, 500,000 American children disappear each year, kidnapped so the Nazis could genetically manipulate them, too; their captors would laugh when they saw the missing kids' photos on the side of milk cartons. Branton adds his own annotations to Terziski's grotesque torture-porn, drawing a similarity between the Nazis' attempts to breed purer Aryans, and the Greys' aim of creating hybrid half-humans to ensure the improvement of their own genetic stock.[13] It should be noted that, as part of their *lebensborn* scheme, the Nazis actually did kidnap children; foreign infants deemed Aryan-looking enough were stolen and handed to new 'racially trustworthy' German parents to expand the Reich's future breeding-stock.[14]

Furthermore, explained Branton, the Illuminati oil-tycoon Nelson Rockefeller (1908-79) had brought 3,000 high-ranking Nazis into the US 'without permission', allowing Dr Mengele to establish his own personal child-abuse centre in Florida. Mengele and his fellow Nazis – there were now 1.6 million hidden across America – had since used this opportunity to develop 'a certain drug' which would prevent children from blacking out during torture, thus forcing them to endure previously unendurable amounts of pain. This was the ideal way for Nazis to break children's psyches and make them into 'sex-slaves for their own kind', most Nazis obviously being paedophiles too. As children's brains were still very small, this made them easier to brainwash. The man responsible for distributing each Nazi with his own baby sex-doll was one Larry King, although 'not the Larry King of the television and talk-show host, but a younger man, a different person, who would barter in human souls.' The Nazis' powerful allies, like President 'George Herbert (The Pervert) Bush', would also be gifted free children to satisfy their 'deviant machinations' by Larry King, to keep them on board. When Nazis got bored of their tiny slaves, they would have them shot in the head and buried in mass graves by bulldozers. Having valuable prior experience in the field, the Nazis were even offering their services as independent genocide consultants to the reptilians, helping them perform mass killings against inferior alien races on other worlds, in a programme of 'joint humanoid-reptiloid interstellar atrocities'. High abortion-rates amongst black Americans were also the result of Nazi racial extermination plans. These fiends turned out to be Satanists too, as in *Spear of Destiny*; some children procured by Larry King were skinned alive and sacrificed to the Devil in bizarre rituals, having their still-beating hearts ripped from their chests as offerings.[15]

* * * * *

The most comically lurid reimagining of Josef Mengele and his fellow Nazis as truly morally alien beings comes in the work of David Icke (b.1952), the former Coventry City goalkeeper and BBC sports reporter turned New Age giant. Following a mystical encounter in a newsagent's, Icke announced he was the 'Son of the Godhead' in 1991, incorrectly predicting the end of the world for 1997 (unless this was simply a reference to the election of Tony Blair). Since then, he has reinvented himself as Britain's leading conspiracy theorist. Icke's breakthrough book was 1999's *The Biggest Secret*, which revealed our planet is run by shape-shifting twelve-foot-tall alien reptile-men who hail from both the constellation Draco (Latin for 'Dragon') and the Lower Fifth Dimension simultaneously, called either the Annunaki or Draconians. Operating as the Illuminati, the Draconians control the CIA,

UN, London School of Economics and the British Royal Family, with most politicians and celebrities either lizards in disguise or mind-controlled by them. As in Branton, the dinosaur-people are violent paedophiles who feed off the chemical adrenalchrone (possibly really *Vril*), which is released by children during pain and psychological torture. The more *Vril* released, the more aliens can pass into our dimension from Draco, with the lizards creating human beings in the first place as an emotional food-source. By maintaining a world full of war, disease, terrorism, crime and poverty, the Illuminati ensure there will be no starvation-rations in the constellation of Draco.

Some Illuminati are full-blooded ETs, others the result of human interbreeding with them, as in Ariosophy, with this humanoid mixed race 'Babylonian Brotherhood' being trained to run the world on the scaly Draconians' behalf. But many of these shape-shifting Babylonian lizard-people are also Nazis, with fascism being their creation. Icke's consequent rewriting of Nazi history, in his chapter 'The Black Sun', is amusing. Although Adolf Hitler was 'officially born' in the Austrian border-town of Braunau-am-Inn in 1889, he may really have been Prince Albert, Duke of Clarence (1864-1892), Queen Victoria's grandson, who ostensibly died of pneumonia in 1892. However, this was a fake death designed to obscure the fact that Albert – and therefore Adolf Hitler – was really Jack the Ripper. Adolf's mistress Eva Braun supposedly described her lover as 'an elderly gentleman of uncertain age' and this may have been because Albert Hitler had really been born in 1864, not 1889. Further proof comes via the fact that 'Albert does not appear to have been "the full picnic", as they say, and Hitler certainly wasn't.' Icke admits that 'I am not saying any of these theories are true because I don't know ... but if you know any more about this, I would be very keen to hear from you' via an address provided at the end of the book. This, it would seem, is how Icke conducts some of his research – by actively soliciting letters from random people.[16]

One of the main ideological inspirations for Adolf the Ripper's anti-Semitism was the English-born writer Houston Stewart Chamberlain (1855-1927), whose obsessive anti-Jewish tirade *The Foundations of the Nineteenth Century* was a pre-Nazi German best-seller. However, did he *really* write this book? In Icke's account, Chamberlain endured several nervous breakdowns, writing in a 'trance' or 'fever', feeling himself 'taken over by demons', a clear reference to being possessed by reptilians 'or another low vibrational consciousness' when he took pen in hand. That Chamberlain died 'after years in a wheelchair, broken in body and spirit' was the inevitable medical consequence of allowing space-dinosaurs into his brain. Having read this book and been primed to hate the Jews by aliens, Hitler subsequently learned 'the esoteric arts' believing this would 'turn him into one of the [Aryan] supermen he had read so much about', but all this really did was open a possession-channel into his mind for Draconians to enter, causing him to transmit ET vibrations into crowds through his 'contorted face and crazed delivery' during speeches, thus making reptoids possess the German people in a 'Pied-Piper principle'. This was reminiscent of Jung's theory about Hitler and the Wotan archetype awakening the Wild Hunt. Hitler was well-suited to become such a human antenna, as he possessed typical 'character-traits of the R-complex, or reptile brain'.[17]

Vril is real and flows within the blood of the Aryan race, being also known as 'serpent force', says Icke. This was the true reason the Nazis wanted to create a *Herrenvolk* Master Race; they were being manipulated by Draconians to create a gigantic human food-larder of blonde, blue-eyed individuals for reptoids to feast upon, as the high levels of *Vril* within Nordics' blood is most nourishing to them. Although Hitler possessed the Spear of Destiny, he was truly being manipulated by the shape-shifting dinosaur-man Josef Mengele, a mere 'reptilian puppet'; when people talk about the Nazis having created 'draconian laws', they don't know how right they are. The mesmerism of the reptoids over mankind continues today, via the modern-day Goebbels of the lying, fake-news media: 'It may not have a swastika on it, but it is still mass hypnotism.' Yet elements of the truth still seep out in the films of Steven Spielberg, particularly the original *Ahnenerbe*-filled *Indiana Jones* trilogy and *Jurassic Park*, 'in which DNA is manipulated to create reptilian dinosaurs'.[18] After the war, the first director of the CIA Allen Dulles (1893-1969), who was 'a Nazi himself', with the aid of 'the Satanist and Rothschild clone, Winston Churchill' and his agents in MI5, Paperclipped Mengele to safety in America, thus demonstrating how 'the CIA was created by Nazis, for Nazis [allowing] the reptile-Aryan-Nazi mentality [to] maintain its power over planet Earth.'[19]

Confirmation came when Icke was contacted by an American lady named Arizona Wilder, who claimed to be a 'Mother Goddess', a high-ranking mind-controlled sex-slave who conducted paedophile murder-rituals for high-ranking members of the Babylonian Brotherhood. So 'high in the Satanic hierarchy' was she that not even the Queen was allowed to speak to her during these sacrificial ceremonies. Arizona was 'genetically bred for this job' by her 'controller', Dr Mengele, whose real name was *Greenbaum*, or 'Green Tree', on account of his invention of a baby-sacrificing ritual known as 'The Last Bulb on the Christmas Tree', performed on Christmas Eve. Mengele once showed his slave a foot-wide genetically modified giant spider he had made to frighten toddlers with, and introduced her to a still-living Adolf Hitler sometime in the 1960s. The shape-shifting part-ET doctor abused Arizona as a child to make her submit to becoming the wife of a high-ranking French Illuminatus named 'Pindar', or 'Penis of the Dragon', who successfully impregnated her (Icke had not yet established Pindar's real name, so once more asked readers 'can you help?'). Arizona sacrificed children to Pindar who made sure to have their faces turned directly towards his at the point of death, so he could use his 'very powerful hypnotic eyes' to eat their souls' *Vril* through an 'evil-eye magnetic process'. However, when Mengele died in the 1980s, Arizona's mental programming began to decay and she 'aborted the foetus' and broke with Pindar and the Illuminati, who unaccountably failed to kill her. This, revealed Icke, was the saurian Mengele's ultimate plan: to create a harem of 'mind-controlled robots' to 'provide bizarre sex for presidents, foreign leaders, politicians and businessmen … [and] when I say bizarre I mean it.'

Arizona described rituals over which she had presided in classically sensationalist terms like those of the old Witch's Sabbat, with infants' blood, livers and eyes being poured into goblets and mixed with arsenic, or allowed to drip from corpses hung on trees for the Illuminati to drink, with victims' fat smeared over attendees' bodies to get them so sexually excited they spontaneously became lizards, as 'at the point of orgasm, the mind-psyche is wide open to access higher or lower dimensions'. Whenever the Queen did this, she revealed her true form of having white scaly skin and a beak like a Triceratops. Children were thrown into water to drown, with their bodies then placed in cages for 'starving sharks' to eat, thus disposing of the evidence. Another way of covering up abuse was for adults and aliens to wear Mickey Mouse masks, as if a victim tells a policeman 'I was raped by Mickey Mouse', they are unlikely to be believed, even if the policeman in question is Bernard Hogan-Howe; but as the adults supposedly performing such acts were meant to include the Queen, Bill Clinton, Kris Kristofferson, Bob Hope, Boxcar Willie and the Pope, surely they were unlikely to be believed anyway? Mickey's House of Mouse was an inherently Satanic organisation, with kids lost during trips to DisneyLand being sacrificed to dinosaurs there once the theme park's doors had closed; many Disneyesque children's films were really intended to plant corrupting subliminal messages in young viewers' minds, with *The Wizard Oz* being a nudge-nudge reference to *The Golden Penis of Osiris*, whatever that is. Traditional witchcraft ceremonies were also performed by Arizona to summon down yet more 'snarling, hideous' aliens from Draco via astral means; whenever occultists raised demons, they were really beaming down reptoids. This, it would seem, is the latest mutant manifestation of Ariosophy.[20]

The true innovation of Icke and Wilder was to merge explicit imagery of medieval witch-trials with more contemporary iconography from the Nazi death camps. How did Mengele's mind-control techniques work? They were perfected in Auschwitz, where he experimented on helpless infant twins to make them do his bidding, under the eyes of Himmler. One crime genuinely committed by Mengele was an attempt to transform brown-eyed gypsies into blue-eyed ones by injecting their irises with dye; Icke suggests the hit country-and-western song *Don't It make Your Brown Eyes Blue* by Crystal Gale ('who is reported to be a mind-controlled slave' herself) is an oblique reference to this. Meanwhile, in Haiti, home of the CIA front-religion of voodoo, the Illuminati continued Mengele's research by turning 'most of the people into little more than zombies'.

The top-secret China Lake Naval Weapons Centre in California also continued Mengele's work, as it contained several 'Woodpecker Grids', giant metal cages, each containing thousands of babies, who were tortured with 'powerful electric shocks' before some were sacrificed on a marble altar by persons 'in black hooded robes' to disturb the prisoners' tiny little minds even further. In Icke's narrative, China Lake was where Mengele worked during Operation Paperclip; some babies and their mothers were even 'used for pornographic films' by his fellow Paperclip Paedos at NASA.

Mengele's basic theory was called 'trauma-based mind control', which exploited the way people often blank out their memory of traumatic or painful incidents. To Icke, the mind coped with such horrors by creating a series of self-compartmentalised alternative mini-selves, as in Multiple Personality Disorder (MPD). Mengele's evil genius was to realise that, by torturing, frightening or raping a child so brutally that their mind shattered into many fragments, it would be possible to get one of their MPD personalities to later perform acts the other ones would not know about or remember – like shooting John Lennon. The true purpose of Auschwitz's medical experiments was thus to create 'a honeycomb of self-contained compartments or amnesiac barriers' in inmates' minds so that, in the future, children could be transformed into compliant Nazi-reptile sex-slaves or political assassins without their everyday selves even knowing about it, thus ensuring total obedience and an inability to inform the police. Simply by implanting trigger-words during torture, separate personalities could be 'pulled forward and pushed back like a mental filing cabinet'. Camp-doctors would discover children's phobias then cover them with snakes or spiders, place them in coffins, force them to kill and eat other children, or immerse them in faeces, urine or blood to warp their minds as appropriate.

Meanwhile, sodomy 'sends a surge of energy up the spine which explodes in the brain' as anyone who has ever tried it will know. 'So, even anal sex has an ulterior motive for those who understand its mental and emotional effects' like Icke does. He had seen paintings done by persons who had themselves been sodomised by Nazis, portraying the 'surge of white energy' which had broken their brains. Disturbed individuals who committed mass school-shootings had also been sodomised by lizard-men, to get governments to pass repressive gun-control laws so the population would be left unarmed and helpless before the space-dinosaurs; Hitler introduced similar Draconian gun-control laws immediately prior to opening the concentration camps, allegedly. To be fair to Icke, he does also say that 'I am convinced ... Tony Blair, with his distant eyes and fixed smile, is under some sort of mental influence', so not all his claims were ridiculous. The fact New Labour's logo was changed to a red rose demonstrated the Party was nothing more than a covert Rosicrucian sex-cult. The less said about the woman who claimed to have been forced to have sex with dogs on film for the benefit of former US Presidents Gerald 'The Porn King' Ford and Ronald 'Uncle Ronnie's Bedtime Stories' Reagan the better, though. 'The psychological ramifications of being raped by a paedophile President are mind-shattering enough,' Icke said, but even worse, if I understand his unclear prose correctly, is that George H. W.

Bush had programmed his own sex-slave into action by use of the trigger-phrase 'Who ya gonna call?' from *Ghostbusters*, thus 'further reinforcing her sense of helplessness'. 'Come on, gang, I know this chapter must have been terribly hard to read,' concluded Icke, 'but it's time to wake up. This has GOT to stop.'[21] Indeed it has, but Icke just goes on writing anyway.

What is his motivation? Anti-hate groups accuse Icke of anti-Semitism, saying his talk about Nazi lizards is actually just code for 'Jews rule the world', but I disagree. His beliefs are no more lunatic than those of Miguel Serrano, Savitri Devi or Jörg Lanz von Liebenfels and they were all totally sincere. It is an unfortunate fact that, like Milton William Cooper (whom he sometimes cites, alongside Branton), Icke has semi-endorsed the *Protocols of the Elders of Zion*, saying their content is real, but that the word 'Jews' should be crossed out and replaced with either 'Nazi reptiles' or 'the Illuminati' depending on your personal taste. In his first conspiracy book, 1994's *The Robots' Rebellion*, Icke condemns Hitler's genocidal use of the *Protocols*, but quotes extensively from them nonetheless, saying they have come true, with the Illuminati (not yet revealed as being lizards) having successfully achieved the stated Jewish aim of creating a One-World Government anyway. Whilst Icke doesn't mean this to condemn the Jews, who he does not think are guilty at all, the effect in some readers' minds might be the direct opposite. Reading the cited anti-Jewish tracts, some may naturally conclude the Jews *are* behind everything bad after all? Icke doesn't always research his data himself, he is fed it by informants, as his public requests for further info about Hitler being Jack the Ripper show, making him open to potential manipulation by those with impure motives. It has been speculated certain Far-Right figures have exploited Icke's credulity to get him to inadvertently promote anti-Semitic tropes by proxy as an innocent dupe, much like Ernst Zündel did with naïve ufologists. Icke's one-time association with the New Age magazine *Rainbow Ark* has aroused suspicion, as the title in question was allegedly a front for enabling anti-Semites to infiltrate Green and New Age milieus to spread their lies to those who may consider themselves open-minded, but are really just gullible. If this is true, then Icke is right, there *is* a conspiracy going on after all – and he's its main victim.[22]

* * * * *

According to the US academic Michael Barkun's book *A Culture of Conspiracy*, there are two types of fringe knowledge. The first are those like belief in UFOs that are officially rejected by academia, politics and science but tolerated as harmless eccentricities and thus free to be promoted for profit by the publishing industry. The second are those deemed actively dangerous, and thus silently excluded even from popular culture, as with Far-Right beliefs about Auschwitz being a hoax. Prior to the Internet-era, if you wanted material about such subjects you had to go underground, to men like Ernst Zündel. By creating a new strand of popular ufology involving such tropes in the 1990s, when the web was still in its infancy, people with extremist views found a vehicle to insert them into the traditionally harmless realm of the mass entertainment media, making them seem less taboo and gaining exposure to a larger potential audience in the marketplace of ideas, making ufology a bridge into mainstream discourse.[23]

This doesn't mean the conspiracy-superstars themselves are necessarily Far-Right or anti-Semitic. Branton frequently warns Jews, blacks, Hispanics and other minorities about the fascist-alien plan for their extermination. But the types of alien being they speak of are sometimes labelled by critics as disguised racial stereotypes in themselves, whether their promoters realise this or not. Milton William Cooper used to argue there were four main types of ETs on Earth, the Greys, a little-seen sub-species with 'a large nose' now known as 'Big-Nose Greys', the Adamski-type Nordics and, not previously mentioned, 'The Orange Ones', like Donald Trump. Michael Barkun points out that the Greys, as unfeeling, hideous, dwarfish, discoloured, malevolent beings, resemble certain anti-Semitic stereotypes, the Big-Nose Greys even more so. The tall, healthy-looking Nordics, however, present a fairy-tale contrast, with such blonde, blue-eyed individuals being thought generally benign. Although 'not a religious man', nonetheless 'the angels [in the Bible] could be the Nordic types and the Greys could well be the demonic ones' Cooper has said.[24]

The *Vril*-seeking Draconians of David Icke, who rape, torture and slaughter white children and drink their blood, fit in perfectly with the old Jewish stereotype of the 'Blood Libel', in which Jews were supposed to kidnap and eat Christian children in medieval Europe, or suck their veins like vampires. Some pro-Jewish organisations have written to politicians and celebrities, informing them Icke has said in print that they are giant Nazi paedophile lizards and inviting them to sue him for libel, but thus far they have had very few takers; Icke maintains this is because these people *are* giant Nazi paedophile lizards, and so know they would lose in court. David Icke is not, in my opinion, an anti-Semite, but he seems to wear any condemnation as being a Jew-hater received from anti-hate groups as a badge of honour, viewing such bodies as yet more Illuminati agents seeking to discredit those who get too close to the truth by shouting 'racist!' at them. The more he is condemned, the more it means he is right. Ordinary Jews are often victims of the Illuminati, Icke argues, and whilst some high-up members are indeed Jewish, these quislings are selling out their own people, not working on their behalf. And yet, when he claims the faked *Protocols* were an invention of the Jewish Rothschild banking family, placed in Hitler's hands to get him to do the lizards' bidding, he is in effect blaming Jews for causing the Holocaust, albeit apparently by mistake. The constant assertion that Nazis, aliens and the Illuminati control finance, education, politics and the media, or are engaged in other forms of mind-control activities – Icke at one point suggested the classically saucer-shaped Millennium Dome was an occult-hypnotic attempt to 'scramble human consciousness' – is also a classic anti-Semitic trope, but remade as something else.[25]

There is something contradictory about these images of competing alien species, in which traditional racial roles are both reinforced and reversed. You would think the Nordic Orthon-type ETs would be the Nazis – but they are often presented as the good-guy peaceniks, albeit so peacenik they actively refuse to intervene. Yet, in the work of people like William Dudley Pelley, maybe this is just a propaganda double-bluff intended to present blue-eyed blonde Nazis positively; the Nordics are the good-guys because, shorn of all the Allied propaganda, so were the actual Nazis. Meanwhile, the Greys have become both Jews and Germans simultaneously. Some death camp doctors resembled them, but the Big-Nose Greys appear to be ET Jews getting their own back on the goyim by performing death camp experiments on them, as if Mengele himself had converted to Zion.

The idea of the interplanetary genetic manipulation programme is equally ambiguous. Is it a Nazi-like attempt to breed a new Master Race? Or is it a recapitulation of Ariosophy's dire warnings about the dangers of humans interbreeding with inferior species? Some interpretations of the Darkside Hypothesis could plausibly be seen as Far-Right in nature; others, the precise opposite. Once these ideas are out there online, there is no level of complete control their originators can maintain over them. How could David Icke know that members of the neo-Nazi skin-head movement Combat-18 would attend one of his lectures and give it a glowing review on the grounds that, in their view, whenever he said 'lizards', he really meant 'Jews' to avoid prosecution? And how did Combat-18 know that, as soon as they printed this opinion, Icke would deny their claims and denounce *them* as being Rothschild-backed members of the Illuminati out to smear him with lies too?[26] And so, like the circular ouroboros snake of alchemy, the Nazi reptiles eat themselves. I shudder to think what certain online commentators might choose to do with this book ...

3

Hell Frozen Over: Melting Down the Myth of the Antarctic Nazi Saucer-Base

When W. A. Harbinson's Nazi ice-base novel *Inception* was released in 1991, he explained in a note how many readers of the first story in the *Projekt Saucer* cycle had sent him letters which 'begged me to tell them which parts of the book were fact and which were fiction'. Actually it was almost all fiction, but the author thought otherwise. Born in Belfast, Harbinson emigrated to Australia aged nineteen, serving six years in the Royal Australian Air Force, a background exploited when later writing war novels like 1973's *Instruments of Death*. It was whilst researching such work in London's Imperial War Museum, Harbinson wrote in 1991, that he spotted an archive newspaper report from 1944 about strange silver spheres looking 'like the glass balls which adorn Christmas trees' infesting the skies over Germany.[1] Harbinson had discovered the foo-fighters. What might these mysterious orbs have been? Harbinson investigated, falling for the post-war lies put out by the likes of Rudolf Schriever, telling his 1991 readers that the Germans probably really had instituted a real-life UFO-building programme called 'Projekt Saucer', from which he took the name of his own thriller-series, with Nazi saucer-scientists ultimately Paperclipped away to build the Allied victors their own discoid flying machines. 'These are some of the facts supporting the fiction' of his novels, Harbinson concluded. 'Ponder them wisely.'[2]

As the sceptical ufological researcher Kevin McClure once pointed out, however, had Harbinson pondered these claims wisely himself, he may have wondered why the Nazis chose to name their scheme 'Projekt Saucer', when the word 'saucer' is demonstrably an English-language one, the correct German term being *untertasser*. Even more impressive was how the Nazis had managed to successfully predict that, two years after the war had ended, a media misinterpretation of Kenneth Arnold's sighting of unknown objects in 1947 would lead to such craft being labelled specifically as 'flying saucers' rather than, say, 'flying discuses' or 'flying coins'. McClure might also have added it was unlikely German intelligence would have helpfully labelled this top-secret plan with a name which gave the entire game away to their enemies. There is a reason 'Operation Barbarossa' was not called 'Operation Let's Invade Russia by Surprise!'[3]

In the foreword to his 1995 non-fiction spin-off *Projekt UFO*, Harbinson accidentally shows how he was taken in by the myth, referring to a one-off issue of 'what at first sight appeared to be an orthodox scientific newspaper' named *Brisant* which he had obtained. The word 'brisant' refers to the latent shattering-power of high-explosive materials, the journal's contents having the potential to smash apart its readers' complacent pre-existing world-views, like swallowing a red pill in *The Matrix*. *Brisant* was distributed for free during a 1978 scientific exhibition in Hanover, and contained 'two seemingly unrelated articles', both written anonymously. One called for the then-West Germany to reclaim a slice of Antarctica known as Queen Maud Land, which the Nazis had supposedly stolen from Norway in 1939 and renamed Neuschwabenland, ostensibly on account of its inherent potential ecological and scientific value to the nation. The second text contained claims about the wartime Nazi creation of flying saucers, complete with technical drawings which had sadly been 'altered by the West German government to render them safe for publication' prior to printing – an excellent way to account for the fact the machines depicted weren't aerodynamically viable.

Here, Harbinson discerned for the first time the suppressed link between Antarctica and Projekt Saucer. Neuschwabenland was the location of the secret 'massive underground complexes' later described in his sci-fi novels where, following German defeat, devoted *Wunderwaffen* scientists had continued their wicked work, before being rumbled and invaded by the Allies. Despite realising *Brisant* was 'written from a neo-Nazi standpoint', with its pleas for reclamation of Neuschwabenland having ulterior nationalist motives, Harbinson guessed the authors had stumbled upon a genuine truth, albeit one 'culled from a variety of fanciful sources', which they were simply abusing for their own Far-Right ends. Harbinson found *Brisant* had been printed by a since-vanished front-company supposedly based in Hamburg, named Lintec GmbH, which strangely 'was not listed with any of the West German Press organisations' as an official State-registered newspaper. Further reading proved *Brisant*'s contents were rewritten wholesale from two books published by a more traceable Canadian organisation based in Toronto – namely, Samisdat Publishers Ltd.[4]

The specific books *Brisant* cribbed from were the German-language editions of *UFOs: Nazi Secret Weapons?* by Mattern Friedrich and *Secret Nazi Polar Expeditions* by Christof Friedrich. Were these two men brothers? Their relationship was even closer. As Harbinson correctly ascertained, the two Friedrichs were two of the many pen names of none other than Ernst Zündel ... Christof Friedrich was almost certainly Zündel, as these were his middle names, but some sources imply Mattern Friedrich was a genuine separate individual named Willibald Mattern, a German émigré living in Chile – if so, he was the Nazi photographer we met in an earlier chapter, claiming to have seen saucers collecting Antarctica-bound supplies of fruit at Colonia Dignidad.[5] A photo of the author in the English-language *UFOs: Nazi Secret Weapon?* is labelled as being Zündel, but this same image is elsewhere listed as showing Mattern. Such confusion was surely intentional. *Brisant* possessed no authorial bylines, and for good reason; West Germany had strict *Volksverhetzung* laws forbidding the promotion of Nazi ideology, so putting your name to such texts would have been legal suicide. That Zündel was ultimately behind *Brisant* can nonetheless be reasonably inferred from a 1994 interview in which he proudly revealed his name was derived from the German word *zundeln*, meaning 'to play with fire'. He thought this 'a very powerful name', with connotations of sparkplugs or arson, 'something that can spark a revolution.' Despite his Far-Right views, Zündel cited the title of one of Lenin's Marxist propaganda journals, *Iskra*, meaning 'The Spark' in Russian. Calling his one-off 1978 newspaper *Zündeln* would have been too obvious, so clearly he settled on the equally explosion-inducing *Brisant* as a rough alternative.[6]

* * * * *

Ernst Zündel may have denied the reality of the Holocaust, but happily asserted the reality of an entirely fictional series of events during 1946-7, when US Rear-Admiral Richard E. Byrd (1888-1957), the first man to fly over the North Pole back in 1926 (a feat some think he faked) had organised a military expedition towards the South Pole named 'Operation Highjump', involving a fleet of thirteen US Navy ships laden with 4,700 troops together with various planes, amphibious tanks and helicopters. Zündel pretended to believe the purpose of Highjump was to encircle and destroy the nearby Nazi UFO-base. In reality, Byrd aimed to establish new polar research facilities, gather scientific data about the frozen continent, and to extend claims for US sovereignty over as much of the landmass as possible, preparing for potential conflict there with the USSR. A programme of long-range aerial reconnaissance was ordered, but the expedition got off to a bad start, with Byrd losing three airmen after their plane crashed during a blizzard on 30 December 1946. By late February 1947, winter was approaching early and the whole mission was abandoned. The Antarctic is an inhospitable place; that's why it hadn't been mapped out before. But to Zündel, the place *had* already been mapped out before – by the Nazis. In 1938-39, German explorer Captain Alfred Ritscher (1879-1963) had led an Antarctic expedition of his own, flying over the future Neuschwabenland region dropping thousands of metal swastika flags onto the snow at regular intervals as proof Hitler owned the place, not the Norwegians. Zündel presented this as a far-sighted plan to build an icy *Alpenfestung* refuge from where war could be waged with the aid of saucers, early versions of which were shipped out there via U-boat. Antarctica, lied Zündel, was the home of his much-hoped-for Last Battalion, hence the Allies' Operation Highjump. The true reason Admiral Richard E. Byrd returned home early was because Nazi saucer-men had shot down his planes.[7]

Zündel blatantly misrepresented certain factual pieces of information culled from the media. On 5 March 1947, Chilean newspaper *El Mercurio* (for which Miguel Serrano used to write, incidentally) ran an authentic interview with Admiral Byrd:

> Admiral Richard E. Byrd warned today that the United States should adopt measures of protection against the possibility of an invasion of the country by hostile planes coming from the polar regions. The Admiral explained that he was not trying to scare anyone, but the cruel reality is that, in case of a new war, the United States could be attacked by planes flying over one or both poles.

By itself, this could indeed have been construed as implying that Byrd had discovered hidden military air-bases there. However, the Admiral then made it clear all he meant was that the post-war development of long-range bombers by the Soviet Union now made the hitherto-inaccessible poles new possible avenues of attack against the previously impregnable North American continent:

> The speed with which the world is shrinking – recalled the Admiral – is one of the most important lessons learned during his recent Antarctic exploration. 'I have to warn my compatriots that the time has ended when we were able to take refuge in our isolation and rely on the certainty that the distances, the oceans and the poles were a guarantee of safety.'[8]

In *Brisant*, though, this interview became garbled, with it being suggested (to cite Harbinson's own account of the rag's findings) that whilst official US reports intended for domestic consumption falsely suggested the expedition had been 'an enormous success', certain 'other, mainly foreign reports' reported that 'many of Byrd's men were lost during the first day; that at least four of his planes inexplicably disappeared; and that while the expedition had gone provisioned for six to eight months, the men actually returned to America in February 1947, after only a few weeks.' Although Harbinson 'could find no verification on this', he said *Brisant* also reported that in a foreign newspaper Byrd warned how it was now 'necessary for the USA to take defensive actions against enemy air-fighters which come from the polar regions', as in any new war, the US would be attacked by 'fighters that are able to fly from one pole to the other with incredible speed.'[9] Evidently, the report being rewritten by *Brisant* here was that of *El Mercurio*, but given a deliberately misleading gloss to imply the actual reason for Byrd's lost aeroplane (or four lost aeroplanes, as they had now become) and early retreat was heroic Nazi resistance against the Allied invaders, not poor weather. Kenneth Arnold's original saucer-sighting, made only a few months following Admiral Byrd's retreat, may thus have been no coincidence; either the Ice-Nazis were taking the war back to America, or America was busy developing its own USAF saucers to counteract the Last Battalion's own air-fleet. Evidently, the Nazis lived on and one day would fly out from Antarctica *en masse*, bringing death from above.[10] Zündel's narrative, conveyed via *Brisant*, became the basic inspiration for Harbinson's own *Projekt Saucer* series. 'This theory,' Harbinson wrote, 'would explain why ... all the nations of the world – even the Soviets and the Americans – had co-operated with one another only in the Antarctic' in terms of joint post-war scientific projects ostensibly aimed at monitoring the continent's weather and geology: to defeat Hitler's resurrected war-machine a second time.[11]

The origins of the notion Hitler personally lay concealed in a polar UFO-base lie in a 1947 – that year again! – book by Ladislas Szabó, a Hungarian refugee living in Argentina, called *I Know That Hitler Is Alive*. But how did Ladislas know? Szabó read how a female visitor saying her last goodbyes to Hitler in the Berlin *Führerbunker* in 1945 noted he had 'changed a great deal', being a complete nervous and physical wreck. During his final hours Adolf had only shaken hands with most visitors and said nothing. Szabó interpreted this as meaning concentration camp doctors had obtained a rough Hitler lookalike and performed plastic surgery and hair transplants to turn him into a true *doppelgänger*, so Hitler could leave a fake corpse behind and escape. Doped with mind-control drugs, the double was unable to speak, thereby disguising his non-Hitlerian voice. However, 'changed into a semi-paralytic' by the operation, Hitler's double came across as an invalid, thus accounting for the Führer's apparent major decline in health.

Taken to Scandinavia by plane, Hitler then jumped into a U-boat and sailed to safety. In July 1945, two German U-boats, the *U-530* and *U-977*, surrendered in Argentina, hoping for a good reception amongst the local German expat community. Szabó saw this as evidence of a 'phantom convoy' which had transported Hitler, Eva Braun and key underlings, first to South America and thence to Neuschwabenland, where a 'New Berchtesgaden' had been established to keep him nice and warm on the direct orders of Admiral Dönitz. Less than a week after the first U-boat surfaced Szabó went to print with his theory in the Argentine newspaper *La Critica*. This article was then reprinted worldwide, the sensational story reaching the receptive ears of Miguel Serrano, who recycled Szabó's claims in his own 1948 book about legends of the Antarctic, before using them as one basis for his bizarre theory about the inherent capability of top Nazis to photocopy themselves like Rudolf Hess. In later years, rumours of strange cargoes of plutonium – ideal for powering nuclear saucers – being found on these submarines have emerged, but at the time the only contraband reported were large quantities of cigarettes. They can't have been for Hitler himself, as he famously didn't smoke. Then again, as other versions of the yarn claim Hitler did commit suicide in Berlin after all, with only his ashes being spirited away by U-boat for enshrinement within a 'very special natural ice-cave' in Antarctica, maybe he was rolled up inside one.[12]

American evangelicals further spread such rumours to imply Hitler would soon stage a fake resurrection and be endorsed as Christ reborn by the wicked Pope in Rome, who would thus claim the power to perform miracles before uniting Europe in a new Catholic-Nazi Empire, only to be stopped by the real Protestant Second Coming of Jesus, probably by 1972 at the latest.[13] Some endorsed the stories as showing Hitler was a coward who ran away; others begged to differ. Ernst Zündel cynically rewrote Szabó's fantasies in his 1975 *UFOs: Nazi Secret Weapon?* book. Forever holding his English-speaking audience in contempt, Zündel argued his hero could not possibly have committed suicide as 'Hitler was not suicide-prone' – after all, he'd never done it before. Furthermore, all top Nazis 'had life-long careers and training in the martial arts and were cool, non-emotional Prussians to the core', so would never have performed such an act of moral weakness. Yes, the Russians found a skull they *said* was Hitler's, but 'There were millions of bones lying all over Germany as the result of mass killing by Allied aerial bombing,' so it could have been anyone's. All they really found at the Berlin bunker were two of Hitler's old hats and a pair of Eva Braun's knickers (some items reputedly corresponding to this description actually were once dug up there). Zündel reproduces a photo of a bomb crater where there happens to be a white cloth, an arrow indicating this to be the underwear in question. Furthermore, the dental records used to identify Hitler's skull were inaccurately drawn up 'from *memory*' by the Führer's dental assistant, with all the leading Nazis' true medical records having been flown away 'to an unknown destination', probably Antarctica. Some of the sources cited by Zündel as evidence for these claims are the German versions of *his own books.*[14]

Zündel presents a prophecy of Nostradamus that one day 'the great one' shall be 'drawn' into an 'iron cage' as proof Hitler did indeed sail to Antarctica in a U-boat; another line of Nostradamus, 'The leader, escaping, shall be safe in a barn on the sea' backed this up.[15] Antarctica made a great lair because its extreme weather rendered it a giant fridge-freezer which would keep Hitler's valuable food supplies 'edible forever' whilst allowing the man himself to remain in a state of elongated, well-cooled youth. There is 'no rust' and are 'no germs' in the Antarctic, good for Hitler's saucers and general health alike, factors 'which would not have been lost on a very health-conscious vegetarian', as Hitler was meant to have been.[16] The 'typically Bolshevik show-trials' held at Nuremberg were a ruse to draw polar saucers out of hiding to rescue the accused so the craft could be shot down by the Allies, but Hitler did not fall for this trap, so 'the orgy of strangulations and torture' went ahead anyway, although a few UFOs were spotted overhead on recon missions. When several UFOs were apparently photographed hovering over the White House in 1952, Zündel saw these as being arranged in a 'typically German' formation, a warning from the Last Battalion that the Yankees' home cities were far more vulnerable than the German underground ice-base, so they had better not try another Operation

Highjump. The Nazis had uncovered a sly new plan to have Antarctica designated a safe zone to conduct atom bomb tests in, thus giving the Allies cover for nuking Hitler's frozen bunker without the public even knowing. Zündel invented yet another quote wholesale, saying that, when asked what the real purpose of Highjump had been, Rear-Admiral Byrd had answered: 'To break the last desperate resistance of Adolf Hitler ... or to destroy him.'[17]

Even if his base was nuked, Hitler could easily escape, though, as at the South Pole the Van Allen radiation-belt 'opens up, funnel-like', creating a radiation-free zone through which Nazi saucers could whizz into space without their crews even needing to wear protective suits; Hitler's wartime 'feasibility studies of space-stations' proved this was so. Zündel hoped to win sympathy from those who feared Cold War nuclear Armageddon, promising polar Nazi saucers would 'undoubtedly prevent atomic war to prevent the extinction of the White Race ... No man of the calibre of Adolf Hitler, deeply committed to the survival and resurgence of Western Culture, would ever allow this tragedy to happen.'[18] Antarctica was therefore humanity's only remaining great white hope.

That the Nazi polar legend has successfully burrowed deep within the skull of our collective unconscious can be seen in the example of Erika Bertschinger (1929-2019), leader of the millenarian German cult Fiat Lux, or 'Let There Be Light'. Erika's story began in 1973 when she fell off her horse and bumped her head like Don Quixote, causing her to believe she was the reincarnation of the Virgin Mary, or 'Uriella', as she now preferred to call herself. Fiat Lux do not maintain a website address, believing the letters 'www' are code for '666' and that the Internet is thus a tool of Satan, but a series of German court-trials involving tax irregularities and fake healing cures ensured some data about them came to light. It appears Uriella/Erika channelled messages from Hidden Masters like the Archangel Uriel, who would appear in her living room, and Jesus Christ, who was an alien. These Masters informed their 'speaking-tube' Erika that, accompanied by a series of global natural disasters such as meteorite strikes, the Third World War would break out in 1998, triggered by the emergence of the Fourth Reich's gigantic saucer-fleet from their Antarctic base. The Nazi saucers would only fight for three days, but kill billions. Yet one third of humanity would be spared, when Christ would send a rescue-fleet of spherical foo-like spaceships to suck the acceptably New Age-minded aboard in a 'Big Beam'. The Nazis would then be defeated by Jesus and our *kali yuga* world become transformed into a *satya yuga* paradise planet named Amora, or 'Love', where sunken continents like Atlantis (and Thule?) would rise from beneath the waves. When 1998 passed without Hitler reappearing, Uriella explained humanity had been gifted an extra 'time of grace' from God to prepare for the genocidal onslaught, due to the immense power of her prayers for salvation.[19]

Similarly disturbed was Norma Cox, a self-described 'crippled and widowed housewife' from Middle America, who possessed the 'awesome and inescapable responsibility' of alerting the white race they were 'targeted for extinction' at the hands of the Jews. Via her many self-published UFO-related tracts and regular newsletter, *Secrets*, Cox spun an elaborate Ariosophy-style yarn in which the pagan gods like Zeus and Apollo were real, belonging to a race of ETs called 'The Watchers', who had formally been stationed above Earth by God to monitor the planet's development from spaceships. Mostly these Watchers stared down rather too closely at 'the comely women of the planet', however, flying down to rape them, siring a race of giants who ate the comparatively tiny normal-sized Earthlings, so God caused the giants to war amongst themselves until all were dead, before imprisoning their pervert pagan fathers within the Hollow Earth. The Bible was full of misprints, with God's true 'Chosen People' being the 'Aryan Christians', not the Jews; the Jews actually worshipped the sun god Apollo and plotted to destroy all Aryans. Allied with Judah was the goddess Diana, who was also the Statue of Liberty; the spikes on her crowned head were truly antennae, transmitting messages to and from alien bases on the moon. The only man who could save white humanity now was Adolf Hitler, who was still alive and safe beneath Neuschwabenland. 'Hitler was not an evil man,' Cox explained, 'except in the eyes of those persons who have had their minds so twisted [by Jewish media] that they have come to regard the … races as equal.' All Hitler did was 'fight to cleanse the planet of the filth that was destroying it' and one day his Fourth Reich would rise and wash the Earth as white as the polar snow.[20]

There are even now purported first-hand accounts, from the likes of ufologist and former USAF Colonel Wendelle Stevens (1923-2010), of B-29 bombers being flown over polar regions looking for 'mysterious objects known as fireballs or foo-fighters'. According to Stevens, these were filmed and footage locked away in Washington. Stevens personally supervised installation of the 'special equipment' used to track them. These frosty foos must have been Nazi in nature, as, whilst working at the US Air Technical Intelligence Centre during the war, Stevens had previously seen a map of Germany marked with nine versions of the astronomical symbol for Saturn, signifying where the initial Nazi saucer-research depots were. The reliability of Stevens' testimony can be gauged by his other claim that full-fledged Nazi UFOs were used 'just once' against the Allies, 'shooting down an unprecedented 200 [Allied bombers] in just one night.' Why didn't they use them again, then?[21]

Antarctica in these stories is really a territory of the mind, a blank, white, icy canvas which, like our similarly Nazi-infested moon, almost nobody will ever actually go to, which you can fill with whatever false images you like. For the academic Joscelyn Godwin (b.1945), writers of fiction – intentional or otherwise – have traditionally equated the North Pole with positive forces like god-men and the South Pole with negative ones like demons and monsters, of whom the Nazis are simply 'their recent representatives'.[22] Yet demons exist to be exorcised, and in 2007 a detailed academic paper by researchers Colin Summerhayes and Peter Beeching appeared in the journal *Polar Record*, demonstrating how the 1938-39 German expedition to Neuschwabenland championed by Ernst Zündel was actually intended to establish a whaling-base there, whales being a vital source of oil and glycerine for use in explosives. Whilst their expedition did find some evidence of surprisingly ice-free lakes, the Germans found no polar openings or inexplicable tropical zones to shelter UFO hangars, as some would later claim. They did not even formally annex the territory from Norway; pretty soon, Germany would be annexing Norway itself in 1940, anyway. As for Operation Highjump, it didn't even occur over Neuschwabenland, but on the other side of the continent, and as usual it turns out many 'factual' UFO texts cite obviously fictional sources like Wilhelm Landig's *Thule* novels for their info. A quotation from Admiral Dönitz that 'The German submarine fleet is proud of having built for the Führer, in another part of the world, a Shangri-La on land, an impregnable fortress ... a paradise-like oasis in the middle of eternal ice' frequently cited by fringe writers turned out to be totally spurious, as did claims the place was powered by geothermal energy, of which there were no possible sources in Neuschwabenland. Photos of the region suddenly acquired completely misleading captions from the likes of Ernst Zündel, whilst wild tales of an atom bomb being personally dropped on the saucer-base by Rear-Admiral Byrd were nixed by the absence of any radiation readings. Operation Highjump was not even a secret mission; journalists accompanied it, and Byrd wrote up his trip-diaries for *National Geographic* magazine. Byrd's premature return really was due to the unexpectedly early onset of winter, not because of his planes being lasered by *Wunderwaffen*. The whole thing was a self-referential cycle of lies.[23]

And yet, from Ernst Zündel's perspective, perhaps none of this mattered. One of the key arguments of Summerhayes and Beeching's paper was that, due to the scale of the hypothetical polar operation, it would have been physically impossible for Germany to keep Antarctica continually supplied with men, materials and supplies throughout the war, when such scarce things were needed back home. Scooping entire mountains out of Antarctica to create an *Alpenfestung* complex would have been nigh-on impossible at the best of times; would the giant industrial machines needed to do so really have been transportable by U-boat, anyway? But the genius of Zündel is that the techniques used by genuine scholars to debunk the idea of Nazi polar UFO-bases mirror precisely the techniques used by pseudo-scholars like himself to debunk the idea of Nazi gas chambers – by careful deployment of facts and figures, Holocaust deniers purport to demonstrate the logistical impossibility of transporting so many Jews by train or fitting so many corpses into ovens. So, when Summerhayes and Beeching ably demonstrate the physical impossibility of the polar base's existence, a lie Zündel did not care about, they inadvertently lend a lie Zündel *did* care about apparent surface credibility. If genuine scholars can demonstrate there were no Nazi UFO-bases by such means, shouldn't it logically follow that, by using similar-looking means, pro-Nazi pseudo-scholars can demonstrate there was no Treblinka? Few reading these words will be technically qualified to make informed judgements about either the load-bearing capacity of wartime German submarines, or the corpse-bearing capacity of death camp ovens; most persons simply accept the standard presented data as a given, believing the UFO-base deniers, and disbelieving the Holocaust deniers. But our justification for doing so is revealed by this comparison simply as being trust and common sense, not actual inherent knowledge or expertise. Once we realise this, maybe we will begin to question the entire basis of our other pre-existing beliefs about history. Thereby, even if his claims are thoroughly disproven, Zündel still wins, in a way.

*****

A further strain of the Nazi Antarctic UFO-base saga centres upon 'Rainbow City', a fabled citadel partly owing its existence to yet more quotes attributed to Rear-Admiral Byrd to the effect that 'I'd love to see that land beyond the [South] Pole. That land beyond the Pole is the centre of the Great Unknown.' This was interpreted by some fantasists not as a simple desire to map uncharted polar territories from the air, but as evidence Byrd had discovered warm, green valleys at the North Pole (these people didn't know the difference between the Arctic and Antarctic) harbouring entrances into the Hollow Earth, where saucers lurked. Somehow, Byrd's innocent words were twisted into proof he had seen a 'monstrous, greenish-hued animal' – apparently a living mammoth – during his explorations.[24] Even weirder was what was done with another of Byrd's quotes, describing his 1947 flight over the Beardmore and Wade Glaciers during Operation Highjump:

> It might have been called the Avenue of Frozen Rainbows. To east and west towered great mountains. Some were free of ice – coal-black and brick-red. Others were completely ice-covered … Where the sun struck their peaks and slopes the light was reflected from them in an indescribable complex of colours. There were blends of blues, purples and greens such as man seldom has seen.[25]

To the mentally unbalanced, this description proved the presence not of reflections of sunlight through the prism of ice crystals, but of a lost polar realm made of gigantic coloured Lego-bricks, in which literally everything, from houses to fabrics, was made of special brightly dyed plastic. In 1947 and 1948 the pulp US sci-fi magazine *Amazing Stories* carried references to a Montana couple, William C. Hefferlin and his wife Gladys, who purported to be in telepathic contact with a reincarnated ancient engineer from this city, named Emery. Supposedly, so the Hefferlins revealed in a privately circulated manuscript, the settlement had its origins millions of years ago, when humans – who actually hailed from another planet – engaged in a thousand-year war against a rival reptilian race called the Snake People. The humans lost and sought refuge on Mars, before the oxygen ran out and they returned to Earth's South Pole, which was then nice and warm and filled with beautiful giant butterflies with wings eight feet wide and bodies the size of turkeys. Here they created seven subterranean cities linked by trains and powered by radium, each named after a colour of the rainbow, with Red City being made from giant red plastic Lego-blocks, Blue City from blue ones, and so on. Towering over them all, containing bricks of every hue, was Rainbow City. As in certain strands of Ariosophy, these ancient humans were giants with special powers, later forced to leave their Golden Age home when the Snake People attacked the planet again, flipping its axis on its side, and bringing ice to our current-day poles. During their long emigration away, the refugees lost their powers and knowledge of advanced super-tech, just like the Hyperborean Aryans of old.

Today, Rainbow City lies protected from prying eyes behind a 10,000-foot-tall ice-wall, whilst its greatest inhabitants, a mini-Royal Family called 'The Ancient Three Who Were, Who Are, Who Will Be, Always', have been reincarnated into the bodies of Hidden Masters living underground in Tibet – or at least they were when the Hefferlins made psychic contact with Engineer Emery. Emery built a fleet of saucers for The Ancient Three so they could soar over Antarctica in 1942, searching for their lost city, since successfully resettled by them and their kin. From here, Hidden Masters still fly out in Emery's circular aircraft, often mistaken for alien saucers, plotting with representatives of the Third World to bring the white race under their control in a sort of legally binding polar UN so as to ensure the end of war, racism and all human ills. 'Thought-machines' contained in their temples ensure the ultimate success of this plan. The fact the Hefferlins are now no longer heard from is not because they are dead, but because they now live in Rainbow City themselves, where, like Zündel's fridge-frozen Hitler, they have become quasi-immortal.[26]

Another source for Rainbow City was the US horror-writer H. P. Lovecraft (1890-1937), whose 1936 novella *At the Mountains of Madness* describes Antarctic explorers unearthing a colossal lost alien metropolis, with some fringe theorists now giving the Hefferlins' original coloured Lego-cities new names stolen directly from Lovecraft's oeuvre, such as 'Kadath', from his 1927 *The Dream-Quest of Unknown Kadath*. Some occultists think Lovecraft's stories about horrific alien demons destroying mankind really told inadvertent truths, as his frequent citing of nightmares as his inspiration for them meant he had actually picked up on telepathic transmissions from the demonic ETs who then appeared in his tales. According to this line of thought, the Lovecraftian Snake People genuinely lie frozen within a 'strange gas' beneath the Antarctic snows like *Doctor Who*'s reptilian Ice-Warriors and Silurians, waiting to be awoken by some foolish human weak enough to obey their subliminal mental commands to dig them all up; *At the Mountains of Madness* becomes a dream-world prediction of this one day occurring. The Snake People are also sometimes linked to Lovecraft's 1921 short-story *The Nameless City*, in which a race of ancient crocodile-men rest Dracula-like in caskets beneath the Earth's crust.[27] Lovecraft's fantasy-writer friend Robert E. Howard (1906-36), creator of Conan the Barbarian, also wrote influential stories about wicked snake-people. Some conspiracists have even tried to link such subterranean serpent-men back to the snake that tempted Eve to eat the Forbidden Fruit in Eden, so giving their ideas biblical 'authority'. The shape-shifting underground lizard-men of Branton and David Icke must have some imaginative roots here too.[28]

Inevitably, Rainbow City has since been become repopulated not by Snake People but by Nazis. The man most responsible was a Far-Right Native American Indian from the Madoc tribe, a former Marine Corps officer and self-styled Bigfoot-witness from Missouri named Tawani Shoush, who contacted newspapers in 1978 to announce his intention to fly a zeppelin into a big hole at the North Pole. Shoush never managed to do this but did release a document chronicling another wholly fake flight of Rear-Admiral Byrd over the North Pole in February 1947, when he was actually busy down at the South Pole with Operation Highjump. In Shoush's forged account, Byrd again sees green vegetation and a mammoth, before spotting 'a large shimmering city pulsating with rainbow hues of colour'. A compulsive diarist, when his plane meets some strange, 'disc-shaped' aircraft with 'a radiant quality' to them, Byrd picks up his pencil and writes 'MY GOD!!! ... They are close enough now to see the markings on them. It is a type of swastika!!! This is fantastic.' In a German accent, radio-operators from the saucers – termed *Flügelrads* or 'flying-wheels' – welcome Byrd to 'our domain', seize remote control of his plane and take him to their Führer inside Rainbow City. The ufonauts, called the Arianni, are indeed all rather Aryan-looking, being 'tall with blonde hair', like Orthon. Their leader, The Master, greets Byrd cordially, warning him the Rainbow Race think mankind should relinquish its nuclear weapons, as they bear 'a certain power that is not for man'. Whilst The Master does promise that, following any future nuclear conflict, the Arianni 'shall come forward again to help revive your culture and your race', Byrd is tasked with delivering this anti-nuclear message to 'the Surface World' anyway.[29]

In the 1990s, Branton of *The Omega File* fame contacted Shoush, who now claimed to be 'a fully fledged Nazi' who had served on one of the U-boats that had fled to South America after the war. Now understanding the difference between the Arctic and Antarctica, Shoush told of how the esoteric SS had hidden the Spear of Destiny in an 'ice-cave' near the South Pole, to 'summon a great leader who will rise out of Europe and finish the work Adolf Hitler began', apparently with the aid of Nazi-loving UN Secretary-General Kurt Waldheim (1918-2007), who wielded the Spear himself on occasion. So, how to explain Rear-Admiral Byrd's encounter with the Arianni at the *North* Pole? Possibly Byrd was a secret Nazi seeking to draw attention away from the alliance of 'Nazis, Greys, Draco, rebel Pleiadians and a few collaborating Sasquatch-people' in Antarctica by diverting interested ufologists northwards instead; the Ariannis' request for humanity to relinquish its nukes was meant to leave us helpless in the face of their own polar *Wunderwaffen*. One person who allegedly suggested this theory to Branton was one Harley Byrd, Rear-Admiral Byrd's supposed grandson!

Alternatively, to Dennis G. Crenshaw, editor of *The Hollow Earth Insider*, the blatant absurdity of Shoush's obvious hoax was intended to discredit the very notion of there being a Hollow Earth at all. Crenshaw blamed not the Nazis for putting Shoush up to this trick, but a shadowy 'New World Order' who actually '*owned* the Bank of Italy and the Bank of America', and who had funded Rear-Admiral Byrd's phoney expeditions in the first place.[30] Clearly, there are some stories too absurd even for Nazi UFO-lovers and Hollow Earth theorists to believe in. At this point, naturally, they turn to the much more plausible narrative of blaming the Jews for it all instead. Somewhere in the depths of Frozen Hell, Ernst Zündel must be laughing through frost-rimed lips.

4

The Half-Life and Half-Death of Captain Blimp: Mr Wilson and the Great American Airship Panic

What have some actual sensible ufologists made of the Nazi UFO myth and its key texts? Generally, they disapprove. Consider a poor review given to W. A. Harbinson's *Projekt Saucer* novel *Genesis*, printed in the leading British UFO periodical *Flying Saucer Review* (*FSR*) by the prominent ufologist Jenny Randles, who thought it a sick rip-off of the Darkside Hypothesis. For Randles, *Genesis* proved 'a horrifying book' because of the 'dreadful image' it gave of ufology, an egregiously 'false picture' which made her 'shudder' far more than any of its shocking plot twists and violent content. She criticised it as 'fanciful and artificial' even in mundane matters, with it being unexplained who actually pays the full-time UFO-hunters in the book, such folk generally being self-funded part-timers in real-life. Randles didn't like the methods employed by Harbinson's ufologists either, which (according to her interpretation) involved beating, raping, drugging and killing people. The reader, argued Randles, is 'forced to assume' the sadistic methodology of the offending ufologists 'is standard'. This is unfortunate, as 'in parts of the text Mr Harbinson actually intermingles real events and characters with fictional ones,' most of whom in reality were 'painstaking researchers and careful documenters', not psychopaths. The end effect of 'this monster novel' is that 'many may read it who could well have their own UFO experience at a later date, and keep their peace when they recall the behaviour of the fictional investigators.' Nobody wants to get raped by a rogue ufologist, do they? Many abductees get quite enough of that kind of thing from the aliens themselves these days. W. A. Harbinson was actually an *FSR* reader and wrote a reply, explaining how he thought few readers would want to examine details of his ufologists' invoices. Also, the 'rape' depicted was no such thing but 'a mutual seduction', he said. Harbinson's ultimate aim was not to demonise ufologists, but to criticise irresponsible scientists like those who helped his Nazis develop their saucers.[1]

Most people don't take such fictions seriously, but we must always remember there are certain individuals who visit crime museums and ask if they have Sherlock Holmes' deerstalker and meerschaum pipe anywhere on display. A similar level of mental tumult was induced in some by the appearance of a final spin-off from the *Projekt Saucer* series self-published by the author in 2017, entitled *The Wilson Papers: Genesis of the World's Most Fearsome Secret*. The cover shows a piece of plain paper bound by a cheap plastic ring-binder, with 'DECLASSIFIED' stamped across it in bold red letters. Adopting an ostensibly non-fiction form, in the shape of a series of retypings of old, once-secret CIA files, these are billed as being 'Edited by W. A. Harbinson', not *written* by him. Instead, apart from Harbinson's own 'editorial interventions' in providing introductions, the purported main author of the book is the titular Mr Wilson. Through Wilson's fake diary entries, now released by the CIA, *The Wilson Papers* retells from a new perspective the story of John Wilson, the original super-genius behind the Nazis' Antarctic saucer programme, who was born in the 1800s in the US but, via a fiendish combination of futuristic genetic techniques and advanced cybernetics, managed to survive into the late 2000s by merging his consciousness with a series of interlinked super-computers kept within underwater Nazi bases, before planning to wipe all fleshly humanity out as inferior to this next, more metallic, stage in the race's evolution. So, in other words, it isn't very realistic. It even features the standard legal disclaimer that 'All characters in this e-book publication are fictitious and any resemblance to real persons, living or dead, is purely coincidental.' Few read such small-print notices, but the blurb should be a dead give-away that the book may not be *entirely* true to life:

> *The Wilson Papers* ... tell the story of a man who was born in the American Midwest of the 19th century, took part in the rise and fall of Nazi Germany, continued [living] into the Space Age of the 20th century and finally entered the late 21st century to unveil a future of unparalleled scientific achievements and unspeakable horrors, a future beyond normal human imagining. *The Wilson Papers*, finally declassified, tell this extraordinary, truly shocking, and almost unbelievable story. Read them and tremble.[2]

Careful readers may have spotted John Wilson was therefore only unplugged from his socket for good in 'the late 21st century', despite this period of time not yet having actually occurred. Less careful readers, however, will have gone instantly onto amazon.com following purchase, there to post outraged one-star reviews like the following [*sic* throughout]::

> This is a FICTIONAL book disguised as factual history until about half the book. Then it goes downhill and becomes pure fantasy ... After reading a few books on classified, nazi and ufo technology, I became adept of the idea that UFOs are man made and that after WWII a lot of germany technology was brought to the backstages to be developed in secrecy ... This book wants to make one believe that all the backstage

activity was ... the product of a single man (Wilson), that lived for 130 years ... and then later cloned himself and ... merged into a biological super computer spread among antarctica and several underwater bases ... Talk about non-credible! Not to mention a few date inconsistencies and the fact the author didnt even mention the co-expedition between USA and USSR to antarctica in the early 1950s to detonate 2 atomic bombs (allegedly to test effects of the bombs on ice melting). This would have made the author's case even stronger, but he never bothers to touch the subject ... To wrap it up: don't waste your time, or if you do, at least read it with a grain (or perhaps a truckload?) of salt[3]

The reviewer here refers to the false rumour that three US nuclear bombs were detonated over the Antarctic under the cover of other experiments during the International Geophysical Year of 1957-58, supposedly to destroy Hitler's ice-base. However, whilst the US did make some secret high-altitude nuclear tests in 1958, they actually took place in the sea near Tristan de Cunha, not over Antarctica. Had such tests happened in the locations usually implied by neo-Nazi fringe theorists like Wilhelm Landig, they would have incinerated a group of international scientists studying there at the time, creating a diplomatic incident.[4] Rubbishing a book as too unrealistic because it fails to mention an event which never occurred is akin to dismissing a history of the Cold War as giving insufficient credit to James Bond's major role in proceedings. The reviewer found *The Wilson Papers* fairly plausible until about half-way through, when he began to experience doubts. But did he really find the following words from 'Paper #1' a realistic account of John Wilson's aberrant childhood psychology, taken direct from the pen of the saucer-builder himself? Complaining that he 'never understood emotions', particularly not 'what they call "love" and its attendant illusions', Wilson proudly explains how he never allowed such fleshly weaknesses get the better of him:

> Even ... as a young man, in the offensive throes of puberty, I would hold my yellow semen in my hand and try to sniff out its properties. The *vas deferens* and the seminal vesicles, the bulbo-urethral and prostate glands; my ejaculations were examined biologically and found to be normal. I thus conquered such distractions. I took the semen on my tongue. Various liquids and sperm, two hundred million spermatozoa: orgasm thus became a form of research and lost its great mystery ... For my birthday, I received a microscope ... In my room, I took my penis in my hand and let the semen stain slides. The mystery of life was in biology. Ejaculation was mere phenomena ... Science. That is all. The pursuit of knowledge was all that mattered.[5]

The point is to establish the young John Wilson as half-robot already, and draw an early analogy between the ice which runs in his veins (and his glands) and the lifeless, cold and icy plains within which he will later build his saucer-base: 'And now, looking out at the glittering ice-caps, I feel deep contentment ... Within the ice is the New World. Beyond it is the Old.'[6] It's certainly an effective literary technique – but did it prove *too* effective for some? Like the contents of John Wilson's teenage hands, you might have thought the above passage would have smelled distinctly fishy.

I don't want to make the disappointed online purchaser feel any more duped, but had he truly 'become adept of the idea that UFOs are man made' he would have been aware of the fact that this 'John Wilson' was inspired by Harbinson's having read about another real-life figure from the distant past of ufology – a real-life figure who, just like Sherlock Holmes, didn't actually exist, but really ought to have done. Harbinson once provided the following interesting information for his fans to contemplate:

> For the purposes of my fiction, I have utilised many real-life people, including the mysterious John Wilson and the Nazi SS generals Artur Nebe and Hans Kammler. The term 'real-life' is used in regard to John Wilson only in the sense that during the first modern UFO sightings – the Great Airship Scare of 1896-97 – when airships of unknown origin were reportedly seen and landed all over the United States – the man whom most witnesses reportedly spoke to had introduced himself simply as 'Wilson' and claimed his airships had been constructed in Iowa and Illinois. He was not seen or heard of after the great scare ended – though C. C. Akers, former sheriff of Zavalia County, Texas, to whom Wilson had referred when speaking to one of the witnesses, claimed that he had known a Wilson who was of 'a mechanical turn of mind'.[7]

In his first Nazi novel, *Genesis*, Harbinson provided data about this Wilson fellow's alleged activities across 1890s America, summaries since used as evidence for the man's literal physical existence by fringe researchers online.[8] In his non-fiction tie-in, *Projekt UFO*, Harbinson made the following ambiguous statement: 'While I have used the mysterious "Wilson" as a major protagonist in my ... *Projekt Saucer* novels, creating what I believe is a plausible explanation for him, it has to be conceded that no proof for his existence, other than [the original 1890s newspaper reports] has ever surfaced.' Yet, 'whether Wilson existed as "Wilson" or was someone else using a pseudonym is of relative unimportance.' What was truly important was this: 'The fact remains that during the Great Airship Scare thousands of people across the United States saw what was clearly a manned, motor-driven airship. The true identity of the genius who built it may never be known.'[9]

Real or not, the enigmatic Wilson – Harbinson arbitrarily christened him 'John' – certainly left a long newspaper-trail behind after him, over half a century before the term 'UFO' was even invented. But was this trail worth the paper it was written on? The Great Airship Scare of 1896-7 was a real social panic which generated thousands of sightings of strange dirigibles speeding across the skies of America, just like Harbinson said. Stereotypically cigar-shaped with an undercarriage equipped with a spotlight to carry passengers and crew, and occasionally with propellers or wings attached, these craft were patently not genuine physical dirigibles. One California airship of 1896 was seen to possess flapping, bird-like wings operated 'by four men, who worked as if on bicycles', whilst in Kentucky, one man pointed his telescope at an airship to see it crewed by winged angels. Some sightings were simply of astronomical phenomena, re-interpreted as airships under influence of prevailing media reports. By the 1890s, the USA was increasingly linked via telegraph, allowing what might have remained as a few baffling local incidents to become a nationwide sensation. Thus, the entire panic was an early mass-media phenomenon. Press reports generated yet more witness reports from readers to feed the journalistic frenzy, in classic circular fashion. Cynics speculated a new medical condition of 'airship neck' might develop, such was the new-found love of searching the skies for things which weren't there.

Some journalists enterprisingly provided the falsehoods themselves, as when a gigantic silver-coated cigar-like dirigible with wings reportedly landed on a Minnesota courthouse in April 1897, before a remarkably exact 135,472 witnesses saw three extraterrestrials emerge. They had 'no line of demarcation between the nose and the mouth', lied a reporter, and possessed gills on the side of their heads which 'resembled the fan-shaped ear of the elephant' as well as 'eyes like boiled eggs' and 'something resembling a huge fin' on their backs. Their feet were 'pointed as tacks' so they didn't float away from the surface of their low-gravity home planet, and their hands 'were simply claws' for when the alien air got too thick they had to literally claw their way through it.

People seeing a bright light in the sky and imagining they could see a shadowy dark black cigar lurking behind it were reasonable enough things to print; an account of a meeting with a 'long-bearded' mystery scientist who refused to reveal his name before pointing to the letter 'M' painted on the side of his zeppelin as a needless hint to his true identity, as reported from Springfield, Illinois, in April 1897, rather less so. Of course, the more detailed a sighting was, the more likely it was to be invented. Some adverts mimicked the dubious reports, claiming airships had dropped leaflets urging residents to attend sales at local stores.

Primitive airships did exist in the 1890s, but the levels of performance attributed to the phantom ones by witnesses far outreached those of the rare genuine ones then undergoing tentative test-flights across the globe. The idea thus arose that a hermit-like genius had developed some means of super-fast airship travel and was busily perfecting it before selling his invention to the highest bidder. Some suggested America's most famous inventor Thomas Edison (1847-1931) might have created a gigantic aerial lightbulb, the 'Electric Star', from which vehicle he hoped to illuminate vast areas from above after dark, like a floating floodlight. In Portland, Maine, in March 1897, crowds gathered to stare at Edison's 'mammoth electric searchlight' hovering eerily in the night sky. It was the planet Venus. Edison just laughed. 'The Wizard of Menlo Park' suggested airships would indeed wing their way across the clouds one day, but not yet outside the pages of Jules Verne. However, since the 1870s, the world had seen the creation of the telephone, steam-turbine, motorcar, cinema, x-ray machine and radio – so why not an airship, too? Accordingly, some publicity-seekers started making implausible claims to get their names in the papers, just like Rudolf Schriever a few generations later; the Nazi saucer legend has many unexpected prior ufological precursors.[10]

* * * * *

Was W. A. Harbinson's Mr Wilson another of these same publicity-seekers? Or a figment of fake-news journalists' fevered imaginations? Historians have investigated, reaching the final conclusion that … nothing can finally be concluded. At 11.00 p. m. on the evening of 19 April 1897, one J. R. Ligon and his son Charley saw lights close to their rural home near Beaumont, Texas, finding a landed airship, over 100 feet long and 20 feet wide, complete with propellers and four large wings. The crew asked for water, which they then fetched from the family's property in buckets, two pails apiece. One aeronaut identified himself only as 'Wilson', saying he was based in Iowa. A report about this exciting event appeared in the *Houston Daily Post* for 21 April, adapted from a local newspaper story (regrettably now lost) printed on 20 April – coincidentally, Adolf Hitler's eighth birthday!

Other witnesses to Wilson's alleged travels across the region then sought their own moment in the limelight. In the *Dallas Morning News*, Dr D. H. Tucker reported these same aeronauts had caused a friend to fall from his buggy after their craft emitted an 'unearthly whistle', scaring his horses. Rushing over to see if he was OK, Wilson, described as having 'the typical face of a genius or an inventor', explained he hoped for proper financing to develop an entire air-fleet to ferry passengers between New York and San Francisco. However, Tucker said, his friend the witness had tragically/conveniently since drowned in a flood, so would be unable to confirm any of this. Yet, twenty-three hours after J. R. Ligon's first sighting of Mr Wilson, at 10.00 p.m. on 20 April, Uvalde County Sheriff H. W. Baylor also claimed to have met a landed airship, with 'fish-like' wings resembling fins, behind his house. A crew member introduced himself again as Mr Wilson, saying that, whilst originally a native of Goshen, New York State, he had formerly been a resident of Fort Worth, Texas, where he had been friendly with former Zavala County Sheriff C. C. Akers, whom Baylor knew, and to whom Wilson asked to be remembered. Once again, Wilson requested buckets of water, then floated away into the night. Local paper the *Galveston Daily News* contacted Sheriff C. C. Akers, who agreed he had indeed once been 'well acquainted with a man by the name of Wilson from New York State' when living in Fort

Worth back in 1876-77, this gentleman being 'a finely educated' young chap 'of a mechanical turn of mind' who had been 'working on aerial navigation and something that would astonish the world'. Wilson seemed of independent means, being able to devote his whole time to his tinkering.

Further reports of Wilson's activities trickled in to Texan newspapers before on 26 April, in the *San Antonio Daily Express*, the *wunderkind* gained a first name – not 'John', as W. A. Harbinson had it, but 'Hiram'. Citing no specific source, the *Express* stated Hiram was the son of an assistant master-mechanic of the New York Central Railroad named Willard H. Wilson, who had entered partnership with a youthful engineer, C. J. Walsh of San Francisco. Leading American UFO historian Jerome Clark has discovered from tax and census records that the man who first met Mr Wilson, J. R. Ligon of Beaumont, Texas, and his son Charley, really did exist. But the person they talked to did not; no Hiram Wilson was traced as living in either Goshen, New York, or Fort Worth, Texas, during the relevant periods. What was going on? As Clark accurately says, 'Since – literally – all we know is what we read in the papers, [any] rationalisations are necessarily speculative and therefore neither provable nor disprovable.' Clark shows how 'oddly and frustratingly, the core details [of the various accounts] both conform and conflict' with one another in terms of how many crew members were aboard Wilson's airship, its size and appearance, geographical origins, methods of fuelling and propulsion, etc – one man said it was powered by gas, another by 'highly condensed electricity'. If the epidemic of phantom Wilsons was an elaborate organised hoax, you may expect its participants to have bothered to get their stories straight; but you could equally argue the inconsistencies just expose the co-conspirators' incompetency. Yet if conspiracy it was, to what purpose?

On 20 June 1897 it was announced in the *Houston Post* that Mr Ligon, as the local agent for the Magnolia Brewery company, planned to mount a special display at a trade-fair on 3 July 'by exhibiting an airship ... not ... the same flying-machine that Mr Ligon saw but ... a fair simile of that remarkable vessel ... complete in every detail ... no charge will be made for examination of the plans of construction or the method of operation.' On 4 July, the *Post* listed the various floats which had paraded during the fair, one being 'Ligon's airship, poised over twenty little girls singing National airs', presumably to fit in with the next day's 4 July celebrations. So, you could plausibly speculate the whole yarn was simply another elaborate attempt at exploiting the 1896-97 airship-wave for advertising purposes, getting free publicity in the local media. But why did all the other named witnesses – most of whom did actually exist – play along? Maybe some were Ligon's friends, eager to help out. Or maybe they were paid, in money or in beer. Possibly they just wanted their name in the papers. But one particular witness, a respected local rabbi named Dr Aaron Levy, might have been unlikely to risk his reputation by becoming publicly involved in such an affair, given the nature of his work. And yet, on 25 April, he, too, was publicly professing to have seen the landed airship, spoken to an occupant and even shaken hands with him, thus implying Mr Wilson possessed some measure of corporeal physical reality – and also proving that, unlike Nazi UFO crews a few decades hence, the craft's captain was thankfully no anti-Semite.

Rather than an advertising-hoax, Jerome Clark himself thinks the wave of Wilson-sightings was an example of what he terms 'experience anomalies', defined as 'something like a collective dream that erupts into consensus reality.' Clark means people can sometimes see – and maybe even touch and otherwise interact with – things that do not exist, like Mr Wilson, who like a ghost was 'there for the duration of a sighting, gone forever afterwards'. 'Such experiences "exist" only in testimony and memory,' proposes Clark, as they usually leave no lasting physical evidence behind after them, which raises profound questions about 'any conventional understanding' of what the verb 'exist' may mean in the first place. 'Put simply,' Clark writes, 'the stories [of Mr Wilson] make no sense. They could not have happened in any way in which the verb "happened" is ordinarily understood.' If such experience anomalies do indeed exist, they do so only within a 'threshold or liminal [borderline] space in which the Otherworld passes from imagination into experience ... a kind of grey zone of ambiguous epistemology.' When this happens, 'it is as if ... a supernatural landscape has briefly overlaid the physical landscape' somehow. For Clark, there is such a thing as 'event-level reality', that physical space in which we live our day-to-day lives, but at rare times some peculiar otherworld may intrude upon it, via mechanisms unknown. You should not take these strange encounters literally, but nor should you blithely dismiss them. Clark argues 'It should be possible to believe one's informants without believing their explanations.' So, just because someone says they have seen an aeronaut named Wilson, this does not mean that what they saw was *actually* an aeronaut named Wilson, any more than someone who says they have seen a fairy has really seen a fairy. 'You can believe your eyes,' says Clark, 'just not what you're seeing.'

Clark is not simply dismissing these things as hallucinations, as sometimes more than one person may encounter a Mr Wilson simultaneously, and they may even appear to tangibly interact with the physical world around them. So, they are something more than fiction, something less than fact: 'Things that can't be, can be, if we don't insist on them as events.' The closest word we could use to describe such encounters is 'visionary'. All that can really be said is that 'Nearly anything can be "seen", though cultural traditions and expectations play a large ... determining role in shaping their particular content ... Protean in nature, experience anomalies change over time and space. In transitional historical and cultural periods, they may fuse motifs in curious ways.' So, a thousand years ago, someone sees a strange light in the sky which resolves into the shape of a shining angel; post-1947, such a light resolves itself into a landing UFO and its attendant aliens; back in 1890s America, a point of transition between these two poles of space-age science and heavenly religion, we get someone pointing their telescope at a star and seeing an airship full of winged angels. In the 1890s, people saw amorphous lights in the sky and felt allowed to identify it as Thomas Edison piloting a flying lightbulb; by 1953, when San Francisco cops witnessed what they specifically described as *being* a flying lightbulb, this option was no longer available. By then, it had become a flying saucer, even though it was not shaped like a saucer at all, but a lightbulb.[11]

There could be some objective, but as-yet unknown, physical phenomenon behind UFOs, Clark suggests, citing an 1887 case from New York State, when a witness saw 'what looked like silver balls, reminding me of silver coin of all denominations, bright and sparkling, tumbling and rushing through the air going towards the east, and finally disappearing beyond the lower stratus of clouds.' These sound not unlike daylight silvery globular wartime foo-fighters. The 1887 witness had no plausible pre-existing cultural lens through which to view these things, but in 1944 an obvious *Wunderwaffe* possibility suggested itself – and so the foo-fighter was born. The experience anomaly, says Clark, occupies a 'parasitic' relationship to such a sighting, as it 'borrows its imagery from the anomalous event'. Maybe these 1887 silver balls were atmospheric phenomena. But if, viewed through the later lens of Nazi UFOs, someone is triggered by unknown means into seeing one 'land' before a German jumps out, then that would be an experience anomaly. The original silver balls, as physical objects of mundane natural origin, could potentially be photographed for posterity. The subsequent manifestation of Hitler in a spaceship could not. And so, somehow, whether in terms of simple hallucination (as a sceptic might maintain) or some unknown paranormal-type process (as a non-sceptic might prefer) an apparent advertising campaign for a local Texas brewery conjured up Mr Wilson from out of nowhere. And, thanks to the best efforts of publishers advertising the fiction of W. A. Harbinson as fact 100 years later, he lives on still – remember, in Branton's *The Omega File*, Wilson became the real-life double-agent who sabotaged Hitler's anti-gravity saucer programme on behalf of Uncle Sam.[12]

Accounts of people's encounters with landed Nazi UFOs and their occupants can bear some resemblance to narratives of the Mr Wilson type. In 1957, the FBI was approached by a former Polish POW whose tractor broke down whilst transporting forced farm-labourers like himself to work in an isolated area one day in 1944. An SS guard appeared, telling the German driver to wait a few minutes. A 'high-pitched whine similar to that produced by a large electric generator' was heard, but once it stopped the tractor started up again. Three hours later, the POW came across a hidden clearing guarded by more SS men, where he observed a strange circular vehicle with three separate sections, each atop the other, the middle of which contained 'a rapidly moving component producing continuous blur similar to an aeroplane propeller'. The high-pitched noise reappeared, and the tractor stopped once more.[13] The obvious conclusion is that this was a lie; but if Jerome Clark is correct that experience anomalies do exist, then even apparently obvious fictions can gain a lifeline of marginal possibility, at least if you're being generous.

What can we make of the Mysterious Mr Wilson, then? Was he nothing more than the accidental by-product of a long-forgotten local advertising campaign, a Marlboro Man come to life? Hopefully one day someone will present a ufologist with some yellow-stained slides from a microscope and demand they be sent off for DNA analysis to solve the entire mess once and for all. Perhaps we could even resurrect Mr Wilson from his own fossilised sperm, like in *Jurassic Park*. The main lesson to be drawn is this: advertising can be used to make ideas become reality, something equally well known by Joseph Goebbels and that other successful fascist ad-man, Ernst Zündel. For Jerome Clark, the usefulness of the concept of experience anomalies is that 'We no longer have to argue for the authenticity or inauthenticity of the described phenomena.'[14] Sadly, there are some less savoury persons out there who have drawn similar conclusions about the rather post-modern ontological status of the paranormal, which they have then used to make people question the degree of 'event-level reality' of other things mentioned within the history-books too – and not only the Holocaust. Now, Nazi ufologists have even begun querying what *really* took place during the First and Second Gulf Wars as well.

5

This Gulf War Did Not Take Place: Nazi Saucer-Pilots Fly Down from Aldebaran to the Aid of Saddam Hussein

Ignorance about what happened several lifetimes ago in wartime Europe can be disturbingly deep. As early as 1977, a German teacher made headlines after setting his children the essay task of writing down everything they knew about Hitler, which turned out to be disarmingly little. 'Hitler was our old Führer,' wrote one fourteen-year-old. 'He did not allow young people to wear their hair long.' Another thought Hitler 'played a leading role in getting Germany back on its feet after World War II'. Ever since, it has been a favourite media game to commission surveys about schoolchildren's knowledge of the Second World War, then complain how dire it is. In 2012, only 43 per cent of British pupils questioned realised the Battle of Britain involved aeroplanes, whilst only 14 per cent were aware of D-Day. A 2009 survey revealed 10 per cent thought Britain's enemy had been France, with incorrect suggestions for Germany's allies ranging from the USA to Scotland and the famously belligerent Switzerland. Another 2009 survey suggested one in twenty thought the Holocaust referred to V-E Day celebrations, whilst one in six thought Auschwitz was an amusement park. However, as 5 per cent supposedly also thought Adolf Hitler was 'a German soccer coach', maybe some kids just enjoy giving deliberately wrong answers to multiple-choice questions.

Or maybe not. 2018 surveys suggested 45 per cent of Americans of all ages could not name a single Nazi concentration camp, whilst one in twenty Europeans had never heard of the Holocaust. In 2017, pro-Palestine Muslim pupils in Germany boycotted International Holocaust Remembrance Day with the active support of their teachers. Rising rates of anti-Semitism in the West are not coincidental.[1] It has not proved difficult to introduce myths about the Holocaust into mainstream public discourse. Further confusion arises when schools use fictional Holocaust-themed novels to teach the subject. Heather Morris' best-seller *The Tattooist of Auschwitz* depicted a football match between prisoners and guards, which was deemed absurd – until historians found the match in question actually did probably occur.[2] As Holocaust survivors rapidly die off, it becomes inevitable such blurrings of fact and fiction will proliferate.

Consider the line of the controversial revisionist British historian David Irving (b.1938) that 'Without Hitler, the State of Israel would probably not exist today, so to that extent he was probably the Jews' greatest friend.'[3] Some left-wing critics have argued that, if only the evil British Empire had not declared war on Germany in 1939, Hitler might just have sent Europe's Jews away for resettlement in Madagascar, as was originally planned, and therefore that appalling racist Winston Churchill was just as guilty for the Holocaust as Hitler was.[4] Coming across such opinions from an ill-informed position, it may be easy for young people to fall for them, particularly if they come wrapped in fashionable anti-Western rhetoric. People whose knowledge of 'history' comes primarily from TV, websites or social media are easy to exploit or brainwash, something realised by neo-Nazis like Ernst Zündel, who were amongst the first to use the web to spin their lies through sites like Jew-Watch. The Far-Right Stormwatch online forum, established in 1995, now ranks in the top 1 per cent of all sites for web-traffic.[5] The image of Nazism propagated online has become deeply ambiguous, as argued by the academic Gavriel D. Rosenfeld:

> While Hitler and the Nazis superficially appear to be everywhere, in a deeper sense, they are nowhere. The inflated use of the Nazi legacy for tendentious purposes threatens to drain it of much of its historical distinctiveness and turn it into an empty signifier … Today, their ubiquity has lent them an aura of normality. For increasing numbers of people, the Nazi era has lost its sense of historical specificity. It has come to mean almost anything. If Hitler and the Nazis once inspired fear, today they are just as likely to elicit laughs. If present-day trends continue, they may soon induce yawns.[6]

Rosenfeld traces the development of online Nazi-related memes, such as the popular *Hipster Hitler* comics, in which Hitler is reimagined as an irritating trendy slacker living in New York, who is admonished in one strip by Goering for wearing a t-shirt saying 'I LOVE JUICE' because it sounds like 'I LOVE JEWS'. You might think this an anti-Semitic meme, but the comic's creators deny any such intent. They just thought it was funny, for reasons they couldn't really articulate, but later offered up the *post-hoc* rationalisation that 'In constructing Hitler as a Hipster we're offering a new way of disliking Hitler and laughing at the lazy dictator he was,' indolence obviously being his chief flaw. In every strip, Hitler wears a new t-shirt emblazoned with an awful pun, such as 'You Make Me Feel Like Danzig' or 'Death Camp for Cutie', which can now be bought from the site's creators. When confronted about his JUICE/JEWS-related shirt, Hipster Hitler replies 'Gah, yeah I know. It's called being ironic, Goering.'[7]

Irony is indeed central to all this, but it is a new kind of all-pervasive, free-floating irony which seems simply to adopt an automatically ironic attitude towards everything under the sun as a matter of course, rather than for any conceivable underlying purpose. When someone wears such a t-shirt, what do they *mean* by it? A small minority may be actual Nazis, but most will mean precisely nothing at all. As Rosenfeld said, such slogans are literally empty signifiers. Such puns can satisfy what Freud called the '*alte Lust am Unsinn*', the old lust for nonsense. But if your meme is indeed an empty signifier, then web-users can do whatever they like with it; the meme's creators cannot control this.[8] Another popular website, Cats That Look Like Hitler, took flak for making the Führer seem appealing by associating him with cute kittens whose facial markings looked like Hitler moustaches, leading to the site's creator to clarify that he thought Adolf 'was an arsehole'. But some complaints were more unpredictable, arguing the site represented animal cruelty, as 'no cat deserves any connection with Hitler' – try telling that to Savitri Devi.[9] As Nazism recedes ever further into the past, and the majority of people come to know of it primarily through films, TV shows, videogames and, just occasionally, actual books, so Hitler and his war increasingly become a purely media phenomenon, experienced at second- or third-hand at best. I have never shot a real Nazi myself, but have wasted legions of pixellated ones in *Wolfenstein 3D*; to me, *Wolfenstein* is more real than D-Day. To the majority of its readers, *The Tattooist of Auschwitz* is more real than Auschwitz. Increasingly, it is coming almost to appear as if the Second World War did not take place.

* * * * *

Some more recent conflicts which did not take place were the First Gulf War against Iraq of 1991 and its action-packed 2003 sequel. We know *The Gulf War Did Not Take Place* because this is the title of a celebrated 1991 book-length essay by the chin-stroking French philosopher Jean Baudrillard (1929-2007) who, contrary to appearances, did accept that the conflict physically occurred somewhere far-away amidst Iraq's desert sands, but that, to the average Westerner sat at home watching it on TV whilst eating crisps, it may as well not have done. To Western viewers, the two Gulf Wars no more took place than the Second World War did to a fifteen-year-old. Viewed from afar, with computer-guided precision bombs eliminating targets from miles above in the sky, with no gory close-up images of shattered Arabs to ruin the illusion, and with virtually no Allied casualties, the 1991 conflict in particular was more like viewing demo-footage of a videogame than anything else – indeed, the tie-in Electronic Arts Mega Drive and SNES title *Desert Strike*, in which you played a helicopter gunship pilot operating in an oil-filled desert country, did great business by treating the nightly TV news as a free wall-to-wall advertising campaign.

So sanitised and clinical was the conflict that Baudrillard mocked it as 'the bellicose equivalent of safe sex: make love like war with a condom!' The war's build-up seemed unreal and staged, as though a fake earthquake was arranged by manipulating measurements on a seismograph, he said.[10] Baudrillard viewed the 1991 war as a simulacrum, a mere geopolitical *doppelgänger*, staged as a giant kinetic advert for competing world-views. America wished to promote its vision of a 'New World Order' in which, following the USSR's fall, its way of life exercised complete hegemony worldwide. The conflict's unofficial spin-off book was political philosopher Francis Fukayama's (b.1952) now obsolete utopian 1992 sci-fi yarn *The End of History*. Iraq's brutal secularist dictator Saddam Hussein (1937-2006), meanwhile, laughably got to sell himself to the Arab world as the Defender of Islam and play to the region's huge anti-Semitic gallery by firing Scuds at Israel. Violence thus became 'a consumable substance', in which 'the media promotes the war, and the war promotes the media.'[11]

War became pure information, interpreted by talking-head pundits as if it were a football match, something to subjectively argue over endlessly; just as some money pundits thought shares might rally 10 per cent by the end of the year, so some war pundits speculated 50 per cent of Saddam's army might have been destroyed by Allied bombs. But others thought the stock market may tumble by 10 per cent, and some said only 20 per cent of Saddam's army may have been destroyed. In this case, asked Baudrillard: 'Whom to believe? There is nothing to believe,' only a series of competing narratives about something which may as well not even have happened to viewers at home. When you see a bombsite and one side says it was a chemical weapons depot and the other says it was a baby milk factory, no viewers will be going out to personally inspect it, so must decide which competing narrative to accept, if any. The Iraqi and Allied armies barely faced one another directly, and many buildings bombed were actually decoys, empty magnets for USAF and RAF bombs. That the planes were often stealth bombers, and thus effectively invisible, only added to the uncanny effect. The uncatchable bombers were like UFOs which also don't show up on radar, the toy soldiers who never actually died like Action Man MIBs; had Western troops just stayed at home, statistically speaking, three times as many would have died in traffic accidents than at Iraqi hands. This was a strange new kind of non-war, one that *saved* a nation lives, not cost them. To Baudrillard, the entire conflict was the military equivalent of a placebo – it only worked if you chose to believe in it. It was almost a Spiritualist séance: 'Event, are you there? Gulf War, are you there?' Some targets which had already been obliterated were re-bombed and re-bombed again, not for any coherent military reasons, purely to ensure there was enough new footage for TV that evening. In a media age, the spectacle replaces that crude and now obsolete thing, the event. Baudrillard recalled the 1977 movie *Capricorn One*, in which NASA fake a Mars landing with actors and TV crews in the US desert.[12]

Baudrillard's book must have sold unexpectedly well amongst ufologists, who quickly constructed a fake narrative around the two Gulf Wars of their own, in which fictional WMD-cum-baby-milk-factories were reconfigured into equally fictional saucer hangars. Soon, the Nazis became involved too, flying down to help Saddam through a rift in space-time in their craft, dubbed Haunebus; these were the very same kind of purported saucers that Orthon had once landed in to meet George Adamski. Naturally, there was also an Iraqi Roswell – even the tiny Federated Island States of Micronesia probably has its own back-engineered spaceships by now. Following the 1991 TV-war, the saucer crash's alien survivors were offered compulsory 'sanctuary' by Saddam in return for building him *Wunderwaffen* to ward off any future military assault, it was said. In 2003, America invaded again anyway, but this time Iraqi troops were armed with sawn-off ET shotguns with vacuum-cleaner nozzles on the end which could pierce the armour of an M1 Abrams tank by firing 'molten yellow metal' at them. Saddam also now had an army of genetically engineered scorpions 'the size of cows' to guard his palace instead of dogs.

Alternatively, in the 1920s archaeologists may have found a 'Stargate' – a portal to another galaxy – buried beneath Iraq, leading to a 1941 rebellion being fostered against British colonial forces there by the Nazis, who wanted access for themselves. Later, Saddam Hussein built a palace over this Stargate, the true reason for the 2003 Gulf War being that Washington feared he was near to opening it. The obscure presence of Thule Society members and Nazi spies in pre-Second World War Iraq was thus explained by *Ahnenerbe*-esque attempts to ferret out the hidden doorway. Mainstream historians explain German spies' presence in the area as efforts to gain Muslim allies for the Reich, but non-mainstream historians know better. As for why Saddam didn't win if he had so many *Wunderwaffen*, the conspiracists' answer was simple: being good judges of character, the ETs didn't trust him with their best stuff, so the dictator was forced to settle for *Ghostbusters*-guns and giant scorpions.[13]

Jean Baudrillard is now dead, but his teachings live on. If the Gulf Wars were simulacra of wars, then the *doppelgänger* of contemporary geopolitics is a pseudo-discipline known as 'exopolitics', tirelessly promoted by one Dr Michael E. Salla, PhD, a former lecturer in genuine international politics at various US and Australian universities, who now lectures in fictional interstellar politics, issuing policy papers via his substantial website. As to which specific policymakers would actually take them seriously, he does not say; in truth, they too are academic simulacra, with plenty of footnotes and citations, but citations of non-books like *One Foot in Atlantis* and *Blindsided: Planet X Passes in 2003*. In *Exopolitics: Political Implications of the Extraterrestrial Presence* and his practical guide for policymakers, *Galactic Diplomacy: Getting to 'Yes' with ET*, Salla argues we must take the existence of aliens seriously, as they explained the true way global political institutions worked. Take the EU. This inhuman body was clearly the work of aliens, hence explaining why its representatives tried to thwart the Brexit vote of 2016. Possibly, just like in *Star Trek*, alien races all belonged to a Galactic Federation, represented on a planet-by-planet basis, not a country-by-country one. Thus, if Earth ever wished to sign up for complete harmonisation with this Space-EU, it must first establish a One-World

Government in line with this non-negotiable regulatory model. Or maybe the European Union is 'a façade for a Nazi Fourth Reich' in cahoots with the lizard-like Draconians.

According to Salla, prior to defeat, top Nazi Martin Bormann instructed German industrialists to siphon cash and assets into a new 'Invisible Reich' to dominate post-war Europe via economic means, whilst other Nazis sought refuge in Antarctic bases, seeking diplomatic alliances with aliens. Shell companies were established by fascist businessmen, who established the European Coal and Steel Community in 1951. The eventual resultant borderless free-trade area provided the ideal basis for using hidden Nazi money to enact hostile take-overs of major European companies like Volvo, whose Hitlerite CEOs would then lobby proto-Brussels politicians to arrange the world to their liking. The end result was the current-day EU, which is really the Third Reich reborn, with an added alien agenda – the anticipated economic success of the Single Market would make other continents copy its model, allowing Nazi corporate lizards to gain control of the world by stealth. Brexit threatened these plans: 'The decision by Britain to end its participation ... puts an end to the fiction that the EU genuinely represents the will of the European populace' rather than that of unelected dinosaur-men, said Salla. Being Nazis, the globalist EU top-brass have bad memories of the last time Britain stood alone against a German-dominated 'United Europe' in 1940, so viewed the Leave vote as a prelude to Blighty 'leading the way in confronting a resurgent Nazi Reich as a global threat' once more. To Salla, 'it does not appear coincidental' that the Brexit vote took place 'at roughly the same time as a [secret] space-war is reportedly being waged against the Fourth Reich and its [lizard] allies, in Antarctica and Deep Space' by the Forces of Freedom. Diplomacy is merely war by other means, so Brexit itself was the contemporary electoral equivalent of the Battle of Britain.[14]

In 2003, Salla released *An Exopolitical Perspective on the Pre-Emptive War Against Iraq: Research Study #2*, arguing that 'the Sumerian scholar' (ancient astronaut theorist) Zecharia Sitchin (1920-2010) had found ancient tablets from what is now Iraq that contained images and descriptions not of gods, as usually thought, but of super-advanced aliens called the Annunaki, who were not to be confused with the evil lizard-men Annunaki/Draconians of David Icke, but more generous god-men from the planet Nibiru who had helped mankind in our early days. Citing the 'independent archaeologist' William Henry's *Saddam Hussein, the Stairway to Heaven and the Return of Planet X*, Salla argued it was the Annunaki who built the Iraqi Stargate to travel easily between Nibiru and Earth. Being the old home of Babylon and Sumeria, Iraq has many archaeological glories, and Henry pointed out Saddam had recently allowed a German team of archaeologists to excavate the ancient Sumerian city of Uruk. Naturally, this was only so they could dig up the Stargate for him. Then, he could 'fulfil prophecy' and let the Annunaki through as his allies, before posing as 'some kind of human saviour facilitating the return of the gods who would solve all humanity's problems'. The presence of German archaeologists was perhaps a diplomatic ruse by Berlin to gain privileged access to the Stargate themselves, as was their general opposition to a second war against Iraq. America was determined to invade and beat Saddam to it but was warned off by the destruction of NASA's Space Shuttle *Columbia* in February 2003, not through technical malfunction as was claimed, but at the hands of 'some clandestine government organisation' wanting to discourage attack on the Stargate. If aliens landed in the middle of yet another Gulf War, this would hardly give the best image of 'a mature humanity responsible enough to continue to exercise sovereignty over the Earth's resources.' So, Salla recommended peace, not war, otherwise we may end up being colonised as wayward, irresponsible children by the aliens again.[15]

* * * * *

1991 saw not only the First Gulf War, but also the release of the final book in Wilhelm Landig's *Thule* trilogy, *Rebellion for Thule*, which exploited that year's headlines by linking the origins of the Nazi Black Sun back to ancient Babylon, the old city-state located south of modern-day Baghdad. In myth, Marduk, the Babylonian god of life and light, once mourned the destruction of the Babylonian Empire until the goddess of love and war Ishtar descended from Venus and commanded the stars shine out a new invisible light to ensure the city's resurrection – surely that of the Black Sun. This legend, said Landig, was really a prophecy that, powered by its ultraviolet rays, the modern-day Babylon of the Third Reich would also rise again. As his novel features schoolboys rebelling against their left-wing teachers for giving them a false depiction of the Aryan race's long and noble history, Landig's message appears an incitement for anti-American neo-Nazi revolution amongst German youth, radicalised anew by events in Iraq. To Landig, the ancient Sumerians were really Aryans from India, so the Iraqis and Germans were kin, with a US-led attack on one an attack on the other. As the poetic Babylonian *Epic of Gilgamesh* is sometimes interpreted as a coded cosmology focusing on the constellation of Taurus and Aldebaran, its largest star, neo-Nazi ufologists soon began claiming that the Aryan race originally hailed from this particular region of space, with the Germans and Iraqis being the Taurian aliens' direct descendants.[16]

The central organisation promoting this new Ariosophist fantasy was the *Tempelhofgesellschaft*, or Temple Society, of Vienna, a supposed successor to the Knights Templar of old. This is a Gnostic-Christian sect of a Marcionite variety, Marcion of Sinope (85-160AD) being a second-century figure who taught a dualistic theology in which a distinction was drawn between the true, loving Christian God of the New Testament and the false Old Testament deity of the Demiurge. The Demiurge was identified with the Jews, and the worship of base matter; the Christian God redeemed men's souls, not their perishable bodies, which went the way of all flesh. Marcion's creed is therefore highly compatible with anti-Semitism. The central figure of the

Tempelhofgesellschaft is Ralf Ettl, an Austrian writer who in the mid-1980s was working on a documentary about Wernher von Braun. One day, the production team received a mysterious brown envelope containing diagrams and photos detailing the construction of flying saucers under Hitler, Ettl has said. Showing these to the Austrian occultist Norbert Jürgen-Ratthofer, the two friends made the 1988 documentary *UFO – The Third Reich Strikes Back?* and its 1990 sequel, *UFO – Secrets of the Third Reich*. In 1992, this was followed up by an extremely influential book, *The Vril Project*. In the years since, Ettl has pumped out numerous solo titles, ranging from *The German UFO Phenomenon: A Journey to the Borders of the Seemingly Inconceivable* to *Isais and Her Revelation from the Light of the Moon* and the CD-ROM *Magical Eroticism* ('with 47 colour photos'). A 2002 600-page novel, *Z-PLAN: A War in the Light of the Black Sun* imitates the old Wilhelm Landig strategy of turning your personal mythology into outright fiction to gain new converts. There are also a series of *Aldebaran Galactic Imperium* pamphlets available.[17]

These texts marked the birth of the Nazi Haunebu craft, clones of Orthon's iconic 1950s saucer, a totally spurious name for Nazi UFOs which is now very popular online. According to the authors, Thule Society founder Rudolf von Sebottendorff had travelled the Middle East, seeking evidence Marcion's Jewish Demiurge of the Old Testament, now dubbed 'El Shaddai', was really the Devil. Sebottendorf uncovered an ancient Babylonian prophecy of a gigantic future battle between good and evil, in which the Jews would have the Kingdom of God wrested from them and handed to its rightful owners, the Aryans – Jesus had once told some Germans serving as Roman legionaries they were God's true Chosen *Volk*. The 1919 book Sebottendorf supposedly said this in, however, *The Inter-Cosmic World War*, does not exist.[18] Also non-existent were the *Vril-Damen* or *Vrilerinnen* ('Vril Maidens'), a group of female psychics of super-model appearance whose images are now all over the Internet. The good looks of their leader Maria Orsic are so supermodel-esque that one common image of her is clearly just the head of the actual super-model Kate Moss Photoshopped onto Adolf Hitler's sexy body, whilst another shows Nena von Schlebrügge (b.1941), Swedish-American mother of the Hollywood actress Uma Thurman, a super-model herself in the 1960s. Photos of Orsic's glamorous assistants Maria, Traute, Sigrun, Gudrun and Heike, with their flowing tresses and pouting expressions, appear to be stolen from shampoo ads, which is highly appropriate as the *Vrilerinnen* would wear their hair in long ponytails to act as 'cosmic antennae' drawing down messages from Aryan-Babylonian aliens from Aldebaran, containing technical plans for Nazi saucers. Blonde women's hair has the ability to tap into *Vril* in the atmosphere, facilitating telepathy with Nordics on other planets, it seems; the word *Vril* now derived not from Bulwer-Lytton, but was Sumerian for 'god-like', this being a good description of Germans on any planet.

Such lies have now spun out of Ettl and Jürgen-Ratthofer's control, with it being claimed in some quarters the Aldebarans' true motives were peaceful ones. By providing the Nazis with *Vril*-powered saucers, they hoped to wean Germany off dependence on British, French and US-controlled oilfields in the Middle East, online theorists say, thus reducing the need for war; if such free-energy devices spread worldwide, they would transform economies and lessen pollution, leading to global harmony. Accordingly, the Green Haunebu worked purely by *Vril*-powered engine-discs spinning opposite one another in clockwise and counter-clockwise fashion, thus generating a directable anti-gravity field. This is why Ezekiel saw something containing a 'wheel within a wheel' in the Bible; he had really seen an ancient Haunebu.

Today, Maria Orsic has gained an entire two-volume pseudo-biography, *Maria Orsic, the Woman Who Originated and Created Earth's First UFOs* by Maximilien De Lafayette, in which it is revealed she was born on Hallowe'en 1895 in what is now Croatia, the daughter of an architect and a beautiful young ballerina. Although an early advocate of pan-Germanism, her true motives in contacting Aldebaran were not wholly pro-Nazi. Wishing to 'fly to the afterlife', Orsic was more interested in using the Haunebu to reach the paradise of Aldebaran, which is why she apparently disappeared in 1945 – she is now on the other side of the galaxy. The only trace Orsic left behind was a note saying 'No one is here,' but she never was there. A total invention of Ettl and Jürgen-Ratthofer, she is often incorrectly said to have been first mentioned in Pauwels and Bergier – spurious works now gaining their own spurious contents. She even has her own Croatian Wikipedia page, which treats her as being real.[19]

The Vril Project's story goes like this. In 1917 Vienna, there existed a precursor Marcionite sect to the *Tempelhofgesellschaft, Die Herren von Schwarzen Stein* (DHvSS), or Lords of the Black Stone, led by a priest named Gernot. Rudolf von Sebottendorff and Maria Orsic met Gernot, who told them about the Black Sun, from which *Vril* emerged at a rate of '75 quintillion oscillations per second' and the age-old battle between the forces of light and El Shaddai, the Jewish Old Testament anti god. In 1919, Rudolf von Sebottendorff founded the Vril Society as an offshoot of his original Thule Society, with Orsic as its chief medium, with the aim of contacting the ancient Babylonian ET gods. At a séance held in Rudolf Hess' flat, Orsic was told by the ghost of the dead Thulean Dietrich Eckart to prepare to hear the voice of Sumi, an Aldebaran alien. As Orsic's eyes rolled backwards into her head, communications emerged from the planet Sumi-Er, sixty-eight light years away in the constellation Taurus, thus explaining why ancient Iraqis were called Sumerians. Consequently, the aliens' language resembled a variant German in its 'tones' and 'frequencies'; the aliens had colonised Iraq 500 million years ago, their descendants being the Nordic-Aryan race, scattered remnants of whom had survived the biblical Great Flood. Proof of this could be found in an Orthon-like prehistoric alien footprint, fossilised alongside a trilobite. Orsic also produced samples of automatic writing in ancient Sumerian.

DHvSS members had contacted what they thought was the Babylonian goddess Isais in the Berchtesgaden Alps during the Middle Ages, but this really represented astral projections from the Empress of Aldebaran. Examining records of Empress Isais' words, which spoke of the Black Sun, the Vril Society discovered these 'Germans in the sign of Taurus' practised 'a kind of National Socialism on a theocratic basis' out in space. The Aldebaran Master Race of 'light god-men' lived on Sumi-Er, but all inferior ET humanoids were confined to the neighbouring ghetto planet of Sumi-An. How did these lesser beings develop? Needing *lebensraum*, the Sumi-Er Nordics colonised other worlds, but differing climatic conditions there turned the settlers less white, whilst atomic warfare mutated some colonisers downwards into 'ape-men'. The Aldebarans had once colonised Earth too, but so had culturally inferior rival space empires from the star-systems Capella and Regulus, who had sired the black and yellow races on our own world. When some colonising white goddesses then mated with the brown monkey-men, as in Jörg Lanz von Liebenfels, they produced racially inferior offspring. Unlike on Earth, the Aldebaran Apartheid races now did not mix, except when the dumb ape-people relied on their wise racial superiors to solve their biggest problems for them, an interplanetary White Man's Burden generously shouldered. Knowing all about the need for strict racial segregation, the Aryan aliens were perfect allies for the Thule Society in their forthcoming cosmic war against the Jews and El Shaddai.

As Rudolf Hess had apparently attended Orsic's séances, Nazi patronage came easily. The consequent secret SS saucer-research department, *Entwicklungsstelle-4,* used the special metal alloy *Viktalen* to build Orsic's channelled blueprints for a time-machine and a wide range of Haunebu fighter-transport saucers, together with the colossal space-zeppelin *Andromeda-Gerät*, from which smaller discs could be launched, the same cigar-like mother ship which had sent Orthon down to bother George Adamski in 1952. The best-in-class Haunebu III could remain flying for eight weeks solid, and carry a crew of thirty-two. Smaller *Vril*-class saucers were also developed purely as circular fighter-planes. Obscure *Wunderwaffen* scientist W. O. Schumann (1888-1974) now became a Vril Society member, too, using Orsic's plans to create the 'Schumann-SM Levitator' anti-gravity engine, with its wheels within wheels generating electromagnetic fields that allowed the first basic German saucers, the RFZs or *RundFlügZeugs* ('Round Aircraft'), to float. Any energy based on explosive principles was 'Satanic', whereas those based on implosive ones were 'divine', he said. In reality, Schumann was an electrical engineer who predicted the discovery of low-frequency atmospheric resonances from lightning, but these authentic 'Schumann Resonances' are now less famous than his fictional anti-gravity engine. As suggested by talk of implosion, Viktor Schauberger and Rudolf Schriever helped the *Vrilerinnen* out too, as they always do. The subsequent Haunebu and Andromeda-class craft were part-powered by even better 'Thule-Tachyonator' engines, which poses rather a problem as the root word 'tachyon', referring to a hypothetical type of sub-atomic particle, was not coined until 1967 by physicist Gerald Fineberg (1933-92).

The rainbow-colours of some Haunebus' exhausts possessed symbolic alchemical significance:

First Stage: White-Yellow = Truth
Second Stage: Yellow-Orange = Benevolence
Third Stage: Orange-Red = Love
Fourth Stage: Red-Green = Compassion
Fifth Stage: Green-Blue = Forgiveness
Sixth Stage: Blue-Violet = Justice
Seventh Stage: Violet-Indigo = Self-Sacrifice[20]

All qualities you would typically associate with Nazis.

Mass production of Haunebus was never achieved for some reason, and in 1946 a joint German-Japanese saucer-crew landed on Mars, hoping to find well-armed Aryan colonists, but discovering only the pyramid ruins of their ancient civilisation and the Face on Mars; the brave Axis pilots died up there, alone. Meanwhile, in 1945, as ordered by Hitler and Himmler, a special new interdimensional SS spacecraft, the *Vril-Odin*, was launched into a 'transdimensional canal' to reach the planet Sumi-Er and request more reinforcements. As the ship travelled faster than the speed of light, only weeks would pass on-board, as in fairyland. In Earth-terms, the spaceship should have reached Aldebaran in 1967, with the joint Nazi-ET invasion fleet of 280 mother ship battle-cruisers, each containing up to 810 flying saucers, appearing in our skies sometime before the end of 2005, thus giving Ettl and Jürgen-Ratthofer's 1992 book thirteen years of solid sales before everyone realised its central prediction was untrue. Even if it was true, though, the 'Anglo-American lobby' who controlled the media and instructed journalists to ridicule UFOs as 'humbug' would never let you know it.[21]

But what happened to the Third Reich's few workable Haunebus left down here on Earth after the war? Possibly they travelled back through time to ancient Babylon, where the German pilots impersonated the original white gods from Aldebaran, being worshipped by the natives.[22] Alternatively, perhaps their crews were sheltered in Iraq by Saddam Hussein (between 1945 and 1979 when Saddam came to power, they primarily hid out in Antarctica). In 1997, Norbert Jürgen-Ratthofer published *The Reichs of Light on Earth*, which features an entire chapter devoted to the First Gulf War. Iraq was 'officially the oldest cultural country on Earth', so if it had been nuked, as at one point gung-ho elements in Washington had threatened, it would have been a tragedy. Yet no nuke came, and Saddam Hussein wasn't even deposed, with the sudden ceasefire on 28 February 1991 surprising many. The 'dangerous, psychopathic' US President George H. W. Bush said that, as Kuwait was successfully liberated from Iraqi occupation, the mission was complete; but was there more to it? Jürgen-Ratthofer provided blurry photos showing an RAF Tornado fighter-jet meeting a German Haunebu disc several times its size, thus demonstrating the Nazis had intervened to save Iraq from nuclear destruction. The Reich had remained a hidden 'Third Power' in the Cold War, waging a 'war of painful pin-pricks' against America, Britain and Russia by sending their saucers out to destroy the electronic detonators on their nuclear stockpiles so they could not be used, either against each other or Antarctica, thus saving the world – and particularly Germany, which would be caught in the European cross-fire – again and again. By forcing Moscow to over-spend to try and catch up with them, the Nazis had bankrupted the USSR and destroyed Communism and now its technological superiority made it the only possible opponent of President Bush's post-Soviet New World Order. When Germany was called cowardly for its refusal to participate militarily in Bush's 1991 war, the Nazis used their Haunebu to disrupt NASA's Space Shuttle programme as a warning for diplomatic pressure on Berlin to cease; which it did, 'very soon'.[23] So, if you subscribe to the unthinking anti-Americanism of our times, and object to all Western military entanglements in the Middle East, you only have one option available to you – support the Nazis instead!

* * * * *

German witnesses have now begun reporting encounters with this wholly invented race of Aryan ETs, proving just how well Ettl and Jürgen-Ratthofer's plan has worked. In 1997, the book *Operation Aldebaran* appeared, detailing the repeated abductions of the Feistel family of Bavaria, who under hypnosis recalled being shown huge 'embryo farms' on a spaceship, intended to breed a 'new race' to replace our fallen humanity. Abductors from Aldebaran first landed on Earth 735,000 years ago, breeding slaves for menial tasks, who revolted and inter-bred with higher humanoid races derived from the Space-Aryans, said the Feistels. Revisiting their abandoned colony in the 1930s, the ETs found racial chaos had bred social chaos. As the Germans represented the purest Earthlings left, the aliens threw in their lot with the Nazis, helping them develop *Wunderwaffen*. Hitler being defeated, they determined to continue his quest to breed a Master Race themselves, through abductions and genetic experimentation.[24] Will Ariosophy never die?

Operation Aldebaran's author was Jan van Helsing, a protégé of Norbert Jürgen-Ratthofer whom we met briefly earlier interviewing Wilhelm Landig about how Hitler was really a dupe of the 'Freemasons'. The leading conspiracy theorist van Helsing is Germany's rough equivalent of David Icke, and a self-styled hunter of vampiric 'bloodsuckers'. Much of his thought is derived direct from *The Vril Project* but updated to relate to contemporary ufological conspiracy trends he saw developing in the US with the likes of Milton William Cooper, whom he knew personally. Talk of the MJ-12 papers, international bankers and AIDS conspiracies mixes seamlessly with Haunebu craft, Aldebarans, Tibetan Masters and the Thule Society predicting the future arrival of a 'Third Sargon', a Messiah destined to save Germany from the Illuminati vampires. Van Helsing's real name is

Jan Udo Holey (b.1967), and the roots of his name-change lie in his teenage years as the son of wealthy, eco-friendly hippie parents. His mother is a clairvoyant and, following his son's ascent to fame, his father Johannes has crafted his own career pumping out New Age books with titles like *God Is in You and Wants to Live, Jesus 2000: The Peaceful Kingdom Approaches, That Does It! How Long Can We Remain Pleased?* and *Let Yourself Be Led*. Holey himself was led into youthful enthusiasm for the paranormal, with his bedroom being full of 'elves, or simple balls of light that danced around'. Aged fourteen, he bought an original edition of Bram Stoker's 1897 novel *Dracula* and, as the elf-haunted teen had a habit of carrying around holy water to dispel unwanted spirits, decided to assume the name of the book's fearless vampire-hunter, Professor Abraham van Helsing.

Once Holey discovered Illuminati 'bloodsuckers' ruled the world, he set out to expose these 'people who do not enrich life, but take life and exist at the expense of other people, energetically' to the sunlight of publicity. The cover of his breakthrough 1993 best-seller, *Secret Societies and Their Power in the 20th Century*, was done in the 'typical vampire colours' of black, red and green, to openly taunt the bloodsucking bastards. By combining bizarre anti-vampire rhetoric with praise of the Green Nazis as eco-warriors, he creates a mad synthesis of New Age and Nazi-friendly spiel. Viktor Schauberger is compared to Jesus, with his free-energy ideas now drawing on *Vril* and the Black Sun, whilst members of a Green 'Master-People' are contrasted with an inferior breed of 'Victim-People' who feel themselves trapped in base matter, not realising that 'life IS movement', as the Austrian creator of implosive anti-gravity engines did. As the Black Sun was not shining so brightly these days, the vibrations of Earth had slowed down, allowing the Victim-People to trap us within a materialist *kali yuga* realm. By suppressing Schauberger's discoveries, these Victim-People were preventing the Master-People building 'airships that can take individuals to other planets ... to give them the opportunity to find out what's going on there', simply to maintain their grip on the oil industry. Thus, 'by their very existence', these individuals and their hide-bound political and financial institutions 'violate life'. No wonder, as they are really undead: 'These people are generally called vampires, bloodsuckers, they live at the expense of others, do not give, but only take – just folk-vampires!' However, the distinction between Master-People and vampiric Victim-People 'has nothing to do with a race or nation', van Helsing says.[25]

The trouble is that the bloodsucking energy-vampire who secretly controlled society was a stock image of Nazi anti-Semitic propaganda pamphlets like 1943's *The Jewish Vampire Brings Chaos to the World*. In *Mein Kampf*, Hitler repeatedly referred to Jews as 'vampires' and 'bloodsuckers'. Himmler's SS occult-advisor Karl Maria Wiligut warned 'dark vampiric creatures ... consumed the blood of sacrificed light creatures,' in terms of Jews bleeding Aryans dry, whilst books like 1939's *Jew and Woman: Theory and Practice of Jewish Vampirism, Exploitation and Infection of Upright Peoples*, argued pollution of the blood through race-mixing was another form of vampirism.[26] Other contemporary authors of an extremely right-wing persuasion have since utilised this same imagery, like the US 'patriot' Jack McLamb (1945-2014) in his *Operation Vampire-Killer 2000*.[27] Claiming your enemies are vampires is a bit different from David Icke claiming his are lizard-men, as the Nazis never made this particular libel against Jews, whereas with vampires, they frequently did. Yet some anti-Semites have since appropriated similar imagery for their own purposes. It could be argued van Helsing is one such man. He claims the vampiric Illuminati have their origins in a 'Brotherhood of the Snake', founded in Mesopotamia in 300,000BC; Bible-style, the Snakes begat the Illuminati, who begat the Rothschilds, who begat the Elders of Zion, who begat the Freemasons, who begat the French Revolutionaries, who begat the Communists, who begat the two World Wars, which begat Israel and the Cold War, which begat the New World Order, which begat the First Gulf War as a prelude to World War III, which will be so bad it will cause everyone to abandon God and embrace 'Luciferic doctrine' instead. The Brotherhood of the Snake, however, actually seems to be a joint fictional creation of ancient astronaut theorists William Bramley in his 1989 *The Gods of Eden* and Peter Tompkins in his 1987 *Mysteries of the Mexican Pyramids*, where the cult's original members are presented as ETs. Today, the Snakes have become bloodsuckers too; David Icke lists 'The Brotherhood' as an alternative name for his flesh-eating, kiddie-fiddling Illuminati Draconians.[28]

Predictably, van Helsing has encountered legal trouble. He denies anti-Semitism, most of his books being apolitical New Age works like *Children of the New Millennium: Middle Children Change the World* (although 2005's *Who Fears the Black Man?* sounds a tad un-PC). Van Helsing poses as a daring defender of free speech, exploiting his dangerous reputation with titles like 2004's *Don't Touch This Book!* and, in reference to two of his titles being banned by German authorities, *The Record of Jan van Helsing – A Documentation of the Prohibition of Two Books in the 'Freest German Land in History'*. In 1996, German prosecutors issued prohibitions on the distribution of his *Secret Societies* and its sequel, alleging they incited hatred against Jews. The problem was that these texts, which alleged a gigantic Illuminati conspiracy was running the entire world, openly borrowed data from known anti-Semites like Wilhelm Landig and Ernst Zündel, as well as *The Protocols of the Elders of Zion*. A report in Germany's *Der Spiegel*, headlined 'Dracula's UFO', characterised van Helsing's first book as 'a mixture of *Mein Kampf*, wild science-fiction and black magic', complaining how it portrayed 'Jewish bankers' and 'Zionists' seeking to make Jerusalem the centre of their 'dictatorship' of 'world domination', and mocking his claim to have 'unmasked the Pope as an AIDS patient'. The Mannheim Public Prosecutor's Office brought charges against van Helsing and his publisher for sedition, whilst a domestic intelligence agency issued a report about his activities, *Right-Wing Extremist Influences Within the Esoteric Scene*. When the first *Secret Societies* book was launched in 1993, a massive PR campaign in fringe magazines made it shift over 100,000 copies in only a few months, so the State feared its potential effect; it is estimated 50 per cent of German UFO literature now shows influence of the vampire-hunter's ideas. Although Mannheim's prosecutors dropped their charges in 1997, van Helsing switched his publishing activities to the Canary Islands before importing books into Austria, where no ban prevailed. Some smuggled them into Germany anyway; allegedly, if you went into certain stores and asked for a copy of 'Cookbook #1', you would be handed an under-the-counter copy. Van Helsing's defence is that his books are not anti-Semitic, they just expose the scheming of the Illuminati – many of whom happen, by chance, to be Jewish.[29]

Van Helsing was a vegetarian anti-fascist activist and punk-rocker in his youth, who experimented with drugs to facilitate astral travel, but things changed when he went to Mexico on a journey of self-discovery and saw a UFO emblazoned with a swastika; his hippie dad once saw the very same thing. Van Helsing then met his grandfather's ghost, who urged him to become an author. This all helped inspire his 1998 novel *The Inner World: The Secret of the Black Sun*, in which the white race's ancient Aryan forefathers, the Atturianer, flee inside the Hollow Earth following a nuclear holocaust 13,500 years ago, in their fleets of swastika-bearing saucers. In the core of the Hollow Earth, whose Atturianer Reich is ruled over by King Haakkuuus III, floats the Black Sun, an artificial crystalline atomic star recharged twice a year by Earth's Golden Sun to beam out invisible beneficial rays. The Atturianer maintain contact with 'true Germans' on the surface down the centuries, culminating in an offer to allow the Nazis to create their own mini-kingdom under the Earth's crust at the end of the war, called Neu-Deutschland. Here, Hitler is King, Eva Braun Queen, and baby Adolf Jr next in line for the throne, alongside his adopted brother, Hans Hitler. That's quite a journey from van Helsing's youthful anti-fascist activism, and all prompted by the sight of a saucer.[30]

Van Helsing speaks of the 'Jewish banking system, that is Rothschild and comrades' and adopts *The Vril Project*'s ideas about the Jews' true god being El Shaddai, or the Devil. On the other hand, maybe the Jews really preferred a race of god-like aliens called the Marcabians, and were willing to betray mankind to them in return for special treatment as their Chosen People. Karl Marx now becomes 'the Jew MOSES MORDECHAI MARX LEVI', a partial truth at best; whilst his mother was indeed of that faith, Marx was baptised a Lutheran and later famously rejected all religion as 'the opium of the people'. Former German Chancellor Helmut Kohl (1930-2017) is also unmasked as a secret Jewish Freemason called Henoch Kohn; van Helsing's source for this is a comic novel about an eccentric inventor who makes impossible claims. Contrary to popular belief, it was the Jews who wanted to exterminate the Germans and not the other way around; van Helsing's source for this information was a book published by Ernst Zündel. Also contrary to popular belief, it was Poland who really started the war by massacring 56,000 ethnic Germans in August 1939 on 'Bromberg Bloody Sunday'. Some Polish killing of ethnic Germans did indeed apparently occur, but a month later, with many, many times fewer victims – it was revenge for Hitler already having invaded in September. His source for this information was even worse: a document from Goebbels' Nazi Ministry of Propaganda. Nonetheless, van Helsing reassured readers he himself was not a neo-Nazi; he would *never* join such people, they were all funded by Israel and Mossad, with skinheads being bribed by provocateurs who 'are almost exclusively circumcised' to commit 'shameful acts' to blacken German honour.[31] But such Jews are not ordinary Hebrews. Instead, they are a specific, obscure subset of Jews called Khazars. Thus, when he thrusts a stake through the heart of the Jews, this is entirely legitimate, says the vampire-killer, as he is only slaying the evil extremist Khazars. However, few of the Jews he claims as having been Khazars actually *were* Khazars at all – especially ones like Helmut Kohl who weren't Jews of any kind in the first place.[32]

Secret Societies explains how media giants like 'the Jewish REUTERS news agency' try to promote widespread moral degeneracy to divert people's attention away from the reality of the paranormal: 'Astrology, the laying on of hands, UFOs and bending spoons are rubbish, it seems, but sex-movies, football on Saturday night and boozing over the weekend are OK.' Even popular songs contain hidden messages aimed at corrupting German youth if you listen to them backwards. Queen's *Crazy Little Thing Called Love* says 'To Hell with the Bible! All I want is magic!' The Beatles' *Revolution No 9* tells kids to 'Start smoking marijuana,' whilst Cindy Lauper's *She-Bop* is amused at how gullible people are: 'You are helpless against evil, against the backwards playing. Ha ha ha.' Even Christians are targeted for moral corruption through melodic 'matrices … charged with Satanic and destructive messages' smuggled into *Jesus Christ, Superstar*. The compliant media just tell people what to think, to fit in with the Illuminati's geopolitical desires: 'Hussein is bad, Bush, Clinton and Kohl are good.' But Saddam Hussein is *not* bad; just as Germany was tricked into war by Poland, so Iraq was tricked into war by America. Washington had falsely promised not to intervene if Saddam invaded Kuwait, but then broke their word as soon as he sent his tanks in to steal all their oil.[33] It may be no coincidence that van Helsing's books became popular in Austria so soon after the nation joined the EU in 1992. Euroscepticism was high, and when people are obliged to join what is arguably an unaccountable transnational pseudo-democracy, they naturally look towards conspiracy theories to find out what is really going on. Under such circumstances, neo-Nazis can conceivably begin to present themselves as the true champions of democracy.[34]

Chapter Forty of *Secret Societies*, 'GERMANY DID NOT SIMPLY LOSE THE WAR!!!' uses UFOs to rewrite history. Just as Pearl Harbor was faked so America could enter the war, so Germany's surrender was faked so America could end it. 'As you know from history books,' explained van Helsing, 'the German Reich never signed a peace treaty, because a peace treaty has to be signed by the leaders of the nation.' The man who signed terms of unconditional surrender following Hitler's suicide was Admiral Dönitz, the most high-up Nazi still in office. But Hitler did *not* commit suicide, he escaped to Antarctica. Thus, he was still the German Führer in May 1945, and so Dönitz had no legal right to sign papers of surrender, meaning the war never officially ended. The current-day German Federal Republic was therefore an 'illegal State' which must be resisted, especially as a Jew like Helmut Kohl 'should never head the *Christian* Democrat Party nor be elected Chancellor of Germany'. At best, Dönitz had signed a temporary ceasefire, but its terms were breached by Rear-Admiral Byrd during Operation Highjump, when once again the Nazis had been subject to an unprovoked military attack, just like Saddam Hussein in 1991. Under 'official NATO law', the Federal Republic was a mere 'substitute nation' and the UFO-base in Neuschwabenland, 'which you will still find on maps of the South Pole of the 1970s', constituted the true legal territory of modern-day Germany, as did Colonia Dignidad and secret underwater Nazi homes beneath the Bermuda Triangle. Bermuda's Nazi mer-men could 'easily float through the water' and 'sit on the ocean floor and ... create underwater domes' to breathe inside by pushing the sea away from them with special devices. In his *The Inner World* novel, van Helsing had earlier explained how the Hollow Earth Aryans had placed Black Sun-powered crystals 'the size of golf-balls' on the seabed there, tiny *Wunderwaffen* able to dissolve ships' metal hulls with laser beams; if the ships were wooden, the crystals made all their nails disappear, with superstitious sailors thinking they had been sucked out by sea-monsters. The Nazis also maintained a base on the Canary Islands, which must have been why van Helsing was still allowed to maintain his publishing operation there.

Nazi sovereign territory also extended into Tibet, which was only annexed by China to kick them all out. Hitler was a puppet of obscure Tibetan 'Yellow Hat' cults, and members of the Black Sun SS still lived with them and certain avatars of the gods within monasteries in the Himalayas, which were 'too high up' for the Chinese military to reach – thank God they didn't possess any aircraft. Even if they had, the Tibetan SS could still have escaped into the Hollow Earth. Iraq, too, contained a Nazi saucer-base near Baghdad. Following the First Gulf War's end, the Allies maintained air superiority over the region, ostensibly to stop Saddam gassing the Kurds, but in January 1993 they attacked his UFO hangars with 434 planes, including RAF Tornados, French Mirage 2000s and USAF F-14s, F-15s, F-111s and B-52 bombers, only to be brutally repulsed by a mere two Nazi VRIL-7 craft bearing the Iraqi flag. An Iranian spy even produced 'very clear photos!!!' of such ships. According to an SS Black Sun informant of van Helsing who currently lived within a giant city inside the Hollow Earth, the scattered worldwide sovereign 'German Reich Network' currently had a standing army of six million troops (some of whom were alien immigrants from Aldebaran) and 22,000 flying saucers which were 'ready to go any minute': 'He told me much, much more, but I'm not allowed to talk about it.'[35]

Why van Helsing focused so much on Iraq is debatable. It could be because he believed the ideas of Landig, Ettl and Jürgen-Ratthofer about the innate

Aryan link between Germany and Babylon. Or, he could just be exploiting the major news story of the day to gain readers. In Chapter 27 of his second *Secret Societies* book, which adopts a Q&A format, the vampire-hunter is asked his opinions about the First Gulf War. 'Only insiders [like me] know that Iraq is an ally of the Germans,' van Helsing replied, with Saddam and his Nazis busily building defences to prevent the Illuminati from causing a Third World War in the Middle East. America now had its own *Wunderwaffen* to facilitate this, such as 'a secret soccer field-sized saucer with US national emblems', but Saddam's 'Germans of the Orient' still held the upper hand. No matter what tactics the Illuminati tried, from economic blockades to halting medicine imports, to poisoning the nation's drinking-water, Herr Hussein's heroes would never submit, due to 'the ingenuity and efficiency of the Iraqi people' and their wonderful semi-fascistic leader. The precise subtext of these claims becomes clear in the following passage:

> Iraq has the highest level of education and training outside of the so-called 'industrialised countries'. The level of education in particular is higher than in various southern European countries and large strata of the USA. The social system is exemplary, the work-ethic is of Central European level. Iraq is thus a country that is becoming a power-factor, a very serious power-factor, from an economic perspective – and all in a quasi-fascist social system. This explains the hope, especially in Israel and the United States, of 'bombing the country back to the Stone Age' [as one US General had reportedly threatened to do]. Saddam Hussein – 'the new Hitler' – is definitely more popular among his people than any democratic politician in his.[36]

The Nazis and Mr Hussein were now the good guys, the only ones resisting US-led military hegemony; by echoing anti-American, anti-military views from a Far-Right rather than a Far-Left perspective, van Helsing sought to hijack kneejerk anti-Western sentiment for his own ends. It is a common claim America only attacked Iraq so it could profit from re-building it; van Helsing says the Allies only attacked Germany in the 1940s to do the same.[37] Yet in 2003 Saddam was toppled, and the moustachioed, ranting, anti-Zionist dictator proved not to have been quite so popular with large sections of his wealthy and highly educated citizenry after all. As such, the whole Iraqi Nazi UFO nexus has now collapsed in popularity – although there is some speculation the Second Gulf War of 2003 was really just a cunning distraction tactic from America nuking a giant metallic city at the South Pole with a new 'boring atomic weapon' designed to penetrate the polar Nazis' 'energy umbrella' bomb-shield – unusual seismological data proves it.[38] That is the awkward thing about history: it just keeps on happening. It could only be maintained Saddam had UFO-related WMD just so long as Saddam himself remained in power. Once Iraq really had been bombed back into the Stone Age, it became confusing just what had happened to all his Haunebus and VRIL-7s ...

6

Round and Round in Circles: Joseph P. Farrell and the Logical Conclusion of Illogical Premises

As something which probably doesn't exist as a literal physical nuts-and-bolts technological object, the UFO is by definition impossible to extricate from the rumours which surround it; the UFO *is* a kind of rumour, in and of itself. This inevitably descends into conspiracy theory, where links proliferate endlessly between everything, until the posited secret plot begins to eat the world and invade actual reality. In an information age, the number of potential dots to be joined is now infinite, the entire world a gigantic 'make your own story' novel. One person 'reads' Roswell or foo-fighters in one way to get one particular conclusion, another person 'reads' them differently and concludes the precise opposite. By even investigating the field, you end up becoming part of the story yourself. In 1997, to mark fifty years since the ufological Year Zero of 1947, the USAF felt the only way to counter the media circus of the Roswell anniversary was to issue a debunking paper, *Roswell Report: Case Closed*, detailing how the 'craft' was just a downed weather-balloon.[1] They may have been correct. But the USAF's mistake was to treat the Roswell Incident primarily as a physical event, not a mythological, media-based one. By demonstrating the Roswell wreckage was a weather-balloon, they only gave conspiracy nuts the chance to slide this fact into the legend, as yet more evidence of a gigantic cover-up. The way the Air Force conclusively proved the spaceship was a weather-balloon only proved all the more conclusively it was a spaceship. Otherwise, why would they have spent so much effort debunking the idea?

The logical *reductio ad absurdum* conclusion of such thinking is seen in the South Dakota-based fringe theorist Joseph P. Farrell's 2011 book *Saucers, Swastikas and Psy-Ops*, described as 'a Hall of Mirrors filled with fog' designed to act as 'the Cliff Notes version of a very complicated story' about an overarching post-war Nazi conspiracy whose army of separate elements he had laid out in a long prior series of texts.[2] These appeared on an annual basis, and included *Reich of the Black Sun: Nazi Secret Weapons and the Cold War Allied Legend* (2005), *The SS Brotherhood of The Bell: NASA's*

Nazis, JFK and MJ-12 (2006), *Secrets of the Unified Field: The Philadelphia Experiment, the Nazi Bell and the Discarded Theory* (2007), *The Nazi International: The Nazis' Postwar Plan to Control Finance, Conflict, Physics and Space* (2008), *The Philosophers' Stone: Alchemy and the Secret Research for Exotic Matter* (2009) and *Roswell and the Reich: The Nazi Connection* (2010). *Saucers, Swastikas and Psy-Ops* drew Farrell's narrative strands up to 2011 neatly together, the key conclusion being that, given the low quality of most evidence for Nazi wartime saucer programmes, it was obvious most of the legend was fake. Yet this only showed Nazi saucers were actually real. Farrell's theory is that the Nazis deliberately provided comically dubious evidence of their non-existent Rudolf Schriever-type craft to act as cover for their real-life ones like The Bell, a purported anti-gravity Nazi time-machine now popular amongst conspiracy theorists online, so their genuine machines would be tainted by association, causing them to be dismissed as rubbish by a sceptical public. So, the less evidence there is for Nazi UFOs, the more evidence there is for Nazi UFOs. This is how conspiracy logic works.

Conspiracy theorists are hard nuts to crack. One who had led a blameless life was given a reward by God when he passed on and stood at the Pearly Gates:

'Ask me anything you like,' said God.
'Who killed JFK?'
'Lee Harvey Oswald.'
'Hmm, this goes higher than I thought.'

From ufologist Richard M. Dolan's (b.1962) 2009 work *UFOs and the Security State*, Farrell borrowed the idea of a 'breakaway civilisation', the notion that, somewhere behind mainstream society, an entire secret parallel State could exist undetected, with access to its own sources of finance, scientific research and political power. Following the Second World War, many defeated Nazis really did begin channelling stashes of stolen cash into front organisations, 'legitimate' industries and secret bank accounts, before infiltrating institutions of civil society, setting up clandestine support networks and, through Paperclipping, embedding themselves within global militaries. Most people would view this as a simple process of self-preservation, with war criminals offering to work for Uncle Sam to gain a living and avoid being hanged, but Farrell sees it as meaning an invisible Fourth Reich continued behind the scenes, acting as a Cold War 'third power' between capitalism and Communism, gradually absorbing both systems from within by making its financial services indispensable to global banking systems, or by feeding the lesser elements of its wartime tech into the military-industrial complex via loyal Paperclipped Nazi double-agents, whilst keeping all the best *Wunderwaffen*, primarily The Bell – of whose legend Farrell is today one of the primary spreaders – for themselves. Farrell rightly perceives the many media stories of 1950s German saucer-inventors were untrue. However, he then speculates that, as post-war CIA intelligence networks in Eastern Europe really were run by ex-Nazis like General Reinhard Gehlen (1902-79), they must have been used to feed the Soviets disinfo about fake inventors like Rudolf Schriever to convince them the US had Paperclipped such men's designs away and so had an unassailable Cold War advantage. The CIA thought that by doing so, Gehlen was working for them; yet, by promoting the ideas of nuts like Schriever, Gehlen was actually steering spies' eyes away from the truth about real-life wartime UFO research.

Sheltered in Nazi-friendly lands like Argentina, the SS's *real* best scientists busily developed an entirely new concept of physics, whilst allowing lesser minds like von Braun to divert the energies of the US and USSR into pointless side-shows like landing on the moon. Probably the 'saucer' that crashed at Roswell was a Fourth Reich *Wunderwaffe* spy-plane, something US authorities knew. The Nazis had already disguised their spy-planes as alien spaceships, and with the US and USSR subsequently colluding in this lie to avoid admitting they had actually lost the war after all, it was guaranteed to succeed. Those who believed in UFOs would think they were aliens, those who did not would dismiss them as a neo-Nazi fantasy. By gradually infiltrating capitalist and Communist power-structures, it then became possible for Nazis to divert taxpayers' money, supplemented by cash from drug-dealing, into so-called 'black' projects of military research, which took place off the official books. If each individual component of *Wunderwaffen* technology was made by a different supply chain manufacturer, nobody would be able to guess what they were being used to build, keeping those who knew what was going on at an absolute minimum. Thus, we are already living within the Fourth Reich, we just don't know it. The Nazis now intend to deliberately ruin their enemies' societies from within by engineering social decay, before later stepping out from genuine *Wunderwaffen* saucers, posing as mankind's Orthon-like ET saviours. A grateful world will then submit to their 'benign' totalitarian rule without a shot being fired.[3]

* * * * *

Farrell mined the old-time US Contactees for supportive evidence, including the ramblings of Dr Frank E. Stranges (1927-2008), who claimed to have befriended a Christian missionary from Venus named Valiant Thor in the 1950s, before availing himself of the facilities in his special space-toilet, which turned Frank's turds into beautiful, sweet-smelling crystals. In 1982, Stranges self-published *Nazi UFO Secrets and Bases Exposed*, in which he said that 'the Top Scientists of Germany' were first inspired to invent flying saucers after seeing discus-throwers at the 1936 Berlin Olympics.[4] He also gave an account of his alleged meeting with a saucer-Nazi in July 1966, which was then reprinted verbatim in Farrell's own book. Tipped off that a 'German Saucer' would soon be landing outside Reno Airport, Stranges went to the promised spot and found the appointment was kept. Standing in the doorway was a 'heavily built man with a deep scar on his cheek and dark heavy eyebrows', who spoke in German, begging for food. Stranges concluded 'he was very desperate,' but the Nazi went unfed as he spotted an approaching police-car, so suddenly closed the UFO's door and initiated lift-off. Farrell admits these 'fantastic claims' sounded pretty dubious, but then, by his own angle, they were *supposed to*.[5]

Meanwhile, descriptions of Venusian Haunebu saucers' propulsion systems from George Adamski sound, to Farrell's ears, rather like those used in The Bell. Why would the Nazis reveal such true *Wunderwaffen* secrets so easily? Maybe to discredit them by association with New Age lunacy, so the US military would never think to imitate them. Alternatively, by advertising their access to such tech, the Nazi 'aliens' meant to seed us with the idea they possessed superior brains and, by implication, superior morality, making it more likely we would eventually accept them as our new rulers once their staged public landing took place. When the Space-Brothers first made friends with the 1950s Contactees, what we were *really* being invaded by were memes. Even though the stories initially seemed comical, the subliminally implanted idea that such blonde, blue-eyed Nordics as Orthon were harmless and wise, came from benignly totalitarian high-tech societies and wished us to destroy our nuclear weapons was a great way to make us later meekly submit to them as our saviours. As there were so many potential contradictions in the ufological data, Farrell even proposed there were two opposing factions in his Invisi-Reich, one promoting the idea Germans really did make UFOs, to prove them a true Master Race, the other saying ETs did it, to hide their secret inventions. Or maybe the Nazis confusingly promoted competing narratives, to see which 'sold' best, like when the same company launches two rival brands of chocolate bar. Tales of benign Aryans made us want to surrender in peace. Tales of evil reptilians made us think resistance was futile. Both made us nix our nukes. Thus, all inconsistencies could be neatly disposed of.[6]

The specific Nazi mastermind behind all this was SS-*Standartenführer* Otto Skorzeny (1908-75), Hitler's most daring commando, who in 1943 had rescued Benito Mussolini from captivity in an audacious glider raid, before settling in post-war Spain under General Franco, where he established a shadowy organisation, 'The Spider', helping SS men escape Europe. With his fingers in many illicit pies, Skorzeny had links to terrorists and acted as a 'security consultant' to repressive Arab regimes, as well as mixing with Miguel Serrano and Savitri Devi. He also had a large scar on his face from a youthful sword duel, so maybe 'Scarface' was the hungry ufonaut once met by Frank E. Stranges?[7] In 1944, Skorzeny was supposedly shown a secret *Wunderwaffe* which he felt could be used in a new form of *Sonderkampf*, or 'special warfare', which would allow the Nazis to win without anyone even knowing. For Farrell, Skorzeny had seen The Bell and realised its innate anti-gravity potential for use in *Weltanschauungskrieg*, or 'world-view warfare', what we now term 'psy-ops' or psychological warfare. The best way to go 'behind enemy lines' was to wait until Allied victory was declared, then fight them when they would least expect it; if the Allies *did not know* they were at war, how could they defend themselves? By infiltrating the military-industrial complex and staging deliberately stupid UFO interactions with Contactees like George Adamski and Frank E. Stranges, Skorzeny's Fourth Reich created a totally false global scientific consensus that only certain things were possible in physics, and that therefore all stories of UFOs must, by definition, be untrue. By creating such a fake 'matrix of interpretation' of reality, the Nazis manipulated rival physicists' worldviews so they would be unable to build their own anti-gravity craft. How could the enemy ever recognise physics papers or sarcastic jokes about little green men as commando tactics? No soldier would view an equation as a deadly weapon. When a teacher tells his pupils objects can't just float in mid-air, he would not know he was actually gunning them all down with Nazi mind-bullets.[8]

Farrell says the post-war UFOs flown by Skorzeny's psy-ops Nazi commandos were 'both an alchemical *technology* and *technique*, for one of the goals of alchemy [as in Jung] has always been the transformation of man and his consciousness, and no one can doubt the UFO has done just that.' UFOs were thus 'an alchemical, psychotronic technology', the weirdest *Wunderwaffe* ever developed. As The Bell emitted radiation, it affected observers' brains, causing hallucinations, giving Skorzeny his whole idea.[9] Farrell cites the theories of Dr Jacques Vallée (b.1939), a French astronomer turned computer-scientist, sci-fi novelist and giant of ufology, the model for one of the lead (human) characters in Steven Spielberg's 1977 blockbuster *Close Encounters of the Third Kind*. Beginning in 1979 with his classic *Messengers of Deception: UFO Contacts and Cults*, Vallée set out a complex new theory of UFOs not necessarily being physical alien craft but some sort of 'control system', designed to manipulate human consciousness and regulate our behaviour. Maybe aliens were ultimately behind this plan, maybe interdimensional beings, or maybe some clandestine human organisation; Vallée did not know. But, as he correctly said, 'it doesn't matter whether [UFOs] are real or not', as they still have a 'social impact'. Some scholars argue Jesus never physically existed either, but this is irrelevant, given 'the effects of the belief in Jesus' on Christians' behaviour-patterns down the centuries.[10] If a ufological equivalent of Christianity could be manufactured, the potential for further mind control would be enormous.

Vallée used computer data to analyse the patterns of UFO behaviour, concluding UFOs *showed* no identifiable patterns of behaviour. This demonstrated UFOs 'behaved like a conditioning process', as 'the logic of [psychological] conditioning uses absurdity and confusion to achieve its goal while hiding its mechanism.' There was a 'genuine technology' at work here, causing directed hallucinations akin to Jerome Clark's 'experience anomalies' amongst witnesses, he said, which could sometimes change their whole outlook on life. If they then went on to achieve positions of social influence, they could inspire other people in their turn too, as when the Emperor Constantine had once converted to Christianity, bringing the Roman Empire along with him. So, the UFOs are pieces of physical technology, probably of some exotic energetic kind, but not necessarily alien, and not necessarily saucer-shaped; they might just *look* like that, due to hallucinations or holograms being projected by the illusion-machines at their centre. As Vallée says, 'When we go to the movies, we look at the objects and the people on the screen; we do not stare at the projector.' Furthermore, in espionage, if you know 95 per cent of info about any topic, you can bet that's the useless 95 per cent; the only valuable part is the 5 per cent you don't know. As 95 per cent of info about UFOs seems to indicate they are UFOs, might the missing 5 per cent of data show that they are *not* really UFOs at all?[11] Vallée identified four key memes being implanted in human minds by the saucer-men:

- *Intellectual Abdication* – the idea that superior moral beings from space would one day solve all our problems for us.
- *Racist Philosophy* – the Arisophist-style belief that some people on Earth were descended from space-men (generally Nordic ones) and were thus innately superior to others.
- *Technical Impotence* – that all mankind's technical advances were gifted to him by ancient astronauts or back-engineered from crashed saucers.
- *Social Utopia* – that, on other worlds, democracy had been replaced by 'utopian' systems of a benignly totalitarian nature which ensured wealth, health and happiness for all.[12]

If Nazi commandos wished to pose as aliens, these are precisely the ideologies they would wish to implant, and Vallée talked with a US intelligence officer who believed UFOs were 'psychotronic devices'. The spy's theory was that Hitler had made saucers which proved useless for delivering ordinary weapons, yet had the unforeseen side-effect of inducing bizarre hallucinations. Vallée found it hard to believe Nazis could have survived the war and begun priming Allied citizens to turn fascist by inducing visions of racially superior ET Hyperborean god-men, but Joseph P. Farrell did not.[13]

Yet if *anything* can now be a weapon, could Farrell be involved in such a Skorzeny-style psy-ops scheme himself, too? If UFOs are not really UFOs, and aliens not really aliens, then might certain books about UFOs and aliens not really be about UFOs and aliens at all? Very possibly Farrell believes everything he says. Another suggestion, however, made by the academic John Stroup in his analysis *Occulture in the Academy*, would be that Farrell secretly wishes to convert his readers to Eastern Orthodox Christianity. Farrell converted to this faith himself from Protestantism, studying patristics at Oxford under a Greek Orthodox professor. Previously, Farrell wrote learned theological discourses and anti-modern cultural criticism, although he now prefers to update his conspiracy theory website, gizadeathstar.com, besides appearing on talk-radio, spouting his regular catchphrase 'See you on the flip-side!' You'd never know, from reading Farrell's Nazi UFO books, anything whatsoever about his religious beliefs, but to Stroup they may represent an attempt to use popular discourse involving sensational topics to gently steer readers away from our fallen modern world and towards more traditional modes of Orthodox thinking, like a non-Nazi Ernst Zündel. (Whilst Farrell was encouraged to write his first Nazi UFO book by the former head of America's National Socialist Party, Frank Joseph, he is certainly not a Nazi himself).

Farrell's breakthrough *Giza Death Star* trilogy claimed the Egyptian pyramids were really alien-built super-weapons, used to fire 'scalar-impulse waves' against invaders from Mars. Like many ancient astronaut books, they reinterpret biblical events as misunderstood ET physics, even including actual mathematical equations. To Stroup, the purpose of this is to rekindle readers' belief in the literal reality of the Bible by reconciling it with cutting-edge physics. In this view, Farrell sees contemporary Western Christianity, unlike its Eastern Orthodox rival, as not a true religion at all, but a fallen parody, polluted by Gnosticism many centuries ago. As Gnosticism, with its rejection of physical matter as evil, also rejects the reality of God's Creation, Western civilisation fell into a foolish quest to gain power over the illusion of matter through technology, culminating in the twin evils of Nazism and Communism, esoteric Gnostic movements in exoteric political disguise which sought to remake the world in their own perverted image – there are shades of Eric Voegelin here.

When the Nazis obtained ancient texts like Grail legends, the *Ahnenerbe* realised they were truly metaphors for a radical new Gnostic-scientific discourse in which the manifestations of physical matter we saw all around us were not truly real at all. Nobody ever sees matter *as* matter, merely as cups, tables, birds or mountains. You never say, 'oh look, there's some matter.' Like the Fourth Reich, pure matter is impossible to see, and in that sense non-existent. Yet, Nazi scientists realised a multi-dimensional substrate of pure matter-*as*-matter did indeed underlie our world and that, by manipulating it, you could reshape reality at will. Things like The Bell thus either stand as real-life *Wunderwaffen* expressions of this new evil Gnostic physics, if Farrell truly believes what he is saying, or else weird popular metaphors for the descent of mankind into new, science-worshipping forms of the Gnostic heresy, if he doesn't. Also, if much of our modern technology is derived from such back-engineered Nazi craft, and funded by crypto-fascist bankers, corporations and politicians, then contemporary Western technocratic society itself stands revealed as the bastard child of the modern-day epitome of all evil, Adolf Hitler. Thus, Farrell's readers may hopefully reject it wholesale and return towards traditional moral and religious values, rejecting the current globalist 'powerlessness repackaged as democracy' within which the oppressed, PC-ridden plebs now lie imprisoned.[14]

The trouble with this supposed plot to use fringe books as disguised literary *Wunderwaffen* against *kali yuga* is that, if Stroup is right, then Farrell's subliminal methods are so subliminal that almost no readers will be able to perceive them. How many viewers of trash US cable-TV shows like *Ancient Aliens* are going to know about the intricacies of the Gnostic heresy as expressed through the complex equations of cutting-edge alternative physics, or conclude that the Roswell spaceship really being a hi-tech Nazi spy-plane means they should embrace the Eastern Orthodox Church? Ernst Zündel's use of Nazi UFO books to make people doubt the Holocaust only worked because it was so crudely done that even the idiots he deliberately aimed them at could get the hidden message. With Farrell, if that hidden message really does exist, then it is hidden far too well to be effective, to the extent that Stroup's idea resembles a paranoid conspiracy theory in and of itself. Maybe Joseph P. Farrell's books really are just about UFOs and Nazis after all, just as a cigar sometimes really is just a cigar.

Conclusion

The War of Ideas

'If the evidence doesn't seem to fit a particular conspiracy theory, just create a bigger conspiracy theory.'
Robert D. Hicks, leading story-technician

Jacques Vallée once quoted a French Air Force officer who admitted the military knew UFOs were real but had no idea what they were. Yet this only made the denial of their reality all the more important, as the revelation scientists and governments didn't know everything about the world, and that such totally inexplicable things could exist in it, might shatter public confidence in authority. Elsewhere, Vallée suggested the absurdity of the phenomenon might be its entire point, as this undermined belief in the wider scientific worldview: 'Where the Establishment is rational, absurdity is dynamite.'[1] This is *Weltanschauungskrieg* indeed.

One of the most unusual ufologists of recent years was Colin Bennett (1946-2014), a free-thinking British theorist who developed a complex post-modern philosophy in which the very idea of a 'fact' was actually a form of fiction, conceiving of all notions of so-called scientific 'reality' as being warring 'idea-animals' with a life of their own – animate memes, basically. Maintaining nothing could ever be known absolutely for certain, he made unfortunate comparisons between the ambiguous evidence for UFOs and the rather more overwhelming evidence for Nazi death camps and the moon-landings, leading some to mistakenly accuse him of Holocaust denial.[2] Possibly, aliens themselves were such idea-animals, having evolved away from primitive corporeal bodies like our own and become disembodied adverts, pinging around the universe hoping to fix themselves within fleshly minds, so gaining a kind of psychic life, he guessed. One criticism of the US-led invasion of Iraq is that we arrogant Westerners thought its inhabitants were just like us and would automatically embrace democracy, as our liberal values are supposedly 'universal'. Likewise, we seem to think ET beings will share our basic rational mindset, a belief which is ironically rather irrational.

If we really did meet an alien, we may be no more able to enjoy an intelligible conversation with it than we could discuss metaphysics with an ant (or perhaps we are the ant, as in the classic Soviet sci-fi parable *Roadside Picnic*). Rather than po-faced sci-fi films like *Contact*, in which alien satellites transmit comprehensible messages for rational human scientists' minds to decode, Bennett thought comedy flicks like *Morons from Outer-Space*, in which the non-human entities are anarchic weirdoes of incomprehensible motives, may be truer to life. Roswell, he says, 'is usually investigated as some kind of traffic-accident', but maybe it would be better to view it as an episode of *You've Been Framed!* crossed with *Police, Camera, Action!* – if ETs act like disembodied memes, then, just like a spectacular motorway pile-up, perhaps the more entertaining and absurdist an alien encounter is, the more likely it is to breed within our minds like rabbits, whereas the duller one is, the more likely it is to go the way of the Dodo.[3] If so, then the idea of Nazi UFOs must be considered very entertaining indeed.

If aliens are adverts, then maybe the more obviously stupid ones, like Orthon, were real after all. Bennett notes that the unforgettable names of many such entities sounded strangely like those of 1950s consumer-products or artificial fabrics – stylish housewives may like to purchase a pure Orthon-woven blouse. Bennett specifically mentions some 1950s ETs as sounding like imaginary brands of shampoo, which reminds me of the *Vrilerinnen* and their wonderful blonde antenna-hair. You needn't actually believe in these creatures' literal existence to aid them in their spread, just find them entertaining enough to remember their names and basic outline. I don't buy L'Oreal shampoo myself, but I still know what it is and recall their ad-slogans. I don't 'buy' Orthon, either, but I do find him memorable, so much so that I've just written a book about him.[4] In a 2009 interview, Bennett explained his thinking:

Many Orthons have appeared throughout history. The equivalents to Adamski's Venusian 'Space-Brother' have appeared on mountain-tops, in deserts, and [like Jesus] have appeared to walk on water, or fly in the sky. Their sole function is to sow seeds in the head; just as a farmer grows a particular crop. These seeds act on the imagination, which replicates and amplifies whatever story-technology [i.e. media] is around at the time … The 'space-folk' are sculptured by wars between rival viral memes competing for prime-time belief. It may be that, as an independent form of non-organic life, memes as active viral information can display an Orthon entity at the drop of a hat … Over a half-century later, we can no more erase the legendary Contactees from our heads than we can erase Elvis Presley or Marilyn Monroe … [who still keep on] turning out scripts and performances in our heads … It might be denied by the social-scientific Left, but the truth is … our moral philosophy and spiritual life are formed by visions and inspirations … As mystics and prophets know, when desert light strikes the retina, anything that can be imagined can happen.[5]

When the David Myatt-inspired O9A once spoke of their Nazi-related Aeonic Magick facilitating 'the creation of new archetypal forms or images and the infection in the psyche of others which results from introducing them', they would seem to have been talking about similar things.[6] Adamski's Aryan aliens proved every bit as excellent ET advertising figures as the Smash mashed-potato Martians of the 1980s. It is not their rationality or plausibility which matters most about myths, but their imaginative power – how plausible are Christianity, Islam, Marxism or fascism? Not very, but all were highly successful; in Jungian terms, all have allowed Wotan to possess millions of men's minds and transform them into his Wild Hunt. In this sense, today's neo-Nazis are quite right to keep pushing their ideologies through mad UFO narratives. Clearly, like many lies, their misleading advert works. The Landig Circles of this world have gained a surprising number of converts down the years, some of whom have turned out to be such true believers they have actually begun *seeing* their impossible Nazi aliens for themselves and even been abducted by them. In this way, as Bennett argues, we all become 'willing hatcheries for particular storylines, each one of us secreting different episodes', which is just how all the different theorists in this book have acted. Bennett views his memetic aliens as being neither 'strictly factual nor strictly fictional', but 'permanently under construction'. As such, their wider narratives may be contradictory or incomplete, just as with the Nazi UFO myth – but this does not mean all the pieces may not fall into place some day. Like 'placeholder assets', where abstract polygons initially stand in for later fully drawn characters in an early build of a videogame, 'bits and pieces of the whole thing may arrive before the main body,' says Bennett, as with 'Darwinism and the nineteenth-century eugenics movement forming eventually into the main body of Nazism in the form of Adolf Hitler.'[7]

Interestingly, Bennett notes the US scientific defence agency DARPA, inventors of the original Internet-prototype DARPAnet, have now launched a spin-off STORyNET project, intending to weaponise narratives in and of themselves, like the 'hybrid warfare' Vladimir Putin's Russia has recently engaged in. According to him, certain online UFO hoaxes involving very professionally made fake photographs of bizarre craft may have been DARPA's own experiments in creating viral online life-forms, or 'story-weapons', of a harmless kind, as a prelude to launching more militarily effective ones as *Weltanschauungskrieg* psy-ops schemes against the West's enemies one day. According to Bennett's analysis, DARPA hope to exploit such narrative-based *Wunderwaffen* to breed new ideologies online that will allow them to manipulate their target-consumers. Maybe, he says, such living memes will be so powerful they could even 'make someone fall in love with Hitler' like Savitri Devi.[8] If so, then the US military have already been beaten to this aim, as this book has shown. Maybe Otto Skorzeny was right after all ...

Invent your conspiracies where you like. Did you know one of the main German air-crew unions is called 'UFO'? Are the Teutons taunting us with this fact, or is there a more innocent explanation? There is indeed: UFO in German stands not only for *Unbekanntes FlugObjekt*, but also *Unabhängige Flugbegleiter Organisation*, or 'Independent Flight Attendant Organisation'. But if you don't like that rather dull explanation yourself, why not invent a better one, post it online and see if it flies, the more lunatic the better? The entire Nazi UFO myth is completely ridiculous and nobody sensible with even half a spoonful of brain-cells could possibly believe a single word of it. And that is precisely why it does so well. I can do no better than to end this book with a quote from its central figure:

'I make a last appeal to reason.'

Adolf Hitler

Bibliography

The Sources of the Saucers

NOTE: Editions listed are ones I personally consulted, not necessarily original publishers or publication dates. Some are online editions for which I have had to provide my own page-numbers.

Books

Appleyard, Bryan, *Aliens: Why They Are Here* (UK: Scribner, 2006)

Bainbridge, William Sims, *The Meaning and Value of Spaceflight: Public Perceptions* (US: Springer, 2015)

Baker, Alan, *Invisible Eagle: The History of Nazi Occultism* (UK: Virgin Books, 2000)

Barker, Gray, *They Knew Too Much About Flying Saucers* (US: IllumiNet Press, 1997)

Barkun, Michael, *A Culture of Conspiracy: Apocalyptic Visions in Contemporary America* (US: University of California Press, 2003)

Battersby, James Larratt, *The Holy Book of Adolf Hitler* (UK: self-published, 1952)

Baudrillard, Jean, *The Gulf War Did Not Take Place* (US: Indiana University Press, 1995)

Beekman, Scott, *William Dudley Pelley: A Life in Right-Wing Extremism and the Occult* (US: University of Syracuse Press, 2005)

Bennett, Colin, *Looking for Orthon* (US: Cosimo, 2008)

Black, Monica & Kurlander, Eric (eds.), *Revisiting the Nazi Occult: Histories, Realities, Legacies* (US: Camden House)

Booth, Nicholas, *Lucifer Rising: British Intelligence and the Occult in the Second World War* (UK: History Press, 2016)

Bowen, Charles (Ed.), *The Humanoids* (UK: Futura, 1977)

Chester, Keith, *Strange Company: Military Encounters with UFOs in WWII* (US: Anomalist Books, 2007)

Clark, Jerome, *The UFO Encyclopaedia Volume I: The Emergence of a Phenomenon* (US: Omnigraphics, 1992)

Clark, Jerome, *Extraordinary Encounters: An Encyclopedia of Extraterrestrials and Otherworldly Beings* (US: ABC Clio, 2000)

Clark, Jerome, *Hidden Realms, Lost Civilisations and Beings from Other Worlds* (US: Visible Ink Press, 2010)

Davis, Erik, *TechGnosis: Myth, Magic & Mysticism in the Age of Information* (US: North Atlantic Books, 2015)

DeConick, April & Adamson, Grant, *Histories of the Hidden God: Concealment and Revelation in Western Gnostic, Esoteric and Mystical Traditions* (UK: Routledge, 2013)

Dem, Marc, *The Lost Tribes from Outer Space [AKA: Jews from Space]* (UK: Corgi, 1977)

Devereux, Paul & Brookesmith, Peter, *UFOs & Ufology: The First 50 Years* (UK: Blandford, 1997)

Devi, Savitri, *The Lightning and the Sun* (India: Temple Press, 1958a)

Devi, Savitri, *Pilgrimage* (India: no publisher listed, 1958b)

Devi, Savitri, *Long-Whiskers and the Two-Legged Goddess* (India, 1965)

Essers, I., *Max Valier – A Pioneer of Space-Flight* (US: NASA, 1976)

Evans, Hilary & Bartholomew, Robert, *Outbreak! The Encyclopedia of Extraordinary Social Behaviour* (US: Anomalist Books, 2009)

Farrell, Joseph P., *Reich of the Black Sun: Nazi Secret Weapons and the Cold War Allied Legend* (US: Adventures Unlimited, 2005)

Farrell, Joseph P., *The SS Brotherhood of The Bell: NASA's Nazis, JFK and MJ-12* (US: Adventures Unlimited, 2006)

Farrell, Joseph P., *Saucers, Swastikas and Psy-Ops: A History of a Breakaway Civilisation – Hidden Aerospace Technologies and Psychological Operations* (US: Adventures Unlimited, 2011)

Farrell, Joseph P., *Hess and the Penguins: The Holocaust, Antarctica and the Strange Case of Rudolf Hess* (US: Adventures Unlimited, 2017)

Gardner, Martin, *Fads & Fallacies in the Name of Science* (US: Dover Books, 1957)

Godwin, Joscelyn, *Arktos: The Polar Myth in Science, Symbolism and Nazi Survivalism* (US: Adventures Unlimited, 1996)

Godwin, Joscelyn, *Atlantis and the Cycles of Time: Prophecies, Traditions and Occult Revelations* (US: Inner Traditions, 2011)

Good, Timothy, *Above Top Secret: The Worldwide UFO Cover-Up* (UK: Sidgwick & Jackson, 1988)

Goodrick-Clarke, Nicholas, *Hitler's Priestess: Savitri Devi, the Hindu-Aryan Myth and Neo-Nazism* (US: New York University Press, 1998)

Goodrick-Clarke, Nicholas, *Black Sun: Aryan Cults, Esoteric Nazism and the Politics of Identity* (US: New York University Press, 2002)

Goodrick-Clarke, Nicholas, *The Occult Roots of Nazism* (UK: IB Tauris, 2009)

Gorightly, Adam & Bishop, Greg, *'A' is for Adamski: The Golden Age of the UFO Contactees* (US: Gorightly Press, 2018)

Guénon, René, *The Reign of Quantity & the Signs of the Times* (US: Sophia Perennis, 2001)

Harbinson, W. A., *Genesis*, (UK: Corgi, 1980)

Harbinson, W. A., *Inception* (UK: New English Library, 1991)

Harbinson, W. A., *Projekt UFO: The Case for Man-Made Flying Saucers* (UK: Boxtree, 1995)

Harbinson, W. A., *The Wilson Papers* (UK: Custom Books Publishing, 2017)

Heller, Steven, *The Swastika: Symbol Beyond Redemption?* (US: Allworth Press, 2008)

Icke, David, *The Biggest Secret* (US: Bridge of Love, 1999)

Jung, C. G., *Flying Saucers: A Modern Myth of Things Seen in the Skies* (US: MJF Books, 1978)

Jung, C. G., *Memories, Dreams, Reflections* (UK: Harper Collins, 1995)

Jung, C. G., *Psychology and Alchemy* (UK: Routledge, 2008)

Kaplan, Jeffrey, *Encyclopaedia of White Power: A Sourcebook on the Radical Racist Right* (US: AltaMira Press, 2000)

Keel, John, *Disneyland of the Gods* (US: IllumiNet Press, 1995)

Kossy, Donna, *Kooks* (US: Feral House, 1994)

Kossy, Donna, *Strange Creations: Aberrant Ideas of Human Origins from Ancient Astronauts to Aquatic Apes* (US: Feral House, 2001)

Kurlander, Eric, *Hitler's Monsters: A Supernatural History of the Third Reich* (US: Yale University Press, 2017)

Lanz, Jörg von Liebenfels, *Theozoology: or, the Science of the Sodomite Apelings and the Divine Electron* (UK: Europa House, 2004)

Lifton, Robert Jay, *The Nazi Doctors* (US: Basic Books, 2000)

Longerich, Peter, *Heinrich Himmler* (UK: Oxford University Press, 2012)

McKale, Donald M., *Hitler: The Survival Myth* (US: Cooper Square Press, 2001)

Melville, Herman, *Moby Dick* (US: Penguin Classics, 2003)

Moore, Patrick, *Can You Speak Venusian?* (UK: David & Charles, 1972)

Moore, Steve (Ed.), *Fortean Studies Volume 2* (UK: John Brown, 1995)

Moore, Steve (Ed.), *Fortean Studies Volume 6* (UK: John Brown, 1999)

McGovern, Una (Ed.), *Chambers Dictionary of the Unexplained* (UK: Chambers, 2007)

Noble, David F., *The Religion of Technology* (US: Penguin, 1999)

Norman, Andrew, *Hitler: Dictator or Puppet?* (UK: Pen & Sword, 2011)

Ouellet, Eric, *Illuminations: The UFO Experience as a Parapsychological Event* (US: Anomalist Books, 2015)

Pauwels, Louis & Bergier, Jacques, *The Morning of the Magicians* (UK: Souvenir Press, 2001)

Pontolillo, James, *The Black Sun Unveiled: Genesis and Development of a Modern National Socialist Mythos* (US: Morryster & Sons, 2013)

Pontolillo, James, *The Black Sun Revisited: Further Chapters in the Development of a Modern National Socialist Mythos* (US: Morryster & Sons, 2017)

Rainey, Lawrence, Poggi, Christine & Wittman, Laura, *Futurism: An Anthology* (US: Yale, 2009)

Redfern, Nick, *Contactees: A History of Alien-Human Interaction* (US: New Page Books, 2010)

Robin, Jean, *UFOs: The Great Parody* (France: Éditions de la Maisnie, 1979) [English translation online at https://www.academia.edu/37695003/UFOS_OR_THE_GREAT_PARODY_by_Mr_Jean_Robin.docx_transl_ated_by_JM_Avril_]

Ronson, Jon, *THEM: Adventures with Extremists* (UK: Picador, 2002)

Rosenfeld, Gavriel D., *Hi Hitler: How the Nazi Past Is Being Normalised in Contemporary Culture* (UK: Cambridge University Press, 2015)

Schmidt, Reinhold O., *The Kearney Incident – Up to Now* (US: Saucer Research Association, 1958)

Schmidt, Reinhold O., *The Reinhold O. Schmidt Story* (US: self-published, 1963)

Sedgwick, Mark, *Against the Modern World: Traditionalism and the Secret Intellectual History of the Twentieth Century* (UK: Oxford, 2009)

Serrano, Miguel, *The Golden Cord: Esoteric Hitlerism* (Chile: Editorial Solar, 1978)

Serrano, Miguel, *Adolf Hitler: The Ultimate Avatar* (Chile: Editorial Solar, 1984)

Serrano, Miguel, *MAYA: Reality is an Illusion* (Chile: Ediciones La Nueva Edad, 2006)

Smith, Michael G., *Rockets & Revolution: A Cultural History of Early Spaceflight* (UK: University of Nebraska Press, 2014)

Snyder, Louis L., *Encyclopedia of the Third Reich* (UK: Wordsworth Military Library, 1998)

Spencer, John & Evans, Hilary, *Phenomenon* (UK: Macdonald, 1988)

Spengler, Oswald, *The Decline of the West* (UK: Oxford University Press, 1991)

Stevens, Henry, *Hitler's Suppressed and Still-Secret Science, Weapons and Technology* (US: Adventures Unlimited, 2007)

Stranges, Dr Frank E., *Nazi UFO Secrets and Bases Exposed* (US: International Evangelism Crusades, 1982)

Tallack, Malachy, *The Undiscovered Islands* (UK: Birlinn, 2016)

Tucker, S. D., *Space Oddities: Our Strange Attempts to Explain the Universe* (UK: Amberley, 2017)

Vallée, Jacques, *Messengers of Deception: UFO Contacts and Cults* (Australia: Daily Grail, 2008)

Van Helsing, Jan [AKA: Jan Udo Holey], *Secret Societies and Their Power in the Twentieth Century* (US: Wake Up! Publications, 2001)

Vesco, Renato & Childress, David Hatcher, *Man-Made UFOs 1944-1994: 50 Years of Suppression* (US: Adventures Unlimited, 1994)

Wells, H. G., *The War of the Worlds* (UK: Penguin Classics, 2005)

Williamson, George Hunt, *The Saucers Speak: Calling All Occupants of Interplanetary Craft* (US: Inner Lights, 2012)

Wilson, Colin, *The Occult* (UK: Watkins, 2006)

Zirger, Michel & Martinelli, Maurizio, *The Incredible Life of George Hunt Williamson* (Italy: Verdechiaro Edizioni, 2016)

Zündel, Ernst, [AKA: Mattern Friedrich] *UFOs: Nazi Secret Weapon?* (Canada: Samisdat, 1975)

Articles, pamphlets, etc (magazines, journals and online)

Bennett, Colin, 'Putting the Noise Back Into the System' in *UFO Magazine*, Vol.23, No.3 (2008)

Bennett, Colin, 'Meme Wars: We Have an Agenda' in *UFO Magazine*, Vol.24, No.1 (2009)

Bennett, Colin, 'Weaponising the Narrative' in *UFO Magazine*, Vol.24, No.5 (2012)

Branton, *The Omega File* (1999) [online at http://pages.suddenlink.net/anomalousimages/images/text/omega4.htm]

Danilina, Anna, 'Shaping Aryan Race: Affect and Embodiment in the Voelkisch Movement, 1900-1935' in *Body Politics 5* (2017)

Fuller, John G., 'Aboard a Flying Saucer: The Adventures of Two Kidnapped Humans' in *Look* magazine, 4 Oct 1966, pp.45-56 & 18 Oct 1966, pp.111-21 (1966)

Guzmán, Gustavo, 'Miguel Serrano's Anti-Semitism and Its Impact on the Twenty-First Century Countercultural Rightists' in *Analysis of Current Trends in Antisemitism* 40, No. 1 (2019)

Ialongo, Ernest, 'Marinetti and the Mafarka Trial: Re-Thinking the Early History of Futurism' in *Mise en Abyme* Vol.II, Issue 2/Vol.III, Issue 1 (2016)

Jung, C. G., 'Wotan', in *Neue Schweizer Rundschau*, March 1936 (1936) [online at http://www.philosopher.eu/others-writings/essay-on-wotan-w-nietzche-c-g-jung/]

Kasten, Len, 'The Nazi/ET Connection: The War for Planet Earth' in *Atlantis Rising* Nos. 65 & 66 (n.d.) [online at https://www.bibliotecapleyades.net/vida_alien/warheaven_warearth12.htm]

Willy Ley, 'Pseudoscience in Nazi-Land', *Astounding Science Fiction* May 1947 (1947) [online at http://www.alpenfestung.com/ley_pseudoscience.htm]

McClure, Kevin, 'The Nazi UFO Mythos: An Investigation – SUFOI UFO Document #5' (2004) [online at http://www.sufoi.dk/e-boger/The%20Nazi%20UFO%20Mythos.pdf]

Miele, Frank, 'Giving the Devil His Due: Holocaust Revisionism as a Test-Case for Free Speech and the Skeptical Ethic' in *The Skeptic* Vol.2, No. 4 (1994) [online at https://www.bibliotecapleyades.net/sociopolitica/sociopol_holocaust06.htm]

Myatt, David, 'VINDEX: The Destiny of the West' in *Liberty Bell* Vol.11, No.5, January 1984 (1984)

Myatt, David, 'The Numinosity of National Socialism' (1995) [online at https://regardingdavidmyatt.files.wordpress.com/2018/11/myatt-selected-ns-writings1.pdf]

Myatt, David, 'The Spirituality of National Socialism: A Reply to Criticism (1998) [online at https://regardingdavidmyatt.files.wordpress.com/2018/11/myatt-selected-ns-writings1.pdf]

Myatt, David, 'The Religion of National Socialism' (2003a) [online at https://regardingdavidmyatt.files.wordpress.com/2018/11/myatt-selected-ns-writings1.pdf]

Myatt, David, 'Towards Identity and the Galactic Empire: Autobiographical Notes' (2003b) [https://regardingdavidmyatt.files.wordpress.com/2018/12/myatt-galactic-empire-v1a.pdf]

Myatt, David, 'A Matter of Honour' (2012) [online at https://davidmyatt.files.wordpress.com/2017/06/a-matter-of-honour.pdf]

Myatt, David, 'The Mythos of Vindex' (2016) [online at https://regardingdavidmyatt.files.wordpress.com/2016/05/myatt-mythos-of-vindex-v1.pdf]

Oberth, Hermann, 'They Come from Outer-Space' in *Flying Saucer Review* Vol.11, No.2, (1955)

Sivier, David, 'Gazurmah's Sons: The Psychopathology of the Nazi Saucer Myth' in *Magonia* 63, May 1998 (1998)

Summerhayes, Colin & Beeching, Peter, 'Hitler's Antarctic Base: The Myth and the Reality' in *Polar Record* 43, (2007) [online at https://www.academia.edu/18894983/Hitlers_Antarctic_base_the_myth_and_the_reality]

Notes

Earlier, shorter versions of the chapters in this book regarding Savitri Devi and Miguel Serrano (plus a few other short, scattered sections) previously appeared in *Fortean Times* magazine and are reprinted here with permission in edited and expanded form. Many thanks to *FT*'s editor, David Sutton, for allowing this to happen.

Introduction: Close Encounters of the Third Reich Kind

1. https://www.historytoday.com/miscellanies/british-church-worshipped-hitler; http://britishguardian.blogspot.com/2019/09/james-larratt-battersby-and-apostles-of.html; https://en.wikipedia.org/wiki/James_Larratt_Battersby
2. Battersby, 1952, pp.11, 15
3. Battersby, 1952, pp.14, 16
4. Battersby, 1952, p.5
5. Battersby, 1952, pp.5, 10, 11, 19, 25, 30, 32
6. Battersby, 1952, p.58
7. Battersby, 1952, p.33
8. Battersby, 1952, p.71
9. See my companion book Nazi UFOs: The Legends and Myths of Hitler's Flying Saucers in WW2 (Pen & Sword/Frontline Publishing, 2022) for full references to all this.
10. Clark, 1992, pp.287-8; Gorightly & Bishop, 2018, pp.265-6; Redfern, 2010, pp.119-20; Schmidt, 1958; Schmidt, 1963; long extracted quotes taken from Schmidt, 1958, pp.10 & 16
11. Zündel, 1975, p.44
12. Goodrick-Clarke, 2002, pp.157-61; McClure, p.55; Miele, 1994; obituary in *The Times*, 26 August 2017; http://nizkor.com/hweb/people/z/zundel-ernst/flying-saucers; https://rense.com/general52/dewi.htm; https://en.wikipedia.org/wiki/Ernst_Z%C3%BCndel; http://vho.org/GB/Journals/JHR/20/1/Zuendel30.html
13. Miele, 1994; https://rense.com/general52/dewi.htm
14. Goodrick-Clarke, 2002, p.159
15. Gorightly & Bishop, 2018, pp.43-4
16. Miele, 1994

17. Miele, 1994
18. http://nizkor.com/hweb/people/z/zundel-ernst/flying-saucers/expedition. html; https:www.h-ref.de/personen/zuendel-ernst/zuendel-hohlerde.php
19. Miele, 1994
20. Zündel, 1975, pp.96-7, 104-5
21. Zündel, 1975, p.151
22. http://nizkor.com/hweb/people/z/zundel-ernst/flying-saucers/ufo-investigator-pass.html
23. http://it.wikiufo.org/index.php?title=UFO_Nazisti
24. https://cvltnation.com/blood-powder-richard-chase-sacramento-vampire/; https://horrorhistory.net/2018/12/26/serial-killer-richard-trenton-chase-dies-in-prison/; http://scholar.ufs.ac.za:8080/bitstream/handle/11660/9764/ NelHT.pdf?sequence=1&isAllowed=y; https://web.archive.org/ web/20070909061627/http://www.crimelibrary.com/serial_killers/weird/ chase/interview_7.ht; https://en.wikipedia.org/wiki/Richard_Chase
25. Goodrick-Clarke, 2002, p171; http://magoniamagazine.blogspot. com/2013/12/eyes-right.html; https://groups.google.com/forum/#topic/ alt.conspiracy/86nqndzbbg0; http://www.ufoupdateslist.com/1999/feb/ m15-019.shtml; https://www.borderland.co.uk/2016-05-06-12-03-40/ at-war-with-the-universe.html; https://www.independent.co.uk/news/ informer-exposes-neo-nazi-football-gangs-tim-hepple-who-infiltrated-the-british-national-party-after-1459707.html
26. https://foreignpolicy.com/2014/01/13/snowden-docs-reveal-nazi-aliens-rule-u-s/; http://www.whatdoesitmean.com/index1730.htm; https://www. rferl.org/a/iran-fars-us-policy-aliens-hitler-snowden/25228985.html; https://drdavidclarke.co.uk/2014/02/23/i-have-some-stuff-you-might-be-interested-in-edward-snowden-and-the-ultimate-secret/
27. Miele, 1994

SEKTION EIN

1 Tyrannosaurus Sex: Ariosophy, the Rape of the White Race by Apes and Dinosaurs and Other Myths of Nazi Occultism

1. https://www.huffingtonpost.co.uk/entry/dinosaur-erotica-author-alara-branwen-interview_n_4049376
2. https://bigjelly.net/ten-amazing-facts-about-william-burroughs-e97aa07d2c57
3. http://www.crystalinks.com/aliensex.html; http://www.reptilianagenda. com/exp/e100799a.shtml; http://www.greatdreams.com/reptlan/reps.htm
4. Bowen, 1977, pp.200–38
5. Norman, 2011, pp.55, 69–74; Goodrick-Clarke, 2009, pp.93–99, 113
6. Goodrick-Clarke, 2009, pp.33-49; Norman, 2011, pp.44-51; Heller, 2008, p.52; Kossy, 2001, p.85
7. Goodrick-Clarke, 2009, pp.106-22; Norman, 2011, pp.49-51
8. Goodrick-Clarke, 2009, pp.18-23, 49-55; Kossy, 2001, pp.7-8
9. http://www.jasoncolavito.com/blog/the-astonishing-racial-claims-of-erich-von-daniken; McGovern, 2007, p.155
10. Goodrick-Clarke, 2009, pp.197-8

11. Norman, 2011, pp.196-9; Heller, 2008, p.55
12. Goodrick-Clarke, 2009, pp.194-8; Norman, 2011, pp.48-54
13. Goodrick-Clarke, 2009, pp.7–16; Kurlander, 2017, pp.20–22
14. Goodrick-Clarke, 2009, pp.93-4
15. Lanz, 2004, p.22
16. Lanz, 2004, p.11
17. Lanz, 2004, p.7
18. Lanz, 2004, p.7
19. Lanz, 2004, p.7
20. Lanz, 2004, p.7
21. Lanz, 2004, p.18
22. Lanz, 2004, p.6-7, frontispiece
23. Lanz, 2004, p.16
24. Lanz, 2004, p.6
25. Lanz, 2004, p.10
26. Lanz, 2004, p.12
27. Lanz, 2004, p.13
28. Lanz, 2004, pp.5, 12, 54, 55
29. Lanz, 2004, pp.20-1
30. Lanz, 2004, p.23
31. Lanz, 2004, pp.8, 16, 22-3
32. Lanz, 2004, p.23
33. Lanz, 2004, p.22
34. Lanz, 2004, p.11
35. Lanz, 2004, p.15
36. Lanz, 2004, p.50
37. Lanz, 2004, pp.14-15
38. Lanz, 2004, pp.18-19
39. Lanz, 2004, p.19
40. Lanz, 2004, pp.30-1
41. Lanz, 2004, pp.26-8
42. Lanz, 2004, pp.8, 10
43. Lanz, 2004, pp.6, 18, 19
44. Lanz, 2004, pp.17-18
45. Lanz, 2004, p.49
46. Lanz, 2004, pp.6, 8, 11-12
47. Lanz, 2004, p.9
48. Lanz, 2004, p.6
49. Lanz, 2004, p.10
50. Lanz, 2004, p.13
51. Lanz, 2004, pp.33, 35, 37-41, 46; Goodrick-Clarke, 2009, pp.95, 101-2
52. Lanz, 2004, pp.34-5
53. Lanz, 2004, pp.35-7
54. Lanz, 2004, pp.31, 45
55. Lanz, 2004, pp.40, 47
56. Lanz, 2004, pp.48-9, 51
57. Lanz, 2004, pp.49-52
58. Lanz, 2004, p.41
59. Lanz, 2004, p.44

60. Lanz, 2004, pp.52-3
61. Lanz, 2004, pp.52-3
62. Lanz, 2004, p.55
63. Lanz, 2004, pp.58-9
64. Lanz, 2004, pp.59-60
65. Lanz, 2004, p.59
66. Lanz, 2004, pp.58-9
67. Lanz, 2004, p.60
68. Lanz, 2004, pp.55-6
69. Norman, 2011, p.63
70. Norman, 2011, p.61
71. Lanz, 2004, p.57
72. Norman, 2011, p.65
73. Norman, 2011, p.59, 60, 64
74. Lanz, 2004, pp.42-3
75. Lanz, 2004, p.45
76. Norman, 2011, p.59; Goodrick-Clarke, 2009, pp.97-8
77. Goodrick-Clarke, 2009, pp.103-4
78. Norman, 2011, p.57
79. Goodrick-Clarke, 2009, p.198
80. https://sites.google.com/site/ufologist52/Home/artiklar/artiklar-1991-1995/-chauffoer-soekes-till-tjaensteman-fraan-venus-; http://malcolmsanomalies.blogspot.com/2018/11/traitors-to-human-race.html; https://www.bayerische-staatszeitung.de/staatszeitung/kultur/detailansicht-kultur/artikel/ausserirdische-heilsbringer.html; https://www.spiegel.de/spiegel/print/d-43159684.html
81. Goodrick-Clarke, 2009, pp.160-2; Norman, 2011, pp.45-6; Danilina, 2017; https://oding.org/index.php/was-lief-verkehrt/1112-der-marby-hokuspokus
82. Theo Paijmans, 'An Ariosophist on Mars', *Fortean Times* 343, pp.28-9
83. Goodrick-Clarke, 2009, pp.201-2
84. Goodrick-Clarke, 2009, p.224
85. Theo Paijmans, 'The Vril-Seekers', *Fortean Times* 303, pp.42-6; Goodrick-Clarke, 2009, pp.218-19; Godwin, 1996, p.54
86. Pauwels & Bergier, 2001, pp.125, 141, 189-91
87. Pauwels & Bergier, 2001, pp.126, 142, 169, 184, 186, 193, 194
88. Pauwels & Bergier, 2001, p.124
89. Goodrick-Clarke, 2009, pp.142-52, 221; Godwin, 1996, pp.48-51, 148; Heller, 2008, pp.46, 56-8
90. Goodrick-Clarke, 2009, pp.219-21; Snyder, 1998, pp.77-8; Godwin, 1996, pp.54, 149; Pauwels & Bergier, 2001, pp.184-8
91. Pauwels & Bergier, 2001, p.190
92. Godwin, 1996, pp.79-85, 95-6, 99, 103-4
93. Goodrick-Clarke, 2009, pp.221-4; http://magonia.haaan.com/2009/spear/; Roy Bainton, 'The Spear Carriers', *Fortean Times* 175, pp.48-52
94. Pontolillo, 2013, pp.14-22; Longerich, 2012, pp.266, 285-6
95. Pontolillo, 2013, pp.23, 34-9, 50-7, 776; Nick Brownlow & Jonathan Turner, 'Himmler's Fortress of Fear', *Fortean Times* 196; Longerich, 2012, pp.294-6
96. Pontolillo, 2013, pp.55-63; Oded Heilbronner, 'The Wewelsburg Effect' in Black & Kurlander, 2019, pp.270-86

2 Heiling Occupants of Interplanetary Craft: William Dudley Pelley, George Hunt Williamson, the Silver Shirts and George Adamski's Aryan Aliens

1. Beekman, 2005, pp.41, 46, 89, 119
2. Beekman, 2005, pp.53-5
3. Beekman, 2005, pp.57-9
4. Beekman, 2005, pp.70-5, 149, 152; Barkun, 2003, pp.154-5
5. Beekman, 2005, pp.1, 76, 80-9, 95, 100-1, 112-15, 120-1, 123, 139, 142, 144, 155, 156
6. Beekman, 2005, pp.153-4
7. Barkun, 2003, p.150; Bennett, 2008, pp.33-7; Devereux & Brookesmith, 1997, p.29; Redfern, 2010, pp.25-6
8. Zirger & Martinelli, 2016, pp.70-1
9. Bennett, 2008, pp.69-70; Zirger & Martinelli, 2016, p.73; http://www.gasite.org/library/basil/index.html
10. Marc Hallet, 'Adamski and His Believers' in Stacy & Evans, 1997, p.67
11. Zirger & Martinelli, 2016, p.268
12. Beekman, 2005, p.155; Zirger & Martinelli, 2016, pp.100-103
13. Kossy, 2001, pp.10-12
14. Zirger & Martinelli, 2016, pp.227, 286
15. Williamson, 2012, pp.40-1; Zirger & Martinelli, 2016, pp.79-80
16. Zirger & Martinelli, 2016, p.294
17. Zirger & Martinelli, 2016, pp.290-9
18. Zirger & Martinelli, 2016, pp.73, 134-6
19. Zirger & Martinelli, 2016, pp.53, 76-85
20. Zirger & Martinelli, 2016, pp.119-23, 147
21. Zirger & Martinelli, 2016, pp.105-117, 129-30, 234, 313-14
22. Williamson, 2012, pp.64, 109-12
23. Williamson, 2012, pp.52, 58, 65, 68, 75
24. Williamson, 2012, pp.104, 49-51, 106-108
25. Barkun, 2002, p.155; Beekman, 2005, pp.161-2; Kossy, 2001, pp.12-15
26. Barkun 2002, p.155; Kossy, 2001, pp.14-15
27. Pontolillo, 2013, p.419
28. Barkun, 2003, pp.155-6; Gorightly & Bishop, 2018, pp.185, 354
29. Barkun, 2003, pp.147-53
30. Beekman, 2005, p.163
31. Kossy, 2001, pp.31-2

3 Springtime for Hitler: Savitri Deviants, the Furred Reich and the Worship of Adolf Hitler as the Stellar Second Coming

1. General unreferenced info about Devi taken from Goodrick-Clarke, 2002, pp.88–106
2. Devi, 1965, p.7
3. Devi, 1965, p.16
4. Goodrick-Clarke, 2002, p.99
5. Devi, 1965, p.91
6. Devi, 1965, pp.61–62

7. Devi, 1965, p.37
8. Goodrick-Clarke, 1998, p.120
9. Goodrick-Clarke, 1998, p.128
10. Goodrick-Clarke, 1998, pp.61-2, 92, 93-5, 99, 103-4, 108
11. Goodrick-Clarke, 1998, pp.123, 154
12. Devi, 1965, pp.134-5
13. Devi, 1965, pp.135–136
14. Devi, 1958a, p.322
15. Devi, 1958a, pp.218, 220
16. Devi, 1958a, pp.350-1
17. Devi, 1965, pp.93–94
18. Devi, 1965, pp.7–8, 26
19. Devi, 1965, pp.130–131
20. Goodrick-Clarke, 2002, pp.89-92; Godwin, 1996, pp.37-45
21. Goodrick-Clarke, 1998, pp.26-7
22. Goodrick-Clarke, 1998, pp.44-5, 69-70, 90, 110, 119
23. Goodrick-Clarke, 1998, pp.76, 107, 129-30
24. Devi, 1958a, p.263
25. Goodrick-Clarke, 1998, p.111
26. Devi, 1958a, pp.420–421; Goodrick-Clarke, 1998, p.114
27. Goodrick-Clarke, 1998, pp.158-9
28. Devi, 1958a, pp.264, 419–420
29. Pauwels & Bergier, 2001, p.172
30. Godwin, 1996, p.70
31. Devi, 1958a, p.427
32. Goodrick-Clarke, 1998, pp.121-2
33. Devi, 1958a, pp.23, 216, 225, 234, 269–270
34. Goodrick-Clarke, 2002, pp.98–100; Goodrick-Clarke, 1998, pp.131, 139, 140
35. Goodrick-Clarke, 1998, pp.135, 139
36. Goodrick-Clarke, 2002, pp.104-105; Goodrick-Clarke, 1998, pp.2, 206-7, 212-13
37. Goodrick-Clarke, 2002, pp.2, 306
38. Goodrick-Clarke, 2002, p.106
39. https://www.savitridevi.org/serrano_letter_1.html
40. https://www.bbc.co.uk/news/magazine-41757047; https://www.nytimes.com/2016/11/21/us/alt-right-salutes-donald-trump.html; http://www.ibtimes.co.uk/savitri-devi-strange-story-how-hindu-hitler-worshipper-became-alt-right-icon-1608413; https://scroll.in/article/823142/bulletins/98/todays-youngsters-could-be-the-most-independent-generation-of-old-people-yet
41. Goodrick-Clarke, 2002, p.43

4 Diplomatic Circles: Miguel Serrano, Circular Nazis, Esoteric Hitlerism and Rudolf Hess Hiding on the Moon

1. General unreferenced info about Serrano taken from Goodrick-Clarke, 2002, pp.173–92; Godwin, 1996, pp.70-3; Guzmán, 2019; Pontolillo, 2013, pp.489-94
2. Serrano, 1984, pp.42–47
3. Serrano, 1984, pp.20–21, 156

4. Serrano, 1984, pp.47, 134–135, 137, 138
5. Jung, 1978, pp.22-3
6. Jung, 1978, pp.108-9
7. Jung, 1978, p.111
8. Jung, 1978, pp.19-21, 117-18
9. Serrano, 1984, pp.455–458, 141
10. Serrano, 1984, p.10
11. Serrano, 1984, p.486
12. Serrano, 1984, pp.123–124
13. Devi, 1958b, pp.1–2
14. Devi, 1958b, p.15
15. Devi, 1958b, pp.16, 18, 32
16. Devi, 1958b, pp.24-5
17. Ulrich Magin, 'Otto Siegfried Reuter & Hermann Wirth: Two Founding Fathers of Nazi Archaeology' in Moore, 1995, pp.177-85; Goodrick-Clarke, 1998, p.166; Longerich, 2012, pp.296-8
18. Devi, 1958b, p.351
19. Devi, 1958b, pp.318–354
20. Serrano, 1984, pp.331–333, 348–352, 484; Pontolillo, 2013, p.13
21. Serrano, 1984, pp.20–21, 147
22. Serrano, 1984, pp.338, 343–344
23. Serrano, 1984, pp.19, 21, 217, 219, 249; Goodrick-Clarke, 2002, p.189
24. Serrano, 1978, p.11
25. Serrano, 1978, pp.2, 7, 8
26. Serrano, 1984, pp.86–105, 118, 120, 133–134, 139, 143–146; http://www.renegadetribune.com/1994-interview-with-miguel-serrano
27. Serrano, 1984, p.144; Pontolillo, 2013, p.490; https://blacksun-sole-nero.net/esoteric-hitlerist-interview-with-miguel-serrano-national-socialism-blacksun/
28. Godwin, 1996, pp.101-2
29. Pontolillo, 2013, p.491
30. Serrano, 1978, pp.11-12; https://blacksun-sole-nero.net/esoteric-hitlerist-interview-with-miguel-serrano-national-socialism-blacksun/
31. Goodrick-Clarke, 2002, pp.117-18, 190, 336; Godwin, 2011, Ch. Two; https://blacksun-sole-nero.net/esoteric-hitlerist-interview-with-miguel-serrano-national-socialism-blacksun/
32. Serrano, 1978, p.8
33. http://www.renegadetribune.com/1994-interview-with-miguel-serrano
34. http://www.renegadetribune.com/1994-interview-with-miguel-serrano; https://blacksun-sole-nero.net/esoteric-hitlerist-interview-with-miguel-serrano-national-socialism-blacksun/; https://oregoncoug.wordpress.com/
35. Goodrick-Clarke, 2002, p.188
36. Serrano, 1984, pp.156-7
37. Goodrick-Clarke, 2002, p.96; Serrano, 2005, p.19
38. Jung, 1936
39. Serrano, 2005, pp.14-18
40. Versions of this interview are online at http://www.oldmagazinearticles.com/carl-jung-studied-hitler-pdf; https://carljungdepthpsychologysite.blog/2019/11/29/carl-jung-on-diagnosing-the-dictators-2/#.Wp1qSzFFflU

41. Serrano, 1984, pp.105-9, 111; Goodrick-Clarke, 2002, pp.178-9
42. Serrano, 1984, p.41
43. Goodrick-Clarke, 2002, p.185
44. http://www.openculture.com/2017/11/carl-jung-psychoanalyzes-hitler.html
45. https://carljungdepthpsychologysite.blog/2019/11/29/carl-jung-on-diagnosing-the-dictators-2/#.Wp1qSzFFflU
46. http://www.renegadetribune.com/1994-interview-with-miguel-serrano; Serrano, 1984, pp.72-3, 125
47. Godwin, 1996, pp.70-3; Goodricke-Clarke, 2002, pp.180-3
48. Serrano, 1984, p.204
49. Serrano, 1984, p.83
50. http://www.renegadetribune.com/1994-interview-with-miguel-serrano
51. Serrano, 1984, p.412
52. Serrano 1984, p.486
53. Serrano, 1984, p.411
54. http://www.antipope.org/feorag/e-prattle/lfn/dem1977.html; Robin, 1979; Dem, 1977
55. Serrano, 1978, p.55
56. Serrano, 1984, p.164
57. Serrano, 1984, p.480
58. Jung, 1995, pp.226-49
59. Serrano, 1984, p.268
60. Serrano, 1984, p.320
61. Serrano, 1978, p.41; http://www.renegadetribune.com/1994-interview-with-miguel-serrano
62. Serrano, 1984, p.456
63. Serrano, 1978, p.13
64. Serrano, 1978, p.24
65. Serrano, 1978, p.46
66. Serrano, 1978, p.7
67. Serrano, 1978, p.41
68. Serrano, 1984, p.499
69. Kurlander, 2017, pp.118-19, 333; Snyder, 1998, pp.139-40, 142-3; Booth, 2016, pp.265-6
70. Serrano, 2006, pp.20-4; Farrell, 2017, pp.88-123
71. Serrano, 2006, pp.6-8; Snyder, 1998, p.36; McKale, 2001, pp.143-4, 150
72. Serrano, 2006, pp.10-12, Serrano, 1984, pp.121-2, 502; McKale, 2001, p.51
73. Serrano, 1978, pp.10, 24, 57; Serrano, 1984, pp.488–491
74. Serrano, 1984, pp.490-1
75. Serrano, 2006, pp.27-8
76. Serrano, 2006, p.32
77. Serrano, 1978, p.9
78. Serrano, 1978, pp.15-16, 19
79. Serrano, 1978, p.16
80. Godwin, 1996, p.126
81. Serrano, 1978, p.26
82. Serrano, 1978, p.21
83. Serrano, 1978, p.25
84. Serrano, 1984, pp.139, 144 (re-ordering and conflating of two separate quotes)

85. Godwin, 1996, pp.20-1, 136; Tallack, 2016, pp.34-6; Serrano, 1978, p.53
86. Serrano, 1978, pp.36, 39; Goodrick-Clarke, 2002, pp.183-4, 336; http://www.jasoncolavito.com/blog/jacques-de-mahieus-daughter-in-law-is-mad-at-me-for-reporting-facts-about-jacques-de-mahieu
87. Serrano, 1978, pp.36-7
88. Serrano, 1978, p.43
89. Goodrick-Clarke, 2002, p.336
90. Serrano, 1984, p.507
91. Serrano, 1984, p.460
92. Serrano, 1984, p.460
93. Serrano, 1984, p.74
94. Serrano, 1984, pp.263-4
95. Serrano, 1978, p.45
96. Serrano, 1984, p.252
97. Serrano, 1984, pp.19
98. Serrano, 1978, p.34
99. Serrano, 1984, pp.262-3
100. Serrano, 1978, p.56
101. Guzmán, 2019
102. Serrano, 1978, pp.47-8
103. Serrano, 1984, p.460
104. Godwin, 1996, pp.127-9
105. Robin, 1979; https://fa.livejournal.com/183495.html#183495.html
106. Vallée, 2008, p.161; Gorightly & Bishop, 2018, p.336; Kossy, 1994, 120-4
107. Goodrick-Clarke, 2002, pp.269-78; Guzmán, 2019

5 The Unholy Grail: Wilhelm Landig, the Flying *Sangraal* and the Polar Reich of the Black Sun

1. General unreferenced info about Landig taken from Goodrick-Clarke, 2002, pp.128-50; Godwin, 1996, pp.62-9; Pontolillo, 2013, pp.465-80
2. Ulrich Magin, 'Otto Siegfried Reuter & Hermann Wirth: Two Founding Fathers of Nazi Archaeology' in Moore, 1995, pp.177-85; Goodrick-Clarke, 2002, pp.129-30, 137; Pontolillo, 2013, pp.465-8; Snyder, 1998, pp.7-8, 73; Kurlander, p.154; Longerich, 2012, pp.275-9
3. Sedgwick, 2009, pp.98-109, 298; Pontolillo, 2013, p.15
4. http://thule-trilogy.blogspot.com/; Pontolillo, 2013, p.472
5. Snyder, 1998, pp.309-10
6. https://archive.org/details/InterviewWithMr.WilhelmLandig/mode/2up
7. https://archive.org/details/InterviewWithMr.WilhelmLandig/mode/2up; http://visupview.blospot.com/2014/09/a-sun-that-never-sets-strange-and_24.html; Pontolillo, 2017, p.467
8. https://rense.com/general52/dewi/.htm
9. Godwin, 1996, pp.57-61; Sedgwick, 2009, pp.107-8
10. Godwin, 1996, pp.21-2
11. Guénon, 2001, pp.128-136
12. Goodrick-Clarke, 2002, pp.129, 130-1; Pontolillo, 2013, p.371
13. Pontolillo, 2013, pp.352-4, 356-7, 361-3; Goodrick-Clarke, 2002, pp.130-1
14. Goodrick-Clarke, 2009, pp.177-91; Kurlander, 2017, pp.176-9; Longerich, 2012, p.284

15. Goodrick-Clarke, 2002, pp.135-6; Pontolillo, 2013, pp.303-35
16. Goodrick-Clarke, 2002, p.136; Pontolillo, 2013, pp.144-52
17. Goodrick-Clarke, 2002, p.136; Pontolillo, 2013, pp.180-7, 209, 215, 219-20
18. Pontolillo, 2013, p.489
19. Pontolillo, 2013, pp.93-103
20. Jung, 1978, p.vii-viii
21. Pontolillo, 2013, pp.473-4
22. Pontolillo, 2013, pp.354-61
23. Godwin, 1996, pp.65-6
24. Goodrick-Clarke, 2002, p.155
25. A partial translation is online at http://thule-trilogy.blogspot.com/
26. http://thule-trilogy.blogspot.com
27. Pontolillo, 2013, pp.469-70
28. Goodrick-Clarke, 2002, pp.137-42; Godwin, 1996, pp.63-9
29. Goodrick-Clarke, 2002, p.158, 160-1
30. Goodrick-Clarke, 2002, pp.137, 143-7
31. Pontolillo, 2013, p.418
32. *Fortean Times* 104, p.20
33. Ley, 1947; Gardner, 1957, pp.37–41; Moore, 1972, pp.66–72; Goodrick-Clarke, 2002, pp.131–4; Wilson, 2006, pp.202–6; Pauwels & Bergier, 2001, 162, 164–5, 168; Essers, 1976, pp.26–7, 220; Kurlander, 2017, pp.30-1, 150-61; Longerich, 2012, pp.279-80, 284; http://www.mpiwg-berlin. mpg.de/en/research/projects/deptiii-christinawessely-welteislehre; http:// en.wikipedia.org/wiki/Hanns_H%C3%B6rbiger; http://en.wikipedia.org/ wiki/Welteislehre
34. Goodrick-Clarke, 2002, pp.131-3
35. Goodrick-Clarke, 2002, pp.133-5; Pontolillo, 2013, pp.367-8, 402
36. Pontolillo, 2013, p.59
37. Pontolillo, 2013, p.384
38. Pontolillo, 2013, p.381
39. Pontolillo, 2013, pp.393-5
40. Pontolillo, 2013, pp.395-6, 410-15; Keel, 1995, p.42; Brian J. Robb, 'The Black Knight Satellite' in *Fortean Times* 377, pp.34-9
41. Pauwels & Bergier, 2011, pp.173-4
42. Godwin, 1996, pp.146-7
43. Godwin, 1996, pp.56-7
44. Pontolillo, 2017, pp.148, 151
45. Pontolillo, 2017, pp.134-41
46. Pontolillo, 2013, p.414
47. Pontlillo, 2013, p. 465

6 To Boldly Go Where No Fascist Has Gone Before: The Faustian Bargain of David Myatt's Galactic Reich

1. Oberth, 1955; Bainbridge, 2015, p.127; Smith, 2014, pp.229-30; Gorightly & Bishop, 2018, pp.15-16; Farrell, 2011, pp.60-9; https://web.archive.org/ web/20101125162907/http://mufon.com/MUFONews/znews_oberth.html
2. Noble, 1999, pp.124-6; Farrell, 2011, pp.60-6
3. Good, 1988, p.370
4. Long, 2012; https://aboutdavidmyatt.wordpress.com/about-2/

5. https://regardingdavidmyatt.wordpress.com/conundrum-of-myatt-and-long/
6. Myatt, 1998
7. Goodrick-Clarke, 2002, pp.223-4
8. Myatt, 2003a
9. Myatt, 2003a
10. Longerich, 2012, pp.267-9
11. Myatt, 1995
12. Myatt, 1995
13. Myatt, 1995; quote slightly re-ordered.
14. Longerich, 2012, p.281
15. Myatt, 2003b; Goodrick-Clarke, 1998, pp.215-16; Goodrick-Clarke, 2002, pp.216-17
16. Devi, 1958b, p.349
17. https://aboutdavidmyatt.wordpress.com/myatt-the-physics-of-acausal-energy/; https://davidmyatt.wordpress.com/theory-of-the-acausal/; I should point out that Myatt does not specifically mention Schopenhauer, his ideas just seem somewhat compatible with him.
18. Myatt, 2016; https://aboutdavidmyatt.wordpress.com/david-myatt-and-the-quest-for-vindex/
19. Myatt, 1984, p.2
20. Myatt, 1984, pp.5-9
21. Myatt, 1984, pp.17-18
22. Myatt, 1984, p.10
23. Myatt, 1984, p.30
24. Myatt, 1984, p.18
25. Spengler, 2001, pp.ix-xii
26. Spengler, 2001, pp.97-100
27. Spengler, 2001, p.174
28. Spengler, 2001, pp.301-3
29. Spengler, 2001, pp.53, 106-7, 111, 220
30. Spengler, 2001, pp.204-5
31. Spengler, 2001, pp.44-5, 55-7, 94-5
32. Spengler, 2001, pp.66-7
33. Spengler, 2001, p.171
34. Spengler, 2001, p.173
35. Spengler, 2001, pp.192-3, 199-201, 209-10
36. Spengler, 2001, p.175
37. https://lapisphilosophicus.wordpress.com/star-game-history-and-theory/star-game-overview/; https://lapisphilosophicus.wordpress.com/star-game-history-and-theory/
38. Myatt, 2016; https://aboutdavidmyatt.wordpress.com/david-myatt-and-the-quest-for-vindex/
39. Kaplan, 2000, p.237
40. Kaplan, 2000, pp.235-8; Goodrick-Clarke, 2002, pp.217-21; https://lapisphilosophicus.wordpress.com/about-2/dialectics-and-aeonic-sorcery/; https://lapisphilosophicus.wordpress.com/about-2/philosophy-of-anton-long; https://en.wikipedia.org/wiki/Order_of_Nine_Angles
41. Melville, 2003, p.178
42. Melville, 2003, p.178

SEKTION ZWEI

1 Abducted to Auschwitz: Cyber-Commandants Meet Doctors of Death as the Nazis Become Even More Inhuman

1. http://it.wikiufo.org/index.php?title=UFO_Nazisti
2. Rosenfeld, 2015, pp.198-203; https://www.bbc.co.uk/news/entertainment-arts-18173708; https://www.telegraph.co.uk/news/newstopics/howaboutthat/ufo/8139811/Nazi-spaceship-film-sparks-UFO-debate.html; https://en.wikipedia.org/wiki/Iron_Sky:_The_Coming_Race; https://www.theguardian.com/film/2019/apr/24/iron-sky-the-coming-race-review-timo-vuorensola-udo-kier
3. https://io9.gizmodo.com/the-legend-of-koizumi-japanese-politics-mahjong-actio-5768702; https://en.wikipedia.org/wiki/Mudazumo_Naki_Kaikaku
4. Pontolillo, 2013, pp.782-3; Jeff Hayton, 'Beyond Good and Evil: Nazis and the Supernatural in Video Games' in Black & Kurlander, 2019, pp.248-69
5. Kasten, n.d.
6. https://en.wikipedia.org/wiki/Richard_C._Hoagland; http://www.enterprisemission.com/Corbett.htm; http://www.enterprisemission.com/catbox.htm
7. *Fortean Times* 376, p.74
8. Tucker, 2017
9. Farrell, 2005, pp.319-30; https://www.ufoinsight.com/the-mussolini-ufo-files-cover-up-in-pre-world-war-two-italy/
10. Harbinson, 1980, pp.565-82; Baker, 2000, Ch.9; Vesco & Childress, 1994
11. http://it.wikiufo.org/index.php?title=UFO_Nazisti p.33
12. Harbinson, 1991, blurb
13. Harbinson, 1991, blurb; Harbinson, 1995, p.5
14. Harbinson, 1995, pp.251-8
15. Harbinson, 1995, pp.156-63
16. Harbinson, 1995, p.180
17. Harbinson, 1995, p.181
18. http://it.wikiufo.org/index.php?title=UFO_Nazisti
19. Kurlander, 2017, p.75
20. Sivier, 1998
21. Pauwels & Bergier, 2001, p.171
22. Fuller, 1966
23. Appleyard, 2006, pp.66-8; Devereux & Brookesmith, 1997, p.197
24. Appleyard, 2006, pp.75, 192
25. Ouellet, 2015, pp.142-6
26. Lifton, 2000, pp.271-8
27. Lifton, 2000, pp.278-4
28. Snyder, 1998, pp.227-8
29. Lifton, 2000, pp.338, 367, 375, 376-7, 380, 418-29
30. Beckley, 1990, pp.44-5, 85, 91, 92, 160
31. *Times Saturday Review*, 15 February 2020, p.16
32. Wells, 2005, p.7
33. Davis, 2015, pp.76-7

34. Bennett, 2008, pp.216-16; 'The Pixels of Roswell' by Colin Bennett in Moore, 1999, pp.76–7
35. Davis, 2015, pp.80-91
36. Davis, 2015, p.251
37. Devereux & Brookesmith, 1997, p.184
38. Appleyard, 2006, p.77
39. Spencer & Evans, 1988, p.168
40. Rainey, Poggi & Wittman, 2009, pp.5, 49-53, 54-61, 181, 308-9
41. Rainey, Poggi & Wittman, 2009, pp.89-92
42. Sivier, 1998; Ialongo, 2006
43. https://thedisorderofthings.com/2013/10/23/junger-meaning-on-the-industrial-battlefield/
44. Sivier, 1998

2 Choose the Darkside, Doctor: The Underground Alliance Between Josef Mengele and the Paedophile Lizards from Outer Space

1. Davis, 2015, p.243
2. McClure, 2004, p.40
3. Devereux & Brookesmith, 1997, pp.110-11, 122-5, Barkun, 2003, p.111-12
4. http://paul.rutgers.edu/~mcgrew/ufo/john.lear.letter; Barkun, 2003, pp.88-91
5. Barkun, pp.36, 60-2, 91-6, 146, 164-5; Kossy, 1994, pp.191-6; Goodrick-Clarke, 2002, pp.284-9; https://newrepublic.com/article/150922/pioneer-paranoia
6. Barkun, 2003, p.119, 123
7. Barkun, 2003, pp.122-3; McClure, 2004, p.33
8. Barkun, 2003, p.222
9. Branton, 1999, Ch. 1, Ch.4, Ch.6, Ch.10, Ch.13, Ch.14, Ch.38
10. Branton, 1999, Ch. 2
11. Branton, 1999, Ch. 2 & Ch.3
12. Branton, 1999, Ch. 15
13. Branton, 1999, Ch.26; McClure, 2004, pp.30-1; Kasten, n.d.
14. Snyder, 1998, p.206
15. Branton, 1999, Ch. 3, Ch. 27, Ch.28, Ch.30
16. Icke, 1999, p.79
17. Icke, 1999, pp.81-2
18. Icke, 1999, pp.82-3
19. Icke, 1999, p.86
20. Icke, 1999, pp.105-107, 113, 114
21. Icke, 1999, pp.110-113, 117, 120, 122, 123
22. Goodrick-Clarke, 2002, pp.290-2; Barkun, 2003, p.104
23. Barkun, 2003, p.83
24. Barkun, 2003, pp.142-7; Kossy, 1994, p.196
25. Barkun, 2003, pp.142-7, 174-5; Ronson, 2002, pp.139-40
26. Ronson, 2002, pp.145-6

3 Hell Frozen Over: Melting Down the Myth of the Antarctic Nazi Saucer-Base

1. Harbinson, 1991, p.1; Harbinson, 1995, pp.6, 45
2. Harbinson, 1991, pp.1-7
3. McClure, 2004, p.29
4. Harbinson, 1995, pp.3-4, 248-51; Harbinson, 1980, pp.565-82; Baker, 2000, Ch. 9; Goodrick-Clarke, 2002, p.332; McClure, 2004, pp.26-7
5. Goodrick-Clarke, 2002, p.159
6. Miele, 1994
7. Summerhayes & Beeching, 2007; Godwin, 1996, pp.122-3, 128; Goodrick-Clarke, 2002, pp.153-4
8. *El Mercurio* (Chile) 5 March 1947
9. Harbinson, 1980, pp.565-82; Summerhayes & Beeching, 2007
10. Goodrick-Clarke, 2002, pp.159-60
11. Harbinson, 1995, p.4
12. McKale, 2001, pp.62-4, 126, 133-9; Summerhayes & Beeching, 2007; Goodrick-Clarke, 2002, pp.153-4, 159, 177
13. McKale, 2001, p.140
14. Zündel, 1975, pp.38-45; McKale, 2001, p.80
15. Zündel, 1975, pp.61-2
16. Zündel, 1975, pp.84-6
17. Zündel, 1975, pp.86, 90, 95
18. Zündel, 1975, pp.98-9
19. Gorightly & Bishop, 2018, pp.54-5; http://wwwuser.gwdg.de/~agruens/UFO/fiatlux.html; https://www.apologeticsindex.org/o08.html
20. Kossy, 1994, pp.210-13
21. McClure, 2004, p.53; Stevens, 2007, p.56
22. Godwin, 1996, p.134
23. Summerhayes & Beeching, 2007
24. Harbinson, 1995, pp.209-11; Godwin, 1996, pp.121-3
25. Cited in Harbinson, 1995, pp.211-12
26. Clark, 2010, pp.47-52; Barkun, 2003, p.117 https://steemit.com/histiry@azzamkhalidi/rainbow-city-2-million-years-amidst-antarctica
27. Godwin, 1996, pp.131-2, 136-7
28. Barkun, 2003, p.121
29. Clark, 2010, pp.43-6
30. Clark, 2010, p.47; Branton, 1999, Ch. 15

4 The Half-Life and Half-Death of Captain Blimp: Mr Wilson and the Great American Airship Panic

1. *FSR* Vol. 26, No.4; *FSR* Vol. 27, No. 1; both online at https://www.sacred-texts.com/ufo/genesis2.htm
2. Harbinson, 2017, blurb
3. Review by 'RMF', posted online at https://www.amazon.co.uk/Wilson-Papers-Genesis-Worlds-Fearsome/dp/1540894819
4. Summerhayes & Beeching, 2007; https://archive.org/details/InterviewWithMr.WilhelmLandig/mode/2up

5. Harbinson, 2017, pp.12-13
6. Harbinson, 2017, pp.15-16
7. Harbinson, 1991, pp.6-7
8. http://curtiseickerman.weebly.com/uploads/1/0/2/7/10270231/the_enigmatic_wilsons_and_john_keely_new.pdf
9. Harbinson, 1995, pp.41-2, 44
10. Devereux & Brookesmith, 1997, pp.18-19; Evans & Bartholomew, 2009, pp.144-5, 214-24; McGovern, 2007, p.9; Spencer & Evans, pp.46-52
11. Barker, 1997, p.39
12. Clark, 2000, pp.270-2; Clark, 2010, pp.274-82; Jerome Clark, 'Experience Anomalies' in *Fortean Times* 243, pp.42-7; Jerome Clark, 'Mr Wilson and the Aeronauts of 1897' in *Fortean Times* 362, pp.38-43
13. McClure, 2004, pp.43-4
14. Jerome Clark, 'Experience Anomalies' in *Fortean Times* 243, pp.42-7

5 This Gulf War Did Not Take Place: Nazi Saucer-Pilots Fly Down from Aldebaran to the Aid of Saddam Hussein

1. https://www.nytimes.com/1977/04/07/archives/west-german-youth-found-to-be-ignorant-about-hitler-period.html; https://www.investigativeproject.org/8422/is-ignorance-about-the-holocaust-connected-to; https://www.thetrumpet.com/9565-british-and-german-children-ignorant-of-world-war-ii; https://www.telegraph.co.uk/history/world-war-two/6034749/Teens-ignorant-of-WWII-poll-finds.html
2. *Sunday Times*, 23 February 2020, p.5
3. Rosenfeld, 2015, p.122
4. Rosenfeld, 2015, p.147
5. Rosenfeld, 2015, pp.301-3
6. Rosenfeld, 2015, p.341
7. Rosenfeld, 2015, pp.316-18
8. Rosenfeld, 2015, pp.316-18
9. Rosenfeld, 2015, pp.319-22
10. Baudrillard, 1995, p.26
11. Baudrillard, 1995, pp.29-31
12. Baudrillard, 1995, pp.41-3, 45, 48, 60, 69
13. https://www.ufoinsight.com/ufo-conspiracies-of-the-gulf-wars/; https://www.ufoinsight.com/iraqi-stargate-conspiracy-nonsense-required-questions/; http://www.ufoinfo.com/roundup/v07/rnd0751.shtml; https://www.pravdareport.com/news/russia/21198-n
14. https://www.exoplitics.org/tag/european-commission/; https://www.exopolitics.org/brexit-britain-challenges-covert-fourth-reich-its-secret-space-program/
15. http://exopolitics.org/archived/Study-Paper2.htm
16. Goodrick-Clarke, 2002, p.147; Pontolillo, 2013, pp.475-8
17. Goodrick-Clarke, 2002, pp.164-5; Pontolillo, 2013, pp.557-8, 571-3
18. Goodrick-Clarke, 2002, p.165
19. https://malcolmnicholson.wordpress.com/2018/08/13/the-maria-orsic-hoax/; https://www.bibliotecapleyades.net/ciencia/ciencia_flyingobjects55.htm; https://ca.wikipedia.org/wiki/Maria_Orsic; http://1stmuse.com/maria_orsitsch/

20. Pontolillo, 2013, p.563
21. Goodrick-Clarke, 2002, pp.165-9; Pontolillo, 2013, pp.557-8 561; https://www.stormfront.org/forum/t381204/; https://www.bibliotecapleyades.net/ciencia/ciencia_flyingobjects55.htm; http://1stmuse.com/maria_orsitsch/; https://en.wikipedia.org/wiki/Winfried_Otto_Schumann
22. Goodrick-Clarke, 2002, p.169
23. Chapter online at https://www.principality-of-sealand.ch/html-2017/busclub/mitglieder_d/brief_d/d_021102_1.html
24. Goodrick-Clarke, 2002, pp.169-70
25. Pontolillo, 2013, p.604; Goodrick-Clarke, 2002, pp.294, 297; Ch. 1 at http://members.kfs.at/kingralf/ufo/buch/buch2/index.html
26. Kurlander, 2017, pp.252-7
27. Goodrick-Clarke, 2002, p.293
28. Goodrick-Clarke, 2002, pp.293-4; http://www.jasoncolavito.com/blog/review-of-ancient-aliens-s03e12-aliens-and-deadly-cults
29. Pontolillo, 2013, pp.604-7; Goodrick-Clarke, 2002, pp.293, 299; https://www.spiegel.de/spiegel/print/d-9133761.html
30. Pontolillo, 2013, pp.605-6
31. https://www.h-ref.de/literatur/h/helsing-jan-van/geheimgesellschaften-1.php
32. Goodrick-Clarke, 2002, p.296
33. Van Helsing, 2001, pp.129-31, 145
34. Goodrick-Clarke, 2002, p.299
35. Van Helsing, 2001, pp.115-117; Pontolillo, 2013, pp.616-17; Goodrick-Clarke, 2002, p.297
36. Ch. 27 at http://members.kfs.at/kingralf/ufo/buch/buch2/index.html
37. Goodrick-Clarke, 2002, p.295
38. Stevens, 2007, pp.221-7

6 Round and Round in Circles: Joseph P. Farrell and the Logical Conclusion of Illogical Premises

1. Davis, 2015, p.243
2. Farrell, 2011, p.vii
3. Farrell, 2011, pp.vii, 1-9, 85-6, 249-52
4. Stranges, 1982, pp.10-11
5. Stranges, 1982, pp.27-9; Farrell, 2011, pp.ix-xi
6. Farrell, 2011, pp.40-1, 45-54, 97, 119
7. Snyder, 1998, pp.322-3; Goodrick-Clarke, 2002, pp.102, 190
8. Farrell, 2011, pp.94-5, 98-9, 104-5
9. Farrell, 2011, pp.115, 133, 252
10. Vallée, 2008, p.54
11. Vallée, 2008, pp.7-9, 30, 73
12. Vallée, pp.112-13
13. Vallée, 2008, pp.166-9
14. John Stroup, 'Occulture in the Academy?: The Case of Joseph P. Farrell' in DeConick & Adamson, 2013, pp.298-311; http://www.jasoncolavito.com/blog/nazi-wonder-weapons-and-their-impact-on-ufology

Conclusion: The War of Ideas

1. Vallée, pp.9-10, 68-9
2. *Fortean Times* 169, p.53; Colin Bennett, 'The Pixels of Roswell' in Moore, 1999, pp.92-3
3. Bennett, 2008
4. Bennett, 2012
5. https://mysteriousuinverse.org/2018/03/ufos-deception-is-the-key-to-this-whole-business/
6. https://lapisphilosophicus.wordpress.com/about-2/dialectics-and-aeonic-sorcery/
7. Bennett, 2012
8. Bennett, 2009